Unequal Europe

This wide-ranging and comparative text reviews the major theoretical and substantive debates on social inequality in Europe. It provides a valuable dual focus on European society and individual societies while placing Europe in its wider global context.

Demonstrating the continued importance of national difference within Europe, the author argues that nonetheless the European social model has softened social inequalities such as those of wealth and income distribution, social class, gender and possibly even ethnicity. However, these achievements are now being undermined, partially by the European Union itself. The book also challenges conventional wisdom on Europe's alleged need for immigration and highlights the UK's distinctiveness within Europe, explaining the country's uneasy relation to the European project.

This book will be of great interest to students and scholars of Politics, European Societies, Social Policy and Comparative Studies.

James Wickham leads the Working Conditions in Ireland project at the Dublin think tank Tasc. He was also Jean Monnet Professor of European Labour Market Studies and Professor in Sociology at Trinity College Dublin, Ireland.

Routledge Advances in European Politics

Unequal Europe

Social divisions and social cohesion in an old continent

James Wickham

Routledge
Taylor & Francis Group

LONDON AND NEW YORK

First published 2016
by Routledge
2 Park Square, Milton Park, Abingdon, Oxon OX14 4RN

and by Routledge
711 Third Avenue, New York, NY 10017

Routledge is an imprint of the Taylor & Francis Group, an informa business

British Library Cataloguing in Publication Data
A catalogue record for this book is available from the British Library

Library of Congress Cataloging in Publication Data
Names: Wickham, James (James John Rufus), author.
Title: Unequal Europe : social divisions and social cohesion in an old continent / James Wickham.
Description: Abingdon, Oxon ; New York, NY : Routledge, 2016. | Series: Routledge advances in European politics | Includes bibliographical references and index.
Identifiers: LCCN 2015036722| ISBN 9781857285512 (hardback) | ISBN 9781315636702 (ebook)
Subjects: LCSH: Europe–Social conditions. | Welfare state–Europe. | Social stratification–Europe. | Equality–Europe.
Classification: LCC HN373.5 .W53 2016 | DDC 306.094–dc23
LC record available at http://lccn.loc.gov/2015036722

ISBN: 978-1-857-28551-2 (hbk)
ISBN: 978-1-315-63670-2 (ebk)

Typeset in Times New Roman
by Wearset Ltd, Boldon, Tyne and Wear

For Lorelei

Contents

Figures

Tables

Acknowledgements

It all started in Frankfurt airport several decades ago where by chance I met my colleague Michael Marsh. We were then both lecturers at Trinity College Dublin, myself in sociology, Michael in political science; we were returning to Dublin from separate academic meetings somewhere in Continental Europe. While waiting for our plane we planned a jointly taught undergraduate course to be entitled 'West European Society and Politics'. Such a course would inform our students about contemporary Europe, it would explore the inter-relationship between those two entities 'politics' and 'society'. Over the years that course changed its name, it began to notice Europe beyond Western Europe, eventually it was no longer taught jointly. In those days in sociology, unlike in political science, there was very little English language empirical material that was specifically about Europe. Consequently the course content seemed destined to be turned into a book. Now that has finally happened, the first acknowledgement should be to Michael for the original idea.

While that undergraduate course was going through different iterations, sections of it morphed into more advanced undergraduate courses, into taught masters' courses and into courses taught in other universities. Accordingly I owe a major debt to my students at Trinity College Dublin whose attentive questioning and discussion helped develop the arguments. An early starting point was working with students and staff on the Erasmus programme on European Labour Market Policies initiated by Bent Greve then of Roskilde University; more recently I have learnt much from international students at Università Carlo Cattaneo in Castellanza on a labour economics course taught with Manuela Samek Ludovici. Many thanks to the teaching assistants and to research assistants who located material for those courses: Aileen O'Carroll, Aine O'Keeffe, Breda Feehan, Clara Thompson, Gemma Carney, Jacqueline Twinem, Paul Candon, Piergiulio Poli and Torben Krings. Special thanks also to Eleanor Russell who checked many sources and located esoteric historical information.

Research on many projects in the Employment Research Centre at Trinity College Dublin has directly or indirectly flowed into the book. My thanks to ERC researchers Alessandra Vecchi, Alicja Bobek, Christian Schweiger, Elaine Moriarty, Gerry Boucher, Gráinne Collins, Ian Bruff, Justyna Salamońska, Lidia Greco and once again Torben Krings. Many of these projects were EU-funded projects involving collaboration with teams across Europe; I have learnt much from David Charles, Erik Latniak, Heike Jakobsen, Jill Rubery, Michael Kuhn and Sven Kesselring. Back in Dublin and outside sociology John Horne and Paul Sweeney have been often unwitting sounding boards for the engagement with history and economic policy respectively.

This book is primarily a work of synthesis and hopefully all more specific references are fully acknowledged in the text. However, special contributions were made by Juliet Webster in our early collaboration on employment in the so-called information society and more recently by Steffen Lehndorff in our work on the political economy of the European crisis. Hopes and fears for the European project have been shared over the years with Catherine Casey and Ronan O'Brien; to both of them a special thanks for all the intellectual encouragement.

At Routledge a series of editors never quite gave up hope that this project would be completed. And above all thanks to Lorelei, who always believed that it would be.

Dublin August 2015

Introduction

In the aftermath of 11 September 2001, *Le Monde* declared '*Nous sommes tous américains.*' In Gaza certainly some briefly celebrated the murders, but in Teheran students lit candles in sympathy with the victims. In Europe, *Nouvel Observateur* and *Spiegel*, leading current affairs journals in France and Germany respectively, each published an article castigating its national intelligentsia for 'anti-Americanism' (Juillard 2001; Broder 2001). The two articles each saw 'anti-Americanism' as a peculiarly French or German stance, in each case allegedly the result of an outdated national view of the world.

Within two years the American government had lost much of that sympathy, forcing people around the world and perhaps particularly in Europe to consider the way in which we are *not* all Americans now. This book starts from that difference.

As the responses to the Iraq War showed, Europeans saw the world differently to Americans. The American invasion was rejected by a majority of the population in every single country, including those whose leaders signed up for it (e.g. Britain, Spain) or tacitly supported it (e.g. Ireland). At the start of the twenty-first century, such differences became the stuff of political commentary. According to one view, Europeans were from Venus, Americans from Mars (Kagan 2003: 3). Europeans believed in the rule of international law and international institutions such as the United Nations; they did not see the world as divided between right and wrong, good and evil. By contrast, especially after 11 September 2001, Americans believed that nations – or at least their own nation – must attack their evil enemies without reference to international institutions.

Conversely, word was spreading among American dissidents that Europe offered something better than the USA. The middle years of the decade saw a veritable Euro-enthusiasm in some nooks and crannies of American intellectual life. For writers such as Reid (2004) and Hill (2010), Europe provided a welcome contrast to the USA. Our social systems did not generate such extremes of wealth and poverty, such crass commercialisation of culture, such naked subordination of democracy to the power of money. These differences have long existed, though they became more marked (or at least more noticeable) during the first presidency of George W. Bush. Europe also seemed to offer a cross-national economic integration which generated regional solidarity and social responsibility – completely unlike the economic integration that the USA promoted in its own hemisphere through NAFTA (Anderson and Cavanagh 2004); European integration appeared to also recognise diversity and the importance of local needs. For the author of *The European Dream* (Rifkin 2004) it was Europe not the USA that was the 'City on the Hill' offering an ideal to the world.

By the end of the decade such admirers of the European project were few and far between. If the global financial crisis started in the USA, it appeared to impact worse on many areas of Europe. In the periphery of the EU15, in Greece, Ireland, Spain, Portugal and even Italy, 'Europe' had once been identified with prosperity and social progress. As the crisis deepened, 'Europe' was now seen as responsible for the politics of austerity. Furthermore 'Europe' became increasingly identified – and negatively – with just one country – Germany. If the decade started with the launch of the euro currency in 2001, saving the euro now seemed to endanger the European project itself. For all the claims that European institutions were being strengthened to tackle the crisis, for ordinary Europeans the entire legitimacy of the project was undermined. Now in 2015 European politics are popularly understood merely as bargaining between national member states; few people can seriously argue any remaining connection between the European project and social progress.

If this is the case, the crisis goes to the heart of the European project. American euro-enthusiasts may appear naive but as outsiders they noticed something crucial. Not only was Europe different, but the nature of this difference, what will be termed in this book the European social model (ESM), was the basis of its legitimacy internally and of its appeal externally. If that is true, then to undermine the ESM is to undermine Europe itself. It is to consign Europe to the status of eighteenth-century Poland, a geographical area where the component parts were so determined to protect merely their own short-term interests that the country was eventually simply divided up between stronger neighbours.

Discussing the European social model is therefore to discuss the possibility of a distinctive European role in the world. It links the traditional concerns of sociologists (social inequality, social cohesion, etc.) to the rediscovery of geopolitics which had begun even before the onslaught of September 2001. Already Huntington (1997) had claimed that a realistic view of the contemporary world must recognise the fundamental divisions between clashing civilisations. More recently, the term 'empire' as a description of the USA's global reach has moved from the margins of political debate ('imperialism') to be used both by critics (e.g. Todd 2004) and by advocates (e.g. Ferguson 2004) of American power. Indeed, Europe's own imperial heritages are now being re-evaluated, not least because of the dawning realisation that empires can construct multi-ethnic polities more easily than nation states (Janoski 2009). And finally the term 'empire' alerts us to the emergence of potentially alternative sources of power in the world. Indeed, with the rapid rise of China and even India to global powers in their own right, the American empire may well turn out to be a brief interlude before the emergence of a more multi-polar – and not necessarily more pleasant – world.

In the nineteenth century Bismarck coined the phrase *Der Primat der Aussenpolitik* (the primacy of foreign policy). In today's geopolitical context the relationship between states makes differences between them more visible and more important. Europe's achievements bring new threats and new responsibilities. The USA long supported European unification in order to bolster Western Europe against the USSR. Now the USA sometimes views European integration with alarm. Especially worrying for the hegemon is that Europe could offer an alternative model of socio-economic development to the free market absolutism which America now incorporates. European integration is no longer just some esoteric pastime of politicians in one corner of the world. Europe finds itself challenged to put forward its development model and above all its understanding of political integration to the wider world.

All of these arguments can be criticised. Politically many – especially in the UK – would claim that 'Europe' as a political entity has already over-reached itself and should revert to – at most – the limited administration of a free trade area. Analytically many would claim that differences between 'European' countries are so great that it is meaningless to talk of 'Europe' as anything more than a geographical expression; such differences make it impossible to compare Europe and the USA as distinct entities.

One reason for the Europeanness of European society is the European Union. The EU's political institutions bring into a common framework nations whose armed quarrels have slaughtered millions of their inhabitants in the past. Here disputes are settled by political bargaining and by rules of procedure; the European Union is the first democratic system in the world which has developed supra-national democratic institutions and supra-national laws. However, this achievement leaves questions open which involve sociology.

First, what is the influence of these institutions back onto society? Whereas popular European national histories see nation states created by pre-existing nations, for decades historians in particular have argued that it might be more appropriate to reverse the causality and talk of state-nations. In one classic account, peasants were turned into Frenchmen through a common currency and tax system, a common school system and a common military service (Weber 1979). Whereas conventional comparative sociology compares different pre-existing European societies with each other and with the USA, it is also important to ask whether the EU itself is creating a European society. If that is too much reminiscent of the construction of European nation states, one can be more adventurous and ask whether the EU is creating distinctively European social processes that cross national boundaries. Should we talk not just of globalisation but of Europeanisation? Posed like this, the social scientific study of 'Europe' is not just about history or economics or political science, it is crucially also a topic for sociology.

Here a key question is the development of the European market itself. The historical European nation states of the nineteenth century broke down social and institutional barriers to the market within their national territories: they abolished internal custom barriers, they standardised currency, they created national markets. While the market itself tore to pieces pre-existing social bonds (Marx's famous phrase about everything solid melting into air), the nation state also created new social bonds. National markets were embedded in and maintained by national societies involving the social solidarity of the national 'we'. From this perspective the key question for Europe is whether it can construct as well as destroy, whether it can create a new social solidarity along with new markets.

However, whatever the European Union is, it is not a single big nation state, it is not even a federal state. The national member states remain centres of political power and social identity. Although at times European leaders may talk of a distinctive European social model, that social model is largely the creation of the separate national welfare states. At the heart of the European social model is a tension between the varied nation states and the EU itself.

Understanding the ESM involves comparisons with the rest of the developed world – and especially the USA. However, what really matters is studying the different forms of social inequality and social cohesion within Europe itself. This involves not just the traditional forms of inequality of income and social class, but also regional inequality, inequality in migration, ethnic inequality and gender inequality. This involves using a wide range of existing studies and this is now easier because there is now a growing European research literature in English as well as scholarly journals such as *European Societies*. In particular, although social research funded directly by the EU through its 'Framework' programmes remains small in comparison to most national programmes, it has made a distinctive contribution. Such research has often attempted to go beyond simply 'comparing and contrasting' individual European societies and to analyse social processes at a specifically European level. Sociologists, like some modern historians, increasingly take as their topic European society rather than European societies.

This growing literature has made it increasingly possible to utilise 'European' research in English, even though there are obvious dangers in such a monolingual approach. Although this book deliberately uses the word 'we' to refer to us Europeans, there are real limitations to a book based primarily on English language sources, and these limitations are conceptual as well as empirical. Precisely the spread of European level research and the parallel move to English as the 'international' language of social science within the European research community may subordinate and even occlude national research traditions such as those of France or Germany, as well as creating new forms of inequality among researchers.

To grasp the diverse forms of social inequality in Europe today requires a synthesis of existing studies. Accordingly this book is almost entirely an interrogation of other scholars' research. Furthermore, since the European social model was a characterisation of what used to be termed Western European society, the study must focus on the EU15 – the so-called old EU before the enlargements of 2004. In a final narrowing of vision, the study uses material from five countries taken to exemplify most of the variety within that first Europe: France, Germany, Italy, Sweden and the UK. However, it does also make some reference to Ireland as a small and (at least in the past) peripheral member state. Some statistical series also compare these case study countries with Poland as the largest of the new member states (NMS). Developments in the NMS are changing Europe as a whole, but analysing the strength of the European social model means examining those countries where it was first developed – and where it is perhaps now ending.

The first chapter puts forward the basic thesis that any definition of Europe involves both the European Union and the specific combination of welfare state, parliamentary democracy and market economy that can be called the European social model. It also outlines the tensions that this involves: between the market-making role of the Union and the need for European solidarity, between the European Union and its constituent national welfare states.

Chapter 2 traces changes in European social structure in the epoch of European unity, from the high point of industrialism in the so-called *trente glorieuses* (thirty glorious years), through the onset of post-industrial society to the emergence of an allegedly knowledge-based society. Within these common frameworks we can highlight differences both between European societies and between Europe and the USA. Switching to a political economy perspective, Chapter 3 brings into sharper focus differences between European societies across time and space as well as the continuing contrast with the USA. The current period can be seen as a period of financialisation and this takes extreme forms in both the USA and the UK. The British question thus goes to the very heart of the European project.

Chapter 4 shows how such financialisation is impacting on European societies, creating pressures towards greater social inequality and greater individualisation, not just in extremes of poverty and wealth, but also in terms of heightened individualisation especially in the 'middle mass' of ordinary Europeans. Against this backdrop, the next five chapters examine the more conventional sociological concerns of social inequality in terms of social class, region, migration, ethnicity and gender. In all five areas we find both the importance of differences within Europe and the contrast with the USA. In each area also we find a limited but real role for the European Union creating a small but significant form of European solidarity.

The concluding Chapter 10 shows that this journey through European social structure does not magically produce any single unambiguous European essence, any more than Europeans share a single common European identity. European societies may be different from the USA, but they are different from each other. They do share the common political framework of the European Union itself, but the very enlargement of the Union threatens to undermine the Union. The forms of solidarity with which the Union binds together new inequalities and new differences could enable Europe to have a distinct role in the world, but realistically this is unlikely. To the relief of some and the disappointment of others, the European Dream will probably remain just a dream.

Bibliography

Anderson, S. and Cavanagh, J. (2004) *Lessons of European Integration for the Americas*, Washington: Institute for Policy Studies.

Broder, H. (2001) Die Arroganz der Demut, *Der Spiegel* 47/2001, 19 November 2001.

Ferguson, N. (2004) *Colossus: The Rise and Fall of the American Empire*, London: Penguin Books.

Hill, S. (2010) *Europe's Promise: Why the European Way is the Best Hope in an Insecure Age*, Berkeley: California UP.

Huntington, S. (1997) *The Clash of Civilizations and the Remaking of World Order*, London: Simon & Schuster.

Janoski, Thomas (2009) The difference that empire makes: institutions and politics of citizenship in Germany and Austria, *Citizenship Studies* 13.4: 381–411.

Juillard, J. (2001) Misère de l'antiamericanisme, *Nouvel Observateur*, 13 November 2001.

Kagan, R. (2003) *Paradise and Power: America and Europe in the New World Order*, London: Atlantic Books.

Reid, T. (2004) *The United States of Europe: The Superpower that Nobody Talks about, from the Euro to Eurovision*, London: Penguin.

Rifkin, J. (2004) *The European Dream*, Cambridge: Polity Press.

Todd, E. (2004) *After the Empire*, London: Constable and Robinson.

Weber, E. (1979) *Peasants into Frenchmen: The Modernization of Rural France 1870–1914*, Stanford: Stanford UP.

1 Where is Europe anyway?

In global terms, Europe is distinctive because of the European social model: its unique combination of market economy, parliamentary democracy and welfare states. Indeed, abandoning this European social model could ensure that Europe itself disintegrated as a distinct polity. This chapter lays the basis for this claim.

The chapter begins with some basic features of Europe in relation to the rest of the world: its geopolitical location, its wealth accompanied by slow economic growth, its apparent demographic crisis and, above all, the European Union itself. However, the second part argues that a key feature of Europe now is its national welfare states and their problematic relation to the European Union. The third part shows how the concepts of *social inclusion* and *social cohesion* allow us to locate Europe in relation to the rest of the world: Europe is an area of the world that, within the framework of parliamentary democracy and on the basis of a market economy, has relative social equality, economic citizenship and a strong public sphere maintained by its national states.

1.1 Definitions of Europe

Europe as a place

Europe is a geographical term, and at first sight this appears comforting: Europe is 'that place' on the map (Figure 1.1). Europe is also a long settled place: Europeans have lived in Europe for a long time. This apparently banal fact does make Europe in many ways very different to the USA and to the other extra-European countries of the Anglosphere, and makes Europe much closer to China and India. An even closer parallel is Japan at the other end of the Eurasian land mass: whereas China and especially India had 'foreign' dynastic rule, this has never been the case for Europe or Japan.

The historical connection with a particular geographical place has a more immediate aspect. Compared to the inhabitants of the USA, and even taking into account variation by class, region, ethnicity and gender, Europeans tend to move house infrequently. When they do move, they usually stay within the same country. Of all the many geographical divisions within Europe, the borders of the European nation states remain the most socially relevant. To a surprising

Figure 1.1 Europe and the European Union (adapted from: www.lib.utexas.edu/maps/cia15/european_union_sm_2015.gif).

Notes
Member states of the European Union (accession date in brackets; Eurozone members in bold; non-Schengen in italic): **France** (1958), **Belgium** (1958), **Italy** (1958), **Luxembourg** (1958), Denmark (1973), *Ireland* (1973), *United Kingdom* (1973), **Greece** (1981), **Portugal** (1986), **Spain** (1986), **Austria** (1995), **Finland** (1995), Sweden (1995), **Cyprus** (2004), Czech Republic (2004), **Estonia** (2004), Hungary (2004), **Latvia** (2004), **Lithuania** (2004), Poland (2004), **Slovakia** (2004), **Slovenia** (2004), Bulgaria (2007), Romania (2007), Croatia (2013).
Non-EU Schengen states: Iceland, Norway, Switzerland.

extent, these national state boundaries still enclose different societies. Most Europeans live their lives within one nation state, which they only leave for holidays or, increasingly, as part of their studies in late adolescence. Although geographical mobility is increasing, it has increased far faster *within* European countries than *between* them.

The problem of course is that the geographical boundaries of 'Europe' continually shift. Until 1989 the Iron Curtain bisected the continent. Within that bipolar world, the centre of gravity for the European countries of the Eastern bloc lay to the east. Their trade was oriented eastwards, their foreign language was Russian, Moscow was their political centre. For nearly fifty years cities such as Prague or Dresden were part of another world, so that for Western Europe 1989 marked a reclaiming of lands that had been lost. Countries such as Poland, Hungary or (then) Czechoslovakia ceased being in 'Eastern Europe' and apparently moved to 'Central Europe'; since 2004 they have become simply part of Europe. Indeed the EU's current eastern boundary is now the traditional religious boundary between the Western and Eastern versions of Christianity, between Rome and Constantinople, between Roman Catholic and Greek Orthodox. With the accession of the Baltic states, the Union now includes territories that were once part of the Soviet Union itself.

As in the nineteenth century, the 'Europeanness' of Russia itself has become a matter of debate. Opposing the division of the Continent, de Gaulle invoked 'Europe from the Atlantic to the Urals', thus defining Russia as both European and Asian. Rather later, Gorbachev envisaged glasnost ensuring Russia's place in 'our common European home', thus defining Russia as firmly European. Today, other parts of the former USSR, especially of course Ukraine, turn to 'Europe' rather than 'Russia'.

Equally, the Europeanness of Turkey is debated by Turks and non-Turks. As in Russia, one story of modern Turkey is the attempt to define itself as 'Western' and 'European', while another story is that this is a betrayal of its true identity. And contemporary Turkey brings up the whole relationship between Europe and Islam. The expansion of Islam for the 500 years after its foundation in the eighth century shut Europe off from the rest of the world, cutting connections to the east and south. In that sense Islam was responsible for the creation of its opposite, 'Christian Europe' (Davies 1997: 257). Halted at Poitiers in 732, the threatened Islamic conquest of Europe was pushed back in the West over the next centuries, and modern Spain was defined through the completion of the *reconquista* and the expulsion of the 'Moors' in the fifteenth century. However, in the same period Asia Minor, present-day Turkey, was conquered by the Ottomans and lost to Christendom. Constantinople finally fell in 1453 and the Balkans and modern Greece were absorbed into the still expanding Ottoman empire, which remained undefeated by Christian forces until the Battle of Lepanto in 1571. In 1683 the Turkish siege of Vienna was lifted; in 1686 Budapest was liberated from the Turks (and its Muslim and Jewish inhabitants systematically massacred). For the next two-and-a-half centuries 'Europe' expanded eastwards and south-eastwards as Hungary and the Balkans were reconquered. In the Danube lands and the Mediterranean, Europe continued to define itself against Islam. In the north and west there were other concerns, even if until the end of the eighteenth century British seafarers' main fear was that they might be captured and enslaved by Barbary (Moslem) corsairs (Colley 2002: 44). Today Romania and Croatia are part of the European Union and Turkey itself could eventually be a member. If only a tiny part of present-day Turkey is in 'Europe', if Europe geographically ends at the Bosporus, then we might remember that much of Asia Minor was part of the 'European' Christian world until the fifteenth century.

And finally there is Europe overseas. While still being invaded from the east, from the fifteenth century onwards Europeans in the west became the invaders. Most European countries have a shared history of colonisation. This meant not simply political rule over foreign territories, for colonisation often meant massive emigration – the 'Great White Plague' (Ferguson 2003: 59) in which Europeans exterminated or marginalised indigenous peoples – and the creation of European societies overseas. Indeed, much of British exceptionalism within Europe is because its links with the world beyond Europe were so strong: its colonies, its British societies overseas in Australia, New Zealand and (more ambiguously) southern Africa, its close connections with the USA (Belich 2010; Darwin 2009). By contrast, nineteenth-century Spain was much more introverted, despite the Latin American connection (and Cuba remained a Spanish colony until 1898). Nonetheless, so long as Algeria remained legally part of metropolitan France, the political boundary of Europe remained on the southern shore of the Mediterranean until 1962. Even today, a French *Département Outre Mer* (Overseas Department) such as Martinique in the Caribbean is legally part of France and hence European Union territory.

The ambiguity of boundaries is not simply a question of faulty terminology. Purely geographical boundaries turn out to be less use than one might expect: Morocco's application for membership of the European Community in 1987 was turned down because it was not a 'European state', yet Turkey's application is officially being processed, while Cyprus, well to the east of Istanbul, is already a member. Europe is a place, but where exactly it ends is impossible to define.

A land of plenty

In global terms Europe is rich. Compared not just to the masses of the 'global South', but also to the inhabitants of nearby middle-income countries, Europeans have a high standard of living. The living conditions of ordinary Europeans are those that represent the normality to which it seems the world's population now aspires.

Europe's wealth is the inheritance of its leadership of the world economy in the nineteenth century. In 1850, 56 per cent of all steam horse power in the world was in Europe (32 per cent in Britain). In 1896 the total had increased more than fivefold, but the European share had even risen to 61 per cent (Great Britain had fallen to 21 per cent) and the US share was approximately a quarter (Landes 1969: 221). The twentieth century is marked by the relative rise and then decline of the USA. At the start of the last century over one-third of the world's Gross Domestic Product (GDP) was produced in Western Europe, as opposed to 15 per cent in the USA. In mid-century the US share had risen to just over one-quarter, while that of Western Europe had fallen; by the end of the century the share of both these established industrial areas had fallen further to around 20 per cent (Figure 1.2). By then the first Asian Tigers (Hong Kong, Singapore, Taiwan, South Korea) had effectively caught up with Europe. More recently there has been the sudden emergence of China and even India, countries

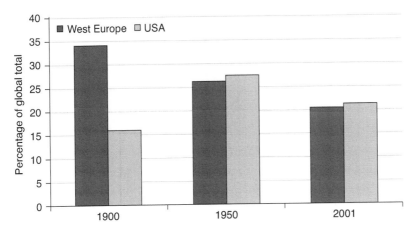

Figure 1.2 GDP as proportion of world total: Western Europe and the USA (derived from Maddison 2003: 233, 259).

so large that their growth makes an impact on the overall shape of the world economy long before their average living standards have approached that of the 'West'.

Europe has been living on inherited wealth in another sense. One alleged reason for slow economic growth has been Europe's relatively low level of innovation compared to the USA. This is clearest in the IT and software industries: the new wave of multinational companies linked to the internet are almost all American (Amazon, Google). European companies with global reach in this sector are few and far between. As Chancellor Merkel commented in a recent interview: 'Ich freue mich, dass wir noch SAP haben' (Merkel 2013). Despite such patches of success, Europe as a whole has become less important in the world economy.

What has mattered for ordinary Europeans is not this relative decline, but rather the staggering improvement in their living standards that occurred during the second half of the twentieth century. The years from the end of World War II to the first oil crisis in 1973 have been named the *trente glorieuses* (thirty glorious years) (Judt 2005: 324). The pace was set by the German *Wirtschaftswunder* with growth averaging 5.9 per cent between 1950 and 1973 (Maddison 1987; also Wehler 2013) but many other parts of Western Europe were not far behind. In Western Europe, but much less so in the increasingly different Eastern Europe, economic growth translated into unprecedented improvements in people's lives. It was during these years that most ordinary people in countries such as Britain for the first time could realistically expect to live in a dry and warm home with separate bedrooms and their own bathroom; they could expect access to medical care; they could afford holidays away from home; they could probably afford their own car. In 1951 in Britain, then the richest country in Europe, in England and Wales 21 per cent of the dwellings still had only outside toilets (General Register Office 1952). This normality, it is important to remember, is less than half a century old.

The enlargement of the EU has increased its internal diversity. All the original six member states were unequivocally some of the wealthiest countries in the world, but GDP per capita in some of the newest member states is similar to those of medium income countries. For example, a household defined as at risk of poverty in Germany has a better living standard than the median household in Romania (see especially Section 4.2). Such differences fuel the argument that denies any commonality between European countries (e.g. Baldwin 2009). There are two responses. First, the overwhelming majority of Europeans live in the richer states. Second, the European Union is a distinct polity, however difficult to classify (more than a nation state, less than a federal super-state). A country such as Romania is a poor member of a rich person's club, not an outsider looking plaintively in. Equally member states have been very differently affected by the post-2008 global economic crisis: at one extreme in Germany the export boom means rising living standards and effectively full employment, while in Greece average real incomes have plummeted and unemployment in June 2013 had reached fully 27.9 per cent (Eurostat 2013). Nonetheless, to date Greece remains part of the European Union: it is a poor member of a rich person's club.

Old Europe: demography

In world terms, the European age is over. Europe's share of the world's population, wealth and military power is smaller than what it was a hundred years ago. In fact the nineteenth century was exceptional. For most of the world's recorded history, Europe was relatively insignificant and isolated from richer civilisations to the east. Only during the nineteenth century did Europe's overseas expansion finally affect its share of the world's wealth and population. Thus in 1750 about a fifth of the world's population was in Europe; by 1900 this had climbed to over a quarter, but by 2000 it had fallen to less than one eighth (Figure 1.3).

During the nineteenth century industrialisation within Europe facilitated population growth. In Britain the initial impact of industrialisation was to lower living standards and life expectancy in the new cities; subsequent industrialisation elsewhere within Europe did not have this pattern. Outside of Europe population grew dramatically in the areas of European settlement, especially in the USA and Australia, but even in southern Africa. Outside these areas, population in the rest of the world initially grew more slowly, not least due to the initial impact of European imperialism itself (Figure 1.3).

By the twentieth century Europe had almost completed its demographic transition: high birth rates and high mortality rates gave way to low birth rates and low mortality rates. By contrast, in what was to become the Third World and is now the developing world, the impact of European medicine led to a dramatic reduction in mortality. Given that fertility there is only now beginning to fall, global population growth continues.

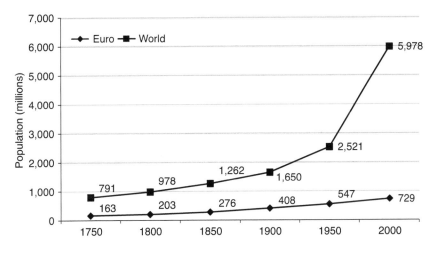

Figure 1.3 Europe and the world population, 1750–2000 (derived from United Nations 1999).

For over thirty years the continuing expansion of the global population has been seen as problematic, but meanwhile in Europe the population problem has been seen as our own declining population in absolute terms. In Europe, people not only continue to live longer, they also have fewer and fewer children. The result is a stagnant population and a novel age structure. In demographic terms Europe has become an old continent. In 2004, 16.4 per cent of the population of the EU28 were at least 65 years old; in 2014 this had already increased to 18.5 per cent (Eurostat 2015). This is very different to Third World countries, but also different even to the USA (Figure 1.4). This version of the population crisis is relatively new, since the immediate post-World War II years saw a 'baby boom' in Europe and in the USA. Furthermore, as Chapter 9 will show, the crisis is very different in different countries. Within the core of Europe it is particularly acute in Germany and above all in Italy, but among others France, the UK and Scandinavia all face an aging population, though not a dramatically declining one.

A zone of peace?

Economically, Europe is no longer the centre of the world. In military terms it is even weaker. Even during the Cold War, West European states always spent relatively less on the military than their American protector. This difference has remained until this day and even applies to the two nuclear-armed powers, France and the UK. Thus in 2003 total US military spending was $405 billion dollars, more than double the $208bn expenditure of the EU15; the US spent over US$1,400 per head of population; even France only spent $800 per head, and for the (then) EU as a whole the figure was only about $500. By 2012 US

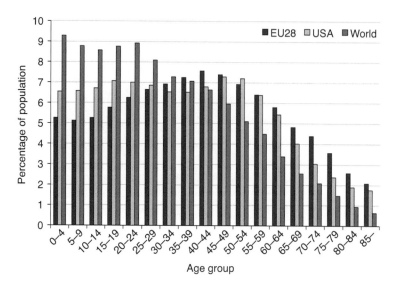

Figure 1.4 Population structure: EU28, USA and world, 2010 (derived from Eurostat, UN databases).

defence expenditure had reached $645.7bn (5.2 per cent of GDP) and remained the largest in the world (International Institute for Strategic Studies 2013). No European country approaches this proportion and Europe's total military expenditure is dwarfed by that of the USA.

It is often claimed that Europe's pacifism is a reaction to the slaughter of the two world wars. There is, however, no automatic connection here – as shown by the fact that after 1918 the same World War I produced much higher levels of anti-war sentiment in Britain and France than in Germany. Nonetheless, it remains true that in these wars far fewer American soldiers died than European soldiers, and of course the USA had virtually no civilian deaths. In World War I about 1.4 million French soldiers and about three-quarters of a million British soldiers lost their lives; the US figure was a mere 114,000. World War II was rather different, but US military losses of just over 400,000 pale into insignificance compared to the 4.3 million German military dead (Figure 1.5). All of this takes no account of the 8.7 million Russian military deaths or the estimated Russian civilian deaths of fully 25 million (Overy 1997: 288), quite apart from the mass murders of the Holocaust. Arguably Americans 'learnt' from World War II that advanced technologies meant they could win wars at relatively little cost; Europeans 'learnt' that advanced technologies simply meant more people died (Sheehan 2008). Certainly today the USA presents a picture of militarism that is often reminiscent of the Imperial Germany. In 1906 an unemployed Berlin shoemaker dressed himself in a captain's uniform, commandeered a troop of soldiers and 'ordered' the mayor of Köpenick to hand over the city funds to him.

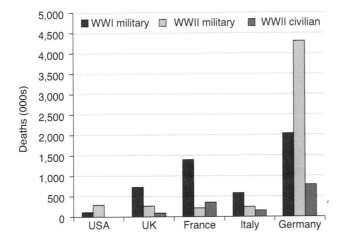

Figure 1.5 Twentieth-century deaths in war: Western Europe and USA (World War I figures from Ferguson 1999: 295; World War II from Davies 1997: 1328 for Europe and from US Department of Veterans Affairs).

Notes
World War II figures in the chart exclude the Holocaust (minimum 4.9 million, maximum 6.3 million); Polish military (0.1 million) and civilian (from 5.7 million to 7 million), Soviet Union military (8–9 million) and civilian (16–19 million) deaths. Some Holocaust victims are presumably also included in the Polish and Soviet Union civilian figures. All figures from Davies (1997).

World War II civilian deaths also exclude deaths in the immediate post World War ethnic cleansings, in particular of German *Vertriebene* (expellees) estimated at least 0.5 million (Douglas 2012).

The Captain of Köpenick remains a symbol of the Kaiserreich's infatuation with military rank. In the USA today, such is the prestige of the military that impostors often claim military experience and to have been awarded medals to which they are not entitled.

The European Union is often credited with making military conflict within Europe obsolete, although this story conveniently ignores the importance of American hegemony (in the 1950s one reason for European unity was that all the participants were American subalterns) (Mearsheimer 2010). Nonetheless, whatever the origins of the peace, it is certainly today the EU that ensures that war between states does not occur within Europe. The problem for Europe is that the world outside is not so pacific. In many ways, Europe's immediate environment is far more threatening than that of the USA. To the east the European borderlands of the old USSR are independent, but Russia perceives the Union's attraction for them as a threat; Russia's southern borderlands are at best unstable, at worst mired in civil war.

Closer to home the Yugoslav wars of the 1990s saw the deliberate destruction of cultural monuments, mass murder, mass rape and ethnic cleansing. This was all reminiscent of Europe in 1945 – and all passively tolerated by 'Europe'. Determination that this would not be allowed to happen again did ensure the intervention of some European states in Kosovo in 1998, but realistically the heavy lifting had to be done by the USA. In the Balkans the peace strategy has been to incorporate the warring states as fast as possible into the Union itself (Slovenia became a member in 2004, Croatia in 2013), but the conflicts in the region remain only just under control. To the south across the Mediterranean and in the Middle East Europe abuts a Muslim world with an exploding population of young men of military age and states with real military potential. And when such states collapse, as in Libya in 2012 or in Syria today (2015), the danger is even more acute and unpredictable. Instability and human rights abuses create pressures for intervention, but the consequences are to say the least unpredictable. Compared to the USA, Europe in fact lives in a more dangerous world.

Multiple political boundaries

European nation states are members of a series of 'European' supra-national organisations which do not have the same membership as the EU. Europe is criss-crossed by a multitude of inter-governmental organisations. In terms of formal international relations, the most important dimension is the military one. Most European states are members of NATO and thus pledged to mutual self-defence. NATO, however, is completely dominated by the USA, and during the Cold War all its European members, with the exception of France, were satisfied with this – the main aim of European military diplomacy was to ensure continued US military presence in Europe. With the end of the Cold War NATO lost its rationale. In 1992 the Treaty of Maastricht entrusted the EU's defence role (whatever that was) to the West European Union, a curious and almost forgotten organisation that had existed since 1954 as an attempt to establish a European military identity. The debacle of Yugoslavia showed that the EU was not even an effective inter-state alliance. In 1995 there was for the first time effective external intervention in Yugoslavia – not by the UN, not by the plethora of 'European' initiatives, but by NATO under clear US leadership, just as recent intervention in Libya was an Anglo-French initiative outside the framework of the EU.

In non-military areas European nation states have, however, developed some effective *European* inter-governmental organisations. Unlike in the case of the EU or the European Court of Human Rights (ECHR), here no sovereignty is ceded 'upwards': the organisations are simply clubs of independent nation states or independent national organisations. Nonetheless, these do seem to be both peculiarly frequent and peculiarly effective within Europe. The European Space Agency (ESA) launches European rockets and puts satellites into space, European state broadcasters meet together in the European Broadcasting Union (EBU) and bring us Eurovision. All these organisations are formally separate from the European Union and do not have the same membership as the EU.

Equally, many interest groups organise at a 'European' level. Since organisations need to lobby the Commission and the Parliament of the European Union, there is a tendency for national pressure groups to collaborate within the boundaries of the EU. Thus COPA (the European Agricultural Union) unites the farming pressure groups of all the member states. However, many 'European' pressure groups have not always had the same boundaries as the EC or the EU. The most obvious example is the ETUC (European Trade Union Congress), the membership of which included all the Scandinavian trade union confederations long before Sweden and Finland joined the EU in 1994 and 1995 respectively. Like the ETUC, BusinessEurope (previously UNICE – the Union of Industrialists and Confederation of Employers) is an official partner in the EU's 'Social Dialogue' and it too has members who are from non-member states. Add to this a multitude of private and professional associations, from European football clubs in UEFA to European sociologists in the European Sociological Association. The growth of these organisations demonstrates the emergence of a European civil society (Fligstein 2008), but the membership of these organisations is not the same as the territorial boundaries of the EU.

Since 1945 firms and, rather more recently, non-governmental organisations (NGOs) increasingly operate on an international level. Here 'Europe' usually includes all of Europe with no respect for political boundaries. Equally, international firms with their headquarters in the USA usually direct their 'European' business from one or more 'European' centres and many also centralise activities into one European location. Microsoft has area offices for all Europe in France and Germany and distributes all its European software from Ireland. On the other side, a non-governmental organisation like Greenpeace organises at national and European and global level: its international headquarters are in Amsterdam.

A zone of multiple polities

The European Economic Community (EEC) was founded in 1957 by the Treaty of Rome. The politicians who brought it into being, above all Jean Monnet, saw its original six members (France, West Germany, the Netherlands, Belgium, Luxembourg, Italy) as the building blocks of a political union; for them the Common Market was the first step towards a United States of Europe. The founding fathers of the Union assumed that the small steps of economic union would almost imperceptibly lead to their grand objective of political union. This belief was taken up in the first academic attempts to understand 'European integration'. The 'neo-functionalist' approach argued that harmonisation in one area of the states' activities would 'spill over' into others (Rosamond 2000). Today the European Union includes twenty-eight nation states, including all of Western Europe and Scandinavia with the exception of Switzerland and Norway. It is probably now both larger and less integrated than its founders would have anticipated.

The original Treaty of Rome committed its signatories to 'an ever closer union' of their peoples. At the same time, however, it was clear that other European countries might join what was then the EEC. The conflict between 'deepening' and 'widening' was built into the Union from its beginnings. Thus the first enlargement in 1973 brought in the UK along with Denmark and the Republic of Ireland. In 1963 and 1967 General de Gaulle had vetoed Britain's application to join, fearing its Anglo-American free trade attitude and its challenge to French influence. In retrospect de Gaulle was right on both counts: the UK has consistently advocated 'free market' policies within European institutions, while by delaying Britain's entry by ten years de Gaulle enabled European institutions to develop French traditions (and language) which they are only now losing. By contrast, Irish national identity and foreign policy influence were strengthened by European membership, and for the next thirty years Ireland became one of the most 'pro-European' member states. For very different reasons to Britain, popular support for European integration has always been weak in Denmark. Right from the beginning, enlarging Europe weakened Europe.

The next two waves of enlargement further increased the diversity of what became, with the Treaty of Maastricht in 1992, the European Union. The acceptance of applications from Greece (1981), Portugal and Spain (both in 1986) was partly because of the political desire to ensure that these countries did not again revert to dictatorships. All three countries were also poorer than the existing member states. By contrast, the enlargement of 1995 brought in Austria, Sweden and Finland, states which were some of the richest in Europe but which also all had strong social democratic and corporatist traditions. By the turn of the century the Europe of the Fifteen was thus already far more diverse than had been the Europe of the Six. Yet all member states had officially been part of the 'West' during the Cold War and in fact enlargement produced fewer strains than the first move from six to nine members. Decisive here was probably the role of the new states of the 1990s: Austria, Finland and Sweden reinvigorated the more socially inclusive aspects of the European project.

In 2004 the Europe of the Fifteen became the Europe of the Twenty-five. The population of this 'Europe' became nearly half a billion (457 million), of which 74 million or 16 per cent were in the new accession states (Eurostat 2015). This enlargement increased diversity still further. Of the ten new member states (Estonia, Latvia, Lithuania, Poland, Czech Republic, Slovakia, Hungary, Slovenia, Malta and Cyprus), all but Malta had a per capita GDP below that of Portugal, hitherto the poorest EU member. Furthermore, with the exception of Malta and Cyprus, all shared a common past within the Soviet empire, as do the most recent new members, Bulgaria (2007), Romania (2007) and Croatia (2013). However much such countries might be 'returning' to Europe, they had not shared in the post-World War II consolidation of the democratic state as welfare state. Furthermore, in such countries the state was seen mainly as a repressive institution, and certainly not as the generator and guarantor of public space. Consequently, in such countries American understandings of the state as an intrusion on a realm of private freedom have much more resonance.

Each new state that joins the Union has to completely accept the *acquis communitaire* (the cumulative legislation of the Union). Yet this common legal framework does not itself create a new European super-state, a 'United States of Europe' that is just a scaled-up version of the existing national states. The age of

European nation states is often dated from the Treaty of Westphalia which ended the Thirty Years' War in Germany in 1648. The Treaty established the principle that states were completely sovereign within their own territory; the borders of the state delimited a single homogenous judicial space: anyone entering this territory was subject to the laws of *this state* and to those of no other. In this Westphalian world, states, of whatever size, were legally self-contained entities.

Today Europe has returned to the Middle Ages, when the legal writ of the monarch, the church and the borough could all co-exist in the same physical territory. The nation state is certainly more important to Europeans' daily lives than is the state in the USA, but utterly unlike Americans, Europeans also participate in the rights and duties of other legal institutions 'above' the nation state. Europeans can appeal over the heads of their national government not only to the EU (in particular to the European Court of Justice), but also to the European Court of Human Rights, a supra-national legal system within Europe which predates the European Community and remains separate from the EU. Citizens of the signatory states are entitled to appeal to it against their own governments on human rights issues.

Furthermore, the EU itself has become internally more varied: not all states participate in all 'European' activities. Most obviously, not all states are members of the Eurozone, which means some member states have only indirect influence on 'European' monetary policy. Equally, although the EU is meant to ensure free movement of goods, services and people within its territory, this itself has become variable. Most but not all of the EU15 are signatories of the Schengen agreement, which reduces frontier controls between them; no sooner was the EU enlarged in 2004 than existing member states imposed restrictions on the movement of labour. Whatever else the EU is, it is not a federal European super-state. This is not because the British Conservatives (or even the French Gaullists) have won the argument in favour of the nation state, but rather because the age of Westphalia has ended in Europe.

1.2 From national welfare states to the European social model

One peculiarity of contemporary Europe is the extent to which national identity has in the last half century become interwoven with the (national) welfare state. For Europeans, part of their Swedishness or Frenchness or Germanness is their involvement in the institutions of their welfare state (Johnston *et al.* 2010). Whereas in the nineteenth century the national schools and the national army made, in the title of Eugen Weber's classic study, 'peasants into Frenchmen' (Weber 1979), in the second half of the twentieth century it has been national education (and not just primary education), national insurance systems and national systems of health provision which made workers and consumers also citizens.

At one extreme the Swedish conception of the welfare state makes the nation state into the *folkhem* (people's home): to be a member of the nation state is to receive and contribute to collective welfare. While here the rhetoric subordinates the market completely to the egalitarian community, the German *Sozialmarkt-wirtschaft* (social market economy) conceptualises the market and society as interwoven. Such an understanding of Germany has been supported, although of course with differing emphases, by both Christian democrats and social democrats. In the early 1980s, when the German economy was an international success story, a social democratic election slogan was 'Modell Deutschland', implying that the *German* social market economy was a source of national pride and a model for other countries. Even Britain, today usually conceptualised within Continental Europe as epitomising Anglo-Saxon liberalism and individualism, has a *National* Health Service, probably more important to national self-identity than the monarchy. Here too we find a remarkable and surprising political consensus – it was after all Margaret Thatcher who declared 'The NHS is safe with us.' Unlike Americans, Europeans define their nationality in part through their involvement in a national welfare state.

Welfare state modelling

The post-World War II settlement in Continental Europe was a political consensus based on those forces which had opposed fascism, or at least which wanted no longer to be identified with it.[1] This meant the political left (the trade unions, the social democrats, the communists), but crucially it also meant the political right (the various forms of Christian democracy). For such people it was axiomatic that the new Europe had to avoid the social conflicts of the inter-war period, and that meant a rejection of both authoritarian dictatorships and naked capitalism. For them the market was not an end in itself and a broadly interventionist stance towards the labour market was desirable.[2] The historical strength of this tradition was shown in the 1980s. When the dictatorships of Greece, Portugal and Spain fell in the 1970s and these countries entered the EU, here too the 'right' was Christian democracy. On the left the new consensus emerged in the late 1940s, with the separation between the communists and the social democrats as the Cold War intensified. This paved the way for social democracy's final commitment to a market economy, recognised above all in the German SPD's Bad Godesberg programme of 1959.

This consensus provided the basis for the development of welfare states. For all the substantial divergences between them in funding, coverage, etc., these states were the building blocks for Europe's system of social and labour market protection. However, these systems remained firmly national. While the European Community was developing as a 'common market', the social model was being built up at national level. In many ways the national states were strengthened during this period (Milward 1999).

Until the 1960s social scientists assumed that the growth of the welfare state was an inevitable part of industrialisation. Authors such as Wilensky (cited in Kleinman 2002: 11) argued that, as societies became richer, they would spend a larger percentage of GDP on welfare. Accordingly, differences between societies were essentially a consequence of the stage of economic development. Since the New Deal, Big Government had become as much a part of the American consensus as it had in Europe. Equally in the immediate post-World War II period within Europe, the most dramatic expansion of the welfare state had occurred in the UK under the Attlee Labour government. In this period it therefore made some sense to see all industrial societies as eventually converging, with the Anglo-Saxon welfare state as the norm.

After the 1960s the role of the USA and the UK changed. With the collapse of the Great Society programme, 'welfare' in the USA came to mean various forms of income maintenance for the poor, concentrated in the inner city ghettoes (see Section 5.3) and had less and less relevance to employed and unionised 'blue-collar' employees. By contrast, it is precisely in the 1970s that the European welfare states matured (Esping-Andersen 1999: 2) into their current configuration. For example, from the late 1960s Scandinavian states provided extensive family services (childcare, residential homes, home help for the aged) and the extent of these services (along with the employment they provide) became the defining characteristic of the Scandinavian welfare states. Whereas in the immediate post-World War II period the British welfare state was often seen as a model for other European countries, by the 1970s, despite considerable expansion, that role had long since ended.

Part of the explanation for the divergence between the USA and Western Europe is the nature of the late 1960s revolt. The obvious similarities of cultural revolution have allowed contemporary historians to ignore a crucial difference between the European and the American popular upheavals of the period. In Europe the 1960s and early 1970s saw the conjunction of the student movement and the alternative sub-culture with a radicalised trade union movement. May 1968 in France was telegenic because of the student riots in the Left Bank of Paris, but those interwove with mass strikes and occupations in factories and other workplaces. The links between students and 'workers' (who actually included many white-collar employees) were also very clear in the Italian 'Hot Autumn' of 1969, but much weaker in Britain or (especially) Germany. Nonetheless, everywhere across Europe this period was the culmination of rank and file initiatives within the trade unions and a politicisation of young working class people.

In Europe a logical response to these challenges was the development of corporatist bargaining between unions, employers and government; a massive expansion of the welfare state providing services, not to mention employment and even careers; the first stirrings of 'social Europe' rhetoric; and last but not least, the expansion of higher education to attract more ambitious young working class people. In many countries the period also saw an expansion of trade union membership (see Section 5.2). By contrast, in the USA the popular movement was above all a resurgence of ethnic politics – the Civil Rights movement developed into black power and the ghetto riots. Political change in the 1970s meant on the one hand a sustained assault on racism on a scale unparalleled in Europe, but on the other hand a form of cultural politics which meant that 'liberal' issues became increasingly disconnected from the overt concerns of the majority of Americans.

By the 1990s scholars accepted that differences between national welfare states were largely self-perpetuating and national developments were path dependent. Even today discussion of these differences remains a debate with the seminal *Three Worlds of Welfare Capitalism* (Esping-Andersen 1990) which classified welfare states into three groups: *liberal* (e.g. the UK, the USA), where the welfare state is a 'safety net', providing means-tested benefits for those who cannot afford an alternative; *corporatist* (e.g. France, Germany), where the welfare state operates to ensure that families can maintain their living standards and position in society despite the vicissitudes of the market; *social-democratic* (e.g. Sweden, Denmark) where the state provides generous benefits to all citizens, who conversely are all expected to work and contribute to society.

Such classifications are central to what has been termed the 'welfare modelling business' (Abrahamson 1999) which has generated detailed comparisons of European welfare states and detailed criticisms of Esping-Andersen's original argument. Crucial for any discussion of European specificity is that Esping-Andersen's typology classifies the UK, Canada, Australia, New Zealand and the USA in one single category. Historically this ignores not only the historical role of Britain in the formation of the post-World War II welfare state, but also the avant-garde role of Australia and New Zealand in the first half of the twentieth century. Freed from the constraints of British deference, these British dominions soon developed a popular radical tradition, contributing to the egalitarianism of the British new world.[3]

Part of the problem here is that whereas Esping-Andersen focused on the purpose of state expenditure, his critics focused on results – the extent to which the welfare state makes a difference to final incomes. This in turn is the result of different conceptions of the role of the welfare state. Within the Anglo-Saxon world the welfare state is meant to be about 'vertical' income redistribution between social classes or at least income categories; accordingly, the welfare state is criticised if it is shown that middle class people benefit most from the state. By contrast, within the 'corporatist' tradition, although much less clearly explicated, the state also has a 'horizontal' role, ensuring 'solidarity' between all citizens. Catholic social thought made an important contribution here, for it accepts social inequality but insists that all members of society nonetheless have mutual obligations: private property is desirable, but comes with responsibilities. Before World War II such responsibilities were seen to be largely exercised through voluntary activity and charity. Roman Catholicism was largely hostile to the state unless – as in Spain or Ireland – it could control it. The experience of World War II and the involvement of the Catholic laity in popular resistance to fascism produced a sea change. Now 'Christian democracy' (the title indicating the weaker formal link to the Roman Catholic Church) accepted that some such solidarity had to occur through the state itself.

Different versions of this history have been shared by most members of the pre-2004 member states of the European Union. By contrast, those new member states which were behind the Iron Curtain until after 1989 have a totally different historical experience. The extensive welfare provisions of their old regime (from subsidised housing and free medicine to income support through full if notional employment) were the most effective way in which the dictatorial and at times totalitarian party state could ensure some limited popular acceptance. Such top-down welfare was thus interwoven with an undemocratic and oppressive state. In what had been East Germany (the DDR) this was simply replaced with the institutions of the West German welfare system, but elsewhere the collapse of the ancien regime initially meant the collapse of any welfare system. Discussions of the European welfare state still often ignore this new divergence within 'Europe'.

Given this multiplicity, it is clearly implausible to talk of any one European model of the welfare state, even within the pre-2004 enlargement member states. Just as a focus on political boundaries does not produce any single definition of 'Europe', nor does a focus on welfare state forms. However, European national societies do seem to have a shared commitment to some form of welfare state, but this is something they share to some extent with some other societies outside of Europe, most obviously in the non-American countries of the Anglosphere. Thus, stressing the UK is not assimilated to the USA does not make it any more part of a distinctive European family of welfare states. The relationship of the UK to the European core remains ambiguous.

European Social Policy and the European social model

Although the EEC was formed as a common market, the founders always believed that economic integration needed to be buttressed by social arrangements: those who lost out (at least in the short term) from market integration should be supported. Thus in 1957 the Treaty of Rome included some rudimentary social provisions for retraining workers affected by industrial change. When the EEC was enlarged in the early 1970s to include Denmark, Ireland and the UK, this was accompanied by the first major expansion of social policy: the Social Action Programme of 1974 which gave employees rights to consultation in relation to mergers, tightened health and safety regulations and above all perhaps, initiated European legislation in equal opportunities (see Section 9.3) (Gold 1993: 22).

Just as in the late 1960s some European politicians such as Willi Brandt had felt that the EU needed a social face, in the lead-up to the Single European Act François Mitterrand began to raise the notion of a 'European social space' and the Maastricht Treaty which founded the European Union also involved the 'Social Charter of Fundamental Rights of Workers'. Yet the Charter highlighted the ambiguities of EU social policy. The Charter was not signed by the UK, even after the other member states had made substantial concessions; it therefore became a voluntary add-on to EU membership, rather than an integral part of it. When New Labour came to power the UK signed the Charter, thus removing its anomalous status. The Charter was, however, essentially declaratory, creating no new rights that were legally actionable. By contrast, successive EU treaties have torn down legal barriers to trade across the EU and created legal rights to fair competition across the EU.

According to Aust *et al.* (2002), from the mid-1980s onwards Jacques Delors as President of the European Commission began to popularise the idea of a 'European Social Model'. For Delors, while the USA represented pure capitalism, the European social model involved protection of the weak against the market as well as the active involvement of business associations and trade unions in socio-economic decision-making – the process known as social partnership. For Delors the development of the EU meant two parallel processes. On the one hand it involved what Scharpf (1999: 45) has called 'negative integration', the removal of national barriers to trade across the EU. On the other hand it involved what Scharpf termed 'positive integration', the creation of European-level institutions, including crucially those concerned with social protection. The paradox of Delors' presidency was that, not least thanks to the determination of Peter Sutherland as Competition Commissioner, the European Commission was successful in negative integration (the completion of the Single Market programme) but achieved far less in terms of positive integration (Grant 1994: 160).

By the mid-1990s the European social model was being actively propagated by the European Commission as defining the distinctiveness of the European Union in the world. Thus the Commission's 1994 White Paper on Social Policy (European Commission 1994) defined its aim as 'Preserving and developing the European Social Model'. The document repeatedly stressed the 'shared values' of Europeans that 'economic and social progress must go hand in hand' (p. 9) and the importance of preserving 'the basis of social protection which the people of Europe have come to prize' (p. 10). Such values and institutions were contrasted with those of the USA, which might have been better at creating jobs but where 'levels of social solidarity' were lower (p. 11).

The term hardly caught on in the UK, but elsewhere in the Union the European social model increasingly became part of normal political discourse. Delors' view can be summarised in Lionel Jospin's slogan, 'a market economy, not a market society', although the ESM began to include notions of 'sustainability' (a term which might simply mean 'sustainable' economic growth, but which also could include environmental concerns). Central to this understanding of the ESM was the claim that high social expenditure not only ensured social solidarity, it was also good for business competitiveness since it ensured a skilled and committed workforce.

In one sense the idea that the EU, as opposed to its member states, could have a 'social policy' is absurd, especially if social policy is defined in the 'Anglo-Saxon' sense, as meaning the collective provision of social services (education, healthcare and personal social services, social security and housing). In all these areas individual European states have extensive policies, budgets and institutions. By contrast, the EU has minimal financial resources and powers to tax; it provides no direct social services; it can at most regulate (and even this, of course, requires the consent of the member states).

In fact the initial focus of EU social policy was the regulation of the employment relationship. There were two reasons for this. First, the origins of the EU in the 'common market' meant that European level institutions dealt with individual Europeans only in so far as they were involved in the market as employees. The Social Charter covered not 'people' or 'citizens' but 'workers'. Second, this was consistent with the 'Continental' tradition of social policy (as opposed to both Scandinavian and British traditions) which historically has seen the 'social question' to be tackled by regulating employment.

Interwoven with the regulation of employment was the involvement of the 'social partners' in developing and implementing legislation. The Economic and Social Committee ('EcoSoc') comprises representatives of employers and employees and gives opinions when the Commission proposes initiatives. It is often criticised as continuing 1970s-style corporatism, in which trade unions and employers make decisions instead of parliament. However, such 'corporatism' was enhanced when the Agreement on Social Policy in the Maastricht Treaty (1992) allowed collective bargaining between unions and employers at EU level to negotiate binding legal agreements, such as the EU Directive on Parental Leave of 1996.

Social policy developed in other ways. First, there were some elements of a transfer union (i.e. a political entity within which resources are transferred from richer to poorer members). In comparison with national budgets, the European Social Fund (ESF) and the European Regional Development Funds were always puny, yet they have had a real impact in some regions of Europe. For example, European funds made a significant contribution to changing Ireland from being one of the poorest to one of the richest member states during the 1990s, Despite the relatively smaller sums involved for the post-2004 enlargements, these are important in most of the new member states. Spending on regional and social cohesion through the European Social Fund, the European Regional Development Fund and the Cohesion Fund comprised 35.7 per cent of the EU 2007–2013 budget. There is no equivalent transfer of resources within a free trade area organisation such as the North American Free Trade Area (NAFTA) which comprises the USA, Canada and Mexico.

The EU has also influenced social policy agendas. Through the ESF in particular the EU has become involved in anti-poverty policy across Europe and so contributed to making issues of poverty and 'social exclusion' more important on the policy agenda of the 'Mediterranean' states. In vocational training, environmental policy and urban policy, the EU is now an actor in its own right: across Europe policy in these areas often involves local, national *and European* institutions. Such institutions and policies do define a European space rather than a simple market. The term 'space' is useful here: it suggests a geographical area across which policies apply (not necessarily evenly) and in which political actors operate. Furthermore, such a space has boundaries, defining what is non-European.

Some observers (e.g. Aust *et al.* 2002) identify a rather different version of the ESM emerging first in the mid-1990s but becoming dominant during this century. In line with the 'Third Way' policies that enjoyed a brief fame under New Labour in the UK, the market has been prioritised as the most efficient way to organise any activity. Whereas the Delorsian understanding of the ESM was identified with what Aust calls a Euro-Keynesian economic strategy (tackling unemployment through European public investment), this new approach was 'neo-liberal' (tackling unemployment by making the labour market more flexible). Thus, while the first version of the ESM sought to strengthen labour market institutions, the second sought to deregulate the labour market. Second, whereas the Delorsian ESM sought to build up European institutions, this new ESM saw progress occurring through inter-governmental agreements. European policy became implemented not through directives but through non-binding agreements and dissemination of best practice – so-called 'soft law'.

At the Lisbon European Summit of 2000 the member states committed themselves to making Europe 'the most competitive and dynamic knowledge-based economy in the world, capable of sustainable economic growth with more and better jobs and greater social cohesion' (Declaration of the European Council, March 2000). The Council set numerical targets for employment such as a total employment rate of 70 per cent by 2010. These were to be achieved through mutual benchmarking, the so-called Open Method of Co-Ordination or OMC (de la Porte and Pochet 2012). Thus instead of imposing a common policy, the European Employment Strategy was expected to encourage both subsidiarity (each state acted autonomously) and integration (each state learnt from the others). A similar approach, involving National Action Plans and annual national reporting, was also developed for the area of social inclusion (Heidenreich and Bischoff 2008).

Even before the global economic crisis hit Europe in 2008 it was clear that these strategies had very little direct impact. At the same time, this second version of the ESM was not simply 'neo-liberal'. There was no convergence towards an American-style minimalist welfare state and no all-out assault on employment protection. In the crisis, however, 'Europe' lacked any explicit social policy and has increasingly become identified with the destruction of national systems of social protection.

1.3 Evaluating European distinctiveness

Given the divergences between European welfare states, and given also the limited impact of European Union social policy, is it really possible to speak of a European social model? Two quotes from prominent European politicians from the middle of the last decade are suggestive:

> Europe has built a distinctive economic and social model that has combined productivity, social cohesion and a growing commitment to environmental sustainability.

> (Kok 2004: 7)

Preserving our European social model – our specific combination of market economy, welfare state and democracy – requires action not only at the European level but also at the global level.

(Lamy 2004:18)

In both these quotes far more is involved than simply the welfare state. I now suggest that the European social model can be taken as a *combination* of features of European national states (see also Mau and Verwiebe 2010: 45). At the same time, there is also a European dimension: European states not only share similarities with others in the same geographical space, they also all participate in a common political system.

The welfare state and social citizenship

The first and most obvious feature of the traditional (West) European state is that it is a welfare state. In the second half of the twentieth century European states became welfare states instead of warfare states. At the macro level, social expenditure vastly outpaces 'defence' expenditure, and while this has also happened in the USA, the shift has been greater in Europe. At the micro level Europeans continually interact with the institutions of the welfare state (education, health, social security) whereas many live their entire lives with only the most minimal contact with the military.

While social policy researchers usually focus on the level of social expenditure as the key index, arguably more important for social integration is the extent to which citizenship involves social rights. Social rights can be counter-posed to charity. Charity and voluntary work are also part of good citizenship, and Americans are justly proud of their traditional generosity in this area. However, while charity may be good for the donor,[4] by itself not even the most supportive tax environment generates enough donations to make a major difference to income distribution. Furthermore, social rights cannot depend on the voluntary goodwill of others, since there is no necessary correlation between the extent of the recipient's need for social support and the intensity of the donor's charitable feeling.

Such rights necessarily have costs, not just in monetary terms but also in terms of restraints on the rights of others. If there is to be free education, then taxpayers have to pay for it. My right to free education constrains your right to spend your income. And frequently, rights and obligations are imposed on the same people (my right to health means I have to pay higher taxes). Furthermore, once people have *rights*, they are also opened up to *duties*. The political right to vote was historically linked to the obligation of universal military service, while today welfare rights are often defined as involving the obligation to look for work. This density of rights *and obligations* in Europe means that Europeans are of necessity more entangled in the state than Americans.

The importance of social rights in Europe also has its converse, the unimportance of group rights. As individuals, citizens have social rights and these rights are by definition universal: they apply to all members of the society. Because social rights have substantial financial costs, they are only sustainable if they are interwoven with notions of mutual responsibility (I am prepared to pay taxes or even 'insurance' to finance my fellow citizen's health needs). In other words, extensive social rights require a strong sense of *national* identity, and are incompatible in the long run with strong multi-cultural policies which prioritise the identities of ethnic sub-groups. Indeed, one of the more effective (and unusual) arguments *against* social rights is the claim that the individualistic USA is far more tolerant of cultural diversity and immigration than is socially cohesive Europe. Historically, inequality has been posed and challenged in the USA in terms of ethnicity and 'race', but in terms of social class in Europe.

For decades European welfare states have allegedly been in 'crisis', but for all the continual talk of cut-backs in fact up from 1982 up until 2007 public social spending as a percentage of GDP had increased in most countries (Figure 1.6). In particular, the main story was the increase in social spending in the Mediterranean states as they caught up with the states of Northern Europe (Greve 2003). However, this stability masks changes in the form of *some* welfare states: the push towards so-called asset-based welfare especially in the UK, the expansion of private finance in education and health, the marginalisation of public housing, the outsourcing of public services to private companies. None of these changes are universal across Europe, and in some areas such as childcare provision social rights have expanded. Equally, more than four years after the onset of the economic crisis there has been no general roll-back of the welfare state.

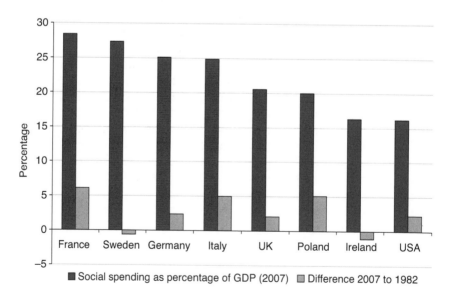

Figure 1.6 Social spending as percentage of GDP, 1982–2007 (derived from OECD 2011: 74).

Restrained income inequality

Social citizenship flourishes where the income distribution is relatively egalitarian. As Section 4.2 will show in more detail, income inequality has been growing in some, but not all, European countries. Nonetheless, no European country approaches the levels of income inequality found in the USA. Data for the late 2000s shows that in no European country is the Gini coefficient for income inequality larger than in the USA and no European country has such a large proportion of the population in poverty. Thus whereas 17.3 per cent of the US population has less than half of the average (median) income, the closest to this level within Europe is Estonia at 13.9 per cent, and in most European countries this applies to less than 10 per cent of the population (OECD 2011). Compared to some (but not all) European countries, the USA also generates greater inequality at the top: it has a larger proportion of people receiving twice the average income. Finally, the USA is the land of the super-rich: no European country has such a concentration of wealthy individuals (e.g. Atkinson and Piketty 2007). Indeed, only in the UK has there been a growth of the 'super-rich' on a scale which begins to match that in the USA so that in both countries very rich private individuals become major social actors in their own right (Section 4.4).

Economic citizenship

European societies have also developed institutions of *economic citizenship*, rights which make employment and the labour market a distinct legal area. This involves the right to representation, most developed in the German tradition of *Mitbestimmung* (co-determination) whereby employees are represented at both workplace level (in the works council) and enterprise level (on the supervisory board). Just as social citizenship is not the same as charity, so economic citizenship is very different to participation as promoted by American-style human resource management. Such 'direct participation' can be much welcomed by employees and of course is claimed by its proponents to increase commitment and productivity. What matters here, however, is that direct participation *is not a right*. To paraphrase the Bible: management giveth, and management taketh away.

Employment rights are also a constituent part of economic citizenship. Compared to American workers, European workers enjoy protection against dismissal; they have rights to maternity leave and even parental leave; their working hours are regulated, as often is 'non-standard work' such as temporary contracts and agency working; their wages are usually determined at national, regional or sectoral level. Furthermore, if they are unemployed or sick, they receive income support and so do not have to work at poverty wages. It has now become an article of faith for many employers, economists, financial journalists and, above all, American commentators that these rights define Europe's 'rigid labour market' and are the cause of European unemployment. Such claims are of course hotly contested, and in any case if made today ignore the significant changes in employment regulation in many countries. The economic consequences can be debated, but distinctiveness of European economic citizenship cannot be denied (Teague 1999).

The key change has been the decline in union membership. Here again there is wide diversity. Whereas in some countries decline started as early as the 1980s, in Sweden trade union density was increasing until the end of the century (Visser 2006). Before the onset of the crisis in 2008 over two-thirds of employees were still in unions in Scandinavia as compared to less than a tenth in France (Figure 1.7). Actual bargaining coverage has not declined to nearly the same extent, so the decline in membership probably exaggerates the decline in union power. Nonetheless, labour market flexibility has clearly reduced the number of employees in secure jobs and hence undermined the workplace as the basis for distinct rights. Everywhere labour market 'reform' has meant just flexibility (the erosion of employment protection) rather than flexicurity (less job security but more vocational training combined with active job placement and support). Especially in Germany, the result has been the emergence for the first time of a low wage service sector on the US model. Just as the key elements of economic citizenship depended on national institutions, so their erosion has had relatively little to do with the EU. The major exceptions are in the construction

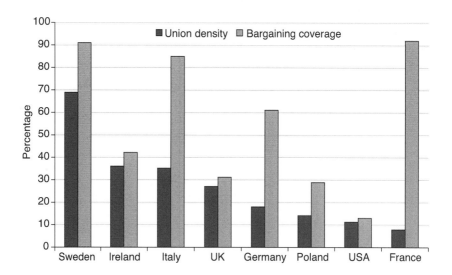

Figure 1.7 Trade union density and bargaining coverage, 2011 (derived from ICTWSS database, Visser 2013).

Notes
Union density: unionised employees as a percentage of wage and salaries in employment; all figures for 2010 or 2011.

Bargaining coverage: employees covered by collective or wage bargaining as a percentage of all wage and salary earners with the right to bargaining (adjusted as proposed by Traxler 1994); figures for most recent available year from 2008.

industry, where the new free movement of workers and the use of various forms of posted workers has enabled wage cutting and erosion of standards in some countries.

The backbone state

Finally, the European social model involves a particular form of state where the state is the *backbone* of society. Welfare states are nationally bounded. Within their territorial boundaries national states raise the taxes that fund the social expenditure; within these same boundaries they define which individuals are entitled to what support. Strong social rights necessitate strong states. These same national states also maintain the public realm. Unlike in dictatorships, where 'civil society' opposes the state, through its public institutions the European state maintains civil society. The public realm is the space, whether virtual or physical, where all citizens have equal rights. In the public realm the ties of family or ethnicity are excluded, but so too is the market. A strong state ensures a broad public realm populated by citizens with equal rights, unlike the market in which consumers exercise their rights by dint of their inherently unequal purchasing power. If politics is the public realm, then each citizen is equal; if politics is a market, then by definition some customers have more money than others. In the public sphere things are done not for profit, but for the general good. A public transport system may not actually be provided by the state, but it is provided *for the public*. 'Public service broadcasting' – a concept almost unknown in the USA – means that some media are considered too important to be run purely for profit, since citizens have a right to good quality entertainment and impartial news which the market cannot be trusted to deliver. Similarly, it is accepted that the state should play a major role in providing education and health, since these involve notions of equity which it would be difficult for a commercial company to apply. This 'public realm' is distinct from both the market and the private spheres. While the public realm is not the same as the public sector, 'central to it are the values of citizenship, equity and service' (Marquand 2004: 27). A strong state has citizens who by definition have equal rights in the public realm.

If the backbone state is perhaps the least noticed of the four pillars of the ESM, it is also where the most decisive changes are occurring, changes which potentially undermine the entire ESM. Health policy, social policy and educational policy are key areas for positive integration. So long as the national state remains the key actor, then a European health policy would require the harmonisation of national systems. Such harmonisation would involve positive integration through the construction of European institutions. This has only happened to a very limited extent. Instead, the very absence of any such institutional development has opened the way for market development: the principle that *any* public service should be open to competitive provision.

The European social model was largely constructed at national level: the European social model is or was a cluster of different national systems. Equally, its dismantling started at the national level, a process which to date has if anything exacerbated differences between the different European countries. Initially the EU supplemented this process and so consolidated the European social model. For the last decade the process has gone into reverse. Having long abandoned its social face, the European Union has begun to destroy the European social model.

1.4 Defining Europe: inclusion and cohesion

Especially within Anglophone discussion, the welfare state is normally thought of as providing a safety net, a floor below which no-one should fall. Even this minimalist conception of the welfare state contains two rather different ideas. The commitment to a minimum level of income has implications for income distribution: we may allow some people to be very wealthy, but we do not allow anyone to be very poor. In these terms, the welfare state can be said to prevent *social exclusion*, to ensure social inclusion. At the same time, the notion of a safety net implies social solidarity: the justification for the income floor is a common mutual responsibility between the members of the society who are tied together by some unspecified social bonds. In these terms the welfare state prevents social atomisation and creates *social cohesion*.

Both 'social inclusion' and 'social cohesion' appear to have entered the English language discussion through European policy debates. The term 'cohesion' was added into the European Treaty by the Single European Act, which enjoined the member states to develop 'cohesion' with the poorer states (Gold 1993). In this case cohesion is something to do with overcoming regional inequalities. By contrast, social exclusion seems to refer more to inequality and poverty within societies, as for example in 1994 when the Commission's White Paper on social policy referred to 'the fight against social exclusion' (European Commission 1994). Yet sometimes the two are treated as synonymous, as in the Lisbon declaration, where 'social cohesion' clearly means more than just regional convergence:

> The Union has today set itself a new strategic goal for the next decade: to become the most competitive and dynamic knowledge-based economy in he world, capable of sustainable economic growth with more and better jobs and greater social cohesion.
>
> (Declaration of the European Council, March 2000)

Yet at least implicitly, some academic discussion differentiates the two terms. For Durkheim, complex societies were always threatened by *anomie*, a sense of normlessness and over-individualisation, a situation that is captured by the contemporary term 'atomisation'. Social cohesion can be seen as going back to Durkheim's concerns and being an essentially 'horizontal' issue about the forms of social solidarity and, in the broadest sense, social values. A cohesive society has high levels of mutual support or, in contemporary parlance, 'social capital'

(Putnam 2000). Such cohesion is compatible with social inequality (those below may defer to those above them, those above may feel obligation and duty to those who serve them). Social cohesion can be measured by the extent to which members of the society trust each other and the state.

By contrast, inclusion is a 'vertical' issue about the extent of social inequality. The socially excluded lack access to material and cultural resources and so are outside of society (see Section 4.2). In a market society where most things and most services can be bought and sold, this is above all a question of money. In these terms, social exclusion can be measured by the distribution of income. The more unequal the income distribution, the greater the level of social exclusion. Even in terms of income, there can be many forms of inequality: there can be a few very well off people, while the rest of the population share a broadly similar situation; one section of the population can be clearly poor but everyone else can enjoy a modest affluence; there can be more or less clear gaps between different groups, etc. Furthermore, income is only one aspect of inequality: inequality encompasses health and mortality rates, chances of access to education, etc. Fundamentally, the exclusion/inclusion dimension therefore involves questions of power. Those who are excluded are pushed to the margins of society, they are kept out of society, while political power may or may not be dependent on economic power.

Each of the two dichotomies cohesion/atomisation and inclusion/exclusion therefore have multiple aspects and raise issues for empirical research. Nonetheless, the analytical distinction between them is fundamental to thinking about the variety of contemporary societies. The extent to which they do vary together is an important empirical question. Thus (if we take for the moment 'social cohesion' and 'social capital' to be equivalents) it is perfectly logical for Putnam to investigate whether there is an empirical relationship between social capital and social inequality (Putnam 2000). Recent work on the social consequences of inequality suggest that highly unequal societies also tend to have more social problems, which we could take to indicate high levels of atomisation (Wilkinson and Pickett 2009). However, the differentiation between social inclusion and social cohesion assumes that *in principle* socially cohesive societies can be either inclusive (egalitarian) or exclusive; socially fragmented societies can also be either inclusive or exclusive.

Figure 1.8 charts these two different dimensions and places societies on them. The differentiation between the two dimensions can be seen clearest in the extreme areas of the chart. Millenarian social movements in the past and in the contemporary world wish to create societies which are cohesive and inclusive: this is above all the dream of the Bolshevik tradition. The attempt to achieve such a society ends in terror and mass slaughter: the Soviet purges, Mao's Great Leap Forward and subsequent cultural revolution, Pol Pot in Cambodia. Whereas these societies aspired to an egalitarian future, the fascist tradition of the twentieth century endorsed and exalted inequality: for the Nazis, hierarchy was no unfortunate aberration but to be desired (*Führerprinzip*). Yet the Nazis and fellow travellers also desired a cohesive society: they castigated the atomisation of liberal democracy and promised a new Volksgemeinschaft.

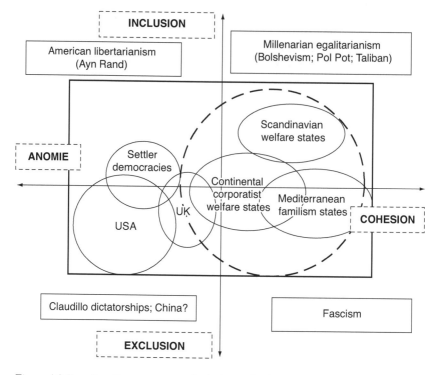

Figure 1.8 Locating European states: inclusion and cohesion.

The left side of the chart is defined by its high level of social atomisation which can also be thought of as the extensive penetration of the market. Because these societies are not cohesive, they cannot be characterised as totalitarian even though they are extremely violent and political order involves frequent use of force. More conventional dictatorships, such as those of twentieth-century Latin America, can be placed in the lower left-hand corner of the chart: such societies enforced political and social inequality but, perhaps precisely because they were economically conservative, made little attempt to create cohesive societies. With the economic changes of the last two decades and the spread of market-based inequality, contemporary China also belongs in this area. Finally, we can imagine a relatively egalitarian but highly individualistic society, in which there is a wide variety of lifestyles, but these are accessible to nearly all members of the society. Social solidarity, however, is, in this model, very limited and low even within the household. Even more so than the other three types, this exists largely as an ideal, since it is difficult to see how a fully developed market economy can avoid levels of economic inequality that in turn generate social exclusion. Although 'only' an ideal, this is a very powerful one: the image of the autonomous equal individual acting responsibly within the market is shared in many ways by most neo-liberal politicians and even some forms of radical feminism (e.g. Hakim on erotic capital). The ideal is particularly powerful when linked with images of the 'frictionless market' and information technology. Such ideas emerged in the rhetoric of cyber-populism of such magazines as *Wired* in the 1990s; they could be found in the 'Pirates' movements in Germany and Sweden. This linkage of individualism, entrepreneurialism and the market was very strong in the 1990s before the dot.com bubble finally burst (see especially Gadrey 2000); in the boom decade of the twenty-first century it resurfaced in a less egalitarian version with the popularity of the radical individualism of Ayn Rand.

All four cases discussed so far are outside the bounds of existing representative democracies and market economies. Within the borders of the solid rectangle on the chart, however, are placed the market democracies of the 'West' (including Japan). Although such societies share these key institutional features, they are nonetheless very different. This can be seen if the different worlds of welfare discussed above are located on the chart.

The top right area within the box is occupied by the Scandinavian welfare states. Sweden, Finland, Denmark and Norway all have low levels of poverty. Virtually all measures of social equality (life chances, social mobility, education access, etc.) put Scandinavian societies in an extreme position among market societies. In terms of cohesion, most studies report higher levels of interpersonal trust in Scandinavia than elsewhere (e.g. OECD 2011). A detailed analysis using European Values Survey data (van Oorschot and Arts 2005) concludes that despite the claim put forward by 'Third Way' advocates that the welfare state 'crowds out' social capital, the evidence is in fact the other way round: universalistic welfare states create social cohesion. Scandinavia shows how a society can therefore be both inclusive *and* cohesive; it can have egalitarian styles of life and also having high levels of formal and informal mutual support.

At the other extreme societies can be exclusive and individualistic, with a wide range of lifestyles of which some are completely inaccessible to significant numbers of the population, while at the same time the society as whole provides little formal or informal mutual support. The contemporary USA is an example of this form of society. Other measures of exclusion certainly point in the same direction as income poverty: the USA has extreme inequalities in access to health and education, the highest incarceration rate of any democratic society, etc. Furthermore, despite its self-image, rates of social mobility are not particularly high in the US and have been declining. Indeed, if exclusion is defined as exclusion from 'normal' lifestyles, in the USA the range of income inequality is so extreme that a 'normal' lifestyle is becoming more and more difficult to define.

The question of cohesion is, however, more complex. Of course the US is (in) famous for its individualism, but it is not clear whether this also means low levels of interpersonal trust and social participation. In his film *Bowling for Columbine* Michael Moore crosses the border to Canada and finds that there, unlike in the USA, normal people do not barricade themselves into their houses and do not threaten to shoot strangers. There is survey evidence that Americans are far more likely than Canadians to believe that 'a little violence is okay' or that sometimes violence is justified in order to 'get what you want' (Rifkin 2004: 31). The complication is that, ever since de Tocqueville's *Democracy in America*, Americans have also been famous for their propensity to join voluntary associations, while individuals and corporations make extensive charitable donations.

The other Anglophone 'settler democracies' of Australia, New Zealand and Canada appear to occupy an intermediate position between the USA and Europe. As we have seen, these 'liberal redistributionist' societies are certainly far more individualistic than European societies, but at the same time none have the extremes of wealth and poverty that characterise the USA.

Historically, however, most capitalist societies have in fact combined social exclusion with some social cohesion. They have had a wide variety of living standards and economic resources, but at the same time quite extensive social solidarity. At the very minimum the nation state involves ideas of commonality. Arguably, Europe's feudal legacy has involved a particularly European notion of the responsibilities of property (Hutton 2002). As we have seen already, 'conservative' or 'corporatist' welfare regimes are about maintaining 'horizontal' cohesion. The history of post-World War II Europe has involved the state in taking greater responsibility for cohesion as well as a movement towards inclusion. Thus each of the four dimensions of the European social model identified in Section 1.3 contributes to the place of European states in the chart. Income equality maps directly onto the vertical axis of the chart; it also contributes indirectly to contemporary (non-deferential) forms of social cohesion. Social citizenship is related to equality but also directly involves social solidarity. At least for those with regular employment, economic citizenship creates cohesion in the workplace and indirectly contributes to greater equality, since it will tend to work against extreme income differentials generated by employment. Finally, the backbone state is important because of its contribution to social cohesion.

If Europe really is to have the 'greater social cohesion' promised in the Lisbon declaration it must move towards the right-hand side of the chart; if it has to 'fight against social exclusion', as social policy documents at least promise, then it has to move towards the top part of the chart. At the same time, if Europe is actually becoming more 'Americanised', as many fear, it is moving in the opposite direction, towards the bottom left-hand corner of the chart, with more social exclusion and greater social fragmentation.

1.5 Conclusion: Europe, the EU and the ESM

Europe's relative income equality, its expansion of social and economic citizenship, as well as its extensive public sphere, are all primarily the creation of the nation states that make up Europe. They may define Europe, but their origins have nothing to do with the European Union. Today, however, they increasingly implicate the EU, but in contradictory ways.

As we have seen, the EU now is involved to some limited extent in some areas of social policy and hence of social citizenship. More importantly, the EU does define basic standards in employment protection and the right to information and consultation. If a country is a member of the EU, its workforce (whether or not they are national citizens) thus acquire rights. The EU is therefore partly constitutive of Europeans' economic citizenship. The situation with respect to the public sphere is much more ambiguous. The creation of the internal market has undermined national states' services such as transport, telecommunications and post, enabling private companies to force states to open these areas to competition.

The ESM is not just a list of characteristics of individual states but is *also* defined by the European Union itself. However, there are two major caveats. First, while all individual states' characteristics vary, within this general diversity even among the old EU15 the UK is far more likely to be the odd one out than any other state. This deviance is all the more important because on issues of social and economic citizenship it is the UK that continually blocks progress and at times even rejects EU institutions. The UK's ambiguous role within the EU is therefore not just about policies, it is also about the very different institutional structure of the UK compared to the rest of Europe.

Second, there is the rather different issue of the new member states (those that joined from 2004 onwards). For nearly all of them (Cyprus and Malta are partial exceptions) membership of the Union has not occurred after the consolidation of national welfare states. Of course, the antecedents of many 'Western' welfare states can also be found before World War II in states such as (then) Czechoslovakia, but war and totalitarian communist rule truncated any developments that would have been similar to those in what became 'the West'. The collapse of communism did not mean the reconfiguration of the extensive social provisions (subsidised transport, housing etc.) of these states into a democratic format. Instead, such rights were reduced or even abolished: social rights became identified with 'socialism' which in turn was equated with the old regime. Similarly, the state is usually seen as simply repressive and so plays little part in the formation of a democratic public realm.

In the middle of the current financial crisis the President of the European Central Bank used an interview with *The Wall Street Journal* to announce that 'The European Social Model is dead' (Draghi 2012). If that really is the case, then much that defined Europe in the world has ended. This study of European social structure asks whether that really is the case. Is the European social model dead, and if so, who killed it? Conversely, if the European social model is alive, does 'our specific combination of market economy, welfare state and democracy', of which Lamy spoke, still produce a relatively inclusive and relatively cohesive society (or even societies)? Is there still, in other words, a distinctive *European society* or, at least, a set of distinctive *European societies*?

Notes

1 The state that later became the Republic of Ireland was not part of these developments. The institutions of the state and the leading political parties have no history of anti-fascism, and this is one reason for the curiously archaic form of much Irish political

discourse. Ireland is for example one of the few countries where terms such as the Irish 'race' can be mentioned without worried foot shuffling.

2 In this regard Christian democracy shares much with the now almost extinct 'One Nation' tradition within the British Conservative Party. However, this British tradition derives from a fundamentally aristocratic distrust of the market and even of 'commerce' (hence its association with 'Tory grandees'). The political achievement of Winston Churchill was to turn British Conservatism into an anti-fascist party; similar conservative traditions in Continental Europe mostly ended up, like the German DNVP, as more or less enthusiastic supporters of fascism. Consequently Christian democracy was a break with conservative tradition that did not have to be made in Britain.

3 Here the differing fates of Irish radicalism are suggestive: whereas in the USA Irish radicalism was soon integrated into American ethnic pressure group politics, in Australia and New Zealand it was a component of a labour movement that forced a democratic franchise (in 1893 New Zealand was the first country in the world in which women had the vote) and narrow income differentials.

4 Most religions stress the value of charity, but they are more concerned with its value to the donor than to the recipient. When writers such as Putnam (2000) see charitable giving in terms of social capital they are adopting the same perspective.

Bibliography

Abrahamson, P. (1999) The welfare modelling business, *Social Policy and Administration* 33.4: 394–415.

Atkinson, A. and Piketty, T. (2007) *Top Incomes over the Twentieth Century*, Oxford: Oxford UP.

Aust, A., Leitner, S. and Lessenich, S. (2002) Konjunktur und Krise des Europäischen Sozialmodells. Ein Beitrag zur politischen Präexplanationsdiagnostik, *Politische Vierteljahresschrift* 43.2: 272–301.

Baldwin, P. (2009) *The Narcissism of Minor Differences: How America and Europe are Alike*, Oxford: Oxford UP.

Belich, J. (2010) *Replenishing the Earth: The Settler Revolution and the Rise of the Anglo World 1783–1939*, Oxford: Oxford UP.

Colley, L. (2002) *Captives: Britain, Empire and the World 1600–1850*, London: Jonathan Cape.

Darwin, J. (2009) *The Empire Project: The Rise and Fall of the British World System 1830–1970*, Cambridge: Cambridge UP.

Davies, N. (1997) *Europe: A History*, London: Pimlico, second edn.

de la Porte, C. and Pochet, P. (2012) Why and how (still) study the Open Method of Coordination (OMC)? *Journal of European Social Policy* 22.3: 336–349.

Douglas, R. (2012) *Orderly and Humane: The Expulsion of the Germans after the Second World War*, New Haven: Yale UP.

Draghi, M. (2012) Interview in *The Wall Street Journal*, 24 February 2012.

Esping-Andersen, G. (1990) *The Three Worlds of Welfare Capitalism*, Cambridge: Polity Press.

Esping-Andersen, G. (1999) *Social Foundations of Postindustrial Economies*, Oxford: Oxford UP.

European Commission (1994) *Growth, Competitiveness, Employment (White Paper)*, Luxembourg: Office for the Official Publications of the European Communities.

Eurostat (2013) Euro area unemployment at 12.0%. Eurostat newsrelease euroindicators, STAT/13/140 http://europa.eu/rapid/press-release_STAT-13-140_en.htm. Accessed 7 October 2013.

Eurostat (2015) Population database. Accessed 14 July 2015.

Ferguson, N. (1999) *The Pity of War*, London: Penguin Books.

Ferguson, N. (2003) *Empire: How Britain Made the Modern World*, London: Allen Lane.

Fligstein, N. (2008) *Euroclash: The EU, European Identity and the Future of Europe*, Oxford: Oxford UP.

Gadrey, J. (2000) *Nouvelle economie, Nouveau mythe?* Paris: Flanmarion.

General Register Office (1952) Census 1951: *Great Britain: One Per Cent Sample Tables*, London: General Register Office.

Gold, M. (1993) Overview of the social dimension. In M. Gold (ed.) *The Social Dimension*, London: Macmillan, pp. 10–40.

Grant, C. (1994) *Delors: Inside the House that Jacques Built*, London: Nicholas Brealey.

Greve, B. (2003) Ways forward for the welfare state in the twenty-first century, *European Legacy* 8.5: 611–630.

Heidenreich, M. and Bischoff, G. (2008) The open method of co-ordination: a way to the Europeanisation of social and employment policies? *Journal of Common Market Studies* 46.3: 497–532.

Hutton, Will (2002) *The World We're In*, London: Little, Brown.

Institute for International Strategic Studies (2013) *The Military Balance 2012*, London: Institute for International Strategic Studies.

Johnston, R., Banting, K., Kymlicka, W. and Soroka, S. (2010) National identity and support for the welfare state, *Canadian Journal of Political Science* 43.2: 349–377.

Judt, T. (2005) *Postwar: A History of Europe since 1945*, London: William Heinemann.

Kleinman, M. (2002) *A European Welfare State? European Social Policy in Context*, London: Palgrave.

Kok, W. (2004) *Jobs, Jobs, Jobs. Creating More Employment in Europe*, Luxembourg: Official Publications.

Lamy, P. (2004) Europe and the future of economic governance, *Journal of Common Market Studies* 42.1: 5–21.

Landes, D. (1969) *The Unbound Prometheus: Technological Change and Industrial Development in Western Europe from 1750 to the Present*, Cambridge: Cambridge UP.

Maddison, A. (1987) Growth and slowdown in advanced capitalist economies, *Journal of Economic Literature* 25.2: 649–698.

Marquand, D. (2004) *Decline of the Public: The Hollowing-out of Citizenship*, Cambridge: Polity Press.

Mau, S. and Verwiebe, R. (2010) *European Societies: Mapping Structure and Change*, Bristol: Policy Press.

Mearsheimer, J. (2010) Why is Europe peaceful today? *European Political Science* 9: 387–397.

Merkel, A. (2013) Interview in *Die Zeit*, 7 November, www.bundesregierung.de/Content-Archiv/DE/Archiv17/Interview/2013/07/2013-07-11-merkel-zeit.html. Accessed 7 January 2014.

Milward, A. (1999) *The European Rescue of the Nation State*, London: Routledge, second edn.

OECD (2011) *Society at a Glance 2011: OECD Social Indicators*, Paris: OECD Publishing.

Overy, R. (1997) *Russia's War*, London: Penguin Books.

Putnam, R. (2000) *Bowling Alone: The Collapse and Revival of American Community*, New York: Simon & Schuster.

Rifkin, J. (2004) *The European Dream*, Cambridge: Polity Press.

Rosamond, B. (2000) *Theories of European Integration*, London: Palgrave Macmillan.

Scharpf, F. (1999) *Governing in Europe: Effective and Democratic?* Oxford: Oxford UP.

Sheehan, J. (2008) *The Monopoly of Violence: Why Europeans Hate Going to War*, London: Faber and Faber.

Teague, P. (1999) *Economic Citizenship in the European Union: Employment Relations in Europe*, London: Routledge.

Traxler, F. (1994) Collective bargaining: levels and coverage, *OECD Employment Outlook 1994*: 167–194.

United Nations (1999) *The World at Six Billion*, New York: United Nations, www.un.org/esa/population/publications/sixbillion/sixbilpart1.pdf. Accessed 12 August 2015.

US Department of Veterans Affairs (n.d.) *America's Wars*, www.va.gov/opa/publications/factsheets/fs_americas_wars.pdf. Accessed 12 August 2015.

van Oorschot, W. and Arts, W. (2005) The social capital of European welfare states: the crowding out hypotheses revisited, *Journal of European Social Policy* 15.1: 5–26.

Visser, J. (2006) Union membership statistics in 24 countries, *Monthly Labor Review* 129.1: 38–49.

Visser, J. (2013) *Data Base on Institutional Characteristics of Trade Unions, Wage Setting, State Intervention and Social Pacts, 1960–2011 (ICTWSS) Version 4.0*, Amsterdam Institute for Advanced Labour Studies.

Weber, E. (1979) *Peasants into Frenchmen: The Modernization of Rural France 1870–1914*, Stanford: Stanford UP.

Wehler, H.-U. (2013) *Die neue Umverteilung: Soziale Ungleichheit in Deutschland*, Munich: C.H. Beck.

Wilkinson, R, and Pickett, K. (2009) *The Spirit Level: Why More Equal Societies Almost Always Do Better*, London: Allen Lane.

2 From industrial society to the knowledge-based economy

Contemporary Europe is often seen as a 'knowledge-based' society. Sometimes this is aspiration or prescription, sometimes rather smug description. Such rhetoric prevents any analysis of the specifics of Europe's social structure and its development.

The theory – or better, the slogan – of the knowledge-based society is an example of *technological determinism*, the belief that technology shapes society. For over fifty years, this belief has underlaid a series of ideas about how European society has been developing. Back in the 1950s and 1960s, European societies were understood as *industrial societies*, from the late 1970s onwards we encounter *post-industrial society* and from the end of the century onwards the *information society* and the *knowledge-based economy*. Although these theories span fifty years, they have a surprising underlying unity, so that conceptual criticisms of the theory of industrial society from the 1960s apply to a considerable extent to contemporary accounts of the knowledge-based society. A discussion of these ideas allows an alternative history of the recent past and a better understanding of the present. This chapter highlights the decisive mid-twentieth-century compromise of industrial society within Western Europe; it shows the distinctive features of the subsequent growth of the service sector in different European countries; finally, it gives a more realistic picture of the role of education in the social structure of today's society.

2.1 Mid-twentieth-century Europe and industrial society

An intellectual genealogy of the idea of industrial society would trace it back to the works of Saint-Simon, Comte and, to some extent, Marx (see above all Kumar 1978). However, the appeal of the idea had to do with how everyday social theory of the twentieth century was saturated with the belief that technology 'drives' society forward in directions over which we have no control. In the first part of the twentieth century the future was often seen as a regimented, machine-paced, mass society. This after all was the age of the dictators, of the mass political rally, of total war. Two films of the time provide the visuals: Charlie Chaplin's *Modern Times* shows the little man of today caught up in meaningless mass production work; Fritz Lang's *Metropolis* shows the industrial slaves of tomorrow. After the defeat of fascism a more benign vision prevailed, coupling the terms 'modern' 'industrial' and 'democratic'. Within formal sociology this was epitomised by Clark Kerr's *Industrialism and Industrial Man* (Kerr 1973). In summary, Kerr and his colleagues argued that all industrial societies were necessarily developing a similar social structure, similar forms of social mobility and similar politics.

According to Kerr, the core of the society is the workplace. Industrial societies rely on the same industrial technology, and this in turn requires particular jobs: the modern workplace contains the same jobs in whatever country it is located. Accordingly, industrial societies all have a similar range of occupations and so a similar occupational structure. The further one gets away from the workplace, the more room there is for variation, because it is further away from the requirements of technology: differences between national societies may continue at the level of culture but this is essentially the stuff of tourism. Underneath the froth of national costumes and traditions, the core institutions of all industrial societies are becoming more alike. Industrial societies may have different origins, but as a society becomes more industrial it becomes more like other industrial societies. In this sense the theory of industrial society – like the other theories in this chapter – is therefore first and foremost a theory of *convergence.*

The development of technology means that work is becoming more technical and more skilled. The process of industrialisation involves an occupational shift: less manual jobs, especially unskilled ones, more white-collar jobs, especially technical and professional ones. Since the effective use and development of technology requires technical skills and technical knowledge, these societies are ones in which education, rather than an inherited characteristic (religion, race, even class), determines access to jobs. This provides another reason why all such societies have high and rising rates of social mobility: people move into the jobs for which they have gained the necessary qualifications within the free competition of the educational system. These optimistic prognoses of the *upskilling assumption* (rising skill, rising education, rising social mobility) are the second common theme of all the theories of this chapter.

Third, industrial societies are seen as *consensual societies*, in which industrial relations are the politics of organised interest groups rather than overt conflict or direct dictatorship. All participants accept, in Kerr's terms, the 'web of rules' that govern the workplace, and 'memos flow instead of blood'. Where conflict does occur, it is understood as 'anomie' and as a lack of individual social integration. In other words, these theories ignore the possibility of divergent interests and competing rationalities.

The theory of industrial society in particular predicted the 'end of ideology', a view which seemed quite plausible in the 1950s and early 1960s in Europe. However, the student revolt of 1968 coincided with the beginning of a period of trade union militancy in many European countries: the May 1968 general strike in France, the hot autumn of 1969 in Italy, the subsequent strike waves in Germany and Sweden. One common feature of all these movements was that the initiative came from the rank and file trade union members. Sit-downs replaced memos. For student radicals of the 1960s and 1970s the theory of industrial society presented a soporific version of the present, occluding the inequality and conflict which to them was all-pervasive. If, forty years on, their disturbances seem more like childish interruptions of a grown-up dinner party, it is worth noting that the party has ended. While Kerr saw the workplace as governed by consensus between interest groups which accepted each other's legitimacy, now some managers have withdrawn recognition from trade unions altogether.

The traditional European labour movement reached its peak at this time when in terms of social structure Western Europe was genuinely an industrial society. Certainly outside the big cities and apart from in Britain, agricultural jobs were still important even though they were rapidly declining (as late as the 1960s nearly 30 per cent of Italian employment was in agriculture). Crucially, however, several generations of Europeans had now lived and worked in the long-established industrial areas such as South Wales or the Ruhr built around coal and iron and steel. Other 'heavy industries' such as shipbuilding were important and even growing in some countries. Furthermore, starting in the late 1920s in Britain, the newer consumer industries from cars to 'white goods' had been expanding the new manufacturing centres such as Birmingham, Turin or Baden-Württemberg (Table 2.1). In all these new sectors, just as in some older areas of services such as transport, most jobs were manual 'working class' jobs.

This was the social basis for one distinctive feature of the West European trajectory. In the early twentieth century, European social scientists asked, 'Why is there no socialism in the United States?' assuming that a socialist movement based on a 'proletariat' was an integral part of the development of industrial capitalism. A century later it is the European experience that appears historically unusual. First, when industry reached its peak the single most common form of employment was manual work in some form of industry (countries industrialising later had relatively smaller industrial sectors which also contained a higher proportion of non-manual jobs). Second, this occurred within parliamentary democracies that enabled labour to organise in unions and in political parties. To

Table 2.1 Industrial employment (000s): 1940s–2010s

	Coal		Railways			Autos		
	UK	Germany	UK	Germany	Italy	UK	Germany	Italy
1940s	710							
1950s	699	565	333			450	277	
1960s	456	426	462			188	514	
1970s	247	226		381	202	288	567	252
1980s	138	189	369	283	240	281	767	219
1990s	15	137	268	272	120	278	742	183
2000s	6	59	77	246	102	254	1,020	224
2010s	5	31	56	134	73	177	1,142	208

Source: see Appendix: statistical sources.

some extent politics did align with social class, and social class did have some social reality. Of course, social class hardly mapped exactly onto politics, starting with the obvious point that many 'working class' people, especially but not only women, voted Conservative (in Britain) or Christian Democrat (in Germany and Italy). Nonetheless, a leading political scientist of the time could analyse voting patterns in terms of 'the democratic class struggle' (Lipset 1960). This was the socio-political basis for what later appeared as the 'mid-century compromise' (Crouch 1999): the co-existence of a market economy with extensive state employment and basic rights of social citizenship.

By the time state socialism collapsed in Eastern Europe in 1989 it was clear that such societies did not simply have a different political superstructure to what was then the West. Instead, the political system ensured a different occupational structure: Garnsey (1975) had already shown how, for a given level of GNP, Eastern European communist societies had a relatively greater proportion of the workforce in manual work than Western countries. State socialism's central economic planning meant that firms did not need to have the many white-collar jobs in accounting and sales that firms in a market economy required. Equally, in the wider society many 'social' activities that in the West were turned into full jobs (above all social work) were carried out as officially voluntary political activity in the East. In other words, different socio-economic systems, even if they used the same technology, would generate different sorts of tasks and turn different tasks into actual jobs.

The study of social mobility was another fertile testing ground for the convergence thesis (Erikson and Goldthorpe 1992). If the theory was correct, then rates of social mobility should be similar in all industrial societies. For example, the children of working class fathers should have similar chances of reaching a professional or managerial job in all the countries of Europe.[1] Early research seemed to confirm the thesis: rates of movement across the then-important manual/non-manual divide did seem similar. However, nearly all subsequent research challenged this. In particular the 'state socialist' regimes of Eastern Europe had much higher rates of social mobility than the liberal democracies of Western Europe. One cause was simply the fact that they industrialised later and faster. The number of jobs in agriculture fell, the number of jobs in industry and services expanded, so that of necessity many farmers' or peasants' children ended up in industry and some reached skilled manual or white-collar jobs. In addition, one of the ways in which these state socialist regimes tried to ensure they were seen as 'workers' states' was to give better chances of promotion to workers' children. At least in their early years (the 1950s), nearly all Eastern European states gave positive discrimination in favour of proletarian children in access to third-level education. Furthermore, since occupational advancement depended on membership of the Communist Party, party membership was for many workers a route to administrative and managerial jobs that was not available in the West.

Within Western Europe there were also significant differences in mobility rates. Here Sweden continually emerged as an outlier with higher rates of social mobility than other Western European countries. In Sweden the children of working class fathers were more likely to end up in non-manual jobs than are comparable children in other countries; the social origins of professionals and managers are more diverse than elsewhere. To some extent these high rates of mobility can be explained by the rapid growth of industry and of skilled jobs in Sweden in the post-war period. However, the main cause was that social democratic policies, particularly in the area of education, made Sweden a much more equal society. One result is simply that social background has relatively little influence on educational achievement. Since these features of Swedish society have existed now for several decades, they cannot be seen as leftovers from the past that will disappear in the onward rush of technology.

Evidence such as the Swedish case therefore undermined the claim that all industrial societies were converging; it showed that the institutions of the *national state* impact on social structure. Furthermore, since such egalitarian policies stemmed from the trade unions and the Social Democratic Party, it suggests that in different countries the subordinate groups have different political power and that this again has consequences.

Whereas industrial society theory assumed convergence in the core institutions and structures of society, empirical research showed that this was not happening. Whereas industrial society theory saw institutions as adjusting to the dictates of technology, the alternative argument was that institutions matter. The clearest statement of this was the 'societal effect' thesis. In a key study in industrial sociology, Maurice *et al.* (1986) showed that manufacturing firms making similar products and utilising similar technology had different occupational structures in Britain, France and Germany. Because German managers delegated decision-making tasks downwards to manual workers, German factories had proportionately more manual workers and fewer office workers than British or French factories. The main reason was that the German vocational educational system produced highly skilled manual workers who were more competent to take decisions than their French or British colleagues. Even in areas closest to the allegedly all-determining industrial technology, national differences remained.

2.2 From the 1970s: the emergence of post-industrial society

The term 'industrial society' seems archaic today, because there is a widespread awareness industrial-type jobs have been declining – whether in mining, transport or manufacturing (Table 2.1). New jobs are being created in the service sector rather than in manufacturing industry. The theory of *post-industrial* society starts from this change, and remains a powerful statement of changes in social structure that have become clear since the 1970s.

The major formulation of the theory was Daniel Bell's *The Coming of Post-Industrial Society* (1973). Post-industrial society theory stresses a double shift in employment: from the manufacturing to the service *sector*, from manual to non-manual *occupations*. The difference between these changes can be understood using a sector/occupation matrix (Figure 2.1). The columns show areas of economic activity (sectors), the rows groups of occupations (classes). Thus the manufacturing industry column includes everyone who works in manufacturing industry, whether a worker on the factory floor or a clerical worker in a dispatch office. Similarly, the 'services' column includes all who work in the service industry. So, for example, all employees in a hospital would be categorised in the services column, whether they were manual workers (e.g. cleaners) or professionals (e.g. doctors). It is normally assumed that at any one point in time the movement from primary to secondary to tertiary sectors involves a decreasing proportion of manual work and an increasing proportion of professional work. Thus in agriculture most occupations are manual, but at the other extreme white-collar and above all professional occupations predominate in the service sector.

Sociologists of stratification now frequently apply the term 'service class' to the upper layers of professional and managerial occupations (see Section 5.4). Conceptually, this has nothing to do with the 'service sector': 'service class' occupations occur in all three sectors. Even more confusingly, researchers sometimes use the term 'service work' or even 'tertiary work' to refer to non-manual occupations wherever they occur. Thus Bosch and Wagner (2004a, 2004b) describe the growth of sales and design functions in manufacturing as the 'tertiarisation' of industry. I shall not use this term, since it conflates sector and occupation.

In Bell's argument, technological change involves two shifts. First, within each sector there is a process of upskilling: over time the proportion of unskilled and manual work within each sector falls, and that of professional and managerial rises (Figure 2.1 vertical arrow). For example, in manufacturing industry there are relatively fewer manual workers on the factory floor and more technicians and engineers. Second, there is a shift between the sectors, so that first employment falls in agriculture and rises in manufacturing; subsequently employment in manufacturing falls as employment in the service sector rises (horizontal arrow). The two processes together produce a movement from the bottom left-hand corner of the chart to the upper right-hand corner.

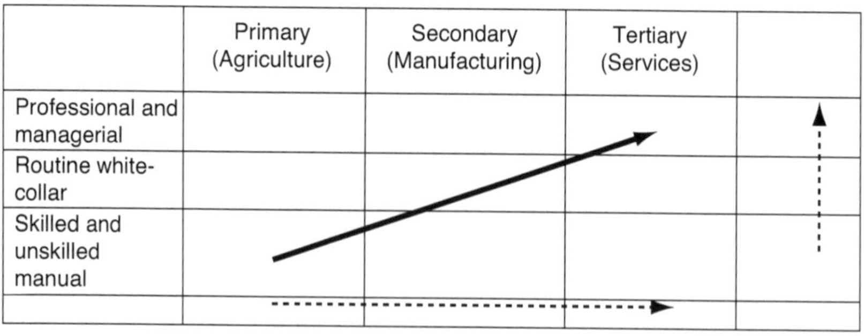

	Primary (Agriculture)	Secondary (Manufacturing)	Tertiary (Services)	
Professional and managerial				
Routine white-collar				
Skilled and unskilled manual				

Figure 2.1 Sectoral and occupational change.

Unlike manufacturing industry, the 'service sector' is a very vague term. Yet it can hardly be treated as a residual category when on most definitions in most European countries it comprises more than 60 per cent of employment. In a crucial early article Singelmann (1978) proposed a six-sector model: (1) agriculture and extractive industry (mining, etc.); (2) manufacturing, construction and utilities; (3) distribution, including both transport and sale of goods; (4) business services, such as banking; (5) social services such as health and education; and (6) personal services (restaurants, domestic cleaning, etc.). There are obvious problems of definition, not least because the same enterprise may operate in several sectors, while especially the distributive sector, defined to include both retail shops and air transport, is particularly heterogeneous. Nonetheless, disaggregating the service sector in this way allows us to see that the form of service sector growth has varied across Europe and the USA.

In the post-war period much of the expansion in the service sector initially occurred in public social services. It is this which gives Bell's claim credibility that work has become less 'economic' and more 'sociologising'. The extent of this expansion in health and education depends massively on political decisions (Doogan 2009). In these terms, far from converging, the employment structure of advanced countries diverged during the final quarter of the last century as the welfare states of Western Europe and especially of Scandinavia expanded their public services. While in the USA employment in public services was 10 per cent of the adult population in 1970 and 11 per cent in 1989, in Sweden it grew from 17 per cent in 1974 to fully 26 per cent in 1989 (Iversen and Wren 1998). These differences continue: in 2008 total public sector employment was 26.2 per cent of the labour force in Sweden, but only 14.6 per cent in the USA (OECD 2011).

Within Scandinavia the caring workforce has been at the centre of this growth of public employment. Estimates of the workforce involved in caring work (defined here as pre-school childcare, institutionalised youth care, elderly care) in the 2000s in Sweden ranged from 9 per cent to fully 13.5 per cent of the workforce, in Denmark 10 per cent and around 5 per cent in the UK (Cameron and Moss 2007). These differences have nothing to do with 'technological change' or even some abstract notion of 'rationalisation', and everything to do with specific institutional configurations. The Scandinavian solution involves wage work by effectively all women, high employment in public social services and relatively egalitarian income distribution. Not surprisingly, in an analysis of service sector employment within the EU15 which focuses not on total employment but on the *volume* of work (i.e. hours worked, whether in part-time or full-time work), Bosch and Wagner (2004a, 2004b) report a strong positive correlation between the extent of work in social services and both women's labour force participation and income equality.

British commentators often claimed that the low level of manufacturing in the UK showed how far the country had 'advanced' to a post-industrial society. In fact Britain's small manufacturing employment today is in part the result of political decisions. British high technology manufacturing had been growing from the 1930s through the 1950s with the emergence of sectors such as aerospace and then nuclear power (Edgerton 2013). The notorious failure of British industry to modernise in the third quarter of the last century, coupled with the country's conflictual industrial relations, led to the Thatcher government's decision to demolish the heartlands of British trade unionism not only in the publicly owned coal industry but also in broad swathes of privately owned manufacturing. Consequently, and despite conventional assumptions of the role of technical and scientific knowledge in economic growth, there was an actual decline in the number of engineers and scientists in the UK in the 1990s (Nolan and Slater 2010).

In Britain the flip side of the destruction of manufacturing was essentially a (so far successful) national wager on global financial services, starting with the 'Big Bang' of financial deregulation in 1986. The high proportion of employment in the UK in financial services is partly because of the pre-eminent global position of Britain – and above all London – in this sector (see Section 6.4). By contrast, the relatively high proportion of German employment in manufacturing industry even today reflects Germany's competitive strength in this sector, itself in part the result of socio-political decisions and choices.

Sector differences are also in part the result of different firm strategies. In Germany in the 2000s there was discussion of what appeared to be a 'services gap' (Bosch and Wagner 2004a): the apparent under-development of the service sector compared to countries such as the UK. In fact, one explanation was the long-established tendency of German firms to keep specialised functions such as design in-house, whereas at the other extreme US firms have long used outside contractors. Thus activities which in Germany will be counted as in the manufacturing sector will be counted as in services in the USA.

The work that is done within the different sectors also depends partly on national state institutions and the overall national context. Thus 'caring work' is very different in different European countries. Everywhere those working to care for the elderly tend to be women with an average age of around 40. However, in the UK such women are mostly in the private sector, on low wages, working part-time, non-unionised and with minimal qualifications and usually returning to work after childbearing. In Sweden, by contrast, women increasingly take up this employment after specialised training, usually work full-time in the public sector and are members of trade unions (Cameron and Moss 2007). While such differences are easily explained by the very different social and employment policies of the states concerned, research in the societal effect tradition showed that national institutional systems also impacted on employment in retail in countries as different as the USA, France and Japan: French and US retailers configured their activities differently, producing not just different levels of employment but different tasks and different jobs (Gadrey *et al.* 1999).

Such arguments undermine the determinist belief that the development of the service sector is simply the automatic result of technological change. The expansion of the service sector in the USA has depended disproportionately on low wages and insecure jobs, especially in the private services sector. This is the world of fast food and domestic cleaning described by Ehrenreich (2002) in her account of low wage America in the early 2000s – where even before the crisis people had to hold down several jobs just to survive. To a very large extent, in many European countries such jobs simply did not exist until recently. First, higher minimum wages and higher social security made them unviable. One response to Bell's original book was to argue that much 'service' activity in fact involves consumers using machinery to service their own needs at home (Gershuny 1978). Today in some countries such self-service is no longer necessary, because low wages mean that once again people can be paid to do such activities. Second, at the other end of the income distribution, high disposable income, more widespread in the USA than in Europe, creates the demand for new forms of labour-intensive services, from dog-walking to personal physiotherapists. Not surprisingly, therefore, there appears to be a clear relationship between the extent of income inequality and the extent of employment in personal services. Such different 'service landscapes' (Bosch and Wagner 2004b) show the diversity within Europe and the limits of any technological determinism.

Post-industrial theory also claimed that greater material prosperity creates a platform for a move towards 'post-materialist' social values. Thus Inglehardt (1977) argued that as people's material needs for food and shelter become satisfied, they are able to tackle their non-material needs for participation and self-fulfilment. The left–right political division is now, so he argued, overlaid with a 'materialist' versus 'non-materialist' one. Whereas the old left versus right division is about the distribution of the gains of economic growth, the new division opposes economic growth with environmental and similar concerns. This in turn involves a shift in the political basis of radicalism: whereas the old left was based on an identifiable social group (the working class), the new left (feminism, environmentalism) is allegedly based on values per se.

The most studied example is the German Greens. In the 1994 elections they became the third party in Germany and later entered government in coalition with the Social Democrats; under the *Realo* (realistic) leadership of Joschka Fischer they became *koalitionsfähig* (acceptable to the other parties as potential coalition members). The strength of the German Greens undoubtedly derives partly from features that are specific to Germany. There is a long German intellectual tradition which valorises nature; what used to be West Germany combined a very high standard of living with the obvious negative consequences of industrialisation (car pollution, autobahns destroying urban and rural landscapes, acid rain); the German political system enables a small party, if it can achieve a certain size, to have an impact at local or national level. Furthermore, such (small) left libertarian parties seem to have an identifiable social base among white-collar public sector employees. Arguably the very extent of public sector employment in Europe thus provides a social base for green politics (Tepe 2012). On the international stage the EU has sometimes been a global advocate of green policies. Far from parties such as the Greens showing that the service society produces politics disconnected from social bases, such parties can emerge precisely because of the particular importance of public 'social services' within the new post-industrial *European* society.

2.3 From the 1990s: the information society and the knowledge-based economy

In many ways, the theory of the information society is a computerised version of post-industrial society. Unlike the earlier theories discussed in this chapter, it does not really derive from social science. Perhaps for that reason, it has more popular impact: unconstrained by the obligations of evidence or the pedantry of citation, the theory of the information society now has wider currency than any other view of contemporary society. From the 1990s politicians and public commentators routinely declaimed that we now lived in an 'Age of Information'. In particular, this was the social theory of the information technology industry, justifying why people and organisations must change – and buy its products, as exemplified by none other than the founder of Microsoft himself (Gates 1995). Since the turn of the century these arguments have been morphing into theories of the 'knowledge-based economy' and even the 'knowledge-based society' (KBS) and taken up by politicians on both sides of the Atlantic, all without almost any serious social science discussion.

The theory of the knowledge-based society

Theorists of the information society make two claims. First, they claim that 'information' or perhaps 'knowledge' is the new resource. Second, they claim that 'knowledge workers' are becoming more important numerically or even that such workers now make up the majority of the workforce. As above all Webster (2007) pointed out, these claims have no logical connection with each other. If knowledge (as opposed to capital or land or whatever) is now the key economic resource, it is perfectly plausible that it is concentrated in very few hands. Alternatively, if everyone is now a 'knowledge worker', it is hardly plausible that access to knowledge per se differentiates the weak and the strong.

The focus on knowledge connects back to Bell, for whom codified abstract knowledge was the key economic resource of the post-industrial society. According to him, the economic success of such societies depended on continued scientific and technological innovation. During the 1980s when the 'information society' was first discussed, Bell started also using the term, but without any change of argument. However, theories of the 'information society' are characterised by three new features.

First, whereas post-industrial society theory linked technology and planning (much of Bell's inspiration came from Eastern European scholars), information society theory links technology directly to the role of markets. Information technology is seen as developing in response to the needs of the market; the market is the mechanism that enforces convergence, since the market selects the most efficient form of organisation and the most efficient technology. Particularly in the US in the late 1990s and in the more naive business literature, the market takes on a totemic role. In terms of consumer markets, the internet is seen as allowing unlimited freedom of choice, linking consumers and producers everywhere in the globe. In this vision, the market becomes self-policing, free of any institutional structures, so that Gates talked of the internet providing 'frictionless markets'. The market was also linked to innovation, in that it was claimed that a crucial precondition for the expansion of ICT companies was stock exchange finance, venture capital and hence a market for companies. Just before the dot. com bubble burst in 2001, enthusiasts announced the creation of the 'new economy' of perpetual growth and ever-climbing share values – all thanks to the internet (Frank 2001).

Second, there is the technology itself. Whereas industrial society and even post-industrial society theories made gestures towards 'technology' but never examined it, theories of the information society are quite specific in their focus on ICT. Quite rightly, more sophisticated versions of the theory stress how information technology has become an integral part of human communication and how social interaction has become machine-based and technologically mediated.[2] This technology is part of the 'fibre' of society, in that it is involved in almost all activities and processes (Castells 2000). The electronic infrastructure of the society connects every workplace, every home – indeed, with mobile communications, every person. In this sense Castells argues that contemporary society is a network society.

Third, theories of the information society are theories of globalisation. In the theory of industrial society and in the theory of post-industrial society, change occurred *within* distinct societies. The same process occurs in different societies and makes them more similar. By contrast, theories of the information society claim that the processes of social change span societies. Proponents of globalisation, whether populist futurologists (Friedman 2005) or learned social scientists (Urry 2000) foresee the end of the easy equation of 'society' with the nation state. Its ability to abolish the constraints of distance ensures that ICT is seen as the technology of globalisation. Thus, theories of the information society are not just theories of technological determinism, they are theories which give a determining role to one very particular technology.

The social structure of the KBS

Most of this writing says little about social structure and social inequality. An early exception was Reich (1993). Anticipating the arguments of Castells, Reich argued that large corporations were becoming open networks rather than closed institutions. Furthermore, the corporation was global rather than national, and this globalisation was very different to the 'transnational' or 'multinational' corporation (MNC) of the mid-twentieth century. That MNC was a national (usually US) company that operated in different countries: it was headquartered in one country, its shares were held by individuals and institutions from that country, it carried out its key functions there. By contrast, argued Reich, the global corporation has no real national identity, for its ownership is dispersed across national boundaries. For Reich, this economic context produces a new social structure comprising three essential groups. The *routine production workers* (about 25 per cent of all US jobs) carry out standardised manual tasks (factory work or data entry). By its nature this work can now be carried out anywhere in the globe; routine production workers are threatened both by automation which removes their jobs completely and by international locational competition which transports the jobs to cheaper labour markets. The *in person servers* carry out service jobs which are tied to the specific physical location – a restaurant waiter or a janitor has to be in a particular place. Globalisation threatens these jobs not by relocation but by immigration, which brings cheaper labour to their physical location. Finally, the *symbolic analysts* (less than 25 per cent of all US jobs) are the beneficiaries of the new society. These new professionals can work anywhere in the world because their networks are virtual rather than spatial. Location matters for them in terms of physical environment and services, not work itself. Consequently in the new global society 'as the rest of the nation grows more economically dependent than ever on the fortunate fifth, the fortunate fifth is becoming less and less dependent on them' (Reich 1993: 250).

Reich's account of symbolic analysts prefigured Richard Florida's discovery of the 'creative class'. With important implications for urban development policies, Florida (2004) argued that professionals and innovators ('creatives') are now able to choose where to live and work, so that quality of life becomes key to the economic growth of cities. While for Florida what matters is precisely 'creativity', for Reich symbolic analysts seem to be characterised by the *social* or at least the *organisational* skills of networking. At the same time, however, those who possess these attributes are assumed to inhabit occupational categories, so that 'symbolic analysts' or 'the creative class' are essentially those in professional and managerial jobs. The idea that a quarter of the workforce is now disentangled from large-scale employers and essentially independent networkers is unsustainable, even though this does appear to be a favourite theme of American popular business literature. Certainly, some knowledge workers appear to accept and even want relatively short-term employment; some knowledge workers' careers develop in a more international marketplace; some knowledge workers are self-employed independent consultants. However, Reich's account at times reads as the generalisation to a quarter of the workforce of the lifestyle desired by some of his friends. It is possible to find some groups of professional workers for whom ICT has enabled greater control over their own working lives, but for many more such workers, ICTs mean more detailed monitoring and more precise financial target – and for some ICT-enabled work means both at once.

Reich himself was clear that his estimate of the number of 'symbolic analysts' was very approximate: it used aggregate occupational census categories and excluded the public sector. Subsequent and more detailed analysis of the same US census figures by Brown and Hesketh (2004) overcame both these problems; they estimated that 'no more than 20 per cent' of US jobs could be classified as 'symbolic analysts'. Using similar definitions, they estimated the proportion of knowledge workers (their term for symbolic analysts) among jobs in the UK as roughly similar. Given that the UK government aims to have 50 per cent of young people in higher education, this suggests that many graduates are *over-educated* for the jobs they fill. There is in fact some evidence that this is occurring. Thus a study of graduates in the British service sector reported that many young graduates are employed in 'non-graduate' jobs, even though much such under-utilisation is in fact short-term (Mason 2002).

The assumption that technological progress generates continued upskilling has been formulated within labour economics as the Skill-Biased Technical Change (SBTC) thesis (Katz and Autor 1999): technical change produces rising skill demands within occupations and a rise in the absolute and relative number of skilled occupations. Like Kerr, SBTC advocates seem to simply assume that an increasing technical content of work inherently produces rising skill demands throughout the organisation. Harping back to Bell's assumptions, they assume an equation of 'skill' with technical content. By contrast, the understanding of skill in the later writers Reich and Florida includes social skills and soft skills. More recent work in labour economics has, however, challenged this optimistic account. Goos and Manning (2007) suggest that technical change currently increases the number of both good and bad jobs ('lovely' jobs and 'lousy' jobs), while reducing the number of intermediate jobs. Using UK Labour Force Survey data for 1979 to 1999, they first rank occupations by the median wage in the initial period; they then show that the occupations which have grown by the end of the period are those at the top and (to a lesser extent) at the bottom of this hierarchy. Growing occupations include software engineers and management consultants, but also care assistants and check-out operators. By contrast, jobs have been lost among intermediate occupations, nearly all of which are skilled or semi-skilled occupations in extractive or manufacturing industry (coal mine labourers, grinding machine setters, etc.). Goos *et al.* (2009) find broadly similar results for sixteen (West) European countries: almost everywhere there is a growth at either end of the occupational structure.

The routinisation thesis fits well with the frequently observed growth in low paid service sector jobs. Reviewing occupational change in the USA over the twentieth century, Wyatt and Hecker (2006) document the rise in managerial and professional occupations, the rise in service workers especially in food service, and the decline in craft and operative workers in industry. Whereas the social structure of the industrial society could have been visualised as a pyramid and the post-industrial society as a diamond, the polarisation thesis suggests that the contemporary knowledge-based society is in fact an hour-glass shaped society (Figure 2.2).

All of these arguments assume that at least in the workplace there is continued technological progress. To some extent they also assume that the direction of technological progress is pre-determined: the role of both policy and social research is to study the consequences. This ignores work going back to the 1970s which explores how and in what way technology is itself socially shaped: technology is part of society rather than outside society. Thus across Europe there is considerable variation in the extent of ICT take-up, whether in terms of

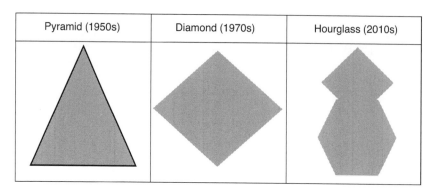

Figure 2.2 Images of social structure.

personal computer ownership, internet connections or level of computer use in the workplace. Intriguingly, some of the countries which score highest on 'information society' indices are also least like the USA on other measures. Thus in 2010 Sweden, Denmark and Finland, a higher proportion of households had internet access than in the USA (OECD 2013b), but these countries have an egalitarian income distribution and extensive public services. The Finnish route to the 'information society' has been based on the country's extensive welfare state and egalitarian educational system. A high standard of basic education for all, free third-level education and high state spending all contributed to turning Finland into a society in which IT-related business (and not just Nokia) became central to economic growth at the start of the new millennium (Castells and Himanen 2002). Given such diversity, it is impossible to sustain the 'myth' (Gadrey 2003) of an umbilical connection between information technology, the market, entrepreneurialism and indeed the American dream.

Indeed, the growth of low paid and unskilled labour in Europe and the USA is in part linked to technological stagnation and even regression (Wickham 2011). In agriculture and food processing, employers' business model depends on low technology and cheap imported labour (Mannon *et al.* 2011). Labour is so cheap that it becomes possible to use older technologies. Where labour has no power, technology can move backwards.[3]

Education and the KBS

As in almost all other countries, educational participation has been expanding continuously in Europe in recent decades. This is especially the case for third-level education and in the new member states such as Poland. Across Europe in most countries at least one-third of the young adult population has now achieved some form of third-level education. This expansion is often used to justify the 'knowledge-based society' label, but this glib slogan masks more complex relationships between education and the wider society – and especially between education and the economy. For example, Table 2.2 shows that Germany has a relatively low level of third-level participation, but this masks the strength of its system of vocational education and training – a strength that could well be undermined by further university expansion (Hirsch-Kreinsen 2013).

While education and conventional social policy such as health or social insurance long remained a jealously guarded prerogative of member states, 'training' could be defined as an area of European policy because it involved employment and the labour market. CEDEFOP (the European Centre for the Development of Vocational Training) was created in 1975 within this policy space as a response to pressure, in particular from European trade unions, for a European social policy (Guasconi 2004). Since the 1970s vocational education and training has been an important component of EU social policy. Across Europe the national variety of training systems remains and there has certainly been no generalisation of the German apprenticeship system (Greinert 2004). EU involvement has been largely limited to rather abstract target setting and calls for enhanced collaboration between systems that remain fundamentally different.

European educational integration has, however, been occurring in other ways. There is now extensive co-operation and exchange between professional educational and academic organisations. The Erasmus programme of student exchanges has ensured that now many European students spend part of their studies in another country (Teichler 2004). The development of European funding has had a massive impact on European research. Since the 1990s through its 'framework programmes' the EU has created a genuine European Research Area in which collaboration between European researchers from different countries has become absolutely normal. European academics and scientists increasingly publish with colleagues from other member states; it is normal for their career to include time in another country, often funded by an EU grant (e.g. Guth 2008).

Through the 'Bologna process' European universities are aligning their qualifications, creating a European third-level system with a standard degree structure (effectively undergraduate, master's and doctorate degrees) and much higher

Table 2.2 Tertiary educational participation: 2000 and 2011, percentage of age group 25–34 attaining tertiary education

	2000	*2011*
France	31	43
Germany	22	28
Ireland	30	47
Italy	11	21
Poland	14	39
Sweden	34	43
UK	29	47
USA	38	43

Source: adapted from OECD (2013a: Table A1.4a).

student and staff mobility. Rather like the European Employment Strategy, 'Bologna' is an example of 'soft law', of decision-making by mutual benchmarking and *governance* rather than old-style 'command and control' government. Probably to the surprise of its original proposers, the Bologna process has been a dramatic success: countries outside the EU are joining up and access to Bologna has become one of the benchmarks used by candidate countries to gauge their own progress towards 'European' standards (Keeling 2006). Meanwhile within the EU all universities have moved towards a common degree structure (the Anglo-American system of bachelor's, master's and doctorate) and the consolidation of the ECTS (European Credit Transfer System).

The origins of the Bologna process, like those of the original Erasmus programme, lie in the attempt to use the European education system as a tool for the creation of European 'identity'. Only more recently has Bologna become linked to the rather different objective of 'competitiveness'. Although the aim of the process is a greater integration of European university systems, this integration is of *national* and state-funded systems. The Bologna process is therefore fundamentally an attempt to reform and integrate European *public* universities. The Bologna process is largely inter-governmental (starting with a declaration of European Ministers of Education in 1998) and remains largely outside of EU institutions. Nonetheless, the process has not only facilitated student mobility (because of the standardisation of degree structures), it has facilitated benchmarking from below. Increasingly European students (and their parents) compare the education in their country with that offered elsewhere – and wonder why 'their' state is inadequate.

Europe's contemporary system of publicly funded universities is part of the backbone state (Chapter 1); for all the mediaeval past of individual institutions the origins of the system really lie with Bismarckian social conservatism. Then in the second half of the twentieth century social democratic parties became committed to university expansion, seeing this as contributing to social equality. By the new century Giddens (2007) could see such national systems in France, Germany and Italy as contributing to these societies' social and economic stagnation. In such 'blocked societies' third-level education was free but underfunded and of generally low quality, teaching was ineffective, students took a long time to complete their studies and many dropped out along the way, a degree brought only limited economic benefits to the individual, levels of research were low and the universities made little contribution to the regions in which they were located. In the last ten years, however, there has been extensive reform, not least through the Bologna process. In particular, teaching is slowly being subjected to quality assurance and universities are acquiring greater institutional autonomy, while by contrast outside of the UK and Ireland there has been relatively little move towards funding through student fees.

One continuity, however, is that different national systems have different relationships to employment. If employability is measured by employers' evaluation of graduates, there are wide variations across Europe: Irish graduates are considered the most employable, those from Slovenia the least (St Aubyn *et al.*

2009). Studies have produced estimates of 20 per cent and more of young people considering themselves over-educated for their current jobs (Lindley 2002: 125). In countries such as Italy and Spain rigid labour market regulation privileges insiders (largely middle-aged males) over outsiders (i.e. young people). At the same time the qualifications produced by third-level institutions are not valued by employers. Many graduates find themselves moving from one short-term temporary job to another, but with little sign that this is developing into anything resembling a traditional career. That this is not just a problem of weak demand is shown by the case of Spain, where this phenomenon was widespread despite an economic boom.

In a very different way the UK has developed an education system which is good at producing both specialist professional and managerial skills and an adaptable graduate workforce, while secondary and vocational education for the rest of the population remains of a relatively low standard (Brown and Hesketh 2004). Combined with the shift of employment to the service sector – greater than in any other European economy – and a deregulated labour market, this has ensured high graduate employment. Importantly, however, students seek out business and management courses, while shunning subjects such as computer science which one might imagine would be more central to a 'knowledge-based society' as conventionally defined.

Compared to the USA, few European countries have universities that are high within the global rankings. Traditionally Germany has an egalitarian university system, with no obvious hierarchy as exists in the UK or the USA. However, in response the German government launched the Excellenzinitiativ focusing research spending on a small number of potentially excellent universities in an attempt to create world leaders. Such emulation of the US, however, ignores the way in which the transformation of American universities has become interwoven with the increasing rigidity of the American social structure.

Competition between American universities has been pushing up student fees. For several decades the cost of college fees, like the cost of healthcare, has become part of the nightmare of Middle America (Frank and Cook 1996). With costs at both public and private universities rising faster than average incomes, 'academic inflation makes medical inflation look modest by comparison' (Hout 2012). The consequence has been predictable:

> In 1979 students from the richest 25 per cent of American homes were four times as likely to attend college as those from the poorest 25 per cent. Now, students from the richest 25 per cent of American homes are more than 10 times as likely to attend colleges and universities as those from the poorest 25 per cent.
>
> (Reich 2004: 11)

Inequality is also growing within the university sector. Across the world elite universities have always been to some extent both socially and intellectually elitist; only at rare moments does intellectual excellence go with an egalitarian recruitment of the student body. However, in America today social and academic elitism are becoming almost synonymous, for access to the leading universities is becoming more and more restrictive. At the top 146 universities, fully 75 per cent of students come from the wealthiest quartile (Marcus 2004; more recently Putnam 2015). At Ivy League colleges only 3 per cent of all students come from the poorest 25 per cent of families and African-Americans have not increased their share of Harvard's student population (Espenshade and Radford 2009). Universities' reliance on private and philanthropic funding means that they cultivate their alumni and other individuals for gifts. Philanthropic funding is massively concentrated on the elite universities and they often fall into the temptation of giving the children of such donors privileged access. While such (covert) 'legacy lists' are often criticised, they are an almost inevitable consequence of the desperate search for private donations (Lewis 2004). The enthusiastic embrace of a market model means a re-calibration of the nature of financial aid for students (Washburn 2005). Originally intended as a means to ensure that less privileged children could reach university, it increasingly is used as a means to simply attract the best and brightest students, *whatever their background.* As a recent study of Ivy League access commented:

> My research suggests that one profound result of higher education's expansion has been the entrenchment of a complicated, publicly palatable, and elaborately costly machinery through which wealthy parents hand privilege down to their children.
>
> (Stevens 2009: 14)

Just as it is the very rich and those on the highest incomes who have benefited most from America's economic growth since the 1970s, so it is these who have benefited most from the 'success' of American higher education (also Sabbagh and van Zanten 2009).

> The first adverse consequence from the marketisation of higher education in the United States concerns social stratification. The most prestigious brands of higher education increasingly are available only to those who can pay for them.
>
> (Reich 2004: 11)

Parents are striving to pay these fees because they assume that elite education leads to elite jobs. Certainly it appears that in many areas (e.g. finance, the judiciary) the hold of elite universities on elite jobs has strengthened, but this does not appear to be universal. Intriguingly, however, elite education is creating social homogomy: graduates of elite universities are likely to have spouses from similar colleges (Hout 2012).

One bizarre feature of the current European enthusiasm for American universities is that it seems to judge the entire system by the achievements of a few elite institutions. This is as absurd as judging the entire UK secondary education system by the achievements of its elite private schools such as Eton. Indeed, claims that the USA is a 'knowledge-based society' sit uneasily with its mediocre levels of basic education and training. The top American universities and business schools may be rated the best in the world, yet in international comparisons a relatively large proportion of Americans fail to acquire a basic education (NCEE 2006). In the first international comparative studies of the effectiveness of education, the USA only scored about average in basic literacy, with fully 18 per cent of fifteen-year-olds only reaching the basic Level 1 on the PISA reading literacy scale (OECD 2003: 69), and having one of the highest proportions of fifteen-year-olds who only achieved the basic Level 1 in mathematical competence (OECD 2006: 82). The most recent international comparisons do show some minor improvements, especially in average mathematical ability. However, compared in particular to Scandinavian countries the US remains remarkable for its long 'tail' of low achievement.

Finally, it is worth reflecting on the implications of defining the USA as the most 'knowledgeable' society in the world. This, after all, is a country of mass religiosity and popular superstition, a country in which 68 per cent of the population believe in the devil (Rifkin 2004: 20) and in which creationism is actually taught in schools. The intellectual vacuity of the entire 'knowledge-based society' argument is highlighted by the fact that it is considered irrelevant to point out that most Americans are notoriously ignorant of anywhere outside the USA or that American mass media has no real tradition of public service broadcasting.

2.4 Conclusion

Education is central to all three sets of theories considered in this chapter – the theory of industrial society, of the service society, of the knowledge-based society. They all share a fundamental optimism in which knowledge equated with formal education becomes the key to economic growth and the key to individuals' advance. Along the way the understanding of 'knowledge' becomes increasingly utilitarian, so that the advocates of the KBS end up with a concept of 'knowledge' that is as limited as that of Dickens' Mr Gradgrind (Casey 2011).

Such discussions also ignore how in a society where education is important, it is important as a positional good. In other words, what matters is not just 'how much' education I have, but how much I have *relative to others.* If educational qualifications are used to queue applicants for jobs, then more education will certainly benefit those individuals who acquire it – *relative to those with less.* This will create a continual pressure for more education, which may or may not benefit the economy or even the society as a whole. Thus expanding university education simply means that competition becomes competition for access to the best universities instead of just to university per se. Furthermore, the American experience suggests that this can be not just a re-jigging of inequality, it can actually exacerbate it.

Finally, it is usually assumed that education is a good thing: more education makes a society more civilised, more liberal, more tolerant. In more mundane terms, education contributes to social cohesion. However, relating education to social inequality suggests that what matters is the form of educational provision and the extent of inequality. In terms of the discussion in Chapter 1, the marketisation of education in Europe will generate greater inequality and greater social fragmentation.

Notes

1 The most basic analysis of social mobility is to compare a man's current occupation with that of his father (father–son mobility). This approach is often criticised as 'sexist' but it simply reflects the sexism of a society in which men have full-time labour force participation while many women do not.
2 In itself, of course, this is nothing new: long before the arrival of the internet we were accustomed to telephone conversations with people we had never met; the ordinary letter reminds us of the extent to which quite traditional communication involves more than face-to-face interaction (i.e. spans time and distance).
3 In world history one recent extreme example of technological regression was Mao's so-called Great Leap Forward. China attempted to produce industrial goods and especially steel with very simple production processes and a terrorised population. The human cost was horrendous, with the direct and indirect death toll running into millions (Dikötter 2010: 58).

Bibliography

Bell, D. (1973) *The Coming of Post-Industrial Society*, London: Penguin.
Bosch, G. and Wagner, A. (2004a) Économies de services en Europe et raisons de la croissance de l'emploi en services, *Sociologie du travail* 46: 451–475.
Bosch, G. and Wagner, A. (2004b) Why do countries have such different service-sector employment rates? In G. Bosch and S. Lehndorff (eds) *Working in the Service Sector: A Tale from Different Worlds*, London: Routledge, pp. 67–93.
Brown, P. and Hesketh, A. (2004) *The Mismanagement of Talent: Employability and Jobs in the Knowledge Economy*, Oxford: Oxford UP.
Cameron, C. and Moss, P. (2007) *Care Work in Europe: Current Understandings and Future Directions*, London: Routledge.
Casey, C. (2011) *Economy, Work and Education: Critical Connections*, London: Routledge.
Castells, M. (2000) Materials for an exploratory theory of the network society, *British Journal of Sociology* 51.1: 5–24.
Castells, M. and Himanen, P. (2002) *The Information Society and the Welfare State: The Finnish Model*, Oxford: Oxford UP.
Crouch, C. (1999) *Social Change in Western Europe*, Oxford: Oxford UP.
Dikötter, F. (2010) *Mao's Great Famine*, London: Bloomsbury.
Doogan, K. (2009) *New Capitalism? The Transformation of Work*, Cambridge: Polity Press.
Edgerton, D. (2013) *England and the Aeroplane: Militarism, Modernity and Machines*, London: Penguin, second edn.
Ehrenreich, B. (2002) *Nickel and Dimed: Undercover in Low-wage USA*, London: Granta.
Erikson, R. and Goldthorpe, J. (1992) *The Constant Flux: A Study of Class Mobility in Industrial Societies*, Oxford: Clarendon Press.

Espenshade, T. and Radford, A. (2009) *No Longer Separate, Not Yet Equal: Race and Class in Elite College Admission and Campus Life*, Princeton: Princeton UP.

Florida, R. (2004) *The Rise of the Creative Class*, New York: Basic Books (first published 2002).

Frank, R. and Cook, P. (1996) *The Winner-Takes-All Society*, New York and London: Penguin.

Frank, T. (2001) *One Market Under God: Extreme Capitalism and the End of Economic Democracy*, London: Secker & Warburg.

Friedman, T. (2005) *The World is Flat: A Brief History of the Twentieth Century*, New York: Farrar, Strauss and Giroux.

Gadrey, J. (2003) *New Economy, New Myth*, London: Routledge.

Gadrey, J., Jany-Catrice, F. and Ribault, T. (1999) *France, Japon, États Unis: L'emploi en détail*, Paris: Presses Universitaires de France.

Garnsey, E. (1975) Occupational structure in industrialized societies: some notes on the convergence thesis in the light of Soviet experience, *Sociology* 9.3: 437–458.

Gates, B. (1995) *The Road Ahead*, New York: Viking.

Gershuny, J. (1978) *After Industrial Society? The Emerging Self-Service Economy*, London: Macmillan.

Giddens, A. (2007) *Europe in the Global Age*, Cambridge: Polity Press.

Goos, M. and Manning, A. (2007) 'Lousy and lovely jobs': the rising polarization of work in Britain, *Review of Economics and Statistics* 89.1: 118–133.

Goos, M., Manning, A. and Salomons, A. (2009) Job polarization in Europe, *American Economic Review* 99.2: 58–63.

Greinert, W. (2004) European vocational training 'systems' – some thoughts on the theoretical context of their historical development, *European Journal of Vocational Training* 32: 18–31.

Guasconi, M. (2004) The unions and the relaunching of European social policy, *European Journal of Vocational Training* 32: 55–62.

Guth, J. (2008) The opening of borders and scientific mobility: the impact of EU enlargement on the movement of early career scientists, *Higher Education in Europe* 33.4: 395–410.

Hirsch-Kreinsen, H. (2013) 'Wie viel akademische Bildung brauchen wir zukunftig? Ein Beitrag zur Akademisierungsdebatte', TU Dortmund, Soziologische Arbeitspapier Nr. 37/2013.

Hout, M. (2012) Social and economic returns to education in the United States, *Annual Review of Sociology* 38: 379–400.

Inglehart, R. (1977) *The Silent Revolution: Changing Values and Political Styles among Western Publics*, Princeton: Princeton UP.

Iversen, T. and Wren, A. (1998) Equality, employment and budgetary restraint: the trilemma of the service economy, *World Politics* 50: 507–546.

Katz, L. and Autor, D. (1999) Changes in the wage structure and earnings inequality. In O. Ashenfelter and D. Card (eds) *Handbook of Labor Economics*, Amsterdam: Elsevier, Vol. 3, Part 1, pp. 1463–1555.

Keeling, R. (2006) The Bologna Process and the Lisbon Research Agenda: the European Commission's expanding role in higher education discourse, *European Journal of Education* 41.2: 203–223.

Kerr, C. (1973) *Industrialism and Industrial Man*, Harmondsworth: Penguin.

Kumar, K. (1978) *Prophecy and Progress: The Sociology of Industrial and Post-industrial Society*, Harmondsworth: Penguin.

Lewis, P. (2004) Dad's old school tie may be just the ticket, *Times Higher*, 24/31 December.

Lindley, R. (2002) Knowledge-based economies: the European employment debate in a new context. In M. Rodriques (ed.) *The New Knowledge Economy in Europe*, Cheltenham: Edward Elgar, pp. 95–145.

Lipset, S. (1960) *Political Man: The Social Bases of Politics*, London: Heinemann.

Mannon, S., Petrzelka, P., Glass, C. and Radel, C. (2011) Keeping them in their place: migrant women workers in Spain's strawberry industry, *International Journal of Sociology of Agriculture and Food* 19.1: 83–101.

Marcus, J. (2004) US fees hike pose threat to access, *Times Higher*, 9 September.

Mason, G. (2002) High skills utilisation under mass higher education: graduate employment in services industries in Britain, *Journal of Education and Work* 15.4: 427–456.

Maurice, M., Sellier, F. and Silvestre, J. (1986) *The Social Foundations of Industrial Power: A Comparison of France and Germany*, Cambridge, MA: MIT Press.

NCEE (National Center on Education and the Economy) (2006) *Tough Choices or Tough Times: The Report of the New Commission on the Skills of the American Workforce*, New York: John Wiley.

Nolan, P. and Slater, G. (2010) Visions of the future, the legacy of the past: demystifying the weightless economy, *Labor History* 51.1: 7–27.

OECD (2003) *Education at a Glance 2003*, Paris: OECD.

OECD (2006) *Education at a Glance 2006*, Paris: OECD.

OECD (2011) *Government at a Glance 2011*, Paris: OECD.

OECD (2013a) *Education at a Glance 2013*, Paris: OECD.

OECD (2013b) *Key ICT Indicators*, www.oecd.org/sti/ieconomy/oecdkeyictindicators.htm. Accessed 22 October 2013.

Putnam, R. (2015) *Our Kids: The American Dream in Crisis*, New York: Simon & Schuster.

Reich, R. (1993) *The Work of Nations: Preparing Ourselves for 21st Century Capitalism*, London: Simon & Schuster.

Reich, R. (2004) The destruction of public higher education in America, and how the UK can avoid the same fate, Second Annual HEPI Lecture, London: Higher Education Policy Institute.

Rifkin, J. (2004) *The European Dream*, Cambridge: Polity Press.

Sabbagh, D. and van Zanten, A. (2010) Diversité et formation des élites: France–USA, *Sociétés Contemporaines* 3.79: 5–17.

St Aubyn, M., Pina, A., Garcia F. and Pais J. (2009) *Study on the Efficiency and Effectiveness of Public Spending in Tertiary Education*, Economic Papers no. 390, Brussels: European Commission, DG Economic and Financial Affairs.

Singelmann, J. (1978) The sectoral transformation of the labor force in seven industrialised countries 1920–70, *American Journal of Sociology* 83.5: 1224–1234.

Stevens, M. (2009) *Creating a Class: College Admissions and the Education of Elites*, Cambridge, MA: Harvard UP.

Teichler, U. (2004) Temporary study abroad: the life of ERASMUS students, *European Journal of Education* 39.4: 395–408.

Tepe, M. (2012) The public/private sector cleavage revisited: the impact of government employment on political attitudes and behaviour in 11 West European countries, *Public Administration* 90.1: 230–261.

Urry, J. (2000) *Sociology Beyond Societies: Mobilities for the Twenty-First Century*, London: Routledge.

Washburn, J. (2005) *University Inc.: The Corporate Corruption of Higher Education*, New York: Basic Books.

Webster, F. (2007) *Theories of the Information Society*, London: Routledge (first edn 1995).

Wickham, J. (2011) Low skill manufacturing work: from skill biased change to technological regression, *Arbeit* 20.3: 224–238.

Wyatt, I.D. and Hecker, D.E. (2006) Occupational changes during the twentieth century, *Monthly Labor Review* 129.3: 35–57.

3 The political economy of contemporary European capitalism

In the Anglosphere the 1980s were the years of Reagan and Thatcher: the beginnings of a new neo-liberal orthodoxy in economic policy, the (partial) dissolution of the welfare state, the roll back of state ownership, the deregulation of the economy. The process was led by regime change in New Zealand and in the UK, although the initial model was Chile, where American economic advisers had counselled the Pinochet dictatorship to sell off nationalised enterprises. In New Zealand a Labour government privatised state companies, reduced welfare and ended tariff protection. In the UK the Conservatives attacked the power of trade unions, reduced labour market regulation and developed an ever more ambitious privatisation policy. In both New Zealand and the UK the new policies began as a response to an economic crisis; they developed into a new political project.

Yet the 1980s also marked the apogee of a very different form of capitalism. German and Japanese firms had now successfully challenged American manufacturing dominance. Japanese car firms with their widely admired 'lean production' systems set up branch plants in the UK and the USA (Womack *et al.* 1990). Japanese and German societies appeared as models of economic success and social stability. Their success was widely attributed to those features which differentiated them from the USA: the close relationships between the banks and large-scale enterprises, as well as – in Japan – the active role of the state in industrial policy. Compared to the USA these were also societies which were relatively egalitarian and placed more reliance on informal business relationships based on mutual trust rather than on omni-present competition.

Then during the 1990s Germany and Japan moved from leaders to laggards in the international economic growth stakes; the American and then UK governments and their ideological supporters could claim that *their* countries' economic success showed that they offered the only viable economic model. And soon everything changed again. Just as Germany was being written off by British sociologist Anthony Giddens as a 'blocked society' (Giddens 2007: 32) the German export boom began. Germany became the power house of Europe, and as the financial crisis deepened, its paymaster.

There are therefore different stories that can be told about the contrasting histories of the USA and Europe. They suggest there is no reason why only American institutions are compatible with economic growth today. The *theoretical* issue here is the extent to which different forms of capitalism are possible within the current epoch of 'globalisation'; the *political* issue is the development of a more 'European' version of capitalism, and ultimately the continuation of the European social model. These issues can be addressed through a political economy approach. The first section of the chapter (Section 3.1) uses this to outline the global changes and national specificities since the 1970s; the next three sections focus in more detail on the role of the state, the relationship between firms and the national financial system, the fragmentation of the labour market. In all three areas there have been distinctive European experiences – a distinctiveness that is now being undermined by the European Union itself.

3.1 Periodising capitalism and finding capitalisms

Political economy involves a duality of periodisation and of national comparison. In what ways is capitalism today different to that of the 1960s? In what ways is capitalism in France different to that in the UK? Initially each of these questions was tackled by a different stream within political economy. On the one hand, directly influenced by Marxist arguments and originally developed in France, the so-called regulation school was concerned to identify particular historical relationships between markets and their wider socio-political context. On the other hand, deriving more from the Anglophone reception of Weberian sociology, the 'varieties of capitalism' approach was concerned to identify specific features of different capitalist economies. The difference between the two approaches is far from rigid, not least because there is a growing concern to tackle both the question of periodisation *and* of comparison.

The post-World War II period in Europe was the epoch of 'fordism'. Fordism is first of all the mass manufacture of standardised products (as Henry Ford reputedly said, 'You can have any colour provided it's black') at unprecedentedly high volume and unprecedentedly low prices. The Italian Marxist Gramsci saw the fordist system also as a novel form of consumption: mass production involved mass consumption and a new rationalised way of life. In Europe in the 1930s this became visible in southern England and the English Midlands: this was not the England of Orwell's *Road to Wigan Pier* and the dole queues, it was the England of new car factories in the Midlands, new electrical appliance factories in West London, the England of the traffic jam and the family drive to the seaside. However, mass production and mass consumption only dominated Western Europe from the 1950s. Employment in the car industry rose (see Table 2.1) and car output rose even faster (Figure 3.1); the large car factories with their thousands of semi-skilled assembly line workers were emblematic of work generally. Mass production enabled mass consumption through higher wages and cheaper and/or new products: the family car, the electric fridge, the telephone. From the 1950s onwards car ownership became normalised. In 1965 for the first time white-collar and blue-collar workers were the majority of car registrations in West Germany (Wolf 1996: 106); in 1971 for the first time more than 50 per cent of all British households had access to a van or a car (Department for

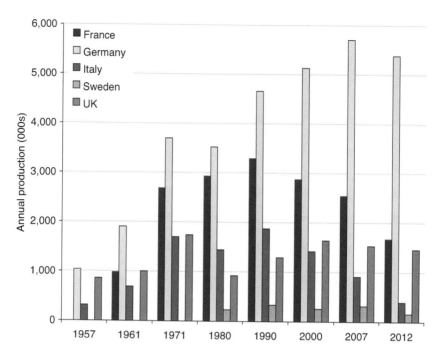

Figure 3.1 Annual car production, 1957–2012: France, Germany, Italy, Sweden and UK (source: see Appendix).

Note
No comparable figures for Sweden until 1980.

Transport 2011). Mass consumption was epitomised by the explosion of mass tourism: new technology (the passenger plane) and new organisations (charter flights) enabled the standardised seaside holiday in southern Europe for ordinary Germans and, especially, ordinary Britons.

Looking back on this period in the 1980s writers identified key features of the period and announced its demise. Following Gramsci, they saw mass production linked to mass consumption through institutions and policies. Lash and Urry (1987) defined organised capitalism as built around Keynesian demand management policies and bargaining between the state, organised business and organised labour. For Piore and Sabel (1984) fordism was structured around the needs of large-scale mass production with its heavy investment in hard (i.e. rigid) automation. Table 3.1 lists these and other features of fordism/organised capitalism; it shows the new features that allegedly replaced them.

While these arguments stressed similarities between European societies at any one point of time, by the new century it had become commonplace to contrast Anglo-American and Continental European capitalisms. Michel Albert (1993) differentiated between Anglo-American capitalism and Rhine–Alpine capitalism.

Table 3.1 Fordism and post-fordism: production and society

	Fordism	*Post-fordism*
Source of competitive strength	**Economies of scale**	**Economies of scope**
Production technology	Mass production, 'hard automation'	Flexible specialisation, 'soft automation'
Labour force	Core: semi-skilled operatives (with small specialised craft and professional groups)	Core: multi-skilled and adaptable 'craft' worker
Firm structure	Vertical integration; 'visible hand' of bureaucratic hierarchy	Networks, supply chain; 'invisible hand' of market between units
Family	Male breadwinner, housewife	Multiple forms
Labour market	Job for life	Fragmented, temporary
Welfare state	Universal security	Individualised benefits, private consumption
Economic policy	Keynesian demand management	Monetarism, supply side policies

For Albert the key to Rhineland capitalism was its financial system. By contrast, in their influential study *Varieties of Capitalism* Hall and Soskice (2001) conceptualise liberal market economies (LME) and co-ordinated market economies (CME) as systems with mutually reinforcing sets of institutions. In each system the firm is involved in four sets of relationships: with the systems of finance, education and training, its employees and industrial relations, and other firms (Table 3.2).

The form of these relationships is significantly different in an LME and a CME. In the LME all relationships tend to be short-term, market-type relationships which

Table 3.2 Liberal and co-ordinated market economies

	Liberal Market Economies (LME)	*Co-ordinated Market Economies (CME)*
Finance system	Stock market-based; 'transparency'	Bank-based; insider information
Inter-firm relations	Long-term relations with rich information flows and extensive co-operation	Markets and contracts; limited information exchange and minimal co-operation
Employment relations	Hire and fire	Long-term employment
Education and training	High general education, further training in marketable skills	Occupation (or industry) specific skills

Source: adapted from Hall and Soskice (2001).

involve explicit financial calculations and legal specifications. The firm relies on the stock exchange for funds, so must provide accurate and transparent information which allows anyone to monitor the activity of the company, above all through detailed publicly available quarterly reports. 'Insider dealing' (where particular shareholders have privileged information) is penalised, since this gives some shareholders unfair advantages. Relations with other firms are limited to what is bought and sold and mutual obligations are specified in contracts. Employees can be easily hired – and equally easily fired; given that they may leave at any moment, the firm makes no attempt to train them apart from for immediate and specific tasks.

The CME is in many ways the polar opposite. Finance is raised through long-term loans and from shareholders, often the founding family or a particular bank. Given that financiers cannot easily (or will not willingly) dispose of their investment, they are committed to the company and attempt to be knowledgeable about it: links between the company and its key shareholders are important mutual sources of information. Similarly, relations with other firms tend to be long term, relatively high trust and again involve two-way flows of information which are not reducible to the immediate contract. In this situation, employees have long-term jobs enabling the company to invest in training, while industrial relations involve mutual bargaining and participation.

The varieties of capitalism approach suggests that different national systems have their own logic. Institutions therefore cannot be simply transplanted or 'benchmarked' from one society to another, since they only function as part of the whole. Within each system firms act with situational rationality, so that a strategy that will produce profits in one situation could be a disaster in another. If the system is self-reinforcing, then it is also 'path dependent'. Firms in LME and CME will develop in different ways according to different trajectories. Firms within a CME tend to be particularly good at incremental innovation, since this involves developing relations with customers over long periods and building up the skills and knowledge of the workforce; by contrast, firms within an LME excel in areas which require radical innovation. Accordingly, German firms (operating in a CME) excel in areas such as engineering, US firms in electronics and software (Hall and Soskice 2001: 41).

The varieties of capitalism approach can show how different sets of institutions fit together: countries where stock exchange is important (as measured by the value of capitalisation relative to GDP) tend to also have deregulated labour markets (Hall and Soskice 2001: 19); countries with longer-term finance tend to have more regulated labour markets and strongly centralised trade union bargaining (Höpner 2005). And most importantly for the analysis of social structure, economies with a high relative stock exchange valuation tend to have high levels of income inequality and be societies in which most people work long hours (Hall and Soskice 2001: 22).

The varieties of capitalism approach has spawned a rich research literature. It has highlighted the extent to which within contemporary Europe 'Anglo-American', 'Atlanticist' or 'liberal market economies' are *not* the norm.

However, research has also undermined the simple contrast between liberal and co-ordinated market economies; it has shown how difficult it is to fit into the model countries such as France, Sweden and Italy, let alone the smaller and often successful European countries such as the Netherlands, Denmark or (briefly) Ireland.

In the 1980s and early 1990s it was perhaps plausible that Germany and the UK as exemplars of respectively co-ordinated and liberal market economies provided different competing models of capitalism, each of which was effective in its own way. Subsequently the apparent stagnation of Germany seemed to suggest that there was indeed only one best (Anglo-American) way. Today (2015) German success has re-opened the possibility of different and competing models, except that, as we shall see, some of the key features of German institutional architecture have been transformed. In many ways the varieties of capitalism thesis was put forward precisely when Germany was changing.

Conceptualising national economies as interlocking institutional systems runs the risk of assuming more coherence than actually exists: it ignores the extent of 'slack' (Thelen 2009) between institutions, such that a variety of combinations may well be possible. Furthermore, identifying the consequences of a particular institution does not necessarily explain its actual origins. German firms may have benefited from, for example, the German training system, but that does not alter the fact that it was largely imposed on them against their wishes. Path dependency does not mean that a trajectory is immutable: there are crises, switching points and turning points. During the 1980s the British Thatcher government wrenched the UK onto a path that brought it much closer to the American model. Much the same may now be happening in other European countries today.

The internationalisation of the financial system involves a key challenge to the nation state. Over the last twenty years global trade flows have been growing faster than GDP, but until the crisis global financial flows were growing faster still: total global capital flows were less than 7 per cent of world GDP in 1998 but had reached over 20 per cent in 2007 (Milesi-Ferretti and Tille 2011). Global financial flows have long since ceased to be simply a means of financing trade. This growing importance of the financial system within economies can also be seen as the financialisation of economies: not only does the financial services sector generate a growing proportion of total wealth, but a growing proportion of non-financial firms' profits comes from their own financial activities. Across the entire society relationships between individuals are increasingly marketised, i.e. explicitly understood in financial terms. This generates new levels of abstraction and isolation, new risks and new uncertainties as the market is shorn of institutional supports and restraints (Deutschmann 2000).

3.2 Back to the watchman state?

In the middle of the nineteenth century Karl Marx described the British state as like a night watchman, providing law and order but little else. This account also fitted the USA, but hardly the rest of Europe. On the Continent the state was always involved in the creation of each national railway system, and in countries such as Germany and Sweden the system was fully state owned; in the early twentieth century the new telephone systems were largely state owned. By the 1970s this national framework had been consolidated in Western Europe: main utilities and infrastructure were usually state owned. In each country the national railway company, the national postal service, the national electricity company, all were part of the framework of the national society. States also directly or indirectly owned many banks and financial institutions as well as some large industrial enterprises. There was, however, much variation. Water has always been provided partly by private companies in France; coal and steel were never nationalised in Germany; in Sweden, despite its advanced welfare state, virtually all industry always remained in private hands. While such state ownership remained minimal in the USA, after 1945 state ownership became more widespread in Britain, with the nationalisation of industry (railways, coal and temporarily steel). The expansion of the state in Europe after 1945 exacerbated the division between the two sides of the Atlantic.

The UK was a relatively late entrant to the mixed economy and was the first to leave it. The Thatcher government effectively invented privatisation as a political project by selling off the major utilities (telephones, water, electricity). Even though privatisation spread to all European countries, in the mid-1990s the UK was an extreme case (Saunders and Harris 1994: 6). In France, for example, much of the initial 'privatisation' was simply the undoing of the nationalisation programme of the first Mitterrand government in the early 1980s. While the UK now has no traditional state enterprises left to privatise, the process is still continuing in the rest of Europe, as the example of urban transport shows (Table 3.3). At the same time the UK continues to be one of the most determined advocates of other forms of the expansion of the market within state services. This can take four main forms:

- the outright sale of assets to an existing company or to individuals, as when state or local government housing is sold to existing tenants;
- the transformation of a state-owned company into a privately owned company, possibly with employee share participation ('privatisation' as normally understood);
- the contracting out of services provided by the state to private companies, including the management of assets which remain state owned;
- the introduction of market criteria into state activities (the creation of 'quasi markets') with the intention of subjecting state entities to competition.

In parallel there has been the widespread attempt to change the way state activities are managed. Within the Anglophone world, 'New Public Management' (NPM) has meant the assumption that public sector management should as far as possible operate as if it were private sector: citizens become customers or clients, investment is justified in terms of market-based 'rates of return', etc.

Table 3.3 Transport ownership in capital cities, 1980 and 2014

	1980	*2014*
London	State-owned monopoly (London Transport)	Public transport authority (Transport for London) contracts out bus services; Underground Public Private Partnership
Paris	State-owned monopoly (RATP)	RATP but delegated management
Rome	State-owned monopoly	State-owned monopoly but changed legal form
Stockholm	State-owned monopoly	Private enterprise contractor (Connex/Veolia runs metro)
Berlin	Municipally owned monopoly	Municipally owned monopoly

However, NPM is hardly the only version of public management reform. Especially in Germany, modernisers attempt to reform public management within a judicial framework and a continued regulatory role for the state (Pollitt and Bouckaert 2011).

Interwoven with such transformation of existing state activities, there is also the move towards the involvement of private sector finance in state capital projects through various forms of 'public private partnership'. Projects (e.g. new bridges, new hospitals) can be planned by the state, but then built and/or managed by a private company. Intriguingly enough, such forms of ownership are reminiscent of the 'concessions' granted to foreign companies in nineteenth-century Latin America.

To equate privatisation with an explicit neo-liberal political project is too simplistic. Privatisation did not figure strongly in the initial programme of the first Thatcher government. In the UK privatisation began with the partial sale of the government's holding in British Petroleum (BP) by the Labour government in 1976; the sale of further shares in BP in 1979 was the first privatisation of a major British state enterprise (Florio 2004: 29). In the UK alone, privatisation was justified by, according to one study, thirteen different objectives, from reducing the size of government, through reducing the state deficit, to improving the efficiency of the newly privatised enterprises (Florio 2004: 32). This list does not explicitly include reducing the power of trade unions, but some authors sympathetic to privatisation consider it to have been a major objective (Saunders and Harris 1994: 23) and it seems implausible that this was never an actual consideration. In comparative perspective privatisation in the UK does stand out for being much more ideologically committed and thoroughgoing: elsewhere privatisation has been less extensive and at times more pragmatic. For example, in Sweden partial privatisation of urban public transport has been relatively uncontroversial. Even in France, where the privatisation of the major state enterprises (Air France, Électricité de France, SNCF) is contested, the increasing private provision of many local services, including urban transport outside Paris, is widely accepted.

One major justification for privatisation was to create 'popular capitalism', i.e. an increase in the number of shareholders. In the UK the number of individuals owning shares in British corporations rose from three million in 1979 to eleven million in 1993 when approximately 22 per cent of the adult population owned shares (Florio 2004: 31) The privatisation of Deutsche Telekom in 1996–1997 was promoted with methods such as TV adverts deliberately copied from the large British privatisations, in order to try to create new first-time shareholders. However, privatisation contributed directly to inequality because it nearly always has meant lower pay and increased job insecurity (and hence lower lifetime earnings) for large numbers of unskilled workers. At the same time, managers' pay has increased. In the UK transport sector there was a once-off hike when some individual managers were able, just like Russian nomenklatura after 1989, to take over existing assets through management buy-outs and then sell them on (Wolmar 2001). More importantly, managers' pay in the newly privatised enterprises is based on private sector standards, and those standards have increasingly diverged from average earnings.

Privatisation and more broadly marketisation is ending the role of the public sector as an exemplary employer where unions were recognised and employment protection legislation enforced. As above all Crouch *et al.* have argued, this was important for social structure as a whole, since the public sector has traditionally provided

> work that required relatively modest skills, paid rather low wages, but offered security of employment and (because of the commitment of most public employers to concepts of the 'good employer') freedom from the brutalisation often associated with low-skilled and low-paid work.
>
> (Crouch *et al.* 2001: 239)

Privatisation mattered in the UK because of the sheer numbers involved. In 1979 approximately 1.5 million people worked for state enterprises; over the next twenty years approximately a million employees were transferred to the private sector, somewhere between 3 and 4 per cent of employees. It is far more difficult to enumerate the numbers affected by other forms of marketisation. This ranges from former municipal employees whose work has been outsourced through to those remaining in the National Health Service but now subjected to the discipline of quasi markets.

Such changes in state employment potentially also impact on the welfare state itself, especially in non Anglo-Saxon welfare states. In Scandinavian welfare regimes, employment in caring services by *women* has facilitated the 'defamilisation' of women; it provides regular work outside the home for some women who thus provide support for all employed mothers (and to some extent, even fathers). Such caring work (Section 2.2) has been relatively good employment but this is because it is also state employment. Privatisation and marketisation thus threaten the working conditions of ordinary women on a large scale. In conservative or corporatist regimes, state employment is important because it provides access for the wage-earner's family to social insurance benefits; this is even more important in 'Mediterranean' regimes where welfare coverage has been incomplete and access to secure state employment *by men* is a crucial way in which entire families access social security benefits. As has become especially clear in the Greek crisis, in such regimes privatisation thus undermines the welfare system.

Privatisation reshapes the political field. It clearly weakens the power of trade unions as the discipline of the market (and the threat of dismissal) replaces political bargaining. During the privatisation period in the UK, trade union membership fell faster there than anywhere else in Europe[1]: from 55 per cent of all employed in 1979 to about 30 per cent at the end of the 1990s (Florio 2004: 181). Much less discussed is that privatisation creates a new opportunity structure in which new actors can emerge, develop and in turn push the process forward (Lorrain and Stoker 1997: 12). Thus the last decade has seen the emergence of companies with global reach in areas such as healthcare, transport and general facilities management. The privatisation of transport systems has involved the emergence of companies such as Stagecoach and Veolia (ex-Connex), both of which operate services (bus, rail) in many different countries which used to be provided by state-owned companies. At the same time, many activities previously internal to the state services have been outsourced, stimulating the growth of service companies who in turn lobby for greater market access. The Danish company ISS (Integrated Services Solutions) provides facility services in state-owned institutions such as hospitals and now employs over half a million people worldwide; the Swedish company CAPIO provides healthcare services in countries such as Finland, France and the UK: the US-owned multinational HP Enterprise Services (formerly EDS) provides IT services through major outsourcing contracts in twenty European countries.

The merits and demerits of privatisation are always discussed in economic terms – is private ownership more efficient? Astonishingly, academic assessments find it difficult to locate any clear efficiency gains. Crucially, such discussion ignores the institutional change involved: a fundamental transformation of the relationship between the state, the society and the economy (Frangakis and Huffschmid 2009: 10). Discussing the privatisation of British transport, the late Tony Judt remarked:

> Now, whether or not the trains all run on time, and just as efficiently and safely whether private or public, doesn't detract from the fact that what you've lost is a sense of the collective service which we commonly own and in the benefits of which we share.
>
> (2012: 383)

In particular, national cultural institutions with national reach, above all the national broadcasting companies, one of the crucial innovations of the fordist epoch in Europe, are exposed to competition and/or simply sold. The paradox of the story is that, for all the excitement with popular capitalism, this is remarkably *unpopular.* State enterprises may have been by-words for inefficiency, but there has never been a *popular* movement to sell them. In the UK in the 1980s privatisation was opposed by a majority that grew over the decade (Saunders and Harris 1994: 121). Indeed, after the fiasco of Railtrack in the UK, at one stage fully 76 per cent of the British electorate supported re-nationalisation (Murray 2001: 168). Although new shareholders can in certain circumstances provide a key swing factor for conservative political parties (see Saunders and Harris 1994: 126), it remains the case that shareholding remains the pursuit of a minority – even if a much enlarged minority.

Even where the public sector is more effective, as in France, the equation of private sector with 'liberty' has added plausibility if high youth unemployment means that even for 'middle-class' youth chances of getting a coveted state sector job are limited. At the same time there is an element of self-fulfilling prophecy here. One explanation for public sector inefficiency is that the denigration of the public sector, and even of public service generally, is now integral to increasing areas of elite education in particular due to the American-style business schools, first in the UK, then elsewhere.

Privatisation is presented as part of a programme to reduce state 'interference' in the economy, yet by itself privatisation does not create markets, and further government intervention is thus required to produce them. This has led to increasingly complex legal measures to create markets in areas which are often in economists' terms 'natural monopolies'. For example, to introduce competition in the railways, ownership of the physical track has to be separated from the operators who actually run the trains. This in turn creates the need for complicated mechanisms to hold the two sides together, not least in order to ensure safety. Furthermore, since utilities such as water or even transport are seen to supply public needs, special targeted instruments have to be devised to ensure that the private companies do serve the public interest. As such, privatisation comes full circle. Once again, the state attempts to direct economic activity, but now the state itself has produced new and powerful private economic actors with their own agendas.

Here the European Union has played an important role. The initial Services Directive of 2006 (the 'Bolkestein Directive') would have opened all education and health services to private provision. For once opposition was organised and effective and a more restrictive version came into force in 2007. However, the Commission and the European Court of Justice (ECJ) have made clear that there is no change in the basic principle that *any* public service should be open to competitive provision. European competition policy ensures that state enterprises must be organised like private companies, even if formally state owned. In the current Eurozone crisis the bail-out programmes imposed on Greece, Portugal and Ireland demanded further privatisation of state assets. Whereas the first stages of the European project consolidated European national states, the contemporary European project undermines them.

3.3 The financial system and the firm

Within the varieties of capitalism literature, the financial system is the keystone of a country's interlocking institutional system. Changes in the financial system therefore should be expected to unlock movement elsewhere. In the case of co-ordinated market economies as exemplified by Germany, changes in the financial system could be expected therefore to involve a new convergence towards an Anglo-American system. This in turn could form a tipping point for changes in the rest of the political economy and so undermine the basis of the European social model itself.

In the second half of the nineteenth century Germany industrialised and the banks provided much of the finance for the new enterprises. Historians have used this to explain the speed of German industrialisation (the German banks were founded to ensure plentiful finance for the new industries) and its concentrated nature (in key industries like coal and steel German firms were much larger than their British counterparts). Historians have also seen this institutional configuration as one component of the German *Sonderweg* (special route) to modern society: German industrialisation was elitist and anti-liberal and so pre-disposed the society to Nazism (Blackbourn and Eley 1984).

Today what matters is not Germany's nineteenth-century past, but the history of the pre-reunification Federal Republic. Throughout the twentieth century one peculiarity of Germany was the tight relationship between the three large banks (the Commerzbank, the Dresdner Bank, the Deutsche Bank) and the country's large industrial firms. For advocates of 'stakeholder capitalism', German banks were seen as having had a benign influence, contributing to economic success and social stability. A firm's *Hausbank* (house bank) had a significant shareholding in the company and provided it with long-term credit: these financial links also involved a rich flow of information, enabling banks to monitor and influence the performance of 'their' companies. Since so much capital was in the form of long-term loans, and since in addition the banks held large shareholdings which they did not usually sell, the stock market was 'shallow' compared to that of the UK: relatively few stocks were traded and hostile takeovers were rare. Consequently, managers did not have to worry about short-term fluctuations of the firm's share price and so were free to make long-term plans, while employees knew that the firm was committed to long-term growth.

Such stable ownership was much more common in Continental Europe than in the UK in the entire post-World War II period. In Sweden large firms were closely linked to banks, whose position has often been protected by special voting shares. Among large firms particularly important was the network of companies controlled by the Wallenberg family (Volvo, etc.). In Italy a few individual families such as the Agnellis (owners of Fiat) dominated the corporate landscape so much so that in the mid-1980s over a quarter of all Italian shares were effectively controlled by three families (Faccio and Lang 2002).

The pattern of share ownership and the form of the financial system relate to corporate governance, i.e. the ways in which shareholders and other stakeholders determine company policy. The German two-tier system of company governance legally separates executive and supervisory functions. In all public limited companies or *Aktiengesellschaften* the firm's *Aufsichtsrat* (supervisory board) is responsible for the overall policy of the company and meets several times a year. It is separate from the smaller *Vorstand* (executive board) of full-time managers which is responsible for the normal running of the company. Until the mid-1990s some studies of corporate governance praised this 'insider' governance system as the key to the success of Germany's 'social market economy' (see especially Hutton 1996; also Charkham 1994). In particular it was contrasted with the short-termism of the UK system, in which the financial sector centred on the City of London had little connection with national industry. Today, however, the British system is seen as exemplary and the 'international' standard against which all others are measured.

The most basic change has been how the firm itself is understood, for now it is self-evident to senior managers all across Europe that the firm exists for its shareholders. Shareholder value prescribes an internationalist laissez-faire financial system, dispersed shareholdings within individual firms, and outsider governance. On all three dimensions of firm structure the movement is towards the UK model. The process is clearest in the financial system. In Germany the large banks were already loosening their links with large industrial firms in the 1980s (Deeg 1993), becoming sellers of services instead of the trusted advisers highlighted in the co-ordinated market economy model. Indeed, in 2001 Deutsche Bank went so far as to announce that it would no longer hold any chairmanships of supervisory boards (Lütz 2005). At the same time, the banks moved into international capital markets where they could earn greater profits than from long-term lending to domestic firms. By 2005 Deutsche Bank had a Swiss-born chairman who behaved like an American CEO and explicitly stated that he no longer saw the bank as a component of a *national* German economy. Whereas earlier representatives of the banks had seats on the boards of the major non-financial companies, by 2010 these links and hence the distinctive German corporate networks had all evaporated (Windolf 2014). For their part, from the late 1990s onwards large German firms sought listings on the New York Stock Exchange, thereby accepting US accounting rules. Starting with the highly controversial Mannesmann takeover battle (Garrett 2001), hostile takeovers became accepted in Germany. Unlike before, there is now a market for corporate control in Germany.

The transformation of the financial system went faster and further in Sweden and above all in France. In Sweden deregulation of the financial system began in the 1980s with the abolition of cross-border capital controls. The French state abandoned its attempts to control industrial credit in the late 1980s. French companies began raising increasing amounts of capital on the stock exchange and a market for corporate control ('mergers and acquisitions') emerged on an unprecedented scale. Far more so than in Germany, the French financial system internationalised: French firms pursued aggressive foreign acquisition strategies, while at the same time foreign buyers were purchasing more French firms; by

1998 foreign shareholders held 43 per cent of the total shares of the Paris stock exchange index firms, the CAC 40. France also led the way in a move towards more Anglo-American forms of corporate governance, with a clear rise in the number of outside appointments to company boards (Goyer 2001). Such changes do not mean that all European countries now have identical financial systems, but the direction of change appears to be in only one direction.

A new business populism has also pushed corporate governance in a more Anglo-American direction. This is a crucial and largely unremarked change in European political culture. Up until the 1970s, small business discontent with large companies took the form of the defence of the little man (the small shop-keeper, the peasant farmer) – an important component of right-wing politics in the first half of the century (including Nazism in the 1930s and Poujadism in France in the 1950s). Today shareholder activism is one form of the economic populism of the small man (and the small woman). In Germany in the 1970s the power of the banks over the economy was criticised by the political left, but from the 1980s it began to be challenged in the name of small savers and share-holders. For example, in a series of vituperative books, Günter Ogger savaged the banks' policies towards their customers and claimed that bankers on super-visory boards had neither the will nor the competence to maximise shareholder value (Ogger 1992). The German system was thus under attack for neglecting the small investor, precisely the person left out in the cold by the privileged rela-tions between banks and 'their' companies. Similar arguments were put forward in France by the small shareholders' organisation Adam (Association pour la Défense des Actionnaires Minoritaires), whose leader, Colette Neuville, became a national figure during the 1990s. As she herself openly admitted, although the association took action on behalf of small shareholders, this was often supported and funded by large international investors. While in the 1930s Keynes expected the small investor to be soon extinct, today's small shareholder activism is based on the number of small investors who can be mobilised for quick returns, as shown by the 'demutualisation' of mutual credit associations in the UK. Here voluntary associations were turned into private companies and then sold for the benefit of their immediate 'owners'. Such popular short-termism (for mutual associations were based on the idea of long-term mutual support) resonates well with the short-termism of the global fund manager and is also fuelled by the growing popular business media (Section 4.3).

A more obvious cause of the change is the global financial market. The agents here are institutional fund managers, based in the USA and to some extent the UK. Unlike the patient investors of co-ordinated market economies, such inves-tors do not have the competence to develop detailed knowledge of the products and processes of the companies in which they invest. Instead, they seek institu-tional forms which they believe will ensure that companies are run in the *imme-diate* interests of *all* their shareholders. They demand 'transparency', i.e. detailed financial information available to all shareholders through the quarterly report; they call for an end to the privileged position of particular shareholders and the unwinding of cross-holdings that link companies to other companies about which there is no public information. For them, shareholders' interests are best maintained by independent directors on the company board and companies should be managed by American-style chief executives remunerated through stock options. Needless to say, for such a world view it is axiomatic that employees have nothing to contribute to the enterprise apart from their immediate labour; American-trained fund managers are probably fairly hostile to European traditions of economic citizenship.

Participation in the world capital markets therefore has a totally different price to participation in the world product or even service markets. It appears to involve the imposition of effectively American standards on the internal governance of European companies. In 2005 Franz Münterfering, then chairman of the SPD, claimed that foreign institutional investors were 'locusts' destroying German companies – the result was a political storm complete with (bizarre) accusations of anti-semitism. That the controversy erupted precisely in Germany was hardly surprising: Germany has gone furthest in integrating employees into the enterprise, and shareholder value directly threatens the institutions that secure this. European firms have therefore been changed in significant ways and against relatively little opposition. This is partly because the 'locusts' are not necessarily foreign and the global market provides massive new opportunities for European investment abroad.

Such changes have only occurred because of political decisions at national and EU levels which have both created structures favourable to global business and facilitated the emergence of new political forces. 'Atlantic' capitalism was only also *Anglo*-American capitalism because of Thatcher's political programme: the abolition of exchange controls, the opening of the London Stock Exchange ('Big Bang' of 1986) and the accelerating privatisation programme. Everywhere the transformation of European enterprises has depended on prior political decisions. In Germany, for example, the 1998 Control and Transparency Act (KonTraG) restricted the power of banks and other privileged shareholders; even more importantly, in 2001 taxation on capital gains from sales of shares was ended, thus facilitating the unwinding of cross-shareholdings and the sale of large 'traditional' blocks of shares (Busch 2005).

The role of the EU in this process was almost unnoticed by public debate until the referendums of 2005. Since the Single European Act of 1987 the EU, while vaguely promoting a 'social Europe', has been deliberately opening up to the market areas of activity which were previously regulated by national states. Early attempts to create a single European company law – which would have facilitated the free movement of capital – were always stymied because some countries insisted that it should involve an element of co-determination on the German model. Today movement towards a single company law and a single capital market is entirely in an Anglo-American direction. The EU has become a key creator of a particular form of economic space.

3.4 The labour market

The labour market is the most politically contentious aspect of the European social model. European societies are distinctive partly because of their labour markets, yet employment regulation is also held responsible for Europe's economic problems. However, there is no single European labour market: the level and form of employment varies enormously between member states. Economic citizenship has been undermined in the name of labour market flexibility, but not everywhere and not in the same way.

In Europe after the crises of the 1970s, many governments initially focused on reducing the number of people looking for work, in particular through encouraging early retirement. Subsequently the policy focus changed: the objective became a high rate of *employment*, rather than simply a low rate of *unemployment.* Employment became seen as desirable in itself. Until the 1970s American adults of working age were less likely to be in work than their counterparts in Western Europe, but the pattern then changed. While proportionately more and more Americans were at work, on this side of the Atlantic it seemed that fewer and fewer Europeans had jobs. By 1990, 73 per cent of Americans were in employment but only 62 per cent of Europeans (Figure 3.2). This was 'Euroscelerosis', allegedly caused by Europe's inflexible labour markets.

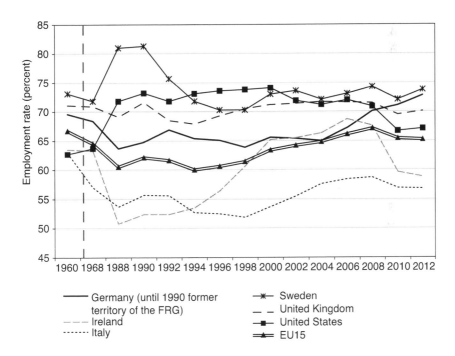

Figure 3.2 Employment rates: EU15, Germany, Ireland, Italy, Sweden, UK and USA (derived from 1960 to 1997 OECD (1999: Table 2.14); 1998 onwards from Eurostat).

One of the most influential explanations of these differences was the OECD (1994) *Jobs Study*. This ranked countries in terms of the stringency of their employment protection legislation (how difficult and/or how expensive it was for the employer to dismiss workers) and how much restriction there was on so-called non-standard employment (part-time work, agency work, temporary contracts). The more employment was protected and the more employment was only full-time and permanent, the more inflexible the labour market. Across Europe the last twenty years have seen a steady stream of so-called reforms which have aimed to reduce employment protection and increase labour market flexibility. However, it is now unclear how much these have been the cause of any increase in total employment (Avdagic and Crouch 2015).

Yet as Figure 3.2 shows, by no means all of Europe was scelerotic. In terms of Esping-Anderson's typology, social democratic Scandinavian societies had high employment with nearly three-quarters of the working age population at work; they were followed closely by the liberal UK with well over two-thirds at work. Continental conservative countries such as Germany or France had a medium level of employment, while in Mediterranean countries such as Italy only just over half of the relevant population was at work. From the mid-1990s onwards there was convergence, with employment increasing in the medium and low employment rate countries. The dramatic change was in Germany, where welfare changes pushed employment up to the level of the UK. A few years later US employment began to decline, so that by the onset of the current crisis the EU15 and the USA had essentially similar levels of employment. In the crisis these trends have continued. Employment in Scandinavia has stayed high and Germany has now almost reached Scandinavian levels of employment, while elsewhere employment has fallen back (though usually not to the low levels of the 1990s).

A labour market that does not privilege full-time work ensures that employers can offer part-time work, enabling people with responsibilities but also students and older people to take employment. Equally, short-term and temporary contracts mean that employers can hire additional workers, without worrying that they will have to be retained even if they are no longer needed. Italy exemplifies what happens when none of this is available (Figure 3.3). Overall employment is low because work is disproportionately the concern of 'prime age' adult males. Few students have part-time work; many women are at home (even if they also have few or even no children); many men have retired early. The 2000 Lisbon Council set an overall employment target of 70 per cent including a rate of 60 per cent for women and 50 per cent for all between fifty-five and sixty-four (Table 3.1). High employment societies such as Sweden and the UK had already achieved these targets, while in the last year before the crisis Germany had nearly done so. Italy by contrast remained way short of the target, with only 59 per cent of the population at work (Table 3.4). The Europe 2020 strategy now sets a target of 75 per cent of all 20–64-year-olds to be employed across the EU, but it is unclear how this is to be achieved.

The UK and Scandinavia have achieved high employment rates in different ways, even though both have flexible labour markets. The UK's high employment

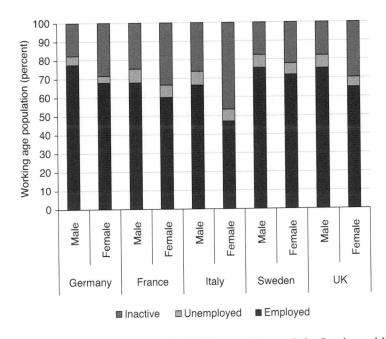

Figure 3.3 Employment status, 2012: Germany, France, Italy, Sweden and UK (derived from Eurostat).

Table 3.4 Employment rates and Lisbon targets, 2007

	All	Women	All 55–64	(Unemployment as % of labour force 15+)
Lisbon target	70.0	60.0	50.0	None
France	64.6	**60.0**	38.3	8.3
Germany	69.4	**64.0**	**51.5**	8.4
Ireland	69.1	**60.6**	**53.8**	4.6
Italy	58.7	46.6	33.8	6.1
Poland	57.0	50.6	29.7	9.6
Sweden	**74.2**	**71.8**	**70.0**	6.1
UK	**71.3**	**65.5**	**57.4**	5.3
EU15	66.9	59.7	46.6	7.0
EU27	65.4	58.3	44.7	7.2*

Source: adapted from European Commission (2008: Table 5).

Note
In bold: target achieved.
* EU25.

rate involves long hours for full-time men and women, but also extensive part-time work, mostly taken by women and much of which is very short hours ('marginal part-time work'). Scandinavian societies have a welfare system financed from general taxation rather than through insurance payments from wages; they have extensive (and expensive) active labour market policies that counsel and retrain the unemployed. Scandinavian social democracies distribute working time relatively evenly: almost everyone works, but full-timers work relatively short hours and part-timers work relatively long hours, and there is also considerable movement between these categories. Furthermore, many young people still in education work part-time and, far more than elsewhere, people return to full or part-time education after having worked full-time. In other words, flexibility is likely to be chosen by Scandinavian employees, but imposed on UK employees.

Flexibility can, however, mean more than just variations in the quantity of work. Thus Atkinson and Meager (1986) argued that firms were increasingly dividing their workforce into a 'core' and a 'periphery'. Workers in the 'core' were employed for *functional* flexibility, required to be adaptable and have a wide range of skills. By contrast, workers on the 'periphery' were employed for *numerical* flexibility, providing quantities of labour which could be purchased in small amounts and/or varied at short notice. If this is the case, then clearly job security for all is undesirable, since it means that firms will be unable to adapt their headcount to fluctuations in demand. However, it also means that *from the point of view of the firm* job insecurity for all is undesirable, since it will undermine core workers' commitment to the enterprise.

Such arguments assumed that functional and numerical flexibility were mutually incompatible. Today, however, employers obtain both functional and numerical flexibility *at the same time.* On the one hand skilled workers are no longer always offered job security. While outsourcing began as a way of getting rid of routine workers, it is increasingly being used by firms to access people with scarce skills *whom they do not wish to permanently employ.* Employment agencies such as Manpower now provide not only unskilled labour, but also skilled workers ranging from fully trained chefs to accountants and computer programmers. On the other hand, many forms of work are not skilled in a traditional sense but demand a particular form of commitment: the fast food server has to smile at the customer, just as the call centre operative has 'to smile down the phone' (Wickham and Collins 2004). This commitment is policed partly by opening up the workplace to the market: the worker answers to the customer, not only to the supervisor. Most fundamentally of all, instead of commitment resulting *from* employment, it becomes a requirement *for* employment (all those advertisements asking for 'dynamic individuals' to 'join our team' – at the local fast food outlet). Commitment is *imposed.* In team work and project work, what is required is now the 'quick trust' of a transitory group of colleagues rather than long-term trust with the employer (Grabher 2002). In retrospect, Atkinson's model located not the future, but a transitional stage between fordism, where permanent employment was the norm, and the current situation of generalised insecurity

Labour market flexibility also refers to flexibility in wages. Where wages are 'flexible' firms have a free hand to adjust employees' wages. Accordingly, 'flexible' wages cover everything from a shift from national to local bargaining through to completely individualised pay systems. While some individuals may well benefit from this situation, flexible wages, even more than other forms of labour market flexibility, clearly involve a shift in power towards the employer. At the same time, since such pay systems force individuals to compete with each other, they may erode trust and co-operation within the workplace.

The flexibility rhetoric assumes that flexibility is an unalloyed good, yet this is not necessarily the case. German high technology manufacturing shows how numerical inflexibility can actually generate functional flexibility. German co-determination (*Mitbestimmung*) places employee representatives on company supervisory boards. In addition, every workplace with more than five employees can also have a *Betriebsrat* (works council) elected by the employees. Since these structures exist alongside conventional trade unions, German employees have a double system of representation. The firm-based institutions mean that the firm is legally partly defined by the people who work in it; it is very different to the Anglo-American concept in which the firm is simply a bundle of assets owned by the shareholders. Employee participation turns the firm into a social as well as a financial entity. These 'beneficial constraints' (Streeck 1997) push employers towards a competitive strategy that relies on quality and technological innovation rather than a 'hire and fire' approach to labour. Job security promotes innovation.

During its heyday there were attempts to copy the German system elsewhere in Europe. In France the Auroux laws of the early 1980s gave employees rights to consultation and information, including a compulsory annual workplace assembly. The European Works Council Directive ensures that the employees of transnational enterprises in Europe can create a European Works Council, although its rights are essentially limited to information. Today, however, works councils are declining in Germany: despite the law many smaller establishments do not have one at all, especially in the new *Länder* of the east. Yet the core of the German system remains. Over the last few years, where firms have restructured and downsized this has mostly been through negotiation which has protected the employment of permanent employees.

Germany is also an example of how numerical inflexibility can create a more qualified workforce. In the German 'dual system' of training, nearly all young people who do not go to university serve an apprenticeship. The system depends on employers co-operating with each other, in particular through the *Industrie- und Handelskammer* (chamber of commerce) and with the state and the unions at both local and national levels. Because employers are involved in designing the curriculum they value the resulting qualification. At the same time, and unlike the UK, German employers are prepared to over-train, providing more skills than the immediate tasks require. One reason for this is the relatively inflexible labour market. Given that skilled workers will probably remain employed by the same firm, employers can assume that in the long term their training investment will be justified (Bosch and Charest 2008).

One explanation for the low levels of employment in Esping-Andersen's 'conservative' welfare states has been the tax system. Insurance-based welfare systems involve significant contributions by employers on behalf of each employee and so can be a strong disincentive to employment. This does not operate where welfare is funded from general taxation. Furthermore, if benefits are previous pay then there is little pressure on many unemployed to accept less well paid jobs.

Until the mid-2000s Germany was a case of this. The large numbers of formerly employed drawing long-term pay-related benefits were bankrupting the social insurance system. The so-called 'Hartz IV' reforms (after the chair of reform commission, Peter Hartz) created a two-tier system. German unemployed now move quickly from pay-related benefits ('Arbeitslosengeld I') to means-tested benefits ('Arbeitslosengeld II') which provide a basic income but with the obligation to seek employment. The result has been a massive expansion of low paid and part-time jobs (so-called mini-jobs). The combination of means-tested benefits and low basic income seems to also function as a threat to those still in well paid jobs (Dörre *et al.* 2013). Like the Thatcher revolution in Britain fifteen years earlier, these changes have profoundly altered the social structure. Social inequality has increased, but unemployment has fallen and more of the population are in employment than ever before (Hassel and Schiller 2010). In France pay-related benefits have also been curtailed, but the changes have not been so far-reaching and the consequences less dramatic (Palier and Thelen 2010).

The ability of an employer to dismiss an employee involves not just the formal legal situation but the constraints of custom and practice and the countervailing power of trade unions. Furthermore, some forms of employment, such as in the state sector, may have the protection of custom or even law which does not apply to the rest of the economy. Thus in the post-World War II period the expansion of state ownership involved the extension of civil service rights to layers of routine workers in the post office, the railways and other utilities. Coupled with strong trade union organisation, this ensured that such employment was effectively permanent. Consequently privatisation has had major consequences for employment rights.

Criticism of employment protection was often linked to criticism of high social expenditure. Implicitly or explicitly, the model was the USA, with its minimal employment protection, minimal welfare state and high employment rate. However, it has become increasingly clear that this is fallacious. A developed welfare state like Sweden not only generously supports those without work, it has been able to maintain high levels of employment even in the crisis (Figure 3.3). In particular Denmark has 'flexicurity' which combines income support *and* very limited employment protection, summarised by the slogan 'Protect the worker not the job'. Employment protection is low and employees can be relatively easily dismissed. Instead of passive income support for the unemployed, there are extensive active labour market policies which counsel and train the unemployed. Income support for the unemployed is relatively high – not least because unemployment is assumed to be temporary. Such countries have shown that today high employment is perfectly compatible with a developed welfare state and consequently with high levels of taxation. Furthermore, it is precisely in these societies that forms of work organisation are prevalent which combine consensual decision-making and flexible working – so-called 'learning organisations' (Holm *et al.* 2010).

However, flexicurity is difficult to generalise. Like other expensive aspects of the social democratic welfare state, it requires high levels of taxation and consequently a committed and cohesive *national* citizenry; it also requires state institutions which are trusted and effective. None are now the norm across Europe.

3.5 Conclusion: the battle for the ESM

With its focus on economic institutions, the political economy approach provides a framework for understanding the differences both between Europe and the USA and within Europe itself. Different responses to the political crisis of the 1960s and to the external shocks of the 1970s pushed the institutional structures of the different European countries and the USA further apart. At the end of the 1970s the UK moved decisively closer towards the USA than ever before, while other European countries continued their in many ways *more* divergent paths. Through the 1980s these differences were consolidated, with European countries apart from Britain offering a different development path to the USA, one that could be summarised as Rhineland as opposed to Atlanticist capitalism.

More recently, political decisions by national states have undermined the institutions of national financial systems. Enterprises have been opened up to external takeover and pressurised towards convergence on an Anglo-American 'shareholder value' model, while at the same time their overseas expansion has been facilitated. The labour markets of European countries remain distinctive, but everywhere change has been in the direction of greater labour market *numerical* flexibility. Reform has meant national-level changes which have weakened the employment conditions of core workers, although there has been some movement towards active labour market policies.

The political economy tradition tends to see institutional systems as self-correcting and so all change as path-dependent. Yet as the Thatcher revolution in Britain in the 1980s and the Hartz IV reforms in Germany in the 2000s both demonstrated, national systems and hence national development paths can be transformed. Furthermore, especially the varieties of capitalism branch of the tradition operates by comparing national systems. This can easily lead to what we could term the League of Nations fallacy: treating nation states as equal, comparing for example Denmark to the USA. Yet because not all nations are equal, some influence others.

Fordism itself is of course American in origin. The post-World War II settlement was largely imposed on Europe by the USA and European unity initially occurred under the protection of the American nuclear shield. What is new is the internalisation of this influence. Under the American umbrella national economies were rebuilt and national institutions were consolidated. US politicians – and US firms – were relatively uninterested in European social arrangements provided they facilitated private property in general and US exports in particular: 'Americans dominated the economic world in the abstract, but the French dominated France, the English England, and the Italians Italy' (Barber 2003: 52).

For Barber, contemporary 'market totalitarianism' destroys all such boundaries. In practical terms today the creation of the 'single market' of the European Union has become increasingly dominated by the exigencies of global enterprises and politicians. This certainly undermines the specificities of each national economy. Even more importantly, by subordinating European economy to the dictates of an abstract market, it risks destroying the infrastructure of the ESM itself, destroying what is specific to Europe without putting anything in its place.

Note

1 With the obvious exception of the ex-state socialist societies.

Bibliography

Albert, M. (1993) *Capitalism Against Capitalism*, London: Whurr Publishers.

Atkinson, J. and Meager, N. (1986) *New Forms of Work Organisation*, IMS Report No. 121, Institute of Manpower Studies, University of Sussex.

Avdagic, S. and Crouch, C. (2015) Symposium introduction: labour market reforms, employment performance, employment quality and changing social risks, *British Journal of Industrial Relations* 53.1: 1–5.

Barber, B. (2003) *Jihad vs McWorld*, London: Corgi Books (first published 1995).

Blackbourn, D. and Eley, G. (1984) *The Peculiarities of German History: Bourgeois Society and Politics in Nineteenth Century Germany*, Oxford: Oxford UP.

Bosch, G. and Charest, J. (2008) Vocational training and the labour market in liberal and co-ordinated economies, *Industrial Relations Journal* 39.5: 428–447.

Busch, A. (2005) Globalisation and national varieties of capitalism: the contested viability of the 'German Model', *German Politics* 14.2: 125–139.

Charkham, J. (1994) *Keeping Good Company: A Study of Corporate Governance in Five Countries*, Oxford: Oxford UP.

Crouch, C., Finegold, D. and Sako, M. (2001) *Are Skills the Answer? The Political Economy of Skill Creation in Advanced Societies*, Oxford: Oxford UP.

Deeg, R. (1993) The state, banks and economic governance in Germany, *German Politics* 2.2: 149–176.

Department for Transport (2011) *Transport Statistics Great Britain: 2011*, www.gov.uk/government/uploads/system/uploads/attachment_data/file/8995/vehicles-summary.pdf. Accessed 6 March 2014.

Deutschmann, C. (2000) *Die Verheißung des absoluten Reichtums: Zur religiösen Natur des Kapitalismus*, Frankfurt: Campus.

Dörre, K., Scherschel, K. and Booth, M. (2013) *Bewährungsproben für die Unterschicht? Soziale Folgen aktivierender Arbeitsmarktpolitik*, Frankfurt: Campus.

European Commission (2008) *Employment in Europe 2008*, Luxembourg: Office for Official Publications of the European Communities.

Faccio, M. and Lang, L. (2002) The ultimate ownership of Western European corporations, *Journal of Financial Economics* 65: 365–395.

Florio, M. (2004) *The Great Divestiture: Evaluating the Welfare Impact of the British Privatisations 1979–1997*, Cambridge, MA: MIT Press.

Frangakis, M. and Huffschmid, J. (2009) Privatisation in Western Europe. In M. Frangakis, C. Hermann and K. Lóránt (eds) *Privatisation Against the European Social Model*, London: Palgrave Macmillan, pp. 9–29.

Garrett, C. (2001) Towards a new model of German capitalism? The Mannesmann–Vodafone merger and its implications for the German economy, *German Politics* 10.3: 83–102.

Giddens, A. (2007) *Europe in the Global Age*, Cambridge: Polity Press.

Goyer, M. (2001) Corporate governance and the innovation system in France 1985–2000, *Industry and Innovation* 8.2: 135–158.

Grabher, G. (2002) Cool projects, boring institutions: temporary collaboration in social context, *Regional Studies* 36.3: 205–214.

Hall, P. and Soskice, D. (eds) (2001) *Varieties of Capitalism: The Institutional Foundations of Comparative Advantage*, Oxford: Oxford UP.

Hassel, A. and Schiller, C. (2010) *Der Fall Hartz IV. Wie es zur Agenda 2010 kam und wie es weiter geht*, Frankfurt: Campus.

Holm, J., Lorenz, E., Lundvall, B. and Valeyre, E. (2010) Organizational learning and systems of labour market regulation in Europe, *Industrial and Corporate Change* 19.4: 1141–1173.

Höpner, M. (2005) What connects industrial relations and corporate governance? Explaining institutional complementarity, *Socio-Economic Review* 3.2: 331–358.

Hutton, W. (1996) *The State We're In*, London: Jonathan Cape (first edn 1995).

Judt, T. (2012) *Thinking the Twentieth Century*, London: Heinemann.

Lash, S. and Urry, J. (1987) *The End of Organised Capitalism*, Cambridge: Polity Press.

Lorrain, D. and Stoker, G. (1997) *The Privatisation of Urban Services in Europe*, London: Pinter.

Lütz, S. (2005) The finance sector in transition: a motor for economic reform? *German Politics* 14.2: 140–156.

Milesi-Ferretti, G. and Tille, C. (2011) The great retrenchment: international capital flows during the global financial crisis, *Economic Policy* 66: 337–342.

Murray, A. (2001) *Off the Rails*, London: Verso.

OECD (1994) *The OECD Jobs Study: Unemployment in the OECD Area 1950–1993*, Paris: OECD.

OECD (1999) *Historical Statistics 1999*, www.oecd-ilibrary.org/economics/oecd-historical-statistics-1999_hist_stats-1999-en-fr. Accessed 21 November 2013.

Ogger, G. (1992) *Nieten in Nadelstreifen: Deutschlands Manager im Zwielicht*, Munich: Droemer Knaur.

Palier, B. and Thelen, K. (2010) Institutionalising dualism: complementarities and change in France and Germany, *Politics and Society* 38.1: 119–148.

Piore, M. and Sabel, C. (1984) *The Second Industrial Divide: Possibilities for Prosperity*, New York: Basic Books.

Pollitt, C. and Bouckaert, G. (2011) *Public Management Reform: A Comparative Analysis. New Public Management, Governance and the Neo-Weberian State*, Oxford: Oxford UP.

Saunders, P. and Harris, C. (1994) *Privatisation and Popular Capitalism*, Milton Keynes: Open University Press.

Streeck, W. (1997) Beneficial constraints: on the economic limits of rational voluntarism. In J. Rogers Hollingsworth and R. Boyer (eds) *Contemporary Capitalism: The Embeddedness of Institutions*, Cambridge: Cambridge UP, pp. 197–219.

Thelen, K. (2009) Institutional change in advanced political economies, *British Journal of Industrial Relations* 47.3: 471–498.

Wickham, J. and Collins, G. (2004) The call centre: a nursery for new forms of work organisation? *Service Industries Journal* 24.1: 1–18.

Windolf, P. (2014) The corporate network in Germany 1896–2010. In T. David and G. Westerhuis (eds) *The Power of Corporate Networks: A Comparative and Historical Perspective*, London: Routledge, pp. 66–82.

Wolf, W. (1996) *Car Mania: A Critical History of Transport*, London: Pluto.

Wolmar, C. (2001) *Broken Rails: How Privatisation Wrecked Britain's Railways*, London: Aurum Press.

Womack, J., Jones, D. and Roos, D. (1990) *The Machine that Changed the World: The Triumph of Lean Production*, New York: Rawson Macmillan.

4 Money, markets and post-modernity

Money matters. In contemporary capitalism the expansion of the market has ensured that more and more relationships are mediated by or even based directly on money. As the first section of the chapter argues, this explains much of the importance of consumption for social and personal identity on which so much contemporary theorising about post-modernity rests. The second section shows how the seamless gradient of income inequality has become steeper both in Europe and especially in the USA. For many in contemporary Europe, so the next section shows, extensive marketisation generates *lite wealth* in the form of exchangeable assets which enable more choice and at least the hope of freedom from the constraints of occupation. However, marketisation also generates *heavy wealth*, the unprecedented wealth of a small number of individuals – whose money frees them from depending on the conventional bases of power. Finally, the shift to a cool economy means a new role for celebrity wealth and allows forms of conspicuous consumption which legitimate this new hyper-inequality.

4.1 Money can buy me love – providing it's on the market

Much sociology – and much political discourse – opposes market and society, contrasting financial relationships to social relationships. However, what happens when social relations are primarily financial relations?

Such a society is in an important sense classless. For class to have a social reality members of the same class must share some form of identity. In the nineteenth and early twentieth centuries the working class of Europe, especially in the areas of heavy industry such as South Wales or the Ruhr, developed its own style of life which was interwoven with its distinctive politics. In these areas the working class was not just an economic category, it was also a distinct status group in Weber's terms.[1] Such forms of identity essentially faced people as pre-given: people like us, *Wir hier unten, die da oben* (us down here, them lot up there), were a certain sort of people. Even more extreme is the case of gender identity. We women, they men: these identities were formed within families in which men and women had clearly defined and apparently 'natural' roles. If the odd political activist, social historian or social scientist suggested these identities were changeable, socially created rather than ahistorical eternities, this analysis diverged from the lived experience of human individuals. People experienced their identities as facts of life.

Now such identities too are up for grabs. Class may be an analytical category, but it no longer has a social reality. What it is to be a man, what it is to be a woman, can be debated, can be changed – in men's groups and women's groups, in therapy and in counselling. Genders can be bent and straightened out again. Inherited identities collapse: people now can self-consciously choose their identity in a way that was not possible before. In particular, consumption style has become uncoupled from occupation. Lifestyles are consciously chosen, not tacitly acquired through socialisation. When we consume, we choose what we want to be.

This image of the free-floating self-actualising individual can all too easily ignore the constraints under which individualisation operates. While the direct role of class (at least in its conventional meaning) and even gender may well be eroding, it hardly follows that social structure is evaporating. Equally, individuals are increasingly reflexive about their situation, but that hardly enables them to wish it away. Consumption, like production, has its history and its structure.

Mass consumer markets first emerged at the end of the nineteenth century. Mass consumption meant a single national market in which the population could all buy the same product, distributed nationwide by a high speed transport system, identified by its brand and usually promoted by national advertising. Within Europe such mass consumption first emerged in Britain and only later and more hesitantly in other major countries. In particular, Britain had the first mass market in Europe for branded food products, a development that was probably helped by the destruction of local culinary traditions by the first stage of the industrial revolution (Kynaston 1976). By contrast, in France the major innovation in consumption, the large department store, served primarily a middle class clientele (Crossick and Jaumain 1998).

Mass consumption for the urban working class only developed intermittently in inter-war Europe. In the 1920s German working class families began to buy mass produced branded clothing and food products for the first time (Wickham 1983). At the end of World War II American troops crossed Europe, throwing chewing gum and stockings at the liberated population while the drab and less well-off British muttered about the Yanks being 'overpaid, over-sexed and over here'. In the subsequent decades a 'normal' form of consumption emerged in Europe. First, new social citizenship delivered *collective* or *public* consumption through the provision of publicly funded housing, health, education and cultural facilities. Second, progressive taxes at the top and basic social welfare at the bottom topped and tailed the income distribution. By the end of the 1950s, a broad equality of consumption standards had been achieved. It was not that everyone had the same standard of living, but that in the advanced societies virtually every household had the same basic equipment: a single family house or apartment with separate living, cooking and sleeping facilities. In the 1930s German working class households were often symbolised by the *proletarische*

Wohnküche – the kitchen-cum-living room with its stove around which the family ate, talked and some even slept. By the end of the 1950s the kitchen and living room were separate functional spaces. Similarly, mass car ownership meant that working class households had access to private transport and so were no longer dependent on large public bureaucracies for their journeys. This was hardly the achievement of some utopian equality, but it did mean that differences were largely of degree rather than of kind – and the working class was no longer a different kind ...

This mass consumption within Europe was essentially national. On the one hand, it depended on the use of the political structures of the nation state to redistribute income and finance social consumption; on the other hand the products for private consumption were themselves national. Barber has spotted the crucial issue:

> In the world before McWorld, the Swedes drove, ate and consumed Swedish; the English drove, ate and consumed English, and the rest of the world's inhabitants either mirrored their colonial masters or developed domestic consumption economies around native products and native cultures.
>
> (Barber 2003: 52)

Today the emergence of global brands of goods and services (from Levis to Facebook) justifies the belief that, at least in the affluent West, we live in the epoch of the global consumer, free from the old structures of nation and class. However, some vestigial differences still remain. Shopping in Rome is not the same as shopping in London and is certainly different to shopping in Los Angeles. Across Europe city centres have retained some viability and suburban shopping is less important. By the 1990s the 'malling of America' (Kowinski 1985) had ensured that American cities had almost all become 'edge cities', with housing, employment and leisure facilities dispersed over a wide metropolitan region (Garreau 1991). By contrast European city centres have remained viable, not least because of the continued public investment in public transport (Bahn 2001). Despite the growing dominance of retail chains, supermarkets, hypermarkets and specialist self-service stores, within Europe there remains a clear north/south divide, with the large chains less dominant in the south (Italy, Greece, Portugal). Even within northern Europe, France and the UK show how differences in employment interweave with differences in shopping experience. In the UK (and Ireland) employees have virtually no product knowledge and training consists in American-style 'smile courses'; labour turnover is high, the labour force is increasingly part-time and/or temporary, and shoppers expect to serve themselves and find assistance intrusive (McGauran 2001).

Different forms of shopping also involve different types of customers. If fordist mass production linked to the family shopping of the post-World War II era, shopping today is more of an individual pursuit. The contemporary slogan 'when the going gets tough, the tough go shopping' is not about the family excursion to the out-of-town supermarket. Theories of individualisation can be justified by the growth of designer shopping – largely involving women – and even from the expanding amount of time that is spent on shopping. However, diverse forms of consumption reflect not just choice, but also inequality. To shop in a smart shopping street in Milan is very different to shopping in ethnic food stalls in Belleville.

Consumption in a market economy necessitates spending money: the more money, the more consumption, and above all, perhaps, the more choice. In popular mythology money is the root of all evil, but also the source of all possible pleasures. Money is abstract. Those who possess money can buy anything that has a price, whether a physical product or, more importantly today, a service; money can be spent, or saved or invested. Money is divisible: any specific amount of money can be used for an almost indefinite number of combinations of purchases and purposes. And finally money is universal: the expenditure of money has no relation to its origin, all money is the same.

For all these reasons, money is corrosive of pre-existing ties. The farm or the shop inherited from the parents, the house in which we grew up, a long-cherished piece of jewellery, even the family pet, all of these things – and animate beings – can be sold. When they are sold the bond between the thing and the owner disappears, the 'sentimental value' evaporates. In the famous words of the *Communist Manifesto*, all that is permanent withers away. Money can do this because, and only because, it involves a market. This 'corrosion' of the market, not some abstract historical tendency, is the root of the individualism trumpeted by theorists such as Beck (e.g. Beck and Beck-Gernsheim 2002).

Money is inherently dynamising and emancipatory. Because money allows individuals to choose, it stimulates multiple thin relationships and removes pre-existing ties. When products and services can be bought, the individual with money can loosen himself – and increasingly herself – from unwanted social relationships. Furthermore, because money allows, indeed demands, choice, it ensures what is fashionably termed 'reflexivity'. The person with money, confronted by the cornucopia of goods and services, must reflect on what he or she 'really' wants. And as any good fashion editor knows, because the choice is never ending, what matters is thinking and reflecting on this apparently mundane activity. Money thus stimulates an aesthetic orientation to the world – the desire to *possess* beauty (Deutschmann 2000: 24). And money profanes. Back in the 1960s the young Beatles sang, 'Money can't buy me love.' In an ever more commodified and sexualised world, where pornography is available at the click of a web browser and sexual trafficking one of the fastest growing industries, that claim is out of date.

If the power of money is to be effective, there must be a market. Accordingly, those with money will attempt to commodify more and more areas of life. Just as rich nations want free trade, whether in opium in the nineteenth century or in GM foods today, so rich individuals demand 'proper service' and 'consumer choice' in all areas of their lives. Those with money wish to expand the area in which they can use it. This generates further inequality, even as it appeals to the freedom of choice of the sovereign consumer.

For Weber, the origins of capitalism lay not in the pursuit of money but in the pursuit of a *Beruf* (vocation). Successful economic activity, so he argued, demanded the long-term perspective and ascetic self-discipline of the calling. Hence the economic success of Protestants in general, and in particular of the Calvinist sects. For Simmel, the relationship between markets and religions was rather different. Because money allows freedom from existing ties, those who operate primarily through money tend initially to be marginalised groups: historically within Europe Jews, elsewhere Parsees, Armenians, ethnic Chinese, etc. Simmel argued that to the extent that the market expands, market relationships move to the centre of the indigenous population. Today self-denial and a long-term perspective are hardly the key virtues of shareholder value capitalism. Instead, the continuing expansion of the market sets individuals' consumption desires free from the constraints of their current resources: the credit card replaces the savings book (Langley 2009). The pursuit of money has now become an end in itself: rather than religion providing the secret basis of capitalism, capitalism itself has become religion (Deutschmann 2000). In 'turbo-capitalism' the religious imperative to expand the market expands the purchasing power of money. The claim that the market can solve everything and that the market itself embodies morality is not only totalitarian, it is chiliastic, it is the belief in the achievability of a fantasy world. *In this sense*, market totalitarianism mirrors the Islamo-fascist utopian fantasies of al Quaeda and ISIS, and has replaced the old (and equally implausible) egalitarian fantasies of the left. In John Gray's words: 'In a curious twist, the utopian mind has migrated from the left to the right, and from the academy to the airport bookshop' (Gray 2005: 15).

However, Deutschmann ignores that this utopianism has been paralleled by a revival of religiosity in the USA, the heartland of his turbo-capitalism. In the USA, rather than capitalism replacing religion as religion, it seems to merge with it. Precisely when theorists of globalisation see the market as global, Americans seem more likely than ever before to identify the market, God *and America* (Frank 2001).

Deutschmann also draws attention to Simmel's stress on the peculiar role of money as power. Because of its divisibility, universality and abstraction, money is a generalised power resource. Money is the power over people, but also over the future. Market economies involve an inherent tension between equality and hierarchy. Where the economy involves market relationships, these are in some sense relationships between equals. The world of the first year undergraduate textbook, with its price-taking individuals, is paralleled by the world of legal subjects equal before the law, including the law of contract. Yet markets also generate their own particular form of inequality. Money begets money. The possession of wealth confers cumulative advantages, from cheaper interest rates through to the purchase of health and education. Assets can be used to leverage further income. Thus, while the next section of the chapter examines income inequality in Europe and the USA, subsequent sections of the chapter look at the new importance of wealth.

4.2 Steepening gradients of inequality

In a market money can apparently buy anything and everything. When differences between people are in terms of the amount of money they have, such differences are always ultimately quantitative: people have more or less of the same 'thing'. The distribution of income is a continuous gradient: groups defined by income are statistical categories, not social groups. The distribution of income is nonetheless about social structure: the extent of inequality (what could be termed the steepness of the gradient of inequality) and how and why it has been changing; the extent to which some people have so little income that they are effectively excluded from normal society. Such issues highlight the continuing difference between Europe and the USA, but also how Europe is losing a key aspect of the European social model.

The most basic question to ask about income distribution is whether there are extremes of rich and poor in a society. Here a measure such as the *Gini coefficient* is a useful indicator. The lower the Gini coefficient, the more equal the distribution: in the limiting case of complete equality, with every person (or every household) having exactly the same income, the coefficient has a value of zero. A relatively egalitarian income distribution is also shown by a low *decile ratio*, which compares the income of the richest 10 per cent of households to the poorest 10 per cent.

Table 4.2 presents Gini coefficient and decile ratios for the USA and selected European countries (household income, after tax and state transfers). Of these countries within Europe, the most egalitarian is Sweden and the least egalitarian is the UK. With a Gini coefficient of 0.38, the USA is far more unequal than any of the European countries. This inequality is expressed more concretely by the P90/P10 ratio. In Sweden the household at the 90th decile has an income three times greater than the household at the first decile; in the USA a similar household is more than *six times* better off. In terms of shares of the total income, the top 10 per cent in the USA receive nearly sixteen times that of the bottom 10 per cent.

In the optimistic 1960s social scientists believed that economic growth would continue indefinitely and that over the long term income distribution became

Table 4.1 Income inequality, 2010

	Gini (at disposable income, post taxes and transfers)	P90/P10 disposable income decile ratio	S90/10 disposable income decile ratio
France	0.303	3.6	7.2
Germany	0.286	3.6	6.7
Italy	0.319	4.3	10.2
Sweden	0.269	3.3	6.1
United Kingdom	0.341	4.1	10.0
United States	0.380	6.1	15.9

Source: adapted from OECD Statistics – Dataset: Income Distribution and Poverty.

Table 4.2 Income inequality, 1970s–2010: Gini coefficients

Year	France	Germany	Italy	Sweden	United Kingdom	United States
Mid-1970s	–	–	–	21.2	26.9	31.6
Mid-1980s	–	25.1	28.7	19.8	30.9	34.0
Mid-1990s	27.7	26.0	32.6	21.1	33.7	36.1
2000	28.7	26.4	32.1	24.3	35.2	35.7
2005	28.8	28.5*	33.0*	23.4*	33.5	38.0
2010	30.3	28.6	31.9	26.9	34.1	38.0

Source: adapted from OECD Statistics – Dataset: Income Distribution and Poverty.

Note
* Figure for 2004.

more equal. The benefits of economic growth, in other words, would be increasingly equally distributed. These assumptions remain powerful today, even though for several decades inequality has been widening in the USA – and *to some extent* also in Europe. In the USA from the 1930s through until the early 1970s incomes became more equal. This began with the New Deal and the recovery from the Depression; it continued through World War II and on into the post-war expansion. For around forty years in the USA three factors came together: the economy grew, real incomes of average Americans grew, and income equality grew. The American dream was a reality. Economic growth translated into growing real wages and rising living standards all round, and this was increasingly the case for all Americans (Ryscavage 1999).

And then it all changed. After the oil crises of the 1970s economic growth was very different to what had gone before. For much of the period since the 1970s the real income of the average American remained constant and at times the real incomes of the poor actually fell. Even when the economy grew, inequality increased, in particular because higher incomes grew faster (Ryscavage 1999). Until recently the European experience has been different. The expansion of the European welfare states meant that whereas in the early 1970s overall income distribution in France and (West) Germany was probably more unequal than the USA (Wilkinson 1996: 84), by the 1980s the situation had reversed.

Until the onset of the current crisis (West) European societies also appeared to be becoming more similar. The more egalitarian societies were becoming more unequal but in a few more unequal societies there were some attempts to raise the incomes of those at the lower end of the income distribution (in the UK through the Family Income Supplement). In the crisis, however, the general experience has been of widening inequality almost everywhere (Table 4.2).

Measures such as the Gini coefficient say very little about the shape of the income distribution, yet this is crucial for understanding the social structure. Figure 4.1 uses data from the 1990s to show the different proportions of the population in different income bands, where these bands are themselves defined as percentages of the median. If the different segments of each horizontal bar

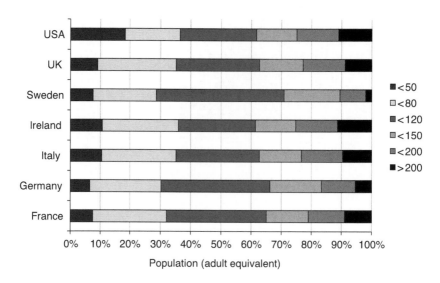

Figure 4.1 Income distribution: USA and selected European countries, mid-1980s (calculated from Atkinson *et al.* (1995: Table 4.2)).

Note
Explanation: the chart shows the proportion of the population in each income band within that
country. Thus in the USA nearly 20 per cent of the population have an income of less than 50 per
cent of the average; no European country comes near this. At the other extreme Sweden has the
largest percentage of the population with between 80 per cent to 120 per cent of the average income.

were placed above each other, then Sweden would indeed resemble the traditional
diamond (more people in the middle band than in each of the bands above and
below the middle). By contrast, even twenty years ago the USA was clearly no
diamond-shaped structure: nearly as many people were in the poorest band as in
the middle income band. All the indications are that since then the relative size of
the middle income group in both the USA and in Europe has fallen (Alderson and
Doran 2013). For example, in Germany there was a small but noticeable decline
between 1991 and 2008 in the proportion of the population in the income bands
between 60 per cent and 140 per cent of the median, while those at both the lower
and (especially) the upper ends grew (Verwiebe 2010: 170). In the crisis evidence
points towards further polarisation with job losses concentrated in construction and
unionised areas of manufacturing, while in many countries the number of well paid
jobs has continued to grow (Eurofound 2013). European societies are not only
becoming unequal, some at least are now moving in the direction of the US model
of inequality, moving from diamonds to egg-timers.

   Within Europe, income distribution data is also central to the definition of
poverty. This is because Europe – or at least European social statistics – define
poverty as having an income below a certain point in the overall distribution of
income. This point is often referred to as the 'poverty line'. Table 4.3 shows the

Table 4.3 At risk of poverty: selected countries, 2010 and 2012

| | Poverty rates after taxes and transfers | | | |
| | *(1)* | *(2)* | *(3)* | *(4)* |
	Poverty Line 60% current median (2010)	*Poverty Line 50% current median (2010)*	*Anchored at fixed point in time – 2008 (2012)*	*% children (under 18) at risk (50% current median) (2010)*
EU27	–	–	18.8	–
France	14.4	7.9	14.2	11.0
Germany	15.3	8.8	–	9.1
Ireland	16.2*	9.0*	22.0**	10.2*
Italy	20.1	13.0	24.0	17.8
Poland	18.1	11.0	11.4	13.6
Sweden	17.4	9.1	11.7	8.2
UK	17.2	10.0	23.4	9.8
USA	24.2	17.4	–	21.2

Source: Columns (1) (2) and (4) from OECD Statistics Dataset – Income Distribution and Poverty, extracted on 27 January 2014. Column (3) from Eurostat SILC [ilc_li22b].

Notes
* Ireland figures for poverty rate at 60 per cent line and 50 per cent line are for 2009, all other country figures for 2010.
** Ireland Anchored at 2008 fixed figure is for 2011.

extent of poverty in seven European countries and the USA using the 60 per cent of median income poverty line. This highlights that in these terms the USA has a far larger proportion of the population in poverty than European societies. Just as with overall income distribution, there is a significant variation within Europe, ranging from France with only 14.4 per cent 'poor' according to this definition to, at the other extreme, Italy with 20.1 per cent poor.

Such simple 'headcounts' of the poor are liable to underestimate the extent of difference in poverty between countries, since they take no account of the *depth* of poverty. Table 4.3 also shows a poverty line calculated as 50 per cent of the median income. Everywhere this reduces the proportion of the population defined as poor, but less so in the USA than in Europe. Thus in the USA fully 17.4 per cent of the population have an income below 50 per cent of the median, as compared to 10 per cent in the UK and 9.1 per cent in Sweden. The USA not only has proportionately more people in poverty, but 'the American poor are really poor' (Alesina and Glaeser 2004: 47).

If poverty is simply related to the median income at one point in time, then an overall fall in the income level in a society could conceivably have no effect at all on the poverty statistics: everyone has become worse off. This seems to be what happened in Ireland in the first years of the crisis: living standards fell, but the proportion in poverty stayed almost the same. Anchoring the poverty line to a fixed point in time shows the impact of such shifts in the overall income level. Table 4.2 for example shows that in Ireland in 2010, 16.2 per cent were at risk of poverty relative to the median income of that year, but if the median income from 2008 is taken the proportion rises to 22.0 per cent.

A low income by itself does not necessarily involve deprivation: income loss can be short term, people may have savings, they may have access to good housing, etc. Since the 1990s poverty research has focused on material indicators such as lack of warm clothing or inadequate housing. Such *Lebenslage* (life situation) research (Verwiebe 2010) has gone along with interest in people's subjective understandings of poverty, such as how difficult they feel it is to make ends meet or their satisfaction with their standard of living (Atkinson *et al.* 2004; Fahey 2007). In the crisis such issues have become more important.

Although a poverty line is defined in monetary terms, its rationale derives from the seminal linkage of poverty with exclusion from normality:

> [People are poor who …] lack the resources to obtain the type of diet, participate in the activities and have the living conditions which are customary, or at least widely recognised or approved, in the societies to which they belong.

> (Townsend 1979: 31)

Income should therefore be adequate to maintain the 'normal' living conditions of the society. To define a poverty line is to find the minimum necessary for normality. The search for such a tipping point in the income distribution is based on the dubious premise that there is a norm in society defining an adequate living standard. As income differences rise, and as the shape of the income distribution changes towards that of an egg-timer, 'normality' itself appears as an achievement of the mid-twentieth century, and one that is again being lost.

Poverty is exclusion from normal social life, but the definition of normality and hence of poverty is largely contained within distinct nation states: the poverty line is 60 per cent of the median *national* income. Developing an EU policy is hampered not just by the fact that national member states control their own taxation policy and social policy, but also by the wide variety of income within the Union, especially after the 2004 enlargements.

Whereas the Commission's extensive powers to enforce competition create a common European economic space, a common European social space remains little more than the lowest common factor of national policies. The Lisbon Council (2000) declared that the EU aimed to 'eradicate poverty and social exclusion by 2010', but even before the crisis there had been little progress. Just as in the European Employment Strategy, the European strategy to combat social exclusion amounted to annual inter-governmental meetings to compare 'National Action Plans' with the aim of exchanging lessons and best practice. The major achievement appears to have been merely more sophisticated measures of poverty (e.g. Atkinson *et al.* 2004).

The Lisbon Strategy was re-launched in 2005. This marked a clear shift to 'employment-anchored social policy' (O'Connor 2005): it was axiomatic that employment was the solution to poverty. This is even more pronounced in the current 'Europe 2020' programme with its grandiose ambition to 'lift at least twenty million people out of the risk of poverty and social exclusion' (European Council 2010). Poverty is defined here as involving three dimensions. The first is the now traditional 'at risk of poverty rate', defined as an income falling below 60 per cent of the national median income. The second dimension is the proportion of jobless households (i.e. households where the level of paid employment is low). This measure assumes that a job solves poverty or at least leads to greater societal participation. However, the Hartz IV reforms in Germany exemplify how a major social change in Europe over the last decade has been the growth of low wage employment.

The third dimension involves material deprivation. Households are defined as 'severely deprived' if they cannot afford at least four of nine basic necessities.[2] Like the second dimension, this is not derived from the income distribution within one national state. The severe deprivation dimension highlights the difference between being 'poor' in purely monetary terms in a poor country and in a rich country. To take the most extreme case: in 2012, 44.1 per cent of Bulgarians were 'severely deprived', as opposed to only 14.5 per cent of Italians, even though the at risk of poverty rate in the countries was very similar (21.2 per cent in Bulgaria and 19.4 per cent in Italy) (European Commission 2014). With increasing physical mobility and awareness of standards of consumption across Europe it becomes increasingly difficult to discuss poverty within purely national terms.

Defining common European measures of poverty implies some European responsibility for social inclusion. However, the extent of differences across

Europe shows the continuing importance of national policies. Different patterns of income distribution and different levels of poverty are massively influenced by the level of taxation and the extent of social transfers, and these are almost entirely the responsibility of national states. The crisis showed how much differences such policies can make. Almost everywhere the crisis has meant widening inequality in market incomes (i.e. incomes before tax and social transfers). However, in some countries, and here Ireland is the outlier, the increase in inequality in disposable income has been quite modest and in Portugal at the start of the crisis it was actually negative. States have been especially vulnerable to the crisis where welfare state expenditure has focused on pensions for former state employees and where coverage of the welfare state is weak. Nearly all countries operate some combination of unemployment benefit (paid when people lose their job) and means-tested social assistance (paid to those who have no other form of support). In 2010 in Greece less than 20 per cent of the long-term unemployed were receiving unemployment benefits, yet over 60 per cent of the jobless poor also were not even covered by social assistance (European Commission 2014: 133). Effective welfare states reduce poverty.

4.3 Lite wealth: assets for the masses?

The majority of European households are now property owners. Thus half of all British households have a net wealth of at least St£218,000 (Table 4.5); across fifteen Eurozone countries overall median household net wealth is €109,200 (ECB 2013: 5). This is *lite wealth*, wealth for the masses. Many households have private housing; individuals own company shares and other financial assets, they have private pensions and certainly own their own private transport. While the wealth of any one individual is insignificant for the wider society, it can alter its owner's life chances and possibly their self-understanding. In aggregate this mass wealth changes the social structure of the society as a whole.

Housing shows how lite wealth is shaped by public policy. Societies have been classified by their 'tenure regimes'. In 'dualist' regimes such as the UK state policy pushes households towards owner-occupation, while in 'integrated' regimes such as Germany state policy does not discriminate between tenures and so home ownership is lower (Kemeny 2006). Societies have also been categorised into 'varieties of residential capitalism' in terms of their levels of home ownership and debt. Thus Italy has high owner-occupation but low mortgage debt, making it an exemplar of the 'familial' variety, while the UK's combination of extensive home ownership and high mortgage debt makes it the European exemplar of the 'liberal market' variety (Schwartz and Seabrooke 2008).

Extensive home ownership in the UK was the result of the inter-war tenurial revolution (Daunton 1987). Until then renting one's home from a private landlord was normal for wide swathes of society, from the most respectable (for example the gentry in Jane Austen's novels) to the very poor. After World War I there was an enormous expansion of 'council housing', as social housing (i.e. state-funded housing built to let) came to be known in Britain. Elsewhere in

Europe, modernist architecture created showcases of healthy housing for the masses which are still a tourist destination for architects today; in Vienna the new housing estates were consciously built as working class fortresses and were the centre of the social democratic armed uprising of 1934. After World War II there was a further expansion of state housing. In Britain by 1981–1982 more than a third of all households were renting from a local council (Frogner 2002). In France as elsewhere, the new housing blocks or *habitations à loyer modéré* or HLM were initially occupied by households with a relatively wide range of incomes (Priemus and Dieleman 2002). Unlike in the USA, social housing was not housing of the last resort.

In the UK the inter-war period mortgage finance funded extensive suburban developments: between the wars over two and a half million houses were built for owner-occupation in Britain (Stevenson 1984: 223). This expansion of owner-occupation also occurred in the USA at the same time, but had no parallel elsewhere in Europe, where high levels of home ownership were largely an inheritance from peasant proprietorship in the countryside. This British exceptionalism was consolidated in the 1980s by the Thatcher government which enabled council house tenants to buy their own houses. No other European country has made such an explicit policy change as the UK, although the trend is towards increasing owner-occupation and a reduction of the state sector (Table 4.4). Some of the most dramatic changes have occurred in Germany as a response to the financial crises of the local authorities. In spring 2006 the city of Dresden sold its entire housing stock to the US private equity group Fortress International (Landler 2006) while elsewhere British and (especially) American finance companies bought up mutual housing associations.

In the UK cheap mortgage finance not only further accelerated home ownership, it enabled housing to be used as an asset to leverage other purchases. The private rented sector expanded as individuals used mortgage finance to 'buy to let'. Between 1998 and 2002, 230,000 such investment mortgages were issued

Table 4.4 Housing tenure, 2011: selected countries (%)

	Owner, with mortgage or loan	Owner, no outstanding mortgage or housing loan	Tenant, rent at market price	Tenant, rent at reduced price or free
European Union (28 countries)	27.4	43.2	18.3	11.1
Germany	28.1	25.3	39.9	6.7
Ireland	34.6	35.7	14.9	14.9
France	29.4	33.7	19.1	17.8
Italy	15.6	57.3	13.3	13.8
Sweden	65.9	3.7	30.0	0.3
United Kingdom	41.9	26.0	13.3	18.8

Source: Eurostat – Distribution of population by tenure status, type of household and income group (source: SILC)[ilc_lvho02].

(Norwood 2003); by 2010–2012, 4 per cent of all British households owned property to let (ONS 2014). EU financial deregulation has expanded property markets beyond national borders and made the boundary between an investment property and a second home even harder to define. During the 'Celtic Tiger' boom Irish investors were reported to own 100,000 properties in Spain and were buying property in Berlin and Bulgaria as well as further afield in Dubai (Wickham 2007).

Across Europe for some time a second home has been a normal part of middle class life. In Scandinavia second home ownership dates back at least to the 1930s and it has been extensive in France and Italy for decades. Second home owners tend to live relatively close to their second home, and many second homes are inherited through the family. In 2005 more than 20 per cent of both Swedish and Finnish households had a second home, as did 14 per cent of households in Italy and over 10 per cent in France (Gallent *et al.* 2005: 93).

Until recently only a few British households owned a second home, usually a distant rural retreat. Now many second homes are actually in metropolitan areas including London itself and purchased for many different reasons: as part of a bi-locating household (where members have jobs in different cities), as student accommodation for family members at university, for income and for capital appreciation (Paris 2009). While in the early 1970s only about 10,000 British residents owned a second home abroad (Gallent *et al.* 2005: 100), by 2010–2012 fully 292,000 British households owned property overseas (ONS 2014).

This dramatic expansion has been driven by British property owners' ability to raise capital in ways that are still largely impossible in less 'sophisticated' markets. The UK has extensive *retail* financial services which, compared to most other European countries, enable consumers to have easy access to retail credit and in particular to mortgage finance. This ensures that many people have been able to turn housing from an immobile and illiquid asset into a financial asset which can be leveraged to access *further* property. In the words of the director of international property at a large UK estate agency: 'We are the first in Europe to see property as an asset class. We use it as a substitute for pensions and now are buying overseas' (Norwood 2003). The Englishman's home may be his castle, but nowhere else is it so likely to be treated as just something to be bought and sold.

Next to housing, share-owning has one of the most widely promoted forms of asset ownership. Extensive small shareholding seems to have emerged first in France as early as the late nineteenth century (Preda 2001). After World War II expanding incomes allowed professionals and managers to invest their spare income and begin to build up property in addition to their homes. In the UK by the mid-1980s approximately 10 per cent all households directly owned some shares. The 1990s saw the outbreak of 'stock market populism' (Harrington 2008), first in the USA and the UK, so that by 1995 share ownership in the UK had reached around 25 per cent of all households (Banks *et al.* 2001). In Germany the increase was slightly later, but by 2008 the ten million individual share-owners outnumbered the seven million trade union members (Deutschmann 2008).

Everywhere small shareholders were facilitated by technological innovations such as web-based trading. In Europe – and here the UK led the way – privatisation of state assets was promoted to popularise shareholding. However, it has hardly created a share-owning democracy. First, most investors hold only one or two stocks and very few are active traders. Second, shares are decreasingly owned by individuals rather than institutions. Thus, in 1964, 54 per cent of all shares by value traded on the London Stock Exchange were held by individuals, but by 2008 this had fallen to 10.2 per cent (Wallop 2010). Third, and most important, most individual holdings are very small, so that shares are of little significance for lite wealth owners. In Britain 2010–2012 the median holding of UK shares for householders was a mere St£4,000 (ONS 2014). Small share-owners are often exposed to substantial losses. In Ireland the privatisation of the national telephone company Eircom saw many first-time share-owners losing money as the value of their shares plummeted. In Germany small investors lost with the collapse of the Neuer Markt (Germany's attempt to replicate NASDAQ).

What really matters is private pensions and associated forms of life insurance. There has been a concerted drive to move away from traditional state-funded pensions to various forms of private pensions. In parallel there has been a move from defined benefit pension schemes to defined contribution schemes. Whereas in the former the benefits are fixed in advance, in the latter only the value of the contribution is fixed and any benefits depend on the final value of the individual's holding. Individual pension wealth thus becomes directly important for people's future living standards. The process has gone furthest in the UK where only 24 per cent of British households now have no private pension wealth at all (Table 4.5) and 50 per cent of all households have at least St£40,400 of pension

Table 4.5 Forms of lite wealth: Great Britain, 2010

	Gini	Median (£)	Households with no participation (%)	Aggregate household wealth (£bn)
Physical assets (excluding housing)	0.45	45,500	(9% all individuals have less than <£8k)	1,102
Property (net)	0.64	150,000 (property owners only)	32	3,528
Private pension	0.73	40,000	24	3,586
Financial assets (net)	0.61	5,900	25% all households have negative financial assets	1,299
Total	0.61	218,400		9,515
Total excluding pension		143,200		5,929

Source: derived from ONS (2014).

wealth. Using a different measure of pension wealth, a recent study gives a median value of €11,900 for all voluntary private pension wealth in the Eurozone. The lower level of this form of wealth in the Eurozone compared to the UK is largely because so much pension provision remains publicly funded. Thus within the Eurozone household participation in voluntary private pensions ranges from 3.8 per cent in Greece to 49.8 per cent in the Netherlands (ECB 2013: 37), but no country approaches the UK level.

Any discussion of private wealth should also include motor vehicles, now an asset owned by the majority of households across Europe. In the post-war period car ownership became the norm in Western Europe: it was assumed that the 'normal' household owned a car. The car remains crucial to post-fordist capitalism, but now for individuals rather than households. As late as 1971, 48 per cent of British households had no car and only 8 per cent had two or more; by 2002, 27 per cent were without a car but 29 per cent had two or more (these proportions have changed very little subsequently) (Department for Transport 2011). Given that the median value of vehicles in Britain is St£5,000 and St£7,000 within the Eurozone, this is a small but significant element of wealth of most European households (ECB 2013).

The expansion of private wealth has been interwoven with a massive expansion of personal debt, especially in liberal market economies. The extreme case was Ireland, where the household debt-to-income ratio immediately before the crisis had reached an astonishing 196.9 per cent (Karamessini 2013: 11). Increasingly households borrow to finance not just the purchase of their home or their cars, but a second home, an investment property, their children's education, and indeed normal consumption. These debts can exceed assets. In Britain 25 per cent of all households have negative financial assets (Table 4.5) as do about 10 per cent of all German households (Deutschmann 2008).

Reliance on mortgage-funded owner-occupation exposes more people to debts they cannot manage. In Britain 'in 2012–13, over half a million (536,000) households had a member(s) who had given up a previous home due to difficulties in paying the mortgage' (Department for Communities and Local Government 2014: 25). This dark side of the push towards home ownership is part of the growing indebtedness of the poor. However, while in general it is the poorest income groups which have the highest levels of debt to income, contemporary Ireland demonstrates how debt-financed property creates risks for new groups. More than five years after the crisis began, 17.3 per cent of all mortgages on Irish principal residences were still in arrears. The collapse of house prices also pushed many such indebted households into negative equity, with their properties now worth less than their mortgages. Furthermore, a massive 27.2 per cent of all buy-to-let mortgages were also in difficulty (Central Bank of Ireland 2014). While most of those with problem mortgages had jobs, they tended to be in relatively weak labour market positons (lower educational standards, irregular or insecure employment, previous experience of unemployment, etc.) (McCarthy 2014). Equally, the more risky investments seem to have been disproportionately made by new entrants to the property market – as in any asset bubble, the outsiders join last and are most likely to fail to get out in time.

Beginning in the UK in the 1980s and accelerating during the 1990s public discourses linked the spread of mass wealth to notions of active entrepreneurial initiative. Just as citizens were replaced by customers, so savers morphed into investors. Individuals were enjoined to actively manage their assets, aided by technologies such as personal financial software, actors such as individual tax consultants and financial advisers, and much increased attention to personal financial advice in the mass media, especially in mid-market daily and weekly newspapers (Langley 2009; Tumber 2004).

This required not just the expansion of wealth per se, but that these assets were commodified. Especially in southern Europe, extensive small property ownership is nothing new. Large numbers of small farmers or small shopkeepers receive income from their property with which their social and personal identity is entangled (the family farm, the family shop). Such *proprietorial* property is in turn one basis for the extensive home ownership, financed through inheritance or savings. By contrast, in financialised societies, property owners are encouraged to treat their assets as a portfolio to be continually reconstituted. Assets are liquid, marketable and have limited emotional value.

Mass wealth is promoted by public policy. Ownership of assets becomes necessary in order to participate in 'normal' society. Thus outside a few main metropolitan areas individual car ownership is essential to get to work, to shop or to socialise (Wickham 2006). Just as transport policy assumes that most people own their own cars, so housing policy in many countries assumes that most people will own their own housing. Increasingly, social policy assumes most people will own their own pensions, while third-level education is also assumed to require private funding. The UK government's Homebuy policy explicitly stated, 'Homes are not just places to live, they are also assets' (P. Smith 2007).

The popular capitalism enthusiasms of the 1990s probably had little major impact on most asset owners. Studies from countries as different as the USA (Harrington 2008) and Germany (Birenheide *et al.* 2005) showed that shareholders understood their trading as demonstrating a new control and autonomy, but that such traders comprised a tiny minority of small shareholders. By contrast, the erosion of the welfare state became for many people an explicit reason to build up their asset portfolio. In the succinct words of one British home-owner: 'I suppose in some ways it's our pension' (S. Smith 2007: 532).

Mass wealth appears to loosen up the class structure. An individual's life chances no longer depend only on their position within the hierarchies of employment, but also on their more or less successful activities as an asset managing entrepreneur. To the extent that this occurs, it marks a further replacement of social categories by monetary gradations – and such relations accentuate individual autonomy (Section 4.1). Yet paradoxically, such autonomy at the individual level generates greater instability for the economy as a whole and this in turn exposes these autonomous individuals to new and greater risks. While individuals acquire assets to try to reduce their exposure to risk, the aggregate effect of such decisions is to enhance the level of risk to which they are exposed.

The expansion of commodified mass wealth is interwoven with the growth of the financial services industry. On the one hand mortgage payments and above all pension contributions become the feedstock for global financial investors, but on the other hand the financial industry develops a wider range of retail financial 'products'. Home purchase stimulates the insurance industry, since for a mortgage life insurance is usually compulsory. Extensive home ownership, especially if combined with high rates of geographical mobility and hence high turnover of housing stock, creates a growth of financial services, not to mention house insurance and above all estate agencies. Thus the expansion of the market for private housing in Germany and Austria led to an enormous expansion in the number of estate agents (Skodacsek 2000; Jones 2014). Equally, cars are often bought with borrowed money and always have to be insured. Individual purchases of shares and private investments in pensions create a new market for professional advice and specialist intermediaries. The growth of lite wealth creates new employment for those involved in buying, selling, financing and insuring these assets.

Here again the UK occupies a peculiar position through its leadership in retail financial services. Whereas international financial services are concentrated in London, retail financial services service local markets and so affect the occupational structure of the entire society. Not surprisingly, UK banks were at the forefront of the redefinition of bank work 'from tellers to sellers' (Regini *et al.* 1999), in which bank workers were transformed into sellers of those financial products for which lite wealth produced a new market. Whereas one element of the different service landscapes is the variety and differential extent of caring work, another element is the variety and differential extent of financial work.

Once people have assets that they can buy and sell they can leave them to their children. Couple this with lower birth rates across Europe, and it becomes clear that more and more people are inheriting relatively substantial assets. As early as 1999 Kohli reported for Germany that '26 per cent of those who owned their home had inherited it or received it as a gift', this in a context where 47 per cent of respondents had already received an inheritance, mostly from parents (in law), and 19 per cent expected one (Kohli 1999).

Slogans such as 'property-owning democracy' link the expansion of mass wealth to greater social equality. However, because wealth can be inherited, the transfer of wealth between generations usually increases the inheritance of social inequality. Across Europe, for the first time a significant number of non-proprietorial households have accumulated fungible wealth which they are now beginning to transfer to their children. At the same time the re-commodification of welfare means that money can now buy more than before. The clearest example is education. When once the 'social capital' of the late twentieth-century middle classes ensured better educational opportunities for their offspring, their successors are simply using their money to buy their children education. Social inequality is financialised.

4.4 Heavy wealth

Many ordinary Europeans now own wealth. This *mass wealth* or *lite wealth* financialises and individualises social relations. A rather similar process has been going on in the more rarefied reaches of the very wealthy. The rich have not only been getting (much) richer,[3] their wealth involves the growing importance of money by itself. This new *heavy wealth* ensures that individuals as well as companies or institutions now matter on the economic stage. Heavy wealth has implications for social structure, since servicing the wealthy creates particular types of jobs; implications for politics, since the new wealthy exercise new forms of influence; and implications for social policy, since it leads to a new role for private philanthropy.

During the glory years of organised capitalism, very wealthy individuals often appeared as an endangered species. Large corporations seemed to control not only existing businesses but innovation as well, so that the self-made man could be written off as a convenient ideological myth. In the period of 'organised capitalism' the economy was dominated by large corporations controlled by salaried managers. There were seriously wealthy families, but they had often inherited their wealth as shares in an established family business. In Sweden the Wallenberg family, owners of much of Swedish manufacturing industry including Volvo, had established their empire by the start of the twentieth century; in Italy Giovanni Agnelli (founder of Fiat) had laid the basis for the family fortune before World War II.

European wealth is old wealth, but not, as one might imagine, in terms of an old landowning aristocracy: only two European billionaires (the Duke of Westminster in the UK and Prince Albert von Thurn und Taxis in Germany) are hereditary landowners. Especially in Germany, many of the super-rich derive their wealth from firms built up during the decades immediately *after* World War II. For example, the Quandt family are one of Germany's richest families: their fortune stems from Herbert Quandt, who turned BMW around in the 1950s. Other German billionaires also made their fortune in the engineering industry, the centrepiece of (West) Germany's post-World War II economy – one reason why the country was for a long time second only to the USA in terms of the total number of billionaires.

When Forbes first counted the number of billionaires in the world nearly thirty years ago, it estimated there were 140 (dollar) billionaires; the 2006 list counted 793, the 2014 list 1,645. The list remains dominated by the USA, with fully 492 billionaires, up from 371 in 2006. There has been a dramatic expansion in the number of billionaires from China (152 billionaires) and Russia (111 billionaires), now at second and third place respectively. Less well known is that over the last ten years the number of billionaires in Europe has been growing faster than in the USA, with for example the number of French billionaires trebling between 2006 and 2014.

There are national specificities to the European super-rich, for the way in which these families have made their fortunes resonate with the national economic structure. The super-rich of France include several families in which the founder made his fortune in luxury goods firms and one arms manufacturer (Dassault) with close links to the state; several Italian billionaires owe their fortunes to luxury goods; Swedish billionaires derive from furniture (Ingvar Kamprad of IKEA) and packaging; British billionaires are disproportionately from finance and real estate and a significant number were born outside the UK. British billionaires are also unusual in that they are relatively young, and as such closer to their American role models, of whom a significant number are still in their fifties and even forties. Partly this is because of the boom of the American ICT and software industries, with SAP co-founder Hasso Plattner one of the very few European billionaires to owe his fortune to information technology.

Below the level of the internationally profiled rich are the humdrum millionaires. In the UK and above all in the USA their wealth has also been increasing significantly faster than that of those below them. This process seems to have started in the 1980s and accelerated in the 1990s. The share of total net worth owned by the wealthiest 1 per cent increased significantly between the early 1980s and the end of the century (Keister 2005), but within this 1 per cent (still several million people) it is in fact the wealth of the top 0.1 per cent (the richest few hundred thousand) that has been increasing fastest. This has been facilitated by taxation changes: in the USA there has been a continual reduction in the taxation on high incomes and a reduction in all forms of inheritance tax. Another cause has been the long-term increase in the value of the stock market relative to the early 1980s. This especially benefits the very wealthy since they already own a disproportionate proportion of all equities.

The third cause of rising wealth inequality is simply that senior executives have been paying themselves more. Once again, the growth is fastest at the top. In the USA the pay of Chief Executive Officers (CEOs) started pulling away from that of ordinary workers in the 1970s but accelerated from the 1980s onwards, peaking at the turn of the century: 'The CEO-to-worker compensation ratio was 20.1-to-1 in 1965 and 29.0-to-1 in 1978, grew to 122.6-to-1 in 1995, peaked at 383.4-to-1 in 2000, and was 272.9-to-1 in 2012' (Mishel and Sabadish 2013: 2).

Other top managers, like Sheryl Sandberg, Chief Operating Officer of Facebook, also have an annual income measured in millions. With a few years at this level of salary, individuals can rapidly amass private fortunes. In turn they become economic actors in their own right – they begin to exercise economic power as individuals, not simply because of their position at the top of managerial hierarchies.

Not surprisingly, such incomes are much envied by European senior managers. While their pay has been increasing faster than that of average employees, nowhere does it reach American heights. Nonetheless, the same trends are at work. Between 2000 and 2006, the remuneration of the directors of the FTSE 100 companies rose 105 per cent more than the retail price index (Taylor 2006). While Germany CEO salaries are still relatively low, they have been catching up fast. In 1987 the average *Vorstandsmitglied* (executive board member) of the top thirty DAX companies received fifteen times as much as the average white-collar employee; by 2012 the figure had increased to fully fifty-three times as much (Krämer 2013: 9).

At the same time, the last twenty-five years *have* been years of entrepreneurial heroes in the classic mode – individuals who have built up enterprises by exercising entrepreneurial talents, exemplified by Bill Gates himself and the new generation of US software entrepreneurs such as Mark Zuckerberg. In Europe these sectors have not played such a leading role, and it has been privatisation and above all deregulation of crucial economic sectors that has provided a similar basis for individual entrepreneurs. For example, entrepreneurs such as Brian Souter of Stagecoach, Sir Stelios Haji-Ioannou of EasyJet and Michael O'Leary of Ryanair have built their companies and made their personal fortunes by seizing the opportunities offered by the deregulation and privatisation of the transport sector.

The growth of heavy wealth, just like the growth of lite wealth, changes the social structure. Not only are a small number of individuals much wealthier than before, but heavy wealth expands some jobs rather than others and so affects the occupational structure. And if the heavily wealthy are few in numbers, their weight makes up for this.

New levels of luxury consumption create new business opportunities. New wealth, including from China, has driven the international art market to new heights (Adam 2014); there is a growing market for super-yachts; the expansion of private air travel now means not just the small corporate jet but the private airliner. Luxury consumption on this scale generates many high skill jobs, analogous to those in the nineteenth-century Italian and French luxury goods industries. The more customised the yacht (or the airliner), the more skilled labour is involved. Furthermore, the very rich create a market for new services, outsourcing not only the design of their home but the choice of their wine cellar. And while some of these tasks are undertaken by new service companies, there does seem to be an expansion of upmarket self-employment. The corporate executive will not only have his (or even her) personal assistant at work, but also a new retinue of personal trainer, personal tutor for the children and even personal chef. A growing number of people are now dependent on the personal whims of a few very rich people, although the households of the very rich employ relatively more skilled and relatively fewer unskilled retainers than their predecessors of the last 'Golden Age'.

Just like lite wealth, heavy wealth also creates new opportunities in finance itself. Banks have identified 'individuals of high net worth' as a group to which they can sell distinctive services. Traditionally the discreet activities of a smaller number of private banks in the UK (e.g. Coutts) and, above all, of Swiss banks, these have now become part of the activities of the normal retail banks. Such services range from the obvious – essentially various forms of portfolio management – to the more imaginative, such as 'boot camps' where the children of the very wealthy learn how to manage their own money (Gott 2008). Heavy wealth means new services and new jobs elsewhere in the society.

In his classic study of power in the USA in the 1950s, C. Wright Mills (1979) argued that three distinct bureaucratic hierarchies (business, politics, and the military) merged at their apex to create 'the power elite'. Subsequently Marxists debated whether the 'capitalist state' supported business because of its structure or because of the social linkages between politics and business. Today the power of wealthy individuals is exercised through money rather than just through their occupation of a particular role.

Studies of traditional corruption differentiate between 'grand' corruption, the direct bribery of officials and politicians for business purposes (usually access to contracts), and 'petty' corruption, where individual citizens routinely pay bribes to go about their normal lives (a job in the state sector, avoiding traffic fines, etc.). Grand corruption is facilitated by the decline of political parties' ideological commitment, the rising costs of political elections, and the erosion of notions of public service among state employees (Della Porta and Pizzorno 1996).

In areas of Italy, especially the Mezzogiorno, both forms of traditional corruption were normal. Paradoxically, in Italy popular revulsion against traditional politicians resulted in the emergence of Berlusconi. Corrupt Italian politicians made their careers without social or educational qualifications apart from their skill in organising bribery. By contrast, Berlusconi entered politics after a successful business career. His wealth was presented as demonstrating his potential political competence: he epitomised the belief that 'business' is more effective than the state (Lane 2004). As one of the richest people in Italy, Berlusconi also demonstrated another feature of the new role of wealthy individuals. They are so powerful and command such resources that they have an 'oligopolistic' relation to the state – they matter as individuals.

The emergence of New Labour in the UK was another dramatic example of the new political power of wealth. Determined to break with its dependence on the trade unions, and at the same time to amass a 'war chest' to run a 'professional' campaign, before the 1997 election, New Labour followed the banks in assiduously courting individuals of high net worth. A few gifts to the party of several hundred thousand pounds became far more important than the dues of its ordinary members. Under New Labour British politics became increasingly Americanised, with a greater acceptance of the legitimacy of private money. Both conditions apply far more in the USA than in Europe, and increasingly they apply more to the UK than to the rest of Europe. Political parties are particularly strong especially where, as in Germany, they are partly funded from public funds and where it is possible for state employees to develop a political career.

The appeal to the alleged competence of 'innovative' or 'entrepreneurial' individuals (Sir Richard Branson, Lord Putnam, Lord Sainsbury, etc.) is based on a distrust of politicians, public sector employees and the civil service. The belief that personal gain provides the only motivation for action and that 'business' provides the only model of organisation lays the basis for the new role of private wealth in politics. Whereas in the past military men were seen to possess superior qualities that made them intrinsically suited to political leadership, today business people (or at least business men) are assumed to be similar. General de Gaulle is replaced by Silvio Berlusconi (or perhaps Richard Branson).

The age of untrammelled capitalism at the end of the nineteenth century was also a golden age of philanthropy. Andrew Carnegie was reviled as one of the 'robber barons' of the USA, but he was convinced that the purpose of amassing large wealth was to contribute to society through philanthropy. Today Carnegie's philosophy is being rediscovered, as his belief that 'philanthropy best promotes American civilisation when endowed in private foundations and stewarded by the wealthy' (Vogel 2006).

One rationale for philanthropy is clearly legitimation. In 2006 private equity buy-outs were increasingly receiving negative publicity for asset stripping firms and sacking employees. Leading figures in the industry therefore set up the Private Equity Foundation to raise money for charity – and their black tie inaugural festivities in London were picketed by members of the GMB trade union whose members they had made redundant (P. Smith 2007). For a few of the new wealthy however, philanthropy has become the rationale for their existence. Like Bill Gates, they at times are described as 'liberal communists', believing that the business abilities which enabled them to amass private wealth will also enable them to use it efficiently to improve the world (e.g. Branson 2000: 329; Lauterbach and Ströing 2012). Private philanthropy, so it is claimed, can also be more innovative than state services and react more quickly to new needs. For example, funds from Chuck Feeney's Atlantic Philanthropies were crucial to expanding Irish higher education when the state did not regard this as a priority. In this case one wealthy individual changed an entire country.

Within Europe private philanthropy is probably most important in the UK, especially within higher education; in some other European countries private philanthropy is growing in importance. In Germany in the mid-2000s there was talk of a *Stifterboom* (philanthropic boom) with in 2006 around 14,000 charitable trusts, nearly half of which had been founded in the previous ten years. Many founders were relatively young (13 per cent under forty-five and a further 26 per cent under sixty) and most were actively engaged in the management of their own trust (*Die Zeit* 2006; Timmer 2006).

The growth of wealth has clearly led to growth of philanthropic funding. In general the wealthier are likely to contribute relatively more from their income than lower income groups (Lauterbach and Ströing 2012), so philanthropic giving does act as a voluntary progressive income tax. However, donations of the wealthy have only very limited redistributive effect and some forms of philanthropy actually accentuate inequality. For example, in the UK Oxford and Cambridge receive around half of *all* UK philanthropic funding for universities (Breeze *et al.* 2011), while their students are disproportionately from affluent backgrounds. US studies also show that, compared to less wealthy donors, the very wealthy are less likely to fund organisations concerned with general welfare and more likely to fund education and the arts (Center on Philanthropy 2010). Like the millionaires who funded New York's Metropolitan Opera in the 1880s, they fund their own recreation (Snowman 2009: 211). If philanthropy replaces the welfare state, it often is a welfare state for the wealthy.

Unlike thirty years ago, it is no longer the case that we can imagine that the entire population shares broadly similar styles of life. In Scandinavia the monarch may still ride a bicycle, but the American super-rich fly around the world in their own private jumbo jets (now joined by billionaires from India and China). The social democratic moment long ago passed in the USA (if it ever existed), it is passing in the UK and is looking perilous in the rest of Europe. At its simplest, heavy wealth now involves a particular form of social exclusion – the wealthy have a different lifestyle such that they are cut off from the rest of society. In this sense, to be super-wealthy, just like to be very poor, is to run the risk of social exclusion. Ordinary citizenship, with its rights and obligations, has *two* boundaries – the boundary of poverty and the boundary of wealth (Dean with Melrose 1999: 69). Journalistic accounts show how, because they have less and less contact with ordinary people, the rich have less and less interest in maintaining the institutions and even the fabric of society as a whole (e.g. Freeland 2013). As even American conservatives are beginning to point out, one reason for this is simply that the rich can buy people, whether as cleaners, security men or politicians, instead of relying on the norms of common sociability. Furthermore, precisely because wealth has become more acceptable, not least because of its coupling with popular celebrity, there is less need for the wealthy to be modest, to even pretend that they are really the same as the rest of us.

In the epoch of 'globalisation' this disconnection takes a new twist. Claiming to be citizens of the world, the rich pay less and less taxes to nation states and have an instrumental approach to national loyalty. At its most obvious, like Rupert Murdoch or Philip Green, they change their citizenship to minimise their taxes. In this internationalism they are similar to the aristocrats of pre-1914 Europe, who also shared a common lifestyle and language. The fortunes of the business dynasties of the mid-twentieth century such as the Agnellis or the Wallenbergs were based on national firms and the families were interwoven with national political structures. Today, however, such families are de-nationalising. Heavy wealth, like lite wealth, has become more abstract – just money.

4.5 Popular wealth – glitzing the rich

As private wealth becomes more important in shaping individuals' life chances, so too wealth is becoming more ostentatious. As in the Gilded Age at the end of the nineteenth century, wealth again becomes self-legitimating. A novelty, however, is the role of celebrity wealth deriving from the creative industries and from sport. Not only are these industries now an important part of the economic structure, especially in the UK, but the globalisation of 'winner-take-all' markets makes them the basis for new forms of personal wealth. This in turn is related to the strange symbiosis between business and celebrity: not only do rock musicians become entrepreneurs, but entrepreneurs dress up as rock stars.

By the 1990s it was already a standard argument that popular music contributed more to British exports than the car industry. By 2013 the UK Department for Culture, Media and Sport estimated that employment in the broad 'creative economy' amounted to 2.6 million, of which 1.71 million worked in creative industries as a whole. The same source estimates that the creative industries create approximately 5.2 per cent of total UK GVA and 8.0 per cent of all UK exports, and that the UK 'music and the performing arts' industry employed 300,000 people (DCMS 2014). The UK appears to be unusual in the extent of the global reach of its popular music industry and, to a lesser extent, of its publishing and electronic industries. No other European country comes near to this scale, even though French popular music, analogous to Spanish and Portuguese popular music, is increasingly part of a different 'global' Francophone music from Africa to Quebec. More so than any other European country, France retains a distinct popular music and a distinct national cinema. Relying heavily on direct subsidies, France has been able to maintain a vibrant national cultural sector.

The transformation of creative and sporting activities into industries means that they become a basis for a new form of heavy wealth – celebrity wealth. This occurs because in these areas commercialisation involves the emergence of winner-take-all markets (Frank and Cooke 1996). In winner-take-all markets the rewards of being the best – the winner – are disproportionately higher than for the runner-up. To the extent that success is seen to depend on having the 'best' expert, other labour markets begin to take on similar characteristics. In a serious court case, no client has ever been happy to hire the second-best lawyer; once consumers can purchase medical care, the same begins to happen to surgeons. As such, the legal labour market begins to resemble the labour market for actors, authors and musicians – a few are very successful, and most cannot even earn a normal living. This is exacerbated by globalisation or, more precisely, by the extent to which electronic communication allows success to occur within an ever greater market. Instead of being a local hero, a football star or a pop musician becomes, as American film stars have been for nearly a century – a global hero. And the rewards of this tiny elite become ever greater relative to the mass of now unsuccessful and local market participants.

For the first time within the history of capitalism, it is now possible for 'creatives' to become seriously wealthy. By the early 1990s there were more show business personalities than 'genuine industrialists' in the *Sunday Times* list of 'The Top 200' richest in Britain; Forbes' 2014 list of (dollar) billionaires includes two film directors (Spielberg, Lucas), but in 2006 J.K. Rowling, the creator of the Harry Potter stories, was richer than all but 745 billionaires in the world. Slightly lower down the scale, national rich lists include pop stars and sporting heroes: it causes no surprise that Bono of U2 is in the list of wealthy Irish. In the late nineteenth century an author like Thomas Hardy could, not least by astute playing of the American market, aspire to a modest middle class lifestyle, even if he mixed socially with the great and glorious of the nation (Tomalin 2006). Today, a few global authors can become seriously wealthy as can pop stars, film stars and footballers and other sporting personalities. They are not only celebrities, they have personal wealth which puts them on a par with more 'serious' wealthy people. Like the rest of the super-rich, such celebrities live an increasingly international lifestyle and have a pragmatic relationship to national citizenship. The 'global band' U2 will sometimes claim to be Irish, but had no compunction moving the registration of its business to the Netherlands to shield its profits from the (low) Irish tax rates, even while at the same time lecturing national governments for not spending money on Third World aid.

The entry of 'trivial' entertainment stars into the world of the very wealthy has consequences for how wealth is understood in the wider society. Celebrities' ability to accumulate further depends in part on remaining celebrities. Of necessity, they have to seek the limelight rather than shun it. The Wallenbergs may try to be ordinary people, Posh and Becks cannot. Part of the publicity depends on conspicuous consumption, typified by the celebrity marriage in a privatised section of the Irish countryside with exclusive rights sold to *Hello!* As such, wealth becomes its own legitimation.

If the wealth of the celebrity is legitimate, surely the corporate executive needs to become a celebrity too. The self-legitimation of the celebrity wealthy spreads to the wealthy as a whole. The process has gone furthest in the USA, where the chief executive as hero goes back to the 1980s, but at the end of the century began to internationalise. When Jean-Marie Messier took Vivendi onto the international markets and declared the end of 'l'exception française' he also bought himself a US$17 million home on Park Avenue in New York and ensured a high media profile for himself.

On the one hand, therefore, just as the emergence of the software industry produced software millionaires, so the transformation of entertainment, popular music and sport into *industries* laid the basis for new forms of individual fortunes. Some heavy wealth is cool simply because it is made in the cool industries. At the same time, heavy wealth also becomes cool because at the end of the twentieth century making money became cool. Especially in the USA, the paradoxical cultural legacy of the counter-culture revolt of the 1960s was to elide the gap between the world of creativity and the world of business. The true legacy of Woodstock was Silicon Valley, the elevation of entrepreneur to popular mythological figure, and above all, the elision of the lifestyles – and even the dress codes – of bohemia and business (Florida 2004: 197).

Outside of the USA, Richard Branson is emblematic of the merger between celebrity wealth and corporate wealth. He made his money at the beginnings of the cool economy with Virgin record stores and then Virgin Music. This was not business as it had been practised. Looking back at his first ventures he described them as a story of how clever cool outsiders took on the Establishment (Branson 2000: 86). Branson exemplifies the new individualisation of heavy wealth in other ways. First, Virgin is not a particular business, it is an abstract brand, and its most concrete manifestation is Branson. When Virgin entered the financial services market, its advertisements featured a photo of Branson himself: Giovanni Agnelli and his family made cars, Branson sells whatever services or products he wants. Second, Branson's companies have been both public and private at different stages, but they are vehicles for his personal wealth, rather than his personal wealth being derived from a company. Third, Branson exercises political influence, with personal access to leading politicians, not because he 'represents' a particular company, but because of his personal fortune. In a study of popular perceptions of wealth and poverty, about one-third of respondents cited Branson by name as an example of somebody who was wealthy, who was a celebrity, but also as a clear example of the 'deserving rich' (Dean with Melrose 1999: 61). The lesson is clear: for those wealthy individuals who wish to become socially acceptable, they need to become famous – and display their wealth.

4.6 Conclusion

Any account of inequality in contemporary Europe has to start with the changed role of the market and of money. Money is the measure of most things, not least the extent of inequality and poverty, but the last decades of the twentieth century were marked by the new role of wealth: the growing importance of *lite wealth*, the changed form of *heavy wealth* and, furthermore, by the novel role of conspicuous consumption by the wealthy themselves.

One theme that unites these changes is the relationship between the market and individualisation. The expansion of the market undermines social divisions ('status groups') and opens the way for greater individual choice, For the mass of the population of contemporary Europe, some limited wealth is now the norm and, crucially, for a significant minority this wealth can be used to generate income and/or more wealth. This new financially based individualism changes the relationship between the market and politics. The decline of ideological politics is interwoven with the deliberate replacement of public provision by the market, thus ensuring that greater areas of social life are determined by the choices of (financially unequal) consumers rather than (politically equal) citizens. Despite populist rhetoric, it is clear that such changes benefit most those who benefit most from the market – i.e. those who can deploy financial resources. Simultaneously and especially in the UK, a very small number of wealthy individuals are given an increasing political role, and their growing importance pushes towards a more plutocratic political system in the American model in which the role of private wealth becomes more and more explicit.

Notes

1 Of course, economic categories and social identities were never completely isomorphic even in these proletarian areas. Furthermore, many manual workers lived outside these areas.
2 Items are currently the inability to afford (1) to pay rent, utility bills or hire purchase instalments or other loan payments: (2) to keep their house warm; (3) to pay unexpected expenses; (4) to eat meat, fish or other protein-rich nutrition every second day; (5) to afford a week-long holiday away from home; to own (6) a car, (7) a washing machine, (8) a colour TV, (9) a car (Eurostat 2014).

3 In the absence of taxation, in a market economy the rich will not only get richer, they will pass on their wealth to their children. Over time inequalities of wealth are exacerbated. This is fundamental to Piketty's crucial study *Capital* (2014).

Bibliography

Adam, G. (2014) *Big Bucks: The Explosion of the Art Market in the 21st Century*, London: Ashgate.

Alderson, A. and Doran, K. (2013) How has inequality grown? The reshaping of the income distribution in LIS countries. In J. Gornick and M. Jäntti (eds) *Income Inequality Economic Disparities and the Middle Class in Affluent Countries*, Stanford: Stanford University Press, pp. 51–74.

Alesina, A. and Glaeser, E. (2004) *Fighting Poverty in the US and Europe: A World of Difference*, Oxford: Oxford UP.

Atkinson, A., Rainwater, L. and Smeeding, T. (1995) *Income Distribution in OECD Countries: Evidence from the Luxembourg Income Study*, Paris: OECD.

Atkinson, A., Marlier, E. and Nolan, B. (2004) Indicators and targets for social inclusion in the European Union, *Journal of Common Market Studies* 42.1: 47–75.

Bahn, C. (2001) Der Einzelhandel als Ressource der Stadtentwicklung. In H. Rudolph (ed.) *Aldi oder Arkaden? Unternehmen und Arbeit im europäischen Einzelhandel*, Berlin: Edition Sigma, pp. 157–176.

Banks, J., Blundell, R. and Smith, J. (2001) *Financial Wealth Inequality in the United States and Great Britain*, Labor and Population Program Working Paper Series 01–01, (DRU-24), Santa Monica, CA: Rand Corporation.

Barber, B. (2003) *Jihad vs McWorld*, London: Corgi Books (first published 1995).

Beck, U. and Beck-Gernsheim, E. (2002) *Individualisation: Institutionalised Individualism and its Social and Political Consequences*, London: Sage.

Birenheide, A., Fischer, M. and Legnaro, A. (2005) *Kapitalismus for alle: Aktien, Freiheit und Kontrolle*, Munster: Westfälisches Dampfboot.

Branson, R. (2000) *Losing My Virginity: The Autobiography*, London: Virgin Publishing.

Breeze, B., Gouwenberg, B., Schuyt, T. and Wilkinson, I. (2011) What role for public policy in promoting philanthropy? The case of EU universities, *Public Management Review* 13.8: 1179–1195.

Center on Philanthropy (2010) *The 2010 Study of High Net Worth Philanthropy*, www.philanthropy.iupui.edu/files/research/2010baml_highnetworthphilanthropy.pdf. Accessed 11 December 2013.

Central Bank of Ireland (2014) *Residential Mortgage Arrears and Repossessions Statistics: Q1 2014*, www.centralbank.ie. Accessed 18 July 2014.

Crossick, G. and Jaumain, S. (1998) *Cathedrals of Consumption: The European Department Store 1850–1939*, Aldershot: Ashgate.

Daunton, M. (1987) *A Property-Owning Democracy? Housing in Britain*, London: Faber and Faber.

DCMS (Department for Culture, Media and Sport) (2014) *Creative Industries: Focus on Employment*, www.gov.uk/government/publications. Accessed 29 July 2014.

Dean, H. with Melrose, M. (1999) *Poverty, Riches and Social Citizenship*, London: Macmillan.

Della Porta, D. and Pizzorno, A. (1996) The business politicians: reflections from a study of political corruption, *Journal of Law and Society* 23.1: 73–94.

Department for Communities and Local Government (2014) *English Housing Survey Headline Report*, London: Department for Communities and Local Government.

Department for Transport (2011) *Transport Statistics Great Britain: 2011*, www.gov.uk/government/publications. Accessed 6 March 2014.

Deutschmann, C. (2000) *Die Verheißung des absoluten Reichtums: Zur religiosen Natur des Kapitalismus*, Frankfurt: Campus.

Deutschmann, C. (2008) *Der Kollektive 'Buddenbrooks-Effekt': Die Finanzmärkte und die Mittelschichten*, Koln: Max Planck-Institut für Gesellschaftsforschung, MPfG WP 08/05.

Die Zeit (2006) Stiften wirkt! Supplement to *Die Zeit* 38, 14 September.

ECB (European Central Bank) Eurosystem Household Finance and Consumption Network (2013) *The Eurosystem Household Finance and Consumption Survey: Results from the First Wave*, Frankfurt: European Central Bank.

Eurofound (2013) *Employment Polarisation and Job Quality in the Crisis: European Jobs Monitor 2013*, Dublin: Eurofound.

European Commission (2014) *Employment and Social Developments 2013*, Luxembourg: Publications Office of the European Union.

European Council (2010) *European Council 17 June 2010 Conclusions*, http://ec.europa.eu/eu2020/pdf/council_conclusion_17_june_en.pdf. Accessed 11 December 2013.

Eurostat (2014) Europe 2020 indicators – poverty and social exclusion, http://ec.europa.eu/eurostat/statistics-explained/index.php/Europe_2020_indicators_-_poverty_and_social_exclusion#Data_sources_and_availability. Accessed 4 November 2015.

Fahey, T. (2007) The case for an EU-wide measure of poverty, *European Sociological Review* 23.1: 35–47.

Florida, R. (2004) *The Rise of the Creative Class*, New York: Basic Books.

Frank, R. and Cook, P. (1996) *The Winner-Takes-All Society*, New York and London: Penguin.

Frank, T. (2001) *One Market Under God: Extreme Capitalism, Market Populism and the End of Economic Democracy*, London: Secker & Warburg.

Freeland, C. (2013) *Plutocrats: The Rise of the New Global Super-Rich*, London: Penguin.

Frogner, M. (2002) Housing tenure and the labour market, *Office for National Statistics, Labour Market Trends* (October): 523–534.

Gallent, N., Mace, A. and Tewdwr-Jones, M. (2005) *Second Homes: European Perspectives and UK Policies*, Aldershot: Ashgate.

Garreau, J. (1991) *Edge City: Life on the New Frontier*, Garden City, NY: Doubleday.

Gott, S. (2008) Heir conditioning, *Financial Times Magazine*, 23/24 February.

Gray, J. (2005) The world is round, *New York Review of Books*, 11 August.

Harrington, B. (2008) *Pop Finance: Investment Clubs and the New Investor Populism*, Princeton: Princeton UP.

Jones, C. (2014) Low interest rates sway German habits towards home ownership, *Financial Times*, 13 July.

Karamessini, M. (2013) Introduction – women's vulnerability to recession and austerity. In M. Karamessini and J. Rubery (eds) *Women and Austerity*, London: Routledge, pp. 1–16.

Keister, L. (2005) *Getting Rich: America's New Rich and How They Got That Way*, Cambridge: Cambridge UP.

Kemeny, J. (2006) Corporatism and housing regimes, *Housing, Theory and Society* 23.1: 1–18.

Kohli, M. (1999) Private and public transfers between generations: linking the family and the state, *European Societies* 1.1: 81–104.

Kowinski, W. (1985) *The Malling of America*, New York: William Morrow.

Krämer, H. (2013) Spitzeneinkommen zwischen ökonomischem und normativem Marktversagen: Marktorientierte und soziale Legitimation von Topmanager-Gehältern, DIW Berlin, SOEP papers on Multidisciplinary Panel Data Research, No. 619, http://hdl.handle.net/10419/92499. Accessed 29 July 2014.

Kynaston, D. (1976) *King Labour: The British Working Class 1850–1914*, London: Allen & Unwin.

Landler, M. (2006) German public housing attracts foreign buyers, *International Herald Tribune*, 4 May.

Lane, D. (2004) *Berlusconi's Shadow*, London: Allen Lane.

Langley, P. (2009) *The Everyday Life of Global Finance*, Oxford: Oxford UP.

Lauterbach, W. and Ströing, M. (2012) Philanthropisches Handeln zu Lebzeiten und über den Tod hinaus, *Berliner Journal für Soziologie* 22: 217–236.

McCarthy, Y. (2014) Disentangling the mortgage arrears crisis: the role of the labour market, income volatility and negative equity, *Journal of the Statistical and Social Inquiry Society of Ireland* 43: 71–90.

McGauran, A.-M. (2001) Retail is detail: cross-national variation in the character of retail selling in Paris and Dublin, *International Review of Retail, Distribution and Consumer Research* 11.4: 436–458.

Mills, C. (1979) *The Power Elite*, Oxford: Oxford UP.

Mishel, L. and Sabadish, N. (2013) *CEO Pay in 2012 was Extraordinarily High*, Washington: Economic Policy Institute, Issue Brief #367 (26 June).

Norwood, G. (2003) UK 'underclass' set to pose problems, *Financial Times*, Special Report Residential Property, 29 October.

O'Connor, J. (2005) Employment-anchored social policy, gender equality and the Open Method of Co-ordination in the European Union, *European Societies* 7.1: 27–52.

ONS (Office for National Statistics) (2014) *Wealth in Great Britain Wave 3, 2010–12*, London: Office for National Statistics.

Paris, C. (2009) Re-positioning second homes within housing studies: household investment, gentrification, multiple residence, mobility and hyper-consumption, *Housing, Theory and Society* 26.4: 292–310.

Piketty, T. (2014) *Capital in the Twenty-First Century*, Cambridge, MA: Harvard UP.

Preda, A. (2001) The rise of the popular investor: financial knowledge and investing in England and France 1840–1880, *Sociological Quarterly* 42.2: 205–232.

Priemus, H. and Dieleman, F. (2002) Social housing policy in the European Union: past, present and perspectives, *Urban Studies* 39.2: 191–200.

Regini, M., Kitay, J. and Baethege, M. (1999) *From Tellers to Sellers: Changing Employment Relations in Banks*, Cambridge, MA: MIT Press.

Ryscavage, P. (1999) *Income Inequality in America: An Analysis of Trends*, Armonk, NY: M.E. Sharpe.

Schwartz, H. and Seabrooke, L. (2008) Varieties of residential capitalism in the international political economy: old welfare states and the new politics of housing, *Comparative European Politics* 6: 237–261.

Skodacsek, K. (2000) The position of estate agent offices in the Austrian property market, *Mitteilungen der Österreichischen Geographischen Gesellschaft* 142: 114–138.

Smith, P. (2007) Union pickets private equity charity, *Financial Times*, 25 January.

Smith, S. (2007) Owner-occupation: at home with a hybrid of money and materials, *Environment and Planning A* 40.3: 520–535.

Snowman, D. (2009) *The Gilded Stage: A Social History of Opera*, London: Atlantic Books.

Stevenson, J. (1984) *British Society 1914–45*, Harmondsworth: Penguin.

Szydlik, M. (2004) Zukünftige Vermögen – wachsende Ungleichheit. In M. Syzdlik (ed.) *Generation und Ungleichheit*, Wiesebaden: VS Verglag fur Sozialwissensechaften, pp. 243–264.

Taylor, A. (2006) No justification for fat cat salaries, say unions, *Financial Times*, 28 December.

Timmer, K. (2006) *Stiften in Deutschland: Die Ergebnisse der Stifter Studie*, Munich: Verlag Bertelsmann Stiftung.

Tomalin, C. (2006) *Thomas Hardy: The Time Torn Man*, London: Viking Penguin.

Townsend, P. (1979) *Poverty in the United Kingdom: A Survey of Household Resources and Standards of Living*, Harmondsworth: Penguin.

Tumber, H. (2004) Scandal and media in the United Kingdom: from Major to Blair, *American Behavioral Scientist* 47: 1112–1137.

Verwiebe, R. (2010) Wachsende Armut in Deutschland und die These der Auflösung der Mittelschicht. In P. Berger and N. Burzan (eds) *Dynamiken in der gesellschaftlichen Mitte*, Wiesbaden: VS Verglag für Sozialwissenschaften, pp. 159–180.

Vogel, A. (2006) Who's making global civil society: philanthropy and the US empire in world society, *British Journal of Sociology* 57.4: 635–655.

Wallop, H. (2010) Share ownership falls to all-time low in Britain, *Daily Telegraph*, 28 January.

Wickham, J. (1983) Working class movement and working class life: Frankfurt am Main during the Weimar Republic, *Social History* 8.3: 315–343.

Wickham, J. (2006) Public transport systems: the sinews of European citizenship? *European Societies* 8.1: 3–26.

Wickham, J. (2007) Irish mobilities. In S. O'Sullivan (ed.) *Contemporary Ireland: A Sociological Map*, Dublin: UCD Press, pp. 48–64.

Wilkinson, R. (1996) *Unhealthy Societies: The Afflictions of Inequality*, London: Routledge.

Wolmar, C. (1999) *Stagecoach: A Classic Rags-to-riches Tale from the Frontiers of Capitalism*, London: Orion Publishing.

5   Employment, occupations and social classes

Within twentieth-century Europe – as opposed to the USA – 'class' was a political reality. 'Class' related people's identity to their economic situation. To be a 'worker' or a member of 'the working class' was a widely understood identity. Parties and organisations of the left claimed to politically articulate the needs and views of working class people. And of course such working class organisations were one influence (although not the only one) on the twentieth-century welfare state. Class mattered, but does it still matter?

Given the growing economic inequality documented in Chapter 4, it might seem bizarre to claim that contemporary Europe is classless. However, such differences of money do not translate directly into observable social groups, and furthermore, mere differences of money, however extreme, in themselves say nothing about the social relations that comprise the structure of society. Social class by contrast suggests that not only are there different social groups in society, but that their mutual relationships are to some extent conflictual ('class conflict') and possibly exploitative. For that reason conservatives usually challenge the very use of the term to describe contemporary societies, however manifestly unequal they may be (Jones 2012).

Class in contemporary sociology is clearly delimited from Marxist or 'strong' class theory (Crompton 2008) in which social classes are seen as social actors (the working class *does* this, the bourgeoisie *does* that). In terms that derive not from Marx but from Max Weber, class is understood as a cluster of market-based economic positions, usually in fact occupations. Thus when Esping-Andersen analysed the different 'occupational hierarchies' of industrial and post-industrial society, he constructed groups of occupations (e.g. 'skilled manuals') that could equally be termed classes (Esping-Andersen 1999: 107). With rather less precision, Reich's account of the changing American economy generated his triple division of 'symbolic analysts', 'routine production workers' and 'in person servers' (Reich 1993); more recently Florida (2004) in rather similar vein announced the rise of the 'creative class' (see Section 2.3). Attempting to grasp the social structure of post-industrial society, Giddens identified eight different 'classes' with such names as ' "Big Mac" workers' and 'wired workers' (Giddens 2007: 62).

Contemporary class theory is over-dependent on models of employment prevalent at the end of the last century. The focus on occupation and employment as key determinants occludes the growing importance of property (Section 4.3) as another economic source of life chances. The assumption that occupations are inherently linked to specific forms of contract ignores the extent to which the nature of employment itself is changing, as we shall see in particular in relation to both the 'intermediate' class and the contemporary 'salariat'. And finally, a purely economic model of class ignores the possible role of 'cultural' and 'social' capital in class formation (Savage *et al.* 2013). Accordingly, this chapter now examines those changes in the structure of European social classes that are important for the European social model: the end of the manual working class as a distinct social category, the emergence of an underclass interwoven with the system of state benefits, a service class that is now essentially a marketocracy, and finally, within the service class, a reconfigured corporate elite possibly disconnected from national institutions.

5.1 From working class to middle mass

Up until the 1970s sociological class theory, whether Marxist or neo-Weberian, tended to assume that there was one major division in society. This division was normally taken to be that between manual and non-manual workers. This has been undermined by changes in the occupational structure, by the fragmentation of political allegiances and by the shifting basis of trade unions. These long-term trends are interwoven with and partially shaped by political changes which, most clearly in the UK, have reduced the political weight of working people or even the working class, however defined.

Strong class theory usually involved a dichotomous theory of social structure: society was divided into two opposing camps of ruling class and working class, bourgeoisie and proletariat. Some early neo-Weberian work also saw the main division in society as being between working class, defined as manual workers, and middle class, defined as non-manual 'workers' of all types. Between the two groups there were differences in income, social mobility and political behaviour, all stemming from differences in power (Parkin 1972). By contrast, later neo-Weberian research was adamant that the class structure of Western market societies involved more than two classes. Even at its simplest, the class model put forward by Goldthorpe comprised three classes: a service class, an intermediate class and a working class, the latter including all manual occupations. The full (seven- or ten-class) model used the manual/non-manual division as one criterion to differentiate social classes (Erikson and Goldthorpe 1992). Up to the turn of the century this retained some plausibility. For example, a study in Holland showed that for all white-collar workers automation increased the skills needed, while for blue-collar workers it involved deskilling (de Witte and Steijn 2000); a Swedish study showed continuing income differences between manual workers and all white-collar workers (Bihagen and Halleröd 2000).

The contrast between blue-collar worker and white-collar worker was based on the situation of the manual worker in manufacturing or extractive industry. Yet such 'proletarian' factory workers – let alone miners – are less and less common. Workplaces have been becoming smaller. The same physical factory employs fewer people than ten or twenty years before. Automation has replaced many physical jobs, while at the same time many activities have been contracted out to sub-suppliers. The result is the end of those large concentrations of manual workers in the same workplace which were so characteristic of mid-twentieth-century Europe. For example, in Turin Fiat employed 49,512 workers in its plants in 1989, but by 2002 this had fallen to 23,980 (Dunford and Greco 2006).

At the same time the transition to post-industrial society in the last decades of the twentieth century involved not only a sectoral shift but also changes in occupations (Figure 2.1). During these decades employment growth was especially in public services (health, education) and in the caring occupations; more recently new customer-facing occupations have emerged especially within private sector services. A contemporary analysis of class divisions in the UK defines social class in terms of shared levels of economic, cultural and social capital; it identifies seven classes including 'new affluent workers', including both 'electricians and electrical fitters' and 'retail cashiers and checkout operatives' and a class of 'emergent service workers' ranging from 'routine operatives' to a plethora of 'customer service occupations'. The 'collar question' appears thus of little use to discriminate between these classes, within which small property ownership is also widespread (Savage *et al.* 2013).[1]

The manual/non-manual divide was more likely to appear as a major social division when it was linked to political divisions. Socialist and communist parties appealed to 'the working class' and manual workers were disproportionately likely to vote for them. However, as early as the 1950s European socialist parties began to become 'people's parties', claiming to speak for all the people rather than just one social group. This deliberate rupture of any explicit link between the party and a social group runs from the Bad Godesberg programme of the German SPD in 1959 to the rebranding of the British Labour Party as New Labour in the 1990s.[2] The shift to people's parties was followed by political fragmentation. The major established parties gain an ever smaller proportion of total votes. Thus in Germany the SPD and the CDU/CSU together polled fully 82 per cent of the votes in 1972, 68 per cent in 1987 and only 62 per cent in 1998 (Paterson 2000); in the 2013 German election the two parties together still polled 67 per cent but the CDU/CSU faced the SPD, Greens, and Die Linke as well as other parties which did not win any seats. In this context, the large European centre-left parties have become increasingly uncoupled from any clearly defined socio-economic base. They may well draw their support disproportionately from manual workers, but they have long ceased to make an explicit appeal to them as a social group.

It is widely believed that trade unions are now out of date and play no important social role. Labour and the manual working class are no longer distinct identities. All over Western Europe union membership and hence union density rose rapidly after the end of World War II, not least because unions were identified with the struggle against fascism. In some countries membership then drifted slowly downwards, and by the 1960s commentators were anticipating –

in language reminiscent of that used today – a permanent decline of trade unions. One argument was that workers were becoming 'middle class' (the so-called embourgeoisement thesis) and hence not interested in the old claims of working class solidarity. Another argument focused on structural change: the growth of white-collar jobs (and somewhat later, the rise in women's employment) ensured an inexorable trade union decline.

Such predictions disintegrated in the late 1960s. The celebrated May events in France in 1968 and the 'hot autumn' of 1969 in Italy were only the peaks of a rank and file mobilisation that occurred in virtually every democratic European country (see especially Crouch and Pizzorno 1978; Streeck 2013: 45). In countries such as Italy and the UK it led to substantial union membership increases and gave the unions a new lease of life (a British pop song in 1973 was 'You can't get me I'm part of the union') (Figure 5.1). Across Europe a new generation of young militants emerged. Especially in France and Germany they had been politicised through connections with the student movement of the time; they would form the core of local leaders until well into the new century. Trade union membership grew both in manufacturing and in service sector occupations. Particularly in Scandinavia, where social democratic governments expanded state sector employment in welfare services, there was a steady increase of union membership among state sector employees.

From the 1980s onwards conditions changed again. Most West European governments did not follow Thatcher in explicitly rejecting co-operation with unions, but they did increasingly abandon Keynesian demand management. This seems to be the reason why factors that explain trade union membership in the previous period do not explain changes after 1980 (Ebbinghaus and Visser 1999). For example, until 1980 social democratic participation in government

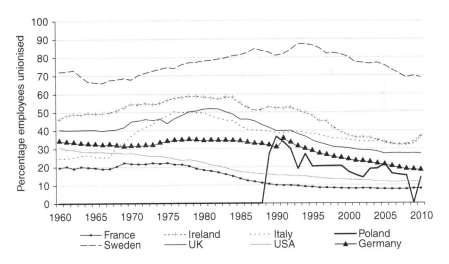

Figure 5.1 Trade union density, 1960–2010: USA, France, Germany, Ireland, Italy, Poland and UK (derived from ICTWSS database (Visser 2013)).

tended to increase trade union membership, but after 1980 this made little difference. Trade union density continued to decline under the Schröder SPD government in Germany and under Blair's New Labour in Britain. The main exception was Sweden and the other Scandinavian countries (as well as Belgium) where the so-called 'Ghent system' involved trade unions in the administration of social insurance, so there only in the new century did union density also begin to decline. As density has declined, so corporatist and tripartite institutions have been either abandoned or marginalised. Whereas in the 1990s unions were brought into policy-making in countries such as Italy and Ireland, in the current crisis these governments have treated them as just another interest group (Baccaro and Howell 2011; Bernaciak *et al.* 2014, Culpepper and Regan 2014).

Everywhere state employment has become the new heartland of trade union membership. Even in Germany, IGMetall (the metalworkers' union centred on the crucial car industry) has been overtaken by Ver.di, essentially the public services union. This has changed the profile of union membership: union members are increasingly likely to be well educated, have 'middle class' jobs and to be women. By the turn of the century trade union density in Sweden was higher among women than among men, as it has been in the UK since 2004; British union members are likely to be middle income earners and, especially among women, the likelihood of union membership increases with education (Grainger and Crowther 2007). Trade unions and trade union membership may remain strong, but unions now recruit from a wide range of occupations. To the extent that support for trade unions does still exist, the manual/non-manual divide is of little importance compared to questions of sector (above all state versus private sector) and gender. Trade unions may represent some employees, but they certainly do not represent the manual working class, whatever that may be.

The distinctive feature of the post-World War II compromise in Western Europe was that the numerical importance of manual working class jobs (see Section 2.1) also involved a distinct identity and social presence of manual workers in the society. At work and in consumption, the social relations of manual workers involved collective power, epitomised by regular and secure employment, the right to housing, social welfare and, perhaps above all, to respect. Arguably in Britain this process went furthest, amounting to a British 'proletarian mode of production' (Offer 2008). Elsewhere in Western Europe Continental corporatism and Scandinavian social democracy were re-configured and could survive into the new century, but in Britain the compromise was challenged head-on by the Thatcher revolution.

In 1957 the sociologists Young and Wilmott published their classic study of the East End of London. Revisiting the area fifty years later, Dench *et al.* commented:

> The year 1957 when *Family and Kinship* was published probably marked a brief golden age: a kind of sunlit upland plateau in which the working class basked in their new found enfranchisement and prosperity.
>
> (Dench *et al.* 2006: 20)

In Britain the destruction of this perhaps nostalgically remembered working class world has recently been highlighted in autobiography and films (starting with *The Full Monty* in 1997) as well as in social history and political commentary.

The most obvious change was in work. Work was real work: work done by men, work involving inherited and informal skills, work in places that were noisy, dirty and recognisably *work* places (Hall 2012). For many manual workers, especially those who identified with the labour movement, manual work was of higher status than white-collar work because it was self-evidently socially useful. Asked to rank occupations in a 1950s study, one respondent from East London replied: 'I've put all people who do physical labour at the top. They're absolutely essential'; 'clerks' were ranked lower since 'Anybody can push a pen along' (Young and Wilmot 1956). From the 1960s women within this male world took action (such as the Ford Dagenham strike in 1968) demanding equality – only to see most regular and union-organised industrial jobs disappear over the next decades.

The transformation was equally significant in housing (Hanley 2012). Until the 1970s access to housing for British manual working class families was a right based on time on a waiting list. However, the 1977 Housing (Homeless Persons) Act prioritised housing in terms of need. Increasingly social housing became charity for the poor, not a right for the worker. Once tenant purchase started in the 1980s, social housing became identified with social problems, not with a social class. Equally, the growth of means-testing transformed the welfare state even further from its roots in working class self-help:

> The evolution of the welfare state had turned it from a mutual aid society writ large, as it seemed at first, into a complex, centralised and bureaucratic system run by middle class do-gooders who gave generously to those who put nothing into the pot while making ordinary working people who did contribute feel like recipients of charity when drawing their own entitlement.
>
> (Dench *et al.* 2006: 208)

While these changes were well under way by the 1970s in Britain, the Hartz IV reforms had the same impact in Germany in the 2000s, replacing insurance and rights-based unemployment benefits with means-tested allowances (Dörre *et al.* 2013). Equally, the current labour market 'reforms' in southern Europe are intended to ensure that everywhere welfare is based on 'need', not rights.

Most difficult to trace, and most easily misunderstood, has been the simple loss of esteem, of the sense that the working class had become 'the People' or even the nation (Todd 2014). In Britain World War II was defined as a 'people's war' (Calder 1969)[3] and the victory as won largely by working people – epitomised by working class London in the Blitz (Dench *et al.* 2006). Yet this new privileging of workers was not restricted to Britain. In France and Italy, to be a 'worker' was a more political identity, linked especially to the mass communist parties (PCF, PCI) and their affiliated trade unions (e.g. Beaud and Pialoux 2003: 385) and to the (somewhat mythologised) anti-fascist struggle of the mid-1940s. Somewhat later, national understanding of the (West) German *Wirtschaftswunder* also gave German *workers* a privileged role in reconstruction. Britain, however, certainly provides the clearest example of disinheritance. Until recently most British people defined themselves as 'working class' (so-called self-ascribed social class), but not now. Now working class means 'chav' and is no longer a label people can wear with pride (Jones 2012). Class has been Americanised.

To all of this have been added the consequences of identity politics, again most clearly in the UK (Goodhart 2013). As claims to rights become based on ethnicity, not class, the indigenous or white members of the working class become conceptualised by social policy-makers, by academics and by politicians as just another minority group. Especially in England the leadership of many local Labour Parties became an alliance between ethnic minority elites and state professionals. Indeed, one left-wing French think tank recently made this explicit, suggesting the left should finally abandon the '*couches populaires*' and focus on an alliance between libertarians and ethnic minorities (Betz 2013). At the same time, the new right-wing populist parties have been jettisoning their earlier free-market enthusiasms and are building a clear base among manual workers. Epitomised by the French Front National, they now combine demands for immigration control and support for the national culture with traditional social democratic demands for income redistribution and for a strong national welfare state. While it is easy to characterise their voters as 'losers of globalisation' or 'the left behind', manual working class support for the new populism in affluent Scandinavia and the prosperous areas of Italy (Betz and Meret 2013) shows that it is not that simple. The coupling of class and politics appears to be re-emerging in unexpected ways.

5.2 The underclass

If the working class in the traditional sense has become part of the middle mass, what is below this amorphous 'middle'? The European working class of the twentieth century was an inherent part of the society, even though it was at times also a basis for opposition to that society. Conceptions of the 'underclass' suggest something very different: the underclass is neither a necessity for the society nor the basis for any movement of social change. The underclass may be threatening, but it is also superfluous.

This section of the chapter begins with the underclass in the USA and that country's explosive mixture of poverty, race and mass incarceration. While some American commentators blamed welfare for the emergence of what they termed the underclass, the cause of American pathologies lies rather in the withdrawal of the state from the lives of the poorer citizens. In Europe recent decades have seen the rise of mass unemployment, and it is often claimed that in Europe too there is now voluntary welfare dependency passed from generation to generation, while, as in the USA, single motherhood has become a viable career for young women. A rather separate issue which may also indicate an Americanisation of European poverty is the eruption of violence in poor housing areas, especially in the banlieus of France.

The origins of contemporary debate – poverty American style

Confronted by the African-American ghettos of the USA – or more recently the suburban 'sink estates' of Britain or the banlieus of France – a widespread response is that the inhabitants of these areas are unemployed because, at its simplest, they do not *want* to work. Allegedly a culture of non-work has developed, not least because of the welfare system. The alternative view puts the causality the other way round, and explains the emergence of the underclass through the disappearance of stable but unskilled employment.

In the 1960s the US government launched its 'War on Poverty' – a systematic attempt to eradicate poverty in the USA. Yet in his influential book *Losing Ground* Charles Murray (1984) argued that by the end of the 1970s not only had the programme failed, it had actually made the situation worse. State welfare programmes, so Murray argued, had made resources available to single women who were bringing up children. Almost for the first time in history, a woman could bring up a child without a man to support her – the man was only needed to conceive the child. Conversely, a man felt no obligation to obtain a regular safe job to support his wife and children, since the state was now prepared to do this for him. Murray argued that family socialises and 'tames' men. Without this constraint young men are likely to seek the more instant gratification of crime. The situation becomes worse as children grow up. In particular, young boys have no father to discipline them, but also no father they can look up to as the family breadwinner. The unemployed have become dependent on welfare: they lack any sense of obligation to the rest of society and lose any desire to better themselves through seeking legitimate employment. An *underclass* is born, with no connection with the mainstream institutions of society.

Given this analysis, the policy prescriptions are clear: welfare needs to be reduced, welfare recipients must be compelled to seek work. Workfare must replace welfare. After all, since the argument assumes that people have in effect chosen to be dependent on welfare, it is perfectly reasonable to remove that support and force them to find jobs. The alternative account developed above all by Wilson (1987, 1996) accepted that social problems in the inner cities had got worse, were increasingly spatially concentrated (i.e. the gap between the ghetto and the rest has widened) and had a clear racial element. However, Wilson reversed the causality. The underclass was the result of what Europeans began to call social exclusion.

For Wilson, the ghettos of American cities emerged because their inhabitants had been abandoned. First, by the government: despite claims of generous welfare levels, the real value of US welfare payments had been declining since the mid-1970s. Even more fundamentally, many state agencies no longer operated, or only operated ineffectively, within the ghetto. Second, by the private sector: unemployment had risen because low skill jobs had been lost, particularly in the ghettoes, and where low skill jobs had been created, they were disproportionately in the service sector in the suburbs and therefore difficult for inner city dwellers to reach. And third, by the black middle class: anti-discrimination and affirmative action policies had benefited and expanded the black 'middle class' who had moved out of the ghetto while entering the mainstream of American life. Historically, black middle class Americans were a ghetto middle class, living in the ghetto and working in jobs which serviced their own community (clergy, lawyers, doctors, etc.). Consequently the social structure of the inner cities had become more homogenous even while black Americans have become more differentiated. Of course, areas like Harlem in the 1950s were poor, they were different to white society, they had relatively high unemployment, but they had functioning families and social institutions:

> In short, unlike the present period, inner-city communities prior to 1960 exhibited the features of social organisation – including a sense of community, positive neighbourhood identification, and explicit norms and sanctions against aberrant behaviour.
>
> (Wilson 1987: 3)

Some thirty years later, much of the underclass debate still oscillates between these two poles of culture and constraint; it still involves the tensions that existed even earlier in the debate over the 'culture of poverty'. Stressing the role of culture gives those in the 'underclass' some power over their own situation, yet also means that they have to be held responsible for it; it runs the risk of blaming the victim and has even been construed as 'racist'. Conversely, stressing the role of structural causes may not blame the poor, but also makes them passive victims of circumstance. Into the argument, however, has come the new feature of US social inequality – mass incarceration.

Up until the 1970s American incarceration rates (the proportion of the population that is in prison at any one time) had been constant for several decades and were broadly comparable with those of Europe. In the next thirty years the incarceration rate more than quadrupled: by the turn of the century there were approximately two million Americans in prison, mostly men and disproportionately poor and black (Uggen and Manza 2002). In the USA now about 12 per cent of black men in their twenties are incarcerated: for unskilled black men, imprisonment has become a normal part of young adult life (Freeman 1996; Petit and Western 2004). Incarceration on this scale means that prison is an integral part of American social structure. As 'part of a novel system of social inequality' (Western 2005: xi) it has implications for inequality, labour market regulation and even democracy. The increase in incarceration has affected those who are already the most disadvantaged by race and class (there has been no increase in the imprisonment rates for black educated men).

For Wacquant (2008) this hyper-incarceration is a key part of US neo-liberal withdrawal of the welfare state. Imprisonment becomes part of the way the

American labour market is regulated: many unskilled young men who would be unemployed are incarcerated, reducing the level of unemployment. Thus, mass incarceration contributed to the explanation for the difference between the USA and Europe in the 1990s (Western 2005: 104). Whereas state institutions (education, the welfare system, etc.) in the past had to some extent ameliorated the inequalities of the market, the American prison system now exacerbates them. This fundamental reversal of the role of the state, the decline of the American nation's 'equalising institutions' (Levy 1999, cited in Wilson 2003), is a basic difference between Europe and the USA.

A European underclass?

Within Europe, too, the terms of debate have been rather different. Often the key concept has not been 'underclass' at all but *social exclusion*.[4] The term itself has important connotations. It suggests that the poor are excluded from society by actions or structures, rather than that they have turned their back on society of their own volition or because of their own culture. Furthermore, social exclusion is implicitly a dynamic process rather than a snapshot of income or wealth at any one point in time. Finally, social exclusion is normally understood to involve a spatial dimension: to be excluded is not just to be poor but to live in a neighbourhood that is isolated from the wider society (Andreotti 2006). Finally, the policy implication of 'exclusion' is to suggest measures to ensure 'inclusion', rather measures that change the values of the underclass so that they finally want to work.

With the return of mass unemployment in Western Europe the number of long-term unemployed also grew. However, during the 1990s it seemed that long-term unemployment across Europe did not in fact have the same implications as in US ghettoes. In the UK Gallie (1995) used survey data to show that while the long-term unemployed were more likely to be in poverty and more likely to suffer a marriage breakdown than those in jobs, they did not form a socially segregated underclass and the experience of unemployment does not lead to any significant ideological shift. With the partial exception of the UK, the European states managed to maintain the standard of living of the long-term unemployed. This was helped by the fact that all European states (again with the exception of the UK) had extensive social housing provision and thus could ensure that the unemployed could usually still be housed in conditions similar to those who had jobs. Finally, while European prisons disproportionately house the poor and those from ethnic minorities, nowhere have they had the impact on the whole society of the American system.

The emergence of single motherhood was for Murray a defining characteristic of the underclass. Within Europe initially the two 'Anglo-Saxon' countries, the UK and Ireland, came closest to the USA with rising rates of single motherhood in the poorest areas. Here the welfare system made it feasible for young women to bring up children by themselves, albeit at great risk of poverty. By contrast, German social policy remained for longer both pro-natalist and supportive of the conventional family, so that single motherhood remained less widespread than elsewhere (Lash 1994). Today the UK still has the highest level of single parenthood (essentially single motherhood) with 18.5 per cent of all households with children being single mother households (European Commission 2014: 9).[5] However, whether single motherhood leads to social exclusion depends crucially on the extent of state support for mothers and the nature of available employment. In these terms, single motherhood is more likely to involve poverty and limited employment opportunities in the UK, while at the other extreme in Scandinavia single motherhood per se involves fewer links to poverty or social inequality.

In the new century and even after the crisis of 2008 these differences between the USA and Europe have remained. There have, however, been two key developments which have increased the size of the potential underclass. First, there has been the growth of youth unemployment. Unlike in the USA, the employment rate was growing up until the crisis (Figure 3.5), but nonetheless young Europeans were increasingly likely to be unemployed, especially in southern Europe. More and more young Europeans now fall into the new social category of 'NEETS' (Not in Employment, Education or Training) while especially in southern Europe many recent graduates have low paid jobs and only survive by living with their parents (Eurofound 2012). Second, in Germany the reforms of the Red–Green coalition were an explicit encouragement of casual service sector jobs and rapidly brought about a whole new glossary of low wage terms: 'Harz-vierer', 'Ein-Euro Jobs'. The combination of labour market deregulation and greater pressure on welfare recipients to accept any job has now created a new 'working poor' in Germany such as already existed in the UK and the USA in the 1990s. At the same time there was a public discovery of the *Unterschicht* (underclass). According to one study, fully 8 per cent of German citizens in the old Bundesrepublik and fully 25 per cent in the new eastern *Länder* could be classified as a 'precarious dependent' group characterised not only by unemployment or irregular employment, but also by a lack of interest in work itself and a disconnection from the institutions and values of the *Leistungsgesellschaft* (achievement society) (Schmidt 2006).

Social exclusion and the Badlands

Unlike in the USA, in northern Europe the worst areas of urban deprivation tend not to be within the inner city. With the partial exception of Inner London, those areas which do show Murray's underclass symptoms (high long-term unemployment, high crime, high illegitimacy) tend to be run-down suburban housing estates (Power 1997). In terms of Murray's indicators, it is the peripheral housing areas of Newcastle or Paris that count. Equally, theories of social exclusion see the excluded as pushed into a part of the city which is seen by the rest of the society as undesirable and even dangerous. The banlieus of the French cities test the extent of convergence between Europe and the USA.

Certainly, there are areas of large European cities with concentrations of both immigrants and unemployed. However, a careful ethnographic comparison of

• French and American 'ghetto' areas (the now demolished *quatre mille* housing project in La Courneuve in Paris, the Woodlawn area of South Side Chicago) brought out important differences in the early 1990s (Wacquant 1996, 2008). Although the 'bad' housing estates of northern Paris were widely perceived from outside as Algerian, in fact Algerians were only a minority. The inhabitants believed they were scorned by the rest of Paris; nobody would willingly admit to living there, but they experienced this in terms of class rather than race. Although there was little available employment, the state had not withdrawn – indeed, state agencies (social welfare offices, etc.) proliferated – and much of the life of the inhabitants was spent queuing for various government and local bureaucratic agencies. In particular, while the American ghetto was dangerous for its own inhabitants, the French 'ghetto' was not.

In the new century such optimism became more problematic, but nonetheless most serious researchers insist on the contrast between European and American ghettos (e.g. Stébé 2009). In 2005 riots started in Clichy-sous-Bois outside Paris and spread to the banlieus of many other cities. There is in fact a long tradition of conflict between young people in the banlieus and the police going back to the 1980s. However, the 2005 riots were unprecedented in scale and duration: across the country over 10,000 cars were burnt and a national state of emergency was imposed. Then in 2007, rioters in another Paris banlieu, Villiers-le-Bel, used fire-arms against police who narrowly escaped with their lives. A police representative commented: 'On assiste à une Americanisation des quartiers' (*Le Point*, 6 December 2007: Moran 2012).

While many politicians were quick to refer to the rioters as *racaille* (scum), some commentators and researchers stressed the apparent shift in state policy which preceded the riots: reduced welfare expenditure and tougher policing. While much of the national and indeed international media saw the riots as 'Islamic', it is clear that at the time there was no real radical Muslim involvement (Dikec 2007; Moran 2012). The relationship between young people in the banlieus is widely reported to be completely antagonistic. The police are seen as provoking conflict by continual identity checks, rudeness and indeed overt racism. Some accounts of the riots insist on seeing them as pre-political protest, as the only way in which the inhabitants of the banlieu can make themselves heard (Sala Pala 2011). In the words of a 20-year-old unemployed young man:

> J'en ai marre moi! Les politiques, ils parlent … ils parlent, tu vois. Mais rien ne change sauf quand on brule des voitures. Après, les médias viennent et tout le monde voit qu'on accepte pas ce qui passe ici.
>
> (cited in Moran 2012: 214)

Similar interpretations were made of the 2011 riots in England. According to some, the riots were excluded young people's response to neo-liberal policing and to scapegoating by conservative politicians (e.g. Tyler 2013). However, the self-understanding of many of the participants seems to have been anything but political. Many rioters were quite aware that their actions (burning shops, looting, etc.) would be seen as protest but they themselves had other ideas: 'It wasn't like I was trying to get back at society, I was taking what I could.' And another summed it up with the simple statement: 'It was a good day for shopping' (Treadwell *et al.* 2013).

The English riots of 2011 thus marked a further move away from explicit politics. In France a previous generation of immigrants had formed the 1983 political movement *Marche pour l'égalité et contre le racisme* which demanded recognition as French citizens (Beaud and Masclet 2006). While *some* accounts see contemporary rioters as still demanding such inclusion, riots are less overtly political and less organised than marches. In this sense the rioters do fit the traditional account of the underclass: riots are the protest of those who are not needed by the rest of the society.

The marginalised housing areas of France and Britain now show more similarities with the American ghetto than when Wacquant made his original comparison. In Britain, levels and styles of gun crime in *some* Afro-Caribbean neighbourhoods have begun to take on American forms: guns as symbols of masculinity are casually used against others from the neighbourhood. In neighbourhoods of both France and Britain in particular, the street economy based on drug dealing has consolidated (e.g. Ocqueteau 2007). In Germany newspapers report growing problems of school discipline: young Turkish school students routinely harass and terrorise teachers. Nonetheless, despite a clear movement towards much more aggressive policing in France and despite threats to welfare and benefits in both Britain and France, in neither country can the state be seen as having shifted purely to a punitive state. In the French banlieus there is still an active associational life and indeed some inhabitants positively identify with their neighbourhood (Kirkness 2014). In the USA neighbourhoods of the poor, whatever their race, now exhibit the features found by Wacquant in the 1990s in the black belt of Chicago: the collapse of community institutions and the rise of intra-community violence, to which must now be added the end of any form of stable family (Putnam 2015). To date, the European poor have not been excluded to this extent.

5.3 Yuppies and their hangers on: the new service class

In the 1980s journalists and advertisers noticed a new social group – the 'yuppies' – 'young upwardly mobile professionals' or 'young urban professionals'. By the end of the decade social researchers had begun to investigate them. Especially in Britain, they highlighted changes not just in consumption but in the economic basis of professional and managerial workers, the group sociologists were beginning to term 'the service class'. Whereas this class had begun as a group at the apex of large, bureaucratic organisations, by the end of the century such organisations were increasingly what the first part of this section terms *marketocracies.* The term highlights the role of the market but, unlike much management orthodoxy of the last twenty years, stresses that business organisations are actually more hierarchical than those they have replaced. Equally, while a 'yuppie' was seen as 'upwardly mobile', in fact one of the features of today's new service class is that the expansion of the market has slowed down social mobility into the elite groups. As the second part of this section shows, this expansion of the market is also implicated in the historically novel forms of household and consumption which characterise the class. However, despite much talk of the increasing cosmopolitanism of service class members' careers, the third part suggests that national frameworks have proved surprisingly resilient.

The rise and decline of bureaucratic organisation

In the nineteenth century European states developed bureaucracies as we would recognise them today. This did not involve the abolition of social privilege: the Prussian civil service and above all the British Imperial civil service were recruited from almost caste-like social groups. Reforms of the nineteenth century such as the Northcote Trevelyan Report of 1854 in Britain created an administrative machine in which access to positions was defined by impersonal criteria (success in exams) independent of particular individuals. The fact that the exam subjects were not 'relevant' was itself irrelevant; the educational criteria both restricted entry to a privileged group and at the same time ensured that between members of this group appointment was impersonal. Crucially, such bureaucracies ensured that the individuals within them were imbued with notions of organisational commitment and disinterested service.[6]

Such systems were only taken over into the private sector as firms began to grown in size. It was no accident that factories were described by contemporaries as involving military discipline and then somewhat later the first large companies, the railway companies, were modelled on military organisations. Professional managers in private companies first became important in the USA before World War I. During the Gilded Age from 1870 to 1900 US firms grew rapidly in size. While in the USA the new bureaucracies emerged in the private sector, in Europe (with the partial exception of Germany) firms remained relatively small. Here modern large bureaucracies were more important in the state (and the military). Accordingly, here the state was the key source of new professional 'middle class' employment. Large private sector bureaucracies really only developed after World War II, while at the same time the state bureaucracies expanded in new areas (welfare, health, education) which generated more professional and managerial jobs. And it was this state employment that provided professional and then managerial opportunities for women (see Chapter 9). In the third quarter of the last century, organisations, whether nominally private or publicly owned, all appeared as bureaucracies. Equally, this bureaucratisation appeared to spread downwards, in that the work of even manual workers became increasingly 'bureaucratised', defined and managed by impersonal rules rather than direct authority (Edwards 1979).

The term 'service class' entered the mainstream of European sociology at the peak of this bureaucratisation of the world. Goldthorpe (1982) and his co-workers in social mobility studies defined those at the apex of these bureaucracies as the 'service class'. Yet the term gained currency in the 1980s just when the basis of the service class began to change. All over Europe large state enterprises have been privatised, while the service sector has grown relative to the manufacturing sector (see Section 2.2). Even more important, the large firm as a coherent bureaucratic structure has been eroded. Firms have introduced market relationships into their internal operations, using accounting methods to identify each unit's contribution to overall profits (units become first identifiable cost centres and then profit centres).

These changes involve changes in organisational structure. In contemporary organisations the post and the occupant are reconnected, since the duties depend on the person who occupies the position. Thus, one contemporary management slogan is that whereas personnel management attempted to recruit people for *jobs*, human resource management recruits people for *companies.* What matters is the whole person and the extent to which they will fit into the company and contribute to it, *whatever they do.* Accordingly, pay should be individualised rather than 'the rate for the job', let alone the 'point on the salary scale'. Salaries also include bonuses for individuals, rather than grades, and furthermore the remuneration package is just that, a salary combined with other asset-based elements such as stock options. For all the rhetoric of flat organisations, this is still a hierarchy, in that some people still give orders to others. Indeed, those at the top of the hierarchy have more power than before because they are less constrained by rules of procedure and by long chains of command. Instead of the bureaucratic hierarchy, we have a marketised hierarchy, a *marketocracy.*

In this context careers have become 'boundaryless' (Arthur 1994). The internal labour market has declined and the external labour market has become more important. Professionals and managers will change employers more frequently over the course of their working life than did those of the preceding generation. Individual success depends more on reputation outside the firm than on perceived achievements within it, and more on connections and networks outside the firm than on 'office politics' within it. Service class careers are no longer about climbing up ladders: many of the rungs have been removed, while other rungs change depending on who is standing on them. The relationship between the professional and 'his' (or increasingly, her) company has become more short term, while both loyalty to the company and detailed knowledge of its workings have become less important.

Although 'service class' members were defined by sociologists as salaried employees, the image of the service class as acting from disinterested loyalty resonates with the traditional understanding of the independent professional, the lawyer or doctor, whose relationship with a client is based on professional knowledge and a certain non-commercial commitment both to the occupation and the client. The location of such skilled professional work has often changed, so that lawyers increasingly are employed in the newly internationalising law firms and within the large corporations. At the same time, there has been a growth of small 'professional' firms in new areas, epitomised by the boom in consultancy in all its forms. Extreme formulations in the USA link this to the internet and suggest that 'everyone' is working for themselves. As in particular Florida (2004) has convincingly demonstrated, this is a wild exaggeration: most 'professionals' are employees. Nonetheless, they are more directly involved in market relations than before.

Until the 1970s trade unions were expanding up the white-collar hierarchies, recruiting more professionals and managers, as the employment conditions of such people became more 'bureaucratised'. Now in some countries (especially the UK) trade union representation has been pushed down the hierarchy. Quite apart from the general political climate, this has been facilitated by the individualisation of pay and the erosion of clear grading systems. Such changes have been slower in the public sector, thus providing another difference between public and private sector professionals, a difference which often is linked to different political support.

Finally, these changes are linked to changes in personality. A professional 'service class' career always involved anticipatory socialisation: candidate members trained themselves to become the right sort of person. But now, as in other areas of employment, more of the personality is involved and this is more self-conscious ('reflexive'). Thus young professionals quite self-consciously conflate friendship and contacts as they 'network' (Collinson and Collinson, 1997)[7] and develop the right personality as they market themselves. Work ceases to be a calling, but part of instant gratification in a new work culture of long hours. The individual understands him- or herself as an active 'player' in the market, navigating a small boat across a largely uncharted and often stormy sea.

These structural changes are interwoven into a new hegemony of the private sector over occupational life. Whereas until the 1970s many organisational innovations came from the state (or the military), now they come largely from the private sector. This is strengthened by government outsourcing, which not only moves activities previously carried out by government into the private sector, but reaffirms the belief that market-based organisations are the source of innovation. The language of the market ('profit', 'customer', 'enterprise') increasingly dominates even those areas of professional employment that remain within the state (Hanlon 1997). The expansion of private relative to public sector professional employment is undermining traditions within the service class of state employment often handed down from generations (Marquand 2004). Instead of moving through a bureaucratic hierarchy, service class individuals traverse a market. And more than ever before, this is how service class individuals understand themselves. Thus in a study of managers' narratives, Martin and Wajcman (2004) note the predominance of what they term a 'market narrative': managers understand themselves as actors in a market, able to make rational market-based choices that shape their own futures.

As successful individuals in an individualised market society, members of the service class can perceive their own success as the result of their own ability and effort. Here too, however, perception and reality diverge. While their incomes have been moving away from those of the mass of society (Savage 2000: 52), so their social origins have been becoming narrower. In his earlier studies of social mobility in Britain, Goldthorpe suggested that while the service class was hetero-geneous in origin, it was increasingly passing on its occupational position to its children. Recent studies do show a slowing of social mobility in both Britain and the USA (Blandel *et al.* 2005; Putnam 2015). The meritocratic rhetoric is under-mined even more when we consider not just the overall rate of mobility but the channels through which it occurs. It has always been the case that the children of the service class had a disproportionate chance of achieving their parents' occu-pational position. Well into the 1980s, mobility studies saw this as *indirect* inheritance. While education was notionally available equally to all, a variety of social and cultural processes ensured that the children of the privileged did better. More recent research suggests that education now has less independent influence than before: inheritance is becoming increasingly *direct*. At least in Britain, this is consistent with the growing importance of private education. The so-called public schools increasingly market themselves on their ability to place children into the more elite universities, as here too a straightforward market ethos (education as a commodity that is purchased because it leads to occupa-tional success) is removing older traditions of education as training for service (Adonis and Pollard 1997). The service class serves only itself.

Households of the successful

British sociologists and social geographers have been exploring the relationship between service class careers, geographical mobility and household form. In the 1990s the centres of most American cities were still being abandoned, but in Europe, especially in Britain, new young professionals had started to renovate old housing stock. This reflects not just the availability of housing, but also new lifestyle choices in which people value the amenities of the city centre and the fact that these can be reached without a car (Buzar *et al.* 2007). It has been argued that for the service class this means a new conception of locality: a residential area is no longer a given place of origin, but an area that has been chosen for its 'elective affinity' with the individual or the household's lifestyle (Savage *et al.* 2005). The area thus becomes a place in which meaning and identity are self-consciously created.

However, this does not mean that the new service class are busy re-creating urban communities or even urban villages. Out in the respectable suburbs it was the role of the woman or the housewife to do this, women being the backbone of voluntary organisations. By contrast, in the urban service class household there is nobody at home: women and men are both likely to be in full-time and indeed professional employment, earning money but short of time. The emergence of the dual career household (as opposed to simply the dual earnings household) has been a major factor in exacerbating the income gap between the *households* of the service class and those of the rest of the society (see also Sections 4.2 and 8.4). Rather less obviously, it has contributed to the disconnection between the household and the locality, with relations being increasingly primarily based on the cash nexus. Instead of neighbours, the 'locals' become simply a source of paid childcare and paid domestic help (see especially McDowell *et al.* 2006).

The new service class is hardly only an inner city class. Urban and suburban households of the new service class area also now likely to use paid domestic labour. Here again, compared to the service class of the mid-century compromise, the service class is new in the extent to which it relies on market relations and the cash nexus for its lifestyle. Professional and managerial work is increasingly time greedy, but to be busy has become itself a sign of high status (Gershuny 2005). Accordingly, the service class makes extensive use of labour-intensive services, from restaurants to nannies. They may enjoy their designer kitchens, but often would rather save time by eating out. Whereas the post-World War II expansion of the middle class suburbs, in Europe as in the USA, involved labour-saving devices, the new re-urbanisation and new service class lifestyles are labour intensive. In particular, once the young professionals have children, they are likely to rejoin their great-grandparents and become employers of domestic servants.

Domestic labour seems to have expanded first in Britain. Citing census figures, Gregson and Lowe (1993: 52) claim that in Britain by 1900 there were approximately two million 'servants' and, rather implausibly, even in 1951 still 1.8 million. The supply of 'domestics' dried up rapidly: the expansion of light manufacturing industry provided better paid jobs for women with none of the dissatisfaction of working under close supervision in someone else's house; the new immigrants went to the factories and the state services. In the 1980s de-industrialisation ended these jobs; many older women welcomed the chance to work for a few hours a week, especially if it was in the black economy and they could continue to draw benefits. From the 1990s onwards the new wave of immigrants also provided another cheap labour force.

Where service class parents have young children, then some form of childcare becomes essential if there is no state provision. Since young professionals have often moved away from their own family networks, such input is unlikely to come from the existing extended family. Given that market-based childcare is expensive, many parents opt for various forms of childcare at home. At times this can be combined with the au pair, who, despite the origins in international exchanges, has now become a cheap form of live-in servant (Mellini *et al.* 2007). For the higher income brackets, especially in the big cities, a multitude of additional services can be purchased: companies can be contracted to do everything from spring cleaning the apartment to landscaping the patio and walking the dog. Thus whereas the mid-century service class purchased appliances, the new service class purchases labour services.

In the USA growing income inequality and the inflow of migrant labour led to a dramatic expansion of domestic labour, especially in the most affluent areas (Hondagneu-Sotelo 2001). Similarly in Britain, minimal state provision of childcare and an increasingly casualised labour market created a situation by the 1990s where: 'The reproduction of the dual career family is both dependent on the existence of female domestics and in turn, generative of major, class based inequalities between women' (Gregson and Lowe 1993: 65).

A decade later, both French and German labour market reforms aimed at creating low paid service sector jobs, and domestic work was explicitly seen as desirable in this context. Labour market regulation was here running after the situation in the labour market itself, where domestic work had become key for many new illegal immigrants, as also in Spain and Italy (Lutz 2002; ILO 2013). Indeed, it is not too fanciful to trace a connection between the new-found enthusiasm of the European service class for immigration and its own need for a cheap labour force to ensure that it is well serviced.

Cosmopolitanism and careers – the new Europeans?

For the new service class, so it has been suggested, the lifestyle involves frequent changes of residence and often migration between countries. Its life is no longer lived within national boundaries and its consumption and members' personal identity become cosmopolitan or European rather than national. As we shall now see, cosmopolitanism is very uneven and in many ways it is a feature of the *British* service class. Furthermore, to the extent that the British service class has moved beyond a national framework it has become international rather than purely European.

Service class work increasingly involves multiple forms of mobility and migration. For many executives, frequent foreign business trips are part of the job (Wickham and Vecchi 2010; Kesselring and Vogl 2010). For the highly skilled, work-related mobility can include commuting across national boundaries, various forms of short-term stays abroad and 'expatriation' (Salt 1997; Mahroum 2000). For the service class, migration in the traditional sense of permanent change of residence from one country to another is part of a much larger picture of mobility.

This mobility can be read in a variety of ways. It can be seen as an exchange of populations within Europe, as part therefore of the emergence of the free movement of professionals within an emerging *European* migratory system. Alternatively, it can be seen rather as a process of internationalisation, in which Europe as such plays no distinctive role. Furthermore, it can be seen as an uneven process, in which the service class of some countries is more mobile than others, whether this is in terms of emigration or immigration.

One way of assessing these arguments is through data on migration (see Dumont and Lemaître 2005). As Figure 5.2 suggests, Britain is in fact extreme among our case study countries in the extent to which its service class is disproportionately foreign-born. In Britain over 16 per cent of all adults with third-level education were born abroad (a proportion exceeded only by Ireland) and many of these immigrants come from outside the EU. Furthermore, only in Britain (and Ireland) is the proportion of foreign-born highest among those with third-level education. If third-level education is taken as a proxy for service class membership, then in Britain to be a member of the service class is to be part of an especially cosmopolitan group in society.

Compared to other countries, therefore, a larger proportion of the British service class is born outside the country. Even more dramatic is the extent of outflow from Britain. The OECD expatriates database shows that there are 3.2

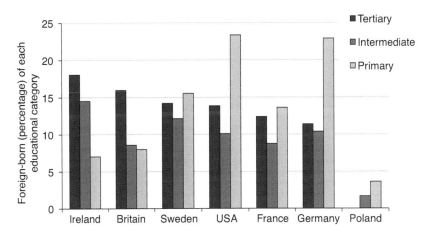

Figure 5.2 Foreign-born as percentage of educational category (early 2000s) (derived from Dumont and Lemaître (2005: Table A4)).

million British expatriates in OECD countries, a number exceeded only by Mexico, more than any other European country and dwarfing India (1.9 million), let alone the USA (a mere 0.8 million). While all Europeans move to the USA in large numbers, only Britain has had large emigration to countries such as Australia. These British expatriates are also especially likely to be highly skilled (defined by the OECD as having completed third-level education). Figure 5.3 shows that nearly 40 per cent of all British expatriates are highly skilled, a larger proportion than from any other European country (US expatriates are even more likely to be highly skilled, but their absolute number is much smaller).

Claims therefore that the European service class *as a whole* is cosmopolitan are exaggerated. If 'cosmopolitan' means mobility beyond the boundaries of the national state, this applies more to Britain than to other European countries, but the British experience is distinctive purely because of the continued importance of old imperial links – both for service class immigration and service class emigration. Even when migration flows within Europe appear as a mutual exchange, they have very different reasons. Thus the number of highly skilled French living in Britain is about the same as the number of equally qualified Britons living in France. However, whereas the French in Britain have been drawn above all to London and to skilled jobs in financial services, the British have moved to France to provide services to the increasing number of British holiday homes.

It is possible that among young adults the situation may be changing: there is some evidence that *in some cities* a European labour market is emerging, partly because there are now no restrictions on the employment of citizens of other EU states. Young European graduates may be moving in greater numbers than before (see Chapter 7) but the careers of their parents have been within a national

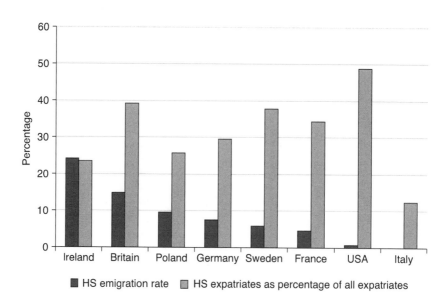

Figure 5.3 High skilled emigration (early 2000s) (derived from Dumont and Lemaître (2005: Tables A4, A6)).

Notes
'High skilled' (HS): all those with tertiary education.
HS emigration rate: HS expatriates as percentage of all domestic-born with tertiary education (no data for Italy).

context and even a local context. Thus, in a study of senior managers in Milan, Paris, Lyon and Madrid most had pursued their careers within the same city, with spells abroad only as a way to advance their career 'back home'. The managers participated in an international world through frequent business travel and intensive electronic communications, but fully 20 per cent of interviewees were actually living in the same neighbourhood of the same city as their own parents (Andreotti *et al.* 2013)! Overall, what is striking is the extent to which, apart from the special case of the UK, service class careers remain national rather than European.

The new service class has been an important theme within British sociology (Bidou-Zachariasen 2000). That is appropriate, because in many ways it is a particularly British phenomenon. Many of the features identified by the discussion are not as salient within the service class of other European countries. The dominance of financial services within the UK service sector (Chapter 2) and changes in corporate governance and firm financing (Chapter 3) all suggest that British enterprises have become more clearly marketocracies than their Continental counterparts. Compared to Scandinavia, but also to France and Germany, the low standards of many state services give the service class a greater incentive to disconnect from the structures of the state. With income inequality greater in the UK, it is hardly surprising that the UK model is attractive to many younger 'professionals' in the rest of Europe, and their desire to emulate their British colleagues has been one reason for the reinvigoration of right-wing political parties across the Continent.

5.4 Globalisation and national business elites

This section examines a particular group within the service class: the managerial elite. The first part shows that while European managers have strikingly similar social origins, there are also clear national differences in how they reached the top. As the second part shows, this especially applied to the role of educational qualifications, so that what was believed to be essential to be a manager in France differed (for example) from Germany or Britain. However, arguably we are only now becoming aware of these differences just when they are being eroded. As the last part of the section shows, European managers are becoming more similar, not because they are becoming 'European', but because they are all becoming more American. Americanisation of management now becomes a move towards greater social inequality.

Social origins and routes to the top

Social studies of 'managers' have to define more closely to whom they are referring. The British term 'senior management' approximates more to the French term *cadres*, the usual translation of 'manager', although the French term has a significance in employment law which the British one lacks. All such managers form part of the service class, out of which climbs the much smaller managerial elite – those who lead the largest companies in Europe. Since some of them are extremely wealthy, they have been to some extent already discussed in Section 4.4, but here the focus is on their occupation rather than their wealth per se. What is striking about the managerial elite is its social homogeneity, compared even to the political, professional or artistic elites.

Studies of the managerial elite gather information (from public sources and sometimes from interviews) on the career and social background of business leaders. Early systematic studies include a comparison of the chief executives of the 200 largest companies in Britain, France and Germany by Bauer and Bertin-Maurot (1999). Similarly Hartmann (2000) studied the most senior managers[8] of the largest 100 companies in France and Germany in both the 1970s and the late 1990s.

Such studies highlighted that until very recently women and members of ethnic minorities have been completely excluded from the European managerial elite. All over Europe, these white male managers still usually come from relatively privileged backgrounds. Thus in one of the first systematic comparative discussions, Lane (1989) focused solely on senior managers of large firms in manufacturing industry in France, Germany and Britain. British and French managers were more likely to come from elite backgrounds than German managers. Below the most senior levels, British managers emerged as more democratically recruited than their colleagues elsewhere. However, one reason for this, which Lane did not consider, was precisely the low social prestige in which manufacturing industry has been held in Britain. By contrast, the high prestige of financial services ('the City') in Britain has long meant that management here is more monopolised by the offspring of the elite groups (Hall 2009). This social inheritance challenges the claim of theorists such as Giddens and Beck that in the post-modern world individuals are loosened from their original milieu. Studies of the managerial elite show it is that precisely those who stress individual achievement most that actually owe it the least.

In the past, most British managers started work without any third-level quali-fication, but this is decreasingly the case. Yet since British undergraduates finish their studies younger than students elsewhere in Europe,[9] British managers are still comparatively young when they enter the workforce. Significantly, Bauer and Bertin-Maurot reported that, of their senior executives, the average age at which the British started in the business world was twenty-two, as against twenty-six in Germany or fully thirty-one in France.

Another key difference is the use of the firm's internal or external labour market. At one extreme, German managers progress almost entirely in the internal labour market of a large company: German managers move up their employing firm's structure but move relatively rarely between firms. German managers therefore have very little experience of other sectors of the large firm economy, let alone of the important *mittelständische* firm sector. At the other extreme, British managers move frequently between firms and indeed between sectors. Career progression involves the external as well as the internal labour market and, conversely, when firms look for managerial recruits they are as likely to recruit from outside as from within their staff. Within the world of work, British managers have a more general experience than managers else-where (see also Hartmann 2009).

The French route is sui generis, with the traditional route to *senior* manage-ment starting with a fast track career in the civil service and a subsequent move across to a senior management post in the private sector (*pantouflage*). Accord-ingly, the state plays a role in the formation of French management that is not found elsewhere in Europe. Given that this career pattern is restricted to senior management, their distinctive career trajectory creates a greater social gap between French senior managers and their immediate subordinates in middle management than is the case in other countries.

Career systems that are based on external labour markets tend to also involve greater pay differentials between senior managers and those whom they manage. More than fifteen years ago, a study cited in the *Financial Times* gave the pay of 'top executives' as a multiple of the pay of 'junior clerks' as follows: Japan ten to fifteen times, Germany fifteen to twenty times, UK twenty to twenty-five, USA forty (Donkin 1999). Today that looks charmingly modest. Already in the 1990s German senior managers pay had been increasing rapidly: 'In the four years between 1996 and 1999 and in the 40 largest German industrial companies, top managers' salaries increased by an average of 66 per cent, plus [*sic*] stock options' (Höpner 2005: 347).

Subsequently senior managers' pay has everywhere been increasing faster than those of ordinary employees. British managers in particular have managed to appropriate an ever greater share of rewards, ensuring that they remain top of the European pecking order. Management pay levels have much to do with the recruitment and reward system in a particular country, and little to do with international differences in 'efficiency' or 'performance'. At the same time, the British managerial elite has become ever more identified with the leading financial service firms of the City of London and their notoriously high salaries and bonuses. Indeed, in France and in Germany, salaries in financial services have been increasing especially fast, with those in international banking increasing fastest of all (Godechot and Fleury 2005).

National qualifications and national careers

For proponents of the knowledge economy, it is self-evident that managerial jobs 'require' educational qualifications. From this view, if educational qualifications are demanded to hold a job, then this shows that they are necessary to actually do the job. An alternative argument already raised in more general terms in Section 2.3 is that educational qualifications are screening devices, and this is quite independent of their actual deployment in the job. Where education is itself understood in terms of its usefulness, then clearly such screening is more likely to be accepted ('legitimate') and the educational qualification can be claimed to be relevant. Across Europe managers have been educated in different sorts of institutions where they gain different types of knowledge. Such knowledge can therefore be seen as a form of legitimation.

One consistent finding of comparative studies is that, compared to their compatriots in all other European countries, British managers have historically had low levels of formal education. Thus Lane (1989) cited several studies, one showing that 24 per cent of British managers were graduates as opposed to about 60 per cent of managers of similar rank in France or (West) Germany. While most of these studies are both relatively old and suffer from problems of definition, Bauer and Bertin-Maurot (1999) reported that the British managers in their study had significantly lower levels of formal education: only 64 per cent had a post-secondary qualification, as opposed to 83 per cent of their French and 88 per cent of their German colleagues.

Britain and France provide two different versions of elite education. Unlike the graduates of French universities, the graduates from France's small number of grandes écoles are assured of the best jobs, especially in the civil service. Accordingly, competition to enter the grandes écoles is fierce, but usually won by those who are themselves from privileged backgrounds. During the 1990s graduates of the grandes écoles actually increased their grip on the leading positions within French business (Hartmann 2000). In Britain, much social selection occurs earlier. Uniquely among major European countries, Britain has a system of private secondary schools separate from the state system. Whereas in the past such schools secured direct entry into the best jobs, now these private schools secure entry to the elite universities. In both France and Britain, privileged parents focus their attention on getting their children access to these elite educational institutions.

By contrast, within German third-level education there is no difference between the universities in terms of social prestige. There are no German universities which are particularly effective at getting their graduates into elite positions, and consequently the offspring of privileged parents are relatively equally distributed across the system. Equally there is no private secondary education and no series of elite secondary schools. Within the school system the reproduction of social privilege occurs through access to Gymnasium (the academically oriented secondary schools) which in turn ensures success in the Abitur (secondary school leaving examination) and entry to university. Since this is a very broad selection, entry to the business elite occurs later, after university.

To the extent that managers do have educational qualifications, these also vary between countries. This was always clear in manufacturing industry. Thus in both Germany and France, senior managers were likely to have an engineering qualification. The education of French managers also had a strong emphasis on science and above all mathematics, for engineering in France is primarily a theoretical discipline, while in Germany engineering has a more applied orientation. In complete contrast, in Britain senior managers in similar industries – if they had any formal third-level qualification at all – were likely to have a qualification in accountancy or even an arts degree (Lane 1989).

Europeanisation and/or globalisation?

The qualification that was needed in order to be a manager thus varied between societies and this was an integral part of national career systems. Today, however, members of the managerial elite share a common educational experience that is shaped by American business schools.

There has been a shift towards business knowledge as part of the formal education of future managers. Subjects such as business studies or management studies have become the norm for degree courses chosen by young people who aspire to a career in management. Conversely, the role of engineering and science (or, in southern Europe, law) as entry qualifications into management has declined. *Betriebswirtschaftslehre* has become more important than engineering as a subject for aspiring German managers. Whereas, in 1970, 31 per cent of the graduates among the chairmen (there were no women) of the top 100 companies had a business degree, already by 1995 this had risen to 40 per cent (calculated from Hartmann 2000). In France, business or management courses have become far more important within the grandes écoles. In the UK the change has been dramatic. A university education has finally become normal for aspiring managers, and at the same time business and management studies are now some of the most popular university degrees. Whereas in the 1960s there were only two business schools in the UK, by the new century there were over 100 and the number of business students had increased from around 1,000 to 156,000 (Tiratsoo 2004).

This business education has itself been increasingly Americanised in terms of content, teaching methods and academic orientation. Management practices and management ideologies have been travelling from the USA to Europe at least since the emergence of Taylorism in the 1920s; the rebuilding of Western Europe through the Marshall Plan also involved a massive imposition of American management techniques, in particular in Germany. Yet although the *Wirtschaftswunder* was popularly associated with American-style management, the period in fact saw the consolidation of *Betriebswirtwissenschaft* as the specific academic education for management and, as we have seen, engineering was considered an appropriate general training for managers (Kieser 2004). In Sweden, business education was originally influenced by German concepts, but American ideas became more powerful after 1945. During the 1970s American influence was probably reduced as specifically Swedish texts were written and the Vietnam War produced a more critical attitude to the USA (Engwall 2004). In other words, it was not just in social policy (see Section 1.4) that the US and Europe diverged in the 1970s.

Since the 1990s, however, the Americanisation of European business education has proceeded apace. By 1997 in the eight oldest Nordic established businesses overall about half of the literature used was American in origin (Engwall 2004). The UK has been at the forefront of this process of Americanisation, aided by the fact that the country had such a limited tradition of academic business education. By contrast, Americanisation was resisted more in France and Germany, where distinctive education for business had developed since the late nineteenth century (Kieser 2004).

The 1990s saw the dramatic growth of the MBA and of business schools as distinct entities within universities – and sometimes outside them. Compared to the rest of European universities, these business schools are standardised, and hence Americanised, using American methods and American texts (Juusola *et al.* 2015). Although EQUIS, the European accreditation for management education, was initially created as an attempt to differentiate European from American business education, it has ended up enforcing the US business school model on European universities. Equally, rankings of business schools such as that of the *Financial Times* ensure that an 'elite' position depends on coming as close to the American ideal as possible (Wedlin 2011).

These changes suggest there is now an international (if strongly Americanised) management culture in Europe. Access to this culture is now facilitated by private universities, and part of the appeal of the few new private universities in southern Europe (such as Bucconi in Milan) is that they can offer business subjects. However, this is not universal: attempts to create private universities in Germany have so far at least been a conspicuous failure. Another route is by accessing fee-paying educational institutions abroad. This is increasingly pronounced at master's level, where British and American universities compete to attract fee-paying students. Another career starting point for the new managerial elite is a job with an international (i.e. American) consultancy company. Indeed, the boundaries between business schools and consultancy companies is becoming increasingly porous. Recruiting elite business graduates, consultancy companies now act as surrogate business schools and as launching pads for careers.

National forms of management education have clearly been eroded, but few of the European managerial elite see their careers as truly transnational. Thus a recent study shows a negligible number of foreigners among the senior management of large French, German, Italian and Spanish companies, and furthermore there is no sign that this has increased over time. A foreign posting, just like some international education, is a career asset, but an asset within a competition that is fought within national boundaries. While 18 per cent of all top managers in the UK are foreigners, this figure falls to 9 per cent in Germany and to only 2 per cent in France (Hartmann 2009). The relative openness of British firms to foreign executives may be related to their greater orientation to shareholder value – a foreigner is less likely to share the domestic managers' commitment to growing the firm and to be more open to short-term gains that can be made by selling assets and business units (Pohlmann and Bär 2009). Once again Britain is a deviant case within Europe, and one that now promotes and legitimates greater social inequality.

Notes

1 In this model 'class' is a name for groups with similar levels and forms of economic, social and cultural capital. As such, a class is not simply an aggregation of occupations. Accordingly, members of the same occupation can be in different social 'classes', although most occupations are concentrated in particular classes.
2 Ironically, while in the 1960s and 1970s reformers in the British Labour Party looked to the German SPD as an example of a 'modern' party, by the 1990s it was the German reformers who attempted to emulate their British counterparts.
3 Despite revisionism, not least by Calder himself, the myth of the Blitz seems to have been quite close to reality (Overy 2013: 177).
4 Significantly, the term first appeared in English-language debates via the policy and research discussions within the European Commission.
5 This study uses European Labour Force Survey data: no data available for Denmark, Finland and Sweden.
6 Notions of service were also generated outside the organisation in education as exemplified by nineteenth-century British 'public' schools.
7 The social networking platform LinkedIn exemplifies this understanding of relationships.
8 *Vorsitzender* (Chairman) in Germany, *PdG – président directeur-géneral* (Chief Executive) in France.
9 Only Ireland has a lower graduation age.

Bibliography

Adonis, A. and Pollard, S. (1997) *A Class Act: The Myth of Britain's Classless Society*, London: Hamish Hamilton.
Andreotti, A. (2006) Coping strategies in a wealthy city of northern Italy, *International Journal of Urban and Regional Research* 30.2: 328–345.

Andreotti, A., Le Galès, P. and Moreno Fuentes, F. (2013) Transnational mobility and rootedness: the upper middle classes in European cities, *Global Networks* 13.1: 41–59.

Arthur, M. (1994) The boundaryless career: a new perspective for organizational inquiry, *Journal of Organizational Behavior* 15.4: 295–306.

Baccaro, L. and Howell, C. (2011) A common neoliberal trajectory: the transformation of industrial relations in advanced capitalism, *Politics and Society* 39.4: 521–563.

Bauer, M. and Bertin-Mourot, B. (1999) National models for making and legitimating elites, *European Societies* 1.1: 9–31.

Beaud, S. and Masclet, O. (2006) Des 'marcheurs' de 1983 aux 'émeutiers' de 2005: deux générations sociales d'enfants d'immigrés, *Annales. Histoire, Sciences Sociales* 61: 809–843.

Beaud, S. and Pialoux, M. (2003) *Violence urbaines, violence sociale: Genèse des nouvelles classes dangereurses*, Paris: Fayard.

Bernaciak, M., Gumbrell-McCormick, R. and Hyman, R. (2014) *European Trade Unionism: From Crisis to Renewal?* Brussels: ETUI. Report 133.

Betz, H.-G. (2013) *The New Front National: Still a Master Case?* RECODE working paper series online no. 30, www.recode.info/wp-content/uploads/2014/01/Final-RECODE-30-Hans-Georg-Betz_Final_fin.pdf. Accessed 27 October 2015.

Betz, H.-G. and Meret, S. (2013) Right wing populist parties and the working class vote: what have you done for us lately? In J. Rydren (ed.) *Class Politics and the Radical Right*, London: Routledge, pp. 107–121.

Bidou-Zachariasen, C. (2000) À propos de la 'service class': les classes moyennes dans la sociologie britannique, *Revue Française de Sociologie* 41.4: 777–796.

Bihagen, E. and Halleröd, B. (2000) The crucial aspects of class: an empirical assessment with Swedish data, *Work Employment and Society* 14.2: 397–330.

Blanden, J., Gregg, P. and Machin, S. (2005) *Intergenerational Mobility in Europe and North America: A Report Supported by the Sutton Trust*, London: Centre for Economic Performance.

Buzar, S., Ogden, P., Hall, R., Haase, A., Kabisch, S. and Steinfiihrer, A. (2007) Splintering urban populations: emergent landscapes of reurbanisation in four European cities, *Urban Studies* 44.4: 651–677.

Calder, A. (1969) *The People's War: Britain 1939–45*, London: Panther.

Collinson, D. and Collinson, M. (1997) 'Delayering managers': time–space surveillance and its gendered effects, *Organization* 4.3: 375–407.

Crompton, R. (2008) *Class and Stratification: An Introduction to Current Debates*, Cambridge: Polity Press (first edition 1993).

Crouch, C. and Pizzorno, A. (eds) (1978) *The Resurgence of Class Conflict in Western Europe since 1968, Volume 1*, London: Macmillan.

Culpepper, P. and Regan, A. (2014) Why don't governments need trade unions any more? The death of social pacts in Ireland and Italy, *Socio-Economic Review* 12.4: 723–745.

de Witte, M. and Steijn, B. (2000) Automation, job content and underemployment, *Work Employment and Society* 14.2 (June): 245–264.

Dench, G., Gavron, K. and Young, M. (2006) *The New East End: Kinship, Race and Conflict*, London: Profile.

Dikec, M. (2007) *Badlands of the Republic: Space, Politics and Urban Policy*, Oxford: Blackwell.

Donkin, R. (1999). Riches for the few: share incentives are widening the pay gap between the top and the bottom, *Financial Times*, 24 February.

Dörre, K., Scherschel, K. and Booth, M. (2013) *Bewährungsproben für die Unterschicht? Soziale Folgen aktivierender Arbeitsmarktpolitik*, Frankfurt: Campus.

Dumont, J.-C. and Lemaître, G. (2005) *Counting Immigrants and Expatriates in OECD Countries: A New Perspective*. OECD Social, Employment and Migration Working Papers, No. 25, Paris: OECD Publishing.

Dunford, M. and Greco, L. (2006). *After the Three Italies: Wealth, Inequality and Industrial Change*, Oxford: Blackwell.

Ebbinghaus, B. and Visser, J. (1999) When institutions matter: union growth and decline in Europe, 1950–1995, *European Sociological Review* 15.2: 135–158.

Edwards, R. (1979) *Contested Terrain: The Transformation of the Workplace in the Twentieth Century*, London: Heinemann.

Engwall, L. (2004) The Americanisation of Nordic management education, *Journal of Management Inquiry* 13.2 (June): 109–117.

Erikson, R. and Goldthorpe, J. (1992) *The Constant Flux: A Study of Class Mobility in Industrial Societies*, Oxford: Clarendon Press.

Esping-Andersen, G. (1999) *Social Foundations of Post-Industrial Economies*, Oxford: Oxford UP.

Eurofound (2012) *NEETs – Young People not in Employment Education or Training*, Luxembourg: Publications Office of the European Union.

European Commission (2014) *Single Parents and Employment in Europe*, Short Statistical Report No. 3, Cambridge: Rand Europe.

Florida, R. (2004) *The Rise of the Creative Class*, New York: Basic Books.

Freeman, R. (1996) Why do so many young American men commit crimes and what might we do about it? *Journal of Economic Perspectives* 10.1: 25–42.

Gallie, D. (1995) Are the unemployed an underclass? Some evidence from the social change and economic life initiative, *Sociology* 28.3: 737–759.

Gershuny, J. (2005) Busyness as the badge of honour for the new superordinate working class, *Social Research* 72.2: 287–314.

Giddens, A. (2007) *Europe in the Global Age*, Cambridge: Polity Press.

Godechot, O. and Fleury, C. (2005) Les nouvelles inégalités dans la banque, *Connaissance de l'emploi* 17 (June).

Goldthorpe, J. (1982) On the service class, its formation and future. In A. Giddens and G. MacKenzie (eds) *Social Class and the Division of Labour*, Cambridge: Cambridge UP, pp. 162–185.

Goodhart, D. (2013) *The British Dream: Successes and Failures of Post-war Immigration*, London: Atlantic Books.

Grainger, H. and Crowther, M. (2007) *Trade Union Membership 2006*. London: Department of Trade and Industry.

Gregson, N. and Lowe, M. (1993) *Servicing the Middle Classes: Class, Gender and Waged Domestic Labour in Britain in the 1980s and 1990s*, London: Routledge.

Hall, D. (2012) *Working Lives: The Forgotten Voices of Britain's Post-war Working Class*, London: Bantam.

Hall, S. (2009) Financialised elites and the changing nature of finance capitalism: investment bankers in London's financial district, *Competition and Change* 13.2: 173–199.

Hanley, L. (2012) *Estates: An Intimate History*, London: Granta.

Hanlon, G. (1997) Commercialising the service class and economic restructuring – a reply to my critics, *Accounting, Organizations and Society* 22.8: 843–855.

Hartmann, M. (2000) Class specific habitus and the social reproduction of the business elite in Germany and France, *Sociological Review* 48.2 (May): 241–261.

Hartmann, M. (2009) Die transnationale Klasse – Mythos oder Realität? *Soziale Welt* 60.3: 285–303.

Höpner, M. (2005) What connects industrial relations and corporate governance? Explaining institutional complementarity, *Socio-economic Review* 3.2: 331–358.

Hondagneu-Sotelo, P. (2001) *Domestica: Immigrant Workers Cleaning and Caring in the Shadows of Affluence*, Berkeley: University of California Press.

ILO (2013) *Domestic Workers across the World: Global and Regional Statistics and the Extent of Legal Protection*, Geneva: ILO.

Jones, O. (2012) *Chavs: The Demonization of the Working Class*, London: Verso.

Juusola, K., Kettunen, K. and Alajoutsijärvi, K. (2015) Accelerating the Americanization of management education: five responses from business schools, *Journal of Management Inquiry* doi: 10.1177/1056492615569352.

Kesselring, S. and Vogl, G. (2010). *Betriebliche Mobilität*, Berlin: Edition Sigma.

Kieser, A. (2004) The Americanization of academic management education in Germany, *Journal of Management Inquiry* 13.2: 90–97.

Kirkness, P. (2014) The cités strike back: restive responses to territorial taint in the French banlieus, *Environment and Planning A* 46.6: 1281–1296.

Lane, C. (1989) *Management and Labour in Europe*, Aldershot: Gower.

Lash, S. (1994) The making of an underclass: neo-liberalism versus corporatism. In P. Brown and R. Crompton (eds) *Economic Restructuring and Social Exclusion*, London: Routledge, pp. 156–174.

Levy, F. (1999) *The New Dollars and Dreams: American Incomes in the Late 1990s*, New York: Russell Sage Foundation.

Lutz, H. (2002) Die neue Dienstmädchenfrage im Zeitalter der Globalisierung. In K. Gottschall and B. Pfau-Effinger (eds) *Zukunft der Arbeit und Geschlecht*, Opladen: Leske and Budrich, pp. 161–192.

McDowell, L., Ward, K., Perrons, D., Ray, K. and Fagan, C. (2006) Place, class and local circuits of reproduction: exploring the social geography of middle class childcare, *Urban Studies* 43.12: 2163–2182.

Mahroum, S. (2000) High skilled globetrotters: mapping the international migration of human capital, *R&D Management* 30.1: 23–30.

Marquand, D. (2004) *Decline of the Public: The Hollowing-out of Citizenship*, Cambridge: Polity Press.

Martin, B. and Wajcman, J. (2004) Markets, contingency and preferences: contemporary managers' narrative identities, *Sociological Review* 52.2: 240–264.

Mellini, L., Yodanis, C. and Godenzi, A. (2007) 'On par'? The role of the au pair in Switzerland and France, *European Societies* 9.1: 45–64.

Moran, M. (2012) *The Republic and the Riots*, Frankfurt: Peter Lang.

Murray, C. (1984) *Losing Ground: American Social Policy 1950–1980*, New York: Basic Books.

Ocqueteau, F. (2007) Les émeutes urbaines de l'automne 2005: cadres d'analyse et points aveugles de la sociologie française, *Sociologie du Travail* 49: 531–543.

Offer, A. (2008) British manual workers: from producers to consumers, *Contemporary British History* 22.4: 537–571.

Overy, R. (2013) *The Bombing War: Europe 1939–45*, London: Allen Lane.

Parkin, F. (1972) *Class Inequality and Political Order*, London: Paladin.

Paterson, W. (2000) From the Bonn to the Berlin Republic, *German Politics* 9.1: 23–40.

Petit, B. and Western, B. (2004) Mass imprisonment and the life course: race and class inequality in US incarceration, *American Sociological Review* 69.2: 151–169.

Pohlmann, M. and Bär, S. (2009) Grenzenlose Karrieren? Hochqualifiziertes Personal und Top-Führungskräfte in Ökonomie und Medizin, *Österreichische Zeitschrift für Soziologie* 34.4: 13–40.

Power, A. (1997) *Estates on the Edge: The Social Consequences of Mass Housing in Northern Europe*, London: Macmillan.

Putnam, R. (2015) *Our Kids: The American Dream in Crisis*, New York: Simon & Schuster.

Reich, R. (1993) *The Work of Nations: Preparing Ourselves for 21st Century Capitalism*, London: Simon & Schuster.

Sala Pala, V. (2011) Quand des jeunes d'un quartier populaire interprètent les émeutes urbaines. In S. Béroud, B. Gobille, A. Hajjat and M. Zancarini-Fournel (eds) *Engagements, rebellions et genre dans les quartiers populaires en Europe (1968–2005)*, Paris: Editions des archives contemporaines, pp. 43–58.

Salt, J. (1997) *International Movements of the Highly Skilled*, Occasional Paper no. 3, Paris: OECD International Migration Unit.

Savage, M., (2000) *Class Analysis and Social Transformation*, Buckingham: Open University Press.

Savage, M., Bagnall, G. and Longhurst, B. (2005) *Globalisation and Belonging*, London: Sage.

Savage, M., Devine, F., Cunningham, N., Taylor, M., Li, Y., Hjellbrekke, J., le Roux, B., Friedman, S. and Miles, A. (2013) A new model of social class? Findings from the BBCs Great British Class Survey experiment, *Sociology* 47.2: 219–250.

Schmidt, T. (2006) Reden über die Unbenennbaren, *Die Zeit*, 19 October.

Stébé, J.-M. (2009) *La crise des banlieus: sociologie des quartiers sensibles*, Paris: PUF.

Streeck, W. (2013) *Gekaufte Zeit: Die vertagte Krise des demokratischen Kapitalismus*, Berlin: Suhrkamp.

Tiratsoo, N. (2004) The 'Americanization' of management education in Britain, *Journal of Management Inquiry* 13.2: 118–127.

Todd, S. (2014) *The People: The Rise and Fall of the Working Class 1910–2010*, London: John Murray.

Treadwell, J., Briggs, D., Winlow, S. and Hall, S. (2013) Shopocalypse now: consumer culture and the English riots of 2011, *British Journal of Criminology* 53.1: 1–17.

Tyler, I. (2013) The riots of the underclass? Stigmatisation, mediation and the government of poverty and disadvantage in neoliberal Britain, *Sociological Research Online* 18.4: 6.

Uggen, C. and Manza, J. (2002) Democratic contraction? Political consequences of felon disenfranchisement in the United States, *American Sociological Review* 67 (December): 777–803.

Visser, J. (2013) *Data Base on Institutional Characteristics of Trade Unions, Wage Setting, State Intervention and Social Pacts, 1960–2011 (ICTWSS) Version 4.0*, Amsterdam: Amsterdam Institute for Advanced Labour Studies.

Wacquant, L. (1996) Red belt, black belt: racial division, class inequality and the state in the French urban periphery and the American ghetto. In E. Mingione (ed.) *Urban Poverty and the Underclass*, Oxford: Blackwell, pp. 234–274.

Wacquant, L. (2008) *Urban Outcasts: Towards a Sociology of Advanced Marginality*, Cambridge: Polity Press.

Wedlin, L. (2011) Going global: rankings as rhetorical devices to construct an international field of management education, *Management Learning* 42.2: 199–218.

Western, B. (2005) *Punishment and Inequality in America*, New York: Russell Sage Foundation.

Wickham, J. and Vecchi, A. (2010) Hierarchies in the air: varieties of business travel. In J. Beaverstock, B. Derudder, J. Faulconbridge and F. Witlox (eds) *International Business Travel in the Global Economy*, Farnham: Ashgate, pp. 125–143.

Wilson, W. (1987) *The Truly Disadvantaged: The Inner City, the Underclass and Public Policy*, Chicago: Chicago UP.

Wilson, W. (1996) *When Work Disappears: The World of the New Urban Poor*, New York: Knopf.

Wilson, W. (2003) Race, class and urban poverty: a rejoinder, *Ethnic and Racial Studies* 26.6: 1096–1114.

Young, M. and Wilmott, P. (1956) Social grading by manual workers, *British Journal of Sociology* 7.4: 337–345.

6 Spatial inequality

Europe of the regions

Europe is not just a *Europe des patries* but also a 'Europe of the regions' or even perhaps a 'Europe of the cities'. One objective of the European Union has always been to enable poorer regions to 'catch up', so regional inequality is a test of the effectiveness of European policies and the European social model. Indeed, the term 'cohesion' first appears in European policy in relation to inequality between rich and poor areas of Europe. Unlike other free trade areas such as NAFTA, the European Union has policies and resources to create this cohesion: the expansion of the European market has involved the expansion of European institutions. This in turn means that European institutions are partly concerned with regions as well as member states.

The rationale for such regionalism is partly the extent of spatial inequality within member states. If the unit of analysis is the region rather than the state, then rich states have poor regions. Thus in Italy, the Mezzogiorno (the south) has always been part of the underdeveloped European 'periphery', while northern Italy has been part of the rich 'core'. Within the UK, there is a contrast between the rich south-east and the old nineteenth-century industrial areas of the north. In Germany, regional inequalities between the prosperous south and the declining industrial area of the Ruhr have now been heightened by the problems of the new *Länder* of the former DDR (East Germany).

Comparing regional differences in Italy and Britain shows there are two different types of 'poor' areas: the rural regions that never industrialised at all (e.g. the Mezzogiorno) and those regions which industrialised in the nineteenth century and have now been left behind (e.g. northern England). The rich regions also differ. In Italy the richest region is now the north-east around Bologna, where economic growth is recent and based primarily on small enterprises. In Britain the wealthy south-east focuses on London, a capital city and a long-established international financial centre. Each of these four types of region (traditional rural, old industrial, growth pole, world city) forms one part of this chapter.

6.1 EU policy and lagging regions

The original six members of the European Union all had broadly similar living standards. Furthermore, they were all part of the core of Western Europe which had industrialised in broadly similar ways at the end of the nineteenth century. However, as the Union has grown, it has become less homogenous. Whole states have joined which are significantly poorer than the existing members and, at the same time, enlargement has highlighted regional differences within some member states.

In 1973, in the first enlargement, Britain, Ireland and Denmark joined the then EEC (see Section 1.1). Their membership confirmed the EU as a rich countries' club. Although Ireland was poorer than the other countries, it was too small to change the nature of the EU and too weak to force any major change in EU policy. However, with the accession of the southern countries (Greece in 1981, Spain and Portugal in 1986) the situation changed dramatically. Inequalities between states now became a major issue and in 1993 the 'Cohesion Fund' was created. The need to transfer resources from the rich to the poor member states was confirmed in the next enlargement when Austria, Finland and Sweden joined the EU in 1995. These new members were wealthy (relative to the rest of the EU), so there were now more resources available for redistribution. At the same time their strong social democratic traditions made them receptive to claims for 'solidarity' between the member states. During the 1990s the poorer member states were catching up with the rest of the EU in purely economic terms. Spain in particular showed how in the space of thirty years a poor country on the periphery of Europe could become integrated into the overall European economy.

The enlargements of 2004 and 2006 might appear more problematic. Taken together, the population of the twelve new member states is significantly larger than that of the countries that joined with the Mediterranean enlargement of the 1980s (approximately 100 million as against about sixty million). Like the Mediterranean countries before them, the new member states bring a large and relatively poor population into the Union. More important is that the political and economic climate has changed. The traditional core member states of the Union, France and Germany, are now less willing to support transfers to poorer 'foreign' regions. The political elites of Europe have shown little interest in proclaiming the benefits of a larger and more cohesive Europe. Enlargement has changed regional policy, but overall has probably meant that it has become *less* important.

For those countries that comprised the EU15 the long-term overall experience has been of converging living standards. However, disparities within countries have been more obstinate. Within the EU itself, regional disparities measured purely in terms of regional GNP per capita decreased somewhat in the 1970s, but most of the evidence suggests that within the EU15 regional inequalities remained constant during the 1980s. During the 1990s, however, regional inequalities again began to narrow, at least within those countries that had joined before the 1990s (Cappelen *et al.* 2003). EU regional policy has had some success.

Creating cohesion through the market or against the market?

Before the advent of the EU, European states tried to reduce regional inequalities within their boundaries. British regional policy dates back to the Depression of the 1930s with the 1934 Distressed Areas Act (Stevenson 1984: 270). Around the same time, Mussolini's government began the first serious attempt to tackle the underdevelopment of the Italian south. In Ireland attempts to develop the poorer areas go as far back as the Congested Districts Board, created by the British government in the late nineteenth century.

As opposed to such state interventionism, expanding the market was central to the original European project: the removal of trade barriers was assumed to ensure economic convergence between European states and regions. However, from the very beginning it was recognised that some would lose out from this process. The Treaty of Rome thus also created the European Social Fund to facilitate the adaptation of workers to industrial change. The contrast to the North American Free Trade Area (NAFTA) created nearly fifty years later is striking. Whereas NAFTA simply aims to remove barriers to trade, even when the European Union was only an aspirant 'common market', it contained new institutions and funds to compensate for the workings of the market.

The EU regional funds are one way in which EU institutions reach below the level of the nation state. Since the 1988 reforms funding has involved an enhanced role for sub-national government and in particular 'European' concepts of partnership between the social partners, civil society organisations, local government and the European Commission. EU regional policy is thus a clear case of multi-level governance, where within a specific policy area EU institutions and spending create a situation where sub-national actors are not only more important, but can by-pass national institutions. The impact was probably greatest in Ireland, where a developing national practice of social partnership interlocked with the expansion of EU funding (Bache and Olsson 2001). In Ireland EU funds did not just mean 'more money', they contributed to institutional and even ideological change. Equally in Britain, EU regional funding strengthened the opposition of Labour controlled local authorities to the neo-liberal Thatcher government (Hooghe 1998). At the other extreme, the expenditure of social funds in Greece and southern Italy seem to have made no difference to existing ineffective and bureaucratic local administrations.

Arguably the high point of the influence of EU regional funds has now passed. Compared to the expenditure of the 1990s, the eastern enlargement has involved no great expansion of the entire cohesion funding budget. Today it is assumed that economic growth will occur in these regions through the privatisation of state enterprises and the 'deregulation' of the labour market, rather than through European funding on social and physical infrastructure. As the ideology of the Commission shifts away from notions of rights to notions of competitiveness, in regional policy there is less and less belief in a specific 'European' approach to regional inequality. There is a diminished focus on social partnership and less ambition to build civil society institutions as part of the regional process of development.

Agricultural change and traditional rural areas

The Common Agricultural Policy (CAP) was one of the central features of the original European Economic Community and until very recently the largest component of the European budget. Because CAP funds flow to rural areas, it has been a regional policy in disguise.

Historically the subsidy of European farmers has been justified because farmers have been seen as embodying national virtues: the real France is the France of the countryside, *la France profonde*. More prosaically, in the post-World War II period farmers were a key electoral basis for Christian democracy in France, Germany and Italy. CAP Europeanised this political support, moving protection (and subsidy) from the national to the European level. Since the core of CAP was production-based subsidies, it ensured that while the small farmers provided the votes, the richer farmers – at first the grain farmers of the Île de France, then the large landowners of East Anglia – made the largest gains. CAP redistributed income from urban consumers to rural producers – especially the largest and most affluent ones.

Once Britain with its historic cheap food policy had joined the EEC pressure to 'reform' the CAP was bound to increase. It was, however, not until the 1990s that the process of reform began: the proposals of Commissioner MacSharry in 1991, the 'Agenda 2000' changes of 2000 and finally those of Commissioner Fischler in 2003 (Chari and Kritzinger 2006: 133ff.). The main objective was to bring European agriculture into line with global production and prices. However, at the same time environmentalists criticised the 'productionist' agricultural regime with its reliance on high fertiliser input and the deliberate undermining of traditional practices. Last but not least, the farm population continued to decline (see Chapter 2) and the rural vote became less important.

Today prices for most agricultural products are in line with world market prices. Support payments to farmers have been 'decoupled' from actual production and thus are essentially a form of social welfare. At the same time there is increased funding for rural development and for the maintenance of the rural environment (Matthews 2015). These changes appeared to open new possibilities for peripheral rural areas. 'Marginal' or 'inefficient' farms could now gain a commercial value from those same 'traditional' methods that had previously been seen as a problem. Turning small farmers into the custodians of the countryside is, however, problematic. Although local traditions do have, to some extent, to be constructed, some raw material is more amenable than others. A traditional dish among poor farmers in northern Sweden, for example, was simply bread soaked in lard, but this is impossible to market to consumers searching for a natural dining experience in new 'traditional' restaurants (Tellstrom *et al.* 2005). Thus it is affluent Austria that has the highest level of organic farming in the EU. In Austria and Italy, increasingly consumers try to assuage their worries about food quality by using locally produced food, but 'local' probably means Tuscany rather than Calabria (Sassatelli and Scott 2001). Much seems to depend on the national context, as shown by the contrast between the success of Irish agriculture in recent decades and the continued failure of Greek agriculture to fulfil its potential.

The EU's acceptance of the principle of free trade in agriculture is now moving most European agriculture towards mass production for a globalised market. This means that European food will increasingly become like the processed food of the USA, where the farmer receives a smaller share of the final product than in Europe. As in Ireland in recent years, some areas may well develop speciality organic and environmentally friendly farming for consumer niches. However, many small farmers from the poorer areas are unlikely to be able to participate profitably in either form of production. Because CAP moved a key element of national budgets to the European level it has been a central component of European integration. At the same time political conflicts over the policy have threatened the entire European project while current policy may well undermine key elements of European identity.

Industrialising the periphery

Fifty years ago the Republic of Ireland and southern Italy (the Mezzogiorno) were 'backward' agricultural areas. Since the 1950s there have been determined attempts to industrialise both regions. Today the Republic of Ireland is one of the success stories of the EU, while the Mezzogiorno, despite some signs of progress, remains one of the poorest areas of the 'old' EU.

Since the end of World War II the Italian state has been attempting to develop the south. From the 1950s onwards the Italian state compelled the large state-owned companies to invest in the south; close relations to the state ensured that they were followed by the car industry. The result was a series of large industrial complexes in cities where previously there had been virtually no industry at all. Key examples included a petrochemical plant in Brindisi, steelworks in Taranto and FIAT's car assembly in Melfi (Dunford and Greco 2007). Until the late 1980s these did create some regular and relatively well paid jobs, but with little other connection to the local economy they became known as 'cathedrals in the deserts'. There has also been extensive investment in infrastructure. The Cassa per il Mezzogiorno was created in 1950 (Dunford and Greco 2006: 87) and funded substantial investment in roads (the Autostrada del Sole), and also in water, telecommunications, etc. Subsequently this has been followed by significant European Union funds. Nonetheless such investment was often ineffective and many large projects remained uncompleted. At its worst this simply created more resources for the Mafia to appropriate and for clientelist politicians to disburse. Comparing differing areas of Italy, Putnam *et al.* (1993) claimed that the failure of investment in the south to generate growth was the result of the region's weak civic institutions, low levels of trust and consequent low *social capital*. The clientelist politics of the south undermine such social capital (Trigilia 2012).

Another form of infrastructure is human capital. Money spent on education, training and research is investment if it enhances the productivity of labour.

Accordingly, one element of industrialisation strategy is to create a more skilled labour force. Much depends both on the content of education and training, and on the institutional connections between the educational institutions and the economy. In Ireland, and to a lesser extent in Portugal, EU funds were used to upgrade the educational system in a way that appears to have be economically relevant. Thus from the 1980s there was a dramatic expansion of sub-degree third-level education in the Regional Technical Colleges (now renamed Institutes of Technology) ensuring that the country had a plentiful supply of technicians; the universities increased their output of engineers and business graduates (Wickham and Boucher 2004). By contrast, in Italy students stay longer in education in the south, but this is largely in order to avoid unemployment.

Since 1956 the Republic of Ireland has been committed to 'industrialisation by invitation': it has attempted to industrialise by enticing foreign firms to create operations in Ireland, but selling to foreign markets. By the 1970s Irish exports were already no longer primarily basic agricultural products (especially live cattle) for the British market, but were manufactured goods exported to the (then) EEC. Irish exports then became increasingly technologically intensive with a growing concentration in pharmaceutical and above all computer manufacturing. The policy was so successful that: 'For most of the 1980s Ireland was the world's second largest exporter of computers, in some years accounting for more than a quarter of all countries' exports of computers' (O'Gorman *et al.* 1997: 1).

Building on this success, Ireland then managed to attract multinational software firms, so that by the mid-1990s Ireland was the world's second largest software exporter and produced more than 50 per cent of all software packages sold in Europe for personal computers (O'Gorman *et al.* 1997: 1). By 2001 employment in 'high technology' services and manufacturing made up a larger proportion of total employment in Ireland than in the EU15 as a whole (Wickham and Boucher 2004). While some of this high tech manufacturing has now relocated to lower wage areas of Europe (Dell closed its Limerick plant and moved production to Poland in 2009), FDI now includes logistics, service support, and even European or regional headquarters. A cluster of high profile US software and internet firms are now located in Ireland. Google now employs over 2,000 people in its European headquarters in Dublin at the centre of a fashionably renovated dockland area (Newenham 2015).

One clear reason for Ireland's success in attracting FDI is clearly that foreign companies have long been subject to very low tax rates. Whereas traditionally foreign firms located in Ireland partly for the low tax on their operations *in Ireland*, high profile American software and internet firms use their Irish operations as a mechanism for ensuring low tax on their operations *across the globe* (Stewart 2014). For example; 'Google's operation in Ireland recorded revenues of €15.5 billion, on which it paid Irish corporation tax of €17 million' (*Irish Times* 2014).

Ireland's success has depended on obtaining a very large share of total foreign investment available in Europe. Any successful emulation by 'competitors' such as the new member states of Eastern Europe will ensure that Ireland's own share is going to diminish. Scooping the lion's share of foreign investment has increasingly depended on tax competition (as well as interpreting EU employment legislation in a way that is acceptable to US employers). Increasingly the larger European countries who contributed so generously through structural funds to Ireland in the 1990s are finding their own tax base eroded as Ireland refuses to countenance any harmonisation of corporate taxation. From being a conduit through which American computers reach Europe, Ireland has become a part of the neo-liberal onslaught on the European model.

6.2 Rustbelt Europe: South Wales to the Ruhr

More than eighty years ago, some of the areas that had been at the core of Europe's initial industrialisation began to be abandoned as new industries developed elsewhere. By the last two decades of the twentieth century in Europe the 'regional problem' was defined by the final collapse of employment in the boom industries of the late nineteenth century: coal, iron and steel, heavy engineering (shipbuilding). These final spasms have been overlaid by the much larger employment losses in manufacturing itself, so that some of the more recent industrial cities of the fordist period have also entered crisis. This section focuses primarily on the more traditional areas. They have a distinctive social structure and are also distinctive politically. If they have a common past, they have divergent futures, for the extent to which economic life is being rebuilt in these areas depends massively on national policy and regional institutional structures, and these vary across Europe.

The social structure of de-industrialisation

By the end of the nineteenth century areas such as the Ruhr in Germany, the Pas de Calais in northern France, South Wales and the Central Belt of Scotland were the centres of European industrialisation. Here rapid employment growth meant these were zones of massive immigration, which often restructured the ethnic as well as the class structure. For example in the 1840s Bochum in the Ruhr was a small town of about 4,000 inhabitants; by 1907 Bochum was an industrial city of 120,000 (Crew 1980: 70). The population came first from the region and then increasingly from the largely Polish areas of the Kaiserreich. Up until World War I Polish trade unions were important in the Ruhr, and Polish family names are still common in the Ruhr today. Equally, language change in the coal-mining valleys of Wales was partly because of the in-migration of English speakers.

In the inter-war period industries such as coal mining remained essential parts of the European economy and in the first years after the end of World War II production expanded to meet the demands of reconstruction. Especially in the Ruhr the 1950s were once again boom years. Soon, however, jobs were again being lost because of technological and organisational change, and then from the 1970s onwards European heavy industries began to be overwhelmed by global competition. Until well into the 1980s Europe's electricity came largely from coal-fired power stations. Then European coal was partly replaced by new energy sources (gas, nuclear), and partly by much cheaper coal imported from the global market.

At the start of the last century coal mining was one of the single largest occupations; coal miners dominated whole regions. In 1920 employment in the South Wales coal mines was well over a quarter of a million (at a time when the total population of Wales as a whole was only just over two million). Other industries were more important in the Ruhr, but here too coal mining shaped the landscape and the culture: the *Ruhrgebiet* (the Ruhr) is colloquially still known as the *Ruhrpott* (the Ruhr mine). As Table 2.1 shows, the dramatic pit closures in the 1980s were only the end of a much longer process of decline which effectively lasted for most of the century. Coal mining has lasted longer in Germany than elsewhere, but even in the Ruhr coal mining as such has ceased (although there are some new strip mines).

In some areas traditional industries gained a new lease of life in the long boom because they were able to utilise immigrant labour: what had once been well paid factory jobs became some of the lowest paid in the country. In the fordist period immigrants went to new car plants but also to the old textile mills, as in Bradford in England. The foreign-born population of the Ruhr also grew, where many Turkish immigrants found jobs in heavy industry. By contrast, north-east England simply declined, so that it is now one of the most ethnically homogenous areas of Britain.

The decline was most dramatic where there was no alternative employment at all. Thus in the pit villages of Yorkshire the entire economy – and much of people's identity – revolved around the mine. With no replacement jobs, families moved from depending on the man's well paid regular employment to a mixture of social welfare benefits and low paid jobs (often taken by women). Gender roles were undermined and even reversed; the traditional authority of the police and trade union collapsed. Such changes were traumatic and scarred a whole generation (Dicks *et al.* 1993; Waddington and Parry 2003).

From working class culture to dependency culture?

In these areas the class structure was polarised. On the one side there were local magnates, the owners of the coal mines and steel mills, on the other side the workers, all employees of a few large companies. Unlike in most areas even of pre-World War II Europe, social groups in between the two large battalions of capital and labour were here either small or non-existent: few professionals and even few clerical workers. Add to this work the distinctive work culture of coal mining, and there was a recipe for 'class consciousness'.

These areas were therefore unusual, but for that very reason they became one core of the European labour movement. Near the northern French coal field, Lille was France's first socialist municipality in 1884. In Germany the *Ruhrgebiet* had a long tradition of class conflict: in the *Ruhraufstand* (Ruhr rising) of

March 1920 workers' militias had controlled the Ruhr and fought pitched battles against the right-wing Freikorps; later in the Weimar Republic the Ruhr was one of the centres of the German Communist Party, the KPD. In such regions smaller towns could be almost one-class societies and sometimes became 'Little Moscows', 'red' bastions controlled by the Communist Party (MacIntyre 1980).

In the immediate post-World War II period the political parties of the left and the trade unions consolidated their position in the heavy industrial districts of Europe. In the Ruhr by the 1950s the SPD and the trade unions were stronger than ever before. In these regions, working class cultural organisations (epitomised by the singing and sporting 'workers' clubs' of Germany) lasted longer than elsewhere. Not only were manual workers more likely to vote left than elsewhere, but there was a spill-over effect with members of other social classes also being more likely to vote for left-wing parties.

This political strength made viable a political strategy which focused on protecting the existing industrial basis of the regions. Thus European coal miners, just like European farmers, campaigned for protection, even though no traditional deep coal-mining industry could compete on equal terms in the world market. Unlike European farmers, however, European coal miners could hardly be turned into custodians of the environment nor, despite the transformation of coal mines into heritage sites (see below), into guardians of the national culture.

Yet the political strength of the old institutions prevented any development of an alternative strategy, especially in France and Britain, where trade unions have no tradition of involvement in strategic policy and no conception, unlike their German and Swedish counterparts, of accepting and steering economic change. Because this protectionist policy used the institutions of the national state, it heightened these regions' dependency on the existing national state. According to some scholars, in areas like the Ruhr the close links between firms and other regional institutions, which had been a source of regional strength in the past, now became obstacles to innovation (Hassink 2007). However, as we shall now see, in the German political context, the institutional structure of the Ruhr in fact has contributed to extensive social change in the region over the last decades. Indeed, a comparative study of three coal-mining areas (the Ruhr, north-east England and Asturias in Spain) ascribed the success of the Ruhr area to its common culture, the institutional 'thickness' of the region, and the tradition of action-oriented consensus (Critcher *et al.* 1999).

Varieties of regions, varieties of nations

From the 1960s onwards, government policy in the Ruhr has been interventionist and proactive, accepting the long-term decline of the region's traditional industries and taking measures to develop alternatives. In the 1960s the programme 'blue skies over the Ruhr' was one of Europe's early attempts to clean up the environmental damage of the first industrial revolution (not surprisingly, the Ruhr is now a centre of environmental engineering expertise). Rather than waiting for the coal mines to close, as in Britain, state policies retrained coal miners while they were still in employment.

Most dramatic of all has been the concerted drive to transform the Ruhr into an educational centre. Until 1965 there was not a single university in the Ruhr. Now there are four universities (Bochum, Essen, Dortmund and Duisburg), a network of *Fachhochschulen* (applied universities) and Germany's national distance education university at Hagen. And these universities have increasingly close links with local enterprises, with local public authorities and with organisations of business such as the *Industrie- und Handelskammer* (chamber of commerce) at city level.

Just as in rural areas, tourism and the heritage industry are other possible bases for economic growth. In the Ruhr, not just the Jugendstil Zeche Zollern (built around 1900), but also the enormous the Bauhaus-style pithead buildings of Zeche Zollverein XII (Zollverein Pit XII) near Dortmund are museums, the latter indeed now a UNESCO world heritage site. In this way, the region begins to import tourists to examine the basis of its previous export industry. Old coal miners become tourist guides to their previous workplaces. Built in the early 1930s, the Zollverein pithead has been recycled into a museum after little more than fifty years.

Heritage has now fed into the more general strategy of culture as a mode of regional revival (Kunzmann 2004) elsewhere in Europe. Thus Bilbao, the capital of the Basque country in Spain, used to be only known for its declining heavy industry (and the depredations of ETA's terrorist campaign of violence). In 1997 the city's Guggenheim Museum of Modern Art was opened. Designed by the famous architect Frank Gehry, the museum was the centrepiece of the city's plan to make Bilbao an international tourist attraction. Urban planners the world over began to talk of a 'Guggenheim effect' – the use of iconic public buildings to entice visitors to the city (or a region), kick-start a high-end tourism industry and perhaps even transform the entire economy (Arruti 2003). Such transformation involves treating the city as an aesthetic experience, while at the same time using this aesthetic to 'rebrand' the city. Cultural development is not just a make-over, it is making a new place (see Jensen 2007).

Other old industrial cities have pursued similar strategies. Glasgow, once known for its dying shipyards and violent gangs, reinvented itself as a city specialising in high-end retail and designer coffee bars. Urban design in Barcelona ensured that the city has become a major tourist destination; in north-east England, the new (and instantly famous) *Angel of the North* statue outside Newcastle points visitors to a city equipped with designer bridges and new arts centres.

Cultural regeneration is sometimes explicitly seen as creating or re-creating regional pride and identity. Nonetheless, by itself it is no magic bullet: it can never provide employment of the scale and quality of industrial jobs that have gone. For all the talk of cultural inclusion, it is plausible that it can actually exacerbate income inequality, attracting well-heeled tourists – and low waged jobs to serve them. Furthermore, the term 'culture' is politically contested, especially perhaps in cities and regions where the workers' movement had once created its own popular counter-culture, memories of which may still (just) linger on (Keating and de Frantz 2003).

A final regeneration strategy is to rely on new middle class consumption. Just as in the nineteenth century the population of the Scottish Highlands was 'cleared' so that the Anglo-Scottish gentry could hunt grouse, so in recent decades docklands have been transformed into marinas, with the existing local population decanted out of sight. The transformation of the London Docklands in the 1980s is often seen as an example of this strategy and was widely resented by existing local communities. Yet the London Docklands have been the more or less explicit model not only for other docklands projects across the world, but also for schemes such as Project Phoenix in Dortmund. In what is now one of the largest urban regeneration projects in Europe, the site of a steelworks which once employed thousands of manual workers has been cleared (after much of the equipment was shipped to China) to create an inland lake, a marina and suitably salubrious housing developments.

Regional regeneration and institutional restructuring

Regional policy for rust belt areas rests on the assumption that these areas cannot be abandoned just because they are no longer centres of economic growth. Today in the USA rust belt areas are essentially abandoned by government: slash-and-burn urban development has become intrinsic to the USA. Urban decay and decline are hardly unknown in Europe, but there are no cities which have been allowed to decline on the scale of Detroit, where the population has halved in the last thirty years and whole areas have been literally abandoned.

The European Union has contributed to this contrast between Europe and the USA. EU spending in declining industrial areas has normally been dependent on some form of matching national expenditure, so that EU policy has been an incentive for national spending. Furthermore, EU regional policy has facilitated the creation of new regional institutions. The effectiveness of regional regeneration has varied across Europe. The Ruhr is probably the most successful case, and the very length of the process highlights how difficult the task has been. Yet the EU as a whole now faces the new challenges posed by the accession states. Here the 'transition' decimated old manufacturing industries with a rapidity unknown in the West. The experience of the EU also suggests that neo-liberalism of the British variety is probably the worst possible strategy. It denigrates local traditions instead of valorising them; it ignores the role of the national state and above all the regional and local state. Perhaps most pernicious of all, its fixation on the virtues of entrepreneurialism ignores how in practice entrepreneurialism and innovation have developed in Europe's regions, as the next section will now show.

6.3 Growth poles: the Third Italy and its imitators

Since the 1980s the economies of some of the more successful regions of Europe have been based on *clusters* of small and medium-sized enterprises from a particular industry or sector. This importance of regions seems paradoxical in an age of globalisation. Many successful regions show a high 'institutional density': firms are embedded in formal and informal local networks. In the 1980s Piore and Sabel's theory of 'flexible specialisation' (Section 3.1) saw areas such as the *industrial districts* of north-eastern Italy as the harbingers of a new form of production. Several decades of research – and change – within the regions have made such claims seem much less plausible. The first part of this section shows the different forms that clusters take and this highlights the specific features of Italian industrial districts; the second and third parts compare the institutional structure and labour market of the classic Italian industrial districts with those of a very different cluster, that of the Metall Industrie of Baden-Württemberg. As the final part of the section shows, Italian industrial districts in particular have largely been transformed, becoming more globalised and less egalitarian.

Place, co-operation and innovation

In 1987 the total GDP of Italy exceeded that of the UK for the first time. Crucial to this *surpasso* (overtaking) was the manufacturing industry of north-east Italy. Dominated by small firms, Emilia-Romagna in particular had the highest living standards in Italy. In trying to explain this phenomenon, scholars returned to the account of 'industrial districts' in nineteenth-century England by Alfred Marshall. Marshall noticed how in England speciality steel manufacturers were concentrated in Sheffield (or in Germany in Remscheid). Such spatial economic specialisation brings *agglomeration effects*. Firms may compete with each other but also benefit from their neighbours: the area can attract specialist labour, specialist suppliers and specialist customers. However, Marshall also showed how such physical proximity involved particular social relations. Frequent local transactions and a constant exchange of news and gossip built up technical knowledge and professional competences: people talked about their work to each other, people learnt. In his famous phrase, knowledge was 'in the air'. There was trust, 'community spirit' or, more formally, 'social capital'.

This interweaving of the social and the economic was stressed by those Italian social scientists who first noticed the emergence of industrial districts (Becattini 2004; Giuliani 2005). The ecology of firms in a geographical area can take different forms. Thus Markusen (1996) identified four types of industrial district: a 'Marshallian industrial district' comprising a multitude of small and medium-sized firms with extensive intra-district trading; a 'hub-and-spoke district' built around one or more large firms with multiple linkages outside the district; a 'satellite industrial platform' district comprising a series of 'branch plants' of large firms which have headquarters outside the district; and 'state-anchored industrial districts' based around large government institutions.

At their peak in the 1980s the Italian industrial districts were clearly Marshallian. In Tuscany, for example, there were clusters of small firms in small towns specialising in textiles (Prato) and furniture (Poggibonso); in Emilia-Romagna clusters included such products as ceramic tiles; in le Marche the shoe-making cluster was studied in detail by Blim (1990). In 1992 fully 20 per cent of all Italian textile exports came from Prato (Dei Ottati 1997: 38). Even in the more high tech areas firm size remained small with usually fewer than fifteen employees. These were family firms. Firms grew not by increasing their size but by subdividing within the family (Lazerson (1988). The industrial district was also a social community: a world in which competitors also co-operated and in which knowledge continually circulated. Thus the economic actor was not so much the individual small firm as a whole. This was a very local economy producing for a continually changing global market. Although individual firms were very small, the network was a major economic actor.

A very different cluster is the Metall Industrie of Baden-Württenberg. First, it is much larger: in the *Land* of Baden-Württenberg as a whole total employment is over four million. Up to the 1950s manufacturing employment was dominated by the textile industry, but then textiles declined continually. In their place came the car industry, above all Mercedes-Benz, and mechanical and electrical engineering. Within the auto industry the dominant role of Mercedes means that the network is primarily one of forced co-operation, but in other industries there is no single dominating firm. The key role is played by *Mittelständische Betriebe* of between 100 and 250 employees (officially classified as SMEs). Like the much smaller Italian firms, these are family owned and have a tradition of innovation. The firms participate in networks which include both other firms and political institutions. By contrast the state-anchored aerospace industry cluster around Toulouse in south-west France has been fuelled by a few large firms in the aerospace industry, producing directly for the global market. Toulouse is the centre not only of the Airbus project, but also the European space industry and a growing electronic and software sector (e.g. Zuliani 2008).

Industrial districts and clusters show the importance of co-operation and institutions for a successful market economy. What fascinated Marshall was that the industrial district did not just learn, it innovated. Thus Silicon Valley in California is the undisputed centre for innovation in information technology in the world. Yet this most free enterprise and individualistic area of the USA, so anthropologists and regional geographers showed over thirty years ago (Rogers and Larsen 1984; Saxenian 1985), depends upon a dense network of informal linkages between engineers, entrepreneurs and venture capitalists that often cross-cuts formal affiliations and ownership structures. Part of the basis for Silicon Valley's success has been that *people in the Valley know each other*.

Innovation depends on people talking to each other, on the 'local buzz' (Bathelt *et al.* 2004): the often excited and even raucous exchange of ideas and anecdotes between practitioners, whether they are artisan shoemakers in northern Italy, software engineers in Silicon Valley or even international bankers in London. Clusters thus involve the local accumulation of uncodified knowledge (Belussi and Pilotti 2002). Today electronic communication facilitates frequent long-range interaction and even familiarity between people who never physically meet, creating virtual communities. Even more importantly, low cost air travel has made it ever easier for people to meet for short periods in business meetings, conferences and trade fairs, creating temporary proximity (Wickham and Vecchi 2008).

External linkages are now seen as decisive for the ability of a cluster to successfully innovate. For example, Bathelt *et al.* (2004) argue that innovative clusters combine local buzz with 'pipelines'. Whereas local buzz is spontaneous and free, pipelines are links which firms deliberately create with selected outside organisations. Clusters which are able to continuously and radically innovate are therefore clusters that contain firms with extensive external linkages (Belussi and Pilotti 2002). The importance of such external linkages does not spell the end of the local advantages of clusters. Rather than making the earth flat, globalisation enhances the importance of the local advantages of specific regions.

Institutional networks in Italy and Germany

Within Europe Emilia-Romagna and Baden-Württenberg are the two best-known industrial districts (e.g. Cooke and Morgan 1994). However, they have different origins, they are based on very different firms in different forms of networks, and have different governance. In many ways these districts are now more important than ever before, since they have been able to change again and so ensure that, as the deputy chair of Confindustria remarked: 'Germany and Italy are now Europe's only true manufacturing countries' (*The Economist* 2008).

Trying to explain the contrast between the effective regional governments of north-eastern Italy and the ineffective governments of the south, Putnam *et al.* (1993) argued that the tradition of the civic autonomy and citizens' involvement of Italian cities in Tuscany (Sienna, Florence, etc.) can be traced back at least to the late mediaeval period. Others have stressed that in these cities artisanal production of luxury goods has always been for international customers and so always had to respond to changes in taste and fashion. In the countryside, too, there are long-standing traditions of small farmers co-operating with each other while producing for a luxury (and hence changeable) market.

Shortening the historical time frame, after the defeat of fascism in Italy there was a strong political consensus for 'a middle way' between socialism and capitalism (Weiss 1988). This resulted in a legal framework which particularly favoured small firms. The two major parties of post-World War II Italy, the Democrazia Christiana – DC (Christian Democrats) – and the Partita Communista Italiana – PCI (Communists) – both developed local strongholds as cross-class organisations, promoting the interests of the local economy and, crucially, strengthening social ties between local entrepreneurs and local politicians (including trade unionists). The PCI made Bologna a showcase for the party; during the 1980s it consolidated its power across Emilia-Romagna (Aiken and Martinotti 1984). At its simplest this meant simply an honest and competent administration. More substantially, the party contributed an institutional framework that facilitated co-operation between local firms and stimulated common associations.

Like Italy, Germany has a long historical tradition of independent cities with local political autonomy and high levels of citizen involvement. It was after all a

German mediaeval proverb that *Stadtluft macht frei* ('City air makes you free'). This tradition of self-regulating *Handwerk* ('artisan') urban guilds fed into the more modern culture of local clubs, associations and *Vereinsmeierei* (the penchant for forming voluntary organisations). These local democratic traditions are an important counter-point to the authoritarian nationalism of the Kaiserreich and the Third Reich. Late nineteenth-century German industrialisation meant German firms were larger than firms elsewhere in Europe, but this was primarily the case for the heavy industries of the Ruhr. In an area like Stuttgart the textile and machinery industries were not on this same scale. And finally the Bonn Republic was both constitutionally and culturally the most decentralised state in Western Europe; its economic *Wiederaufbau* involved a greater role for *Mittelständische Betriebe* (medium-sized enterprises) than in the pre-war period.

In Emilia-Romagna firms developed some formal institutions to share marketing and research. There is some limited formal involvement in these activities by the provincial government and city governments, who to some extent escape the general Italian distrust of the state. Bologna University is one of the most famous universities in Italy, but it has relatively little formal engagement with the region. By contrast, in Baden-Württenberg there is active state involvement at the level of the *Land* government, again based around a political consensus. Baden-Württenberg research institutions and universities are closely integrated with the regional economy. Particularly important also is that under German law, all enterprises have to be members of their local chamber of commerce. The IHK (along with the parallel *Handwerkskammer* for artisanal enterprises) thus provides a legal basis for co-operation between firms.

Employment, skill and the labour market

The Third Italy appeared to show that market dynamism could be coupled with egalitarianism. Furthermore, the skill and autonomy of the employees was also seen as crucial to the success of the model. The towns of the Third Italy developed as clusters of very small enterprises where the artisan-owners worked alongside their employees who often were family members. There was an ethic of hard work but also extensive social mobility with many workers setting up their own enterprises (Blim 1990). The income distribution appears to have been more equal than in the industrial towns of the north (Dei Ottati 1997). Furthermore in the Italian industrial districts small enterprises are usually unionised, as indeed are usually enterprises in Baden-Württenberg.

In Baden-Württenberg an important basis for the industrial district has been the German apprenticeship system which has been ambitiously revamped in recent years. By contrast, in Emilia-Romagna formal education has been notoriously irrelevant to employment (Regini 1997) and the high levels of trust both between enterprises and between employers and employees is cause and effect of extensive on-the-job learning. However, the tradition of mutual support between enterprises in northern Italy has also facilitated employer-initiatives for vocational and professional education up to and including the creation of private universities such as Castallenza. Nonetheless, the continued failure of the national educational system does mean that access to rapidly changing and formal knowledges remains a continuing problem for the Italian industrial districts.

Here Silicon Valley provides an interesting contrast. Silicon Valley began in part as 'spin-offs' from Stanford University; the Valley's continuing success depends on the high standards of American postgraduate education in electronics and software. Within Silicon Valley this formal education is supplemented by high mobility between firms ('innovation on the hoof') and a work culture which facilitates learning on the job. However, unlike the European industrial districts, Silicon Valley has a bifurcated labour force of well paid engineers on the one hand and poorly paid workers on the other. Consequently, income distribution in Silicon Valley has always been more unequal than the US average. Furthermore, charity giving and corporate involvement in community activities appear to be below US averages (e.g. Marquis *et al.* 2007). Silicon Valley is therefore a useful corrective to simplistic ideas of social capital: it shows how *some* forms of social capital, such as the importance of work-related networking, can be limited to some social groups within the same geographical area.

Challenges to local autonomy

The Italian industrial districts grew in order to serve the world market so globalisation was part of their rationale. In this sense to talk of globalisation as challenging industrial districts is absurd. However, at its very simplest the specificity of any cluster is the co-location of economic activities *in the same territorial area.* The advance of manufacturing in Newly Industrialising Countries (NICs), above all China, has exposed all manufacturing to new competition. Searching for ways to reduce their wage costs, Italian firms began to outsource their manufacturing to lower wage countries, especially in Eastern Europe and North Africa. In Germany, too, many middle-sized enterprises began to move manufacturing abroad, including to China. Although most design and finishing work remains in the cluster, this is a dramatic change in the overall role of the industrial district in that it becomes part of a value chain rather than the clustering of all activities in one area. For example, the Italian town of Montebelluna still describes itself as the world centre of the sports shoe industry, even though now most firms in the cluster have relocated much of the simpler manufacturing tasks to Romania (Sammara and Belussi 2006).

There have also been changes in the ecology of clusters, not least the entry of large multinationals into the districts. However, while there were originally fears that MNCs would simply take over the districts, in fact they seem to have entered precisely in order to benefit from the existing social and economic infrastructure. As such they have contributed to the more general trend which has been summed up as an increasing 'hierarchialisation' of relationships between firms (Rinaldi 2005). There is a clear tendency for leading companies to emerge, taking on more leadership roles especially in relation to innovation.

In both Germany and Italy local banks have played an important role in the development of the industrial districts: in Germany the *Landesbanken*, (banks funded by the local state), and in Italy the local *Casse dei Risparmio* (savings banks). These banks mobilise local funds for local entrepreneurs, they have local knowledge and are involved in high trust local relationships. These local banks have been undermined by the mergers in financial services and in particular by the EU's Banking Directive which opens up the financial services to direct competition.

The 'Marshallian' dimension of the industrial districts has been fatally undermined by two further developments (de Marchi and Grandinetti 2014). First, immigration has changed the workforce. By 2003, for example, in some leather working communities in Vicenza over 10 per cent of the population were foreign (Andall 2007: 291). Immigrants often enter southern Italy illegally and then move north in the hope of better jobs and eventual legalisation. A section of the workforce is not only badly paid, it has a different legal and social status. The relationship between employers and employees is no longer mediated through family and other social connections; the enterprise community disappears.

Second, in Germany and especially in Italy family-run firms have been facing a growing succession problem. As the number of children falls – and Italy is now below ZPG (Zero Population Growth) – so the number of family members who can be called on is also reduced. At the same time, cultural changes ensure that the succession generation are less likely to consider ties of obligation to either family or locality (Betts 2000). Consumerist individualism and instant gratification replace the famous north Italian work ethic and family solidarity. Another institution that supported economic dynamism is weakened.

In their original form, Italian industrial districts were perhaps quite close to a twentieth-century version of the communities of independent artisans praised by French socialist Proudhon in the early nineteenth century. Perhaps Third Italy was just a brief passing phase, a historical oddity appearing in some limited geographical areas at the dusk of fordism, highlighting the possibilities of trust in economic relations just as on a worldwide-scale market conservatism pushed it back. Writing in the late 1980s, Blim could already comment almost nostalgically on the 'short shelf life' of the Italian model (Blim 1990: 267); two decades later the same scholar was writing the model's epitaph (Blim 2004). Nonetheless, these areas are still somewhat distinctive today and, more generally, industrial districts can be seen as *one* articulation of a more general *European* approach to economic activity, one that embeds the market in social institutions. From this perspective, it is significant that US examples of industrial districts are limited not just geographically but also socially: we have seen the contrast in income distribution between Silicon Valley and Emilia-Romagna and even Baden-Württemberg. In Europe, more so than in the USA, industrial districts can be one economic element of social inclusion.

6.4 Global cities, world cities: London today, Berlin tomorrow?

Within Europe the emergence of London as a global financial centre shows that 'place' and 'geography' are not hangovers from a previous epoch, but instead are generated anew in each period. In her path-breaking work on 'global cities' Sassen (1994) linked the new role of leading cities within financial networks with their specific social structures. This section begins by showing how London became a node of activity for international financial services. The second part assesses Sassen's claim that as a global city London has a polarised social structure, with large numbers of very well paid jobs especially in financial services and large numbers of poorly paid workers in personal services. As the third part shows, artistic and symbolic production is now also concentrated in London and New York, despite Berlin's re-emergence as a cultural centre. The section concludes by briefly considering the extent to which European world cities remain distinctively European.

The global city in the global economy

In the twenty years from 'Big Bang' of 1986 to the financial crash of autumn 2008, London became Europe's undisputed financial services centre. This peculiar importance of one city is paradoxical. Unlike manufacturing industry, the 'products' of financial services are by definition almost entirely weightless: their production is not tied to any particular location. Even before the gurus of globalisation were announcing that the world was flat, global financial integration was seen to herald 'the end of geography' (O'Brien 1992).

The reality, however, is different. Technological and regulatory change merely facilitates that even on a flat surface, 'money flows like mercury': it is spatially sticky, it concentrates in specific places (Clark 2005). The financialisation of the economy has gone in parallel with the increasing importance of a few financial centres. A very small number of cities have become 'global cities', dominating the global financial system. Even more strikingly, within these cities, there is a remarkable concentration of financial service activities in a very small area (Wall Street, the 'City' of London).

The simplest explanation for this importance of proximity is the need to maintain face-to-face social relationships. Financial firms are especially 'hungry' for social connectivity (Wojcik 2007). Elite decision-makers need to be able to meet each other at short notice; expertise has to be kept up to date:

> While intellectual capital is networked, knowledge is still communicated face-to-face and through informal means, by chance meetings in City streets, in bars and on transport. Respondents in both cities [London and Frankfurt] emphasised the importance of proximity for knowledge transfer between firms, within and across industries.
>
> (Beaverstock *et al.* 2001: 37)

Marshall's description of the industrial district as having 'knowledge in the air' applies even more to the financial experts of Wall Street or the City of London than to the furniture makers of Poggibonso or the sports shoe makers of Parma (see Section 6.3).

Interwoven with such relationships is the importance of a wide and deep labour pool. Firms can move to a financial centre knowing that they have a good chance of being able to recruit highly specialised labour (Beaverstock and Hall 2012). Only in a few cities in the world is it possible to recruit – sometimes in large numbers – experienced people in a multitude of esoteric specialisms. Firms are also attracted to financial services centres because such centres have a wide range of specialist business services (corporate law, advertising, real estate, etc.). Conversely, as more financial firms move to or develop in a specific centre, they add to the demand for business services and provide markets for further specialist companies.

Global cities are also defined by their mutual linkages. Two technologies are crucial for global connectivity: air travel and electronic communication. The networks these two technologies create are strikingly similar, with London and New York being more closely connected to each other than to other cities (Choi *et al.* 2006; Taylor 2005). While it may appear that the networks of physical and virtual communication reinforce the status quo, the position of cities within the global networks can change over time. Sassen initially identified New York, London and Tokyo as three 'global cities', but international finance has been increasingly dominated by just two cities, New York and London. Especially over the last ten years international financial services have been growing in Singapore, Hong Kong and Shanghai, while there have been signs of the resurgence of Tokyo. At the same time London and New York (or rather their financial districts) have become increasingly interconnected. The links between them are far closer than each city's links with more subordinate cities, with some business executives commuting weekly between London and New York.

The differences between the global cities are not simply differences of size. Even when the size of its financial sector made Tokyo seem in the same league as London and New York, it was in fact more oriented towards its domestic national market than New York or London. Historically London's role as a financial centre was based around the stock exchange, but its contemporary international importance stems from the 1970s with the growth of the eurodollar market (i.e. transactions in dollars held outside the USA) (Stafford 1992: 33). This growth involved an influx of foreign, especially American, banks. During the 1980s London gained a further advantage as it was the first centre to deregulate its stock exchange (the 'Big Bang' of October 1986). Once again, however, this meant that the established firms of the City lost business to American-owned companies. The end of 'gentlemanly capitalism' was also the end of the dominance of London by *British* companies (Augar 2000; Faulconbridge and Muzio 2008). This question of ownership means that London and New York have different relationships to the national states within which they are located. London's dominance by American banks is not reciprocated by any British ownership of American banks.

A newly polarised occupational structure?

Employment growth in London's financial services began to accelerate in the 1980s. According to Thrift and Leyshon (1992) total employment in the City of London was growing by over 7 per cent a year in the middle 1980s; in 1991 financial services employed over 600,000 people in the Greater London area – nearly one-fifth of total employment (McDowell 1997: 71) As a previous Governor of the Bank of England pointed out, this is about the same as the total *population* of Frankfurt, Europe's next most important financial centre. More recent estimates identify approximately 300,000 people in wholesale financial services – the core 'City jobs' (Butcher and Hamann 2013).

Some areas of financial services now generate quite astonishing incomes. The young men (and very few young women) working in the dealing rooms of the money markets earn 'serious money' – the only other ways you can earn so much so young is by dealing in hard drugs or becoming a sporting or entertainment celebrity. And those slightly older managers who direct them earn even more. In the early 1990s in the new-style international banks in London and New York, salaries for top managers became a multiple of what they had been only two decades earlier. By the end of the boom the 'bonus culture' of financial services came under public attack, first for the sheer scale involved (by 2006 annual bonuses to top City of London managers could reach several millions of pounds) (Seager 2006) and then, as the crisis hit in 2008, for the alleged short-term behaviour which these bonuses encouraged.

While average wages and salaries in south-east England were growing faster than the national average, those from employment in the City area were growing faster still. As one study summarised: 'The rich are not only getting richer, there are more of them' (Hamnett 2003: 2407). This in turn ensured that house prices rose fastest in the most expensive areas. In areas of London such as Barnsbury, where vaguely trendy types had begun gentrification in the late 1960s, by the turn of the century a new breed of 'urban ranchers' were pushing house prices out of reach of all but the best paid corporate lawyers and City financiers (Butler and Lees 2006). Expensive residential property in London is also increasingly owned by foreigners: the highly paid immigrants in financial services, international property investors and the new global super-rich. Prices are now pushed up further still by foreign investors who have bought expecting further asset appreciation and meanwhile leave the properties unoccupied.

Employment in the global city has, however, its dark side. According to Sassen, employment is polarised: there are well paid jobs and poorly paid jobs, but little in the middle. As the middle has been hollowed out, low paid service sector employment has grown. The new high earners create new personal service jobs, from waiters in restaurants to dog-walkers and servers in speciality shops. Much of this work is informal and deregulated, so allowing easy access to immigrants. Immigrants also provide most of the labour force for the only sort of manufacturing that can survive in the city, sweated workshops (especially in clothing) which rely on massive exploitation of family labour. Finally the new low wage population, often with a disproportionate level of ethnic minorities, generates its own demand for low cost services and products.

However, research in the 1990s suggested that in terms of occupational structure London, like other advanced urban areas of Europe, was undergoing not polarisation but professionalisation – a general upgrading of the occupational structure with a decline in unskilled jobs and a growth in upper and lower professional jobs. There was growing income inequality, but this seemed unrelated to occupational changes (Hamnett and Butler 2013). A review of occupational change across London in the last two decades of the twentieth century argued that the 'big story' was the growth of elite occupations and the growth of the 'middle middle mass' (Butler *et al.* 2008). Where London was unusual was in its high level of unemployment, but this was of course utterly at odds with Sassen's image of the global city with its allegedly disproportionate masses of *working* poor (Hamnett 1994; Buck 1997).

For Sassen the growth of lowly paid employment in the global city was the result of the changed demand for services by the elite. An alternative explanation would focus on the supply of labour. Unlike an American city such as New York or Los Angeles, London had few newly arrived immigrants ready to work at low wages. Equally, the social welfare system was just generous enough to ensure that the unemployed and existing ethnic minorities were not forced into such low paid jobs (Hamnett 1996).

In the new century, however, London changed as immigration suddenly reached unprecedented levels. This new migration involved first, increased numbers of highly skilled workers in areas such as financial services; second, large numbers of refugees and asylum speakers (especially around the turn of the century); and, third, skilled and semi-skilled workers from other poor countries and from Eastern Europe. Unlike in the early 1990s, London now had a large labour force of newly arrived immigrants ready to take up low paid jobs. Real wages for low paid jobs fell and were probably below those in the rest of the country (Gordon *et al.* 2007: 57). These falling wages clearly allowed the *number* of low paid jobs to increase: lower wages made more low paid jobs viable.

By the end of the boom, therefore, the social structure of London had become close to Sassen's original global city image, but for different reasons. Low paid immigrant jobs expanded everywhere. Cleaning on the London Underground, for example, became a standard job for new immigrants. Working long hours, often without holiday entitlement or overtime pay, living in rented accommodation and scraping to save money to send home, the new immigrants serviced the London population as a whole, not just the elite (May *et al.* 2007; Datta *et al.* 2007). At the same time, paradoxically, unemployment in London remained high by comparison with the rest of the UK. Furthermore, despite the fact that the East European migrants were nearly all employed, migrants from poorer countries tended to have very low levels of employment. Here cultural assumptions about the role of women coincided with the support provided by the welfare system to keep many of the unskilled out of the labour market altogether. In other words, even if there was some occupational polarisation, London's social structure was very different to that imagined by Sassen. Spatial inequality is partly shaped by the institutional context, the national welfare state and national immigration policy.

The global tastemakers – the NY-LON axis

By the turn of the century London was the financial centre of Europe. Although some might have challenged this, it was also Europe's centre of cultural production. High art – museums, opera, ballet and classical music – were certainly well represented in London: according to Arts Council England the city had 'two opera houses, more than 150 galleries and museums, nineteen national museums and above 2,600 music companies' (Currid 2007a). Yet, as this quote suggests, in London traditional high culture interlocked with popular music, the visual arts and the more obvious 'industries' of advertising and the media. London had also become a centre for the global fashion industry, despite competition from Paris and Milan. Since the 1960s British pop music had been the only seriously global European popular music and, despite the brief effervescence of local centres starting with Liverpool in the 1960s, London was always the industry's centre. From the mid-1990s the so-called Young British Artists (above all Damien Hirst) had conquered global art markets, London auction houses had a turnover second only to New York and the global high art market was dominated by the two London houses of Sotheby's and Christie's.

Although Sassen stressed the extent to which financial services employment is centralised within the global city, in fact compared to the cultural industries financial services employment is relatively evenly spread across the UK. Equally, examining New York Currid calculates Location Quotients (the extent to which a group is over-represented in a particular area) for occupations. New York certainly has a higher concentration of overall employment in finance than any other major metropolitan area, but the LQ for financial services occupations is only 2.41; by contrast New York's LQ for 'Arts and Culture' overall is 4.38 (by far the highest in the USA) (Currid 2006).

At least since the mid-nineteenth century, cultural production has required not only rich patrons but also a bohemian infrastructure. Art arrives from the margins. So accounts of the late twentieth-century post-modern art boom in New York trace its origins to the 'train bombing' graffiti artists of the 1970s (Currid 2007b). In popular music, whether rock or hip-hop, the tension between' real' music and 'selling out' to commercial success is notorious. So one part of the story of a city's cultural success is the extent to which it can provide not just art galleries but cheap studios, not just concert halls but casual gigs. Here, too, place matters: casual encounters on the street, at parties or cool clubs ensure a continual flow of information and contacts. And this can only happen if 'everybody' is in the right place. One reason for Berlin's sudden re-emergence on the global cultural landscape is its lively – and cheap – counter-culture.

Other European cities also play an important cultural role. Historically, national capital cities have been cultural centres, not least because of the monarchy as a source of artistic patronage. In the more recent past media centralisation has been tied to the role of the nation state with employment in TV and radio concentrated in the capital cities. Today despite all the discussion of tele-cottages, new multimedia firms also tend to be located in the national capital. In Germany after reunification Berlin has not only become the political capital, but it has challenged Munich as the centre of German cultural industries (Krätke 2004).

Global cities and European cities of the world

In many ways the debate about global cities detracts from specific features both of European cities and of the European city system. Compared to the USA, Europe is remarkable for its large number of medium-sized cities. It is these cities which make Europe an urban continent. Cities have been decisive in Europe since the Middle Ages. Indeed, for Max Weber the distinctiveness of the European city seems to have been as crucial for the origins of capitalism as his much more well-known claim linking Protestantism and capitalism. Utterly unlike the larger historical Oriental cities, the European city had a legal system that protected private property and citizens who were voluntary members of its urban guilds.

In the nineteenth century the elites of the new industrial cities often saw the mediaeval city as a model of economic success and active citizenship, but they believed that their cities were the proud heirs of this tradition. When it was built, Leeds Town Hall was described as 'not inferior to those stately piles which still attest the ancient opulence of the great commercial cities of Italy and Flanders' (Hunt 2004: 186). The European nineteenth-century city was also distinctive for its new municipal enterprise. It was the nineteenth-century European city which municipalised services and utilities, and also, especially where there was a strongly organised labour movement, increasingly took on welfare state roles.

All of this contributes to the distinctiveness of the contemporary European experience (Kazepov 2005). The European city has a historic centre, a place of administration and culture; the American city has only a business centre (Bagnasco and Le Galès 2000: 9). European cities remain more compact than US cities, despite suburbanisation, and have continued to invest in their city centres; they are less car dependent and have far more extensive pedestrianisation.

As cities begin to vie with each other for mobile investment and above all mobile people, they then begin to re-emerge from within nation states. For this the European dimension has been important. The EU has provided a framework in which the political and above all the administrative leaders of Europe's cities can relate directly to each other. A series of EU initiatives and research programmes explicitly address European cities, there is a network of European capital cities and, most famously, the annual European 'city of culture' programme, a programme which is now copied in the Americas.

At the same time the European city is threatened. Continued suburbanisation and car-based development undermine the specific structure of the European city. In the second half of the twentieth century much of the distinctiveness of

European cities was because they were embedded in national welfare states. The national welfare state ensured funding for municipal services and utilities; it imposed its relatively egalitarian income distribution and social supports that limited social polarisation, probably above all through funding social housing; the expanded welfare systems provided state employment so that European cities contained a broad middle class with regular employment relatively protected from the market (Häussermann 2005). Paradoxically, therefore, challenges to the national welfare state threaten to undermine the distinctive role of Europe's cities.

Bibliography

Aiken, M. and Martinotti, G. (1984) The turn to the Left among Italian cities and urban public policy. In I. Szelenyi (ed.) *Cities in Recession*, London: Sage, pp. 238–275.

Andall, J. (2007) Industrial districts and migrant labour in Italy, *British Journal of Industrial Relations* 45.2: 285–308.

Arruti, N. (2003) Introduction: the Guggenheim effect six years on, *International Journal of Iberian Studies* 16.3: 141–144.

Augar, P. (2000) *The Death of Gentlemanly Capitalism*, London: Penguin.

Bache, I. and Olsson, J. (2001) Legitimacy through partnership? EU policy diffusion in Britain and Sweden, *Scandinavian Political Studies* 24.3: 215–237.

Bagnasco, A. and Le Galès, P. (2000) Introduction: European cities, local societies and collective actors? In A. Bagnasco and P. Le Galès (eds) *Cities in Contemporary Europe*, Cambridge: Cambridge UP, pp. 1–32.

Bathelt, H., Malmberg, A. and Maskell, P. (2004) Clusters and knowledge: local buzz, global pipelines and the process of knowledge creation, *Progress in Human Geography* 28.1: 31–56.

Beaverstock, J. and Hall, S. (2012) Competing for talent: global mobility, immigration and the City of London's labour market, *Cambridge Journal of Regions, Economy and Society* 5: 271–287.

Beaverstock, J., Hoyler, M., Pain, K. and Taylor, P. (2001) *Comparing London and Frankfurt as World Cities: A Relational Study of Contemporary Urban Change*, London: Anglo-German Foundation for the Study of Industrial Society.

Becattini, G. (2004) *Industrial Districts: A New Approach to Industrial Change*, Cheltenham: Edward Elgar.

Belussi, F. and Pilotti, L. (2002) Knowledge creation, learning and innovation in Italian industrial districts, *Geografiska Annaler Series B, Human Geography* 84: 125–139.

Betts, P. (2000) Globalism calms family feuding, *Financial Times*, 29 June.

Blim, M. (1990) *Made in Italy: Small Scale Industrialisation and Its Consequences*, London: Greenwood.

Blim, M. (2004) A death in the family: reflections on economic decline in an industrial district, paper presented at Università di Milano-Biccocca, 23 May 2004, http://anthropology.commons.gc.cuny.edu/michael-blim/. Accessed 26 July 2015.

Buck, N. (1997) *Social Divisions and Labour Market Change in London: National, Urban and Global Factors*, Working Papers of the ESRC Research Centre on Microsocial Change, Paper 97–25, Colchester: University of Essex.

Butcher, S. and Hamann, F. (2013) Financial services headcount down 30% in London … 2% in Frankfurt? 18 March. Efinancialcareers, http://news.efinancialcareers.com/ie-en/en/news-analysis. Accessed 25 July 2015.

Butler, T. and Lees, L. (2006) Super-gentrification in Barnsbury London: globalisation and gentrifying global elites at the neighbourhood level, *Transactions of the Institute of British Geographers* 31.4: 467–487.

Butler, T., Hamnett, C. and Ramsden, M. (2008) Inward and upward: marking out social class change in London 1981–2001, *Urban Studies* 45.1: 67–88.

Cappelen, A., Castellacci, F., Fagerberg, J. and Verspagen, B. (2003) The impact of EU regional support on growth and convergence in the European Union, *Journal of Common Market Studies* 41.4: 621–644.

Chari, R. and Kritzinger, S. (2006) *Understanding EU Policy Making*, London: Pluto.

Choi, J., Barnett, G. and Chon, B. (2006) Comparing world city networks: a network analysis of internet backbone and air transport intercity linkages, *Global Networks* 6.1: 81–99.

Clark, G. (2005) Money flows like mercury: the geography of global finance, *Geografiska Annaler Series B.* 87.2: 99–112.

Cooke, P. (1997) Global clustering and regional innovation: systematic innovation in Wales. In H.-J. Braczyk, P. Cooke and M. Heidenreich (eds) *Regional Innovation Systems*, London: UCL Press, pp. 245–262.

Cooke, P. and Morgan, K. (1994) Growth regions under duress: renewal strategies in Baden-Württemberg and Emilia-Romagna. In A. Amin and N. Thrift (eds) *Globalization, Institutions and Regional Development*, Oxford: Oxford UP, pp. 91–117.

Crew, D. (1980) *Bochum: Sozialgeschichte einer Industriestadt 1860–1914*, Frankfurt: Ullstein.

Critcher, C., Parry, D. and Waddington, D. (1999) Regulation, restructuring and regeneration in coalfields: three European cases. In P. Edwards and T. Elger (eds) *The Global Economy*, London: Mansell, pp. 87–110.

Currid, E. (2006) New York as a global creative hub: a competitive analysis of four theories on world cities, *Economic Development Quarterly* 20.4 (November): 330–350.

Currid, E. (2007a) The new Bohemia and how we must save it, *Times Higher*, 14 September.

Currid, E. (2007b) *The Warhol Economy: How Fashion, Art and Music Drive New York City*, Princeton: Princeton UP.

Datta, K., McIlwaine, C., Evans, Y., Herbert, J., May, J. and Wills, J. (2007) From coping strategies to tactics: London's low pay economy and migrant labour, *British Journal of Industrial Relations* 45.2: 404–432.

De Marchi, V. and Grandinetti, R. (2014) Industrial districts and the collapse of the Marshallian Model: looking at the Italian experience, *Competition and Change* 18.1: 70–87.

Dei Ottati, G. (1997) The remarkable resilience of the industrial districts of Tuscany. In H.-P. Braczyk and P. Cooke (eds) *Regional Innovation Systems*, London: UCL Press, pp. 28–47.

Dicks, B., Waddington, D. and Critcher, C. (1993) The quiet disintegration of closure communities, *Town and Country Planning* 62(7): 174–176.

Dunford, M. and Greco, L. (2006) *After the Three Italies: Wealth, Inequality and Industrial Change*, Oxford: Blackwell.

Dunford, M. and Greco, L. (2007) Geographies of growth, decline and restructuring: steel localities in the Italian Mezzogiorno, *European Urban and Regional Studies* 14.1: 27–53.

Economist, The (2008) Face value: woman of steel, 15 March, p. 82.

Faulconbridge, J. and Muzio, D. (2008) Organizational professionalism in globalising law firms, *Work Employment and Society* 22.1: 7–25.

Giuliani, E. (2005) Cluster absorptive capacity: why do some clusters forge ahead and others lag behind? *European Urban and Regional Studies* 12.3: 269–288.

Gordon, I., Travers, T. and Whitehead, C. (2007) *The Impact of Recent Immigration on the London Economy*, London: London School of Economics for City of London.

Hamnett, C. (1994) Social polarisation in global cities: theories and evidence, *Urban Studies* 31.3: 401–424.

Hamnett, C. (1996) Social polarisation, economic restructuring and welfare state regimes, *Urban Studies* 33.8: 1407–1430.

Hamnett, C. (2003) Gentrification and the middle-class remaking of Inner London 1961–2001, *Urban Studies* 40.12: 2401–2426.

Hamnett, C. and Butler, T. (2013) Re-classifying London: a growing middle class and increasing inequality, *City* 17.2: 197–208.

Hassink, R. (2007) The strength of weak lock-ins: the renewal of the Westmunsterland textile industry, *Environment and Planning A* 39.5: 1147–1165.

Häussermann, H. (2005) The end of the European city? *European Review* 13.2: 237–249.

Hooghe, L. (1998) EU cohesion policy and competing models of European capitalism, *Journal of Common Market Studies* 36.4: 547–477.

Hunt, T. (2004) *Building Jerusalem: The Rise and Fall of the Victorian City*, London: Weidenfeld & Nicholson.

Irish Times (2014) Corporate tax calculations, 13 February, p. 17.

Jensen, O.B. (2007) Culture stories: understanding urban cultural branding, *Planning Theory* 6.3: 211–236.

Kazepov, Y. (2005) Cities of Europe: changing contexts, local arrangements and the challenges to social cohesion. In K. Kazepov (ed.) *Cities of Europe*, Oxford: Blackwell, pp. 3–42.

Keating, M. and de Frantz, M. (2003) Culture-led strategies for urban regeneration: a comparative perspective on Bilbao, *International Journal of Iberian Studies* 16.3: 187–194.

Krätke, S. (2004) City of talents? Berlin's regional economy, socio-spatial fabric and 'worst practice' urban governance, *International Journal of Urban and Regional Studies* 28: 511–529.

Kunzmann, K. (2004) Culture, creativity and spatial planning, *Town Planning Review* 75.4: 383–404.

Lazerson, M. (1988) Organisational growth of small firms; an outcome of markets and hierarchies? *American Sociological Review* 53: 330–342.

McDowell, L. (1997) *Capital Culture: Gender at Work in the City*, Oxford: Blackwell.

MacIntyre, S. (1980) *Little Moscows: Working Class Militancy in Inter-war Britain*, London: Croom Helm.

Markusen, A. (1996) Sticky places in slippery space: a typology of industrial districts, *Economic Geography* 72.3: 293–313.

Marquis, C., Glynn, M. and David, G. (2007) Community isomorphism and corporate social action, *Academy of Management Review* 32.3: 925–945.

Matthews, A. (2015) *Food Security as a Driver of Integration in Europe*, IIIS Discussion Paper No. 466, Dublin: Institute for International Integration Studies.

May, J., Wills, J., Datta, K., Evans, Y., Herbert, J. and McIlwaine, C. (2007) Keeping London working: global cities, the British state and London's new migrant division of labour, *Transactions of the British Institute of Geographers* 32.2: 151–167.

Newenham, P. (ed.) (2015) *Silicon Docks: The Rise of Dublin as a Global Tech Hub*, Dublin: Liberties Press.

O'Brien, R. (1992) *Global Financial Integration: The End of Geography*, New York: Council on Foreign Relations Press.

O'Gorman, C., O'Malley, E. and Mooney, J. (1997) *Clusters in Ireland: The Irish Indigenous Software Industry*, NESC Research Series, Paper no. 3, Dublin: NESC.

Putnam, R. (2000) *Bowling Alone: The Collapse and Revival of American Community*, New York: Simon & Schuster.

Putnam, R. with Leonardi, R. and Nanetti, R. (1993) *Making Democracy Work: Civic Traditions in Modern Italy*, Princeton: Princeton UP.

Regini, M. (1997) Different responses to common demands: firms, institutions and training in Europe, *European Sociological Review* 13.3: 267–282.

Rinaldi, A. (2005) The Emilian model revisited: twenty years after, *Business History* 47.2: 244–266.

Rogers, E. and Larsen, J. (1984) *Silicon Valley Fever*, New York: Basic Books.

Sammarra, A. and Belussi, F. (2006) Evolution and relocation in fashion-led Italian districts: evidence from two case-studies, *Entrepreneurship and Regional Development* 18.6: 543–562.

Sassatelli, R. and Scott, A. (2001) Novel food, new markets and trust regimes: responses to the erosion of consumers' confidence in Austria, Italy and the UK, *European Societies* 3.2: 213–244.

Sassen, S. (1994) *Cities in a World Economy*, Thousand Oaks, CA: Pine Forge/Sage Press.

Saxenian, A. (1985) The genesis of Silicon Valley. In P. Hall and A. Markusen (eds) *Silicon Landscapes*, London: Allen & Unwin, pp. 20–34.

Seager, A. (2006) City bonuses reach record £19bn, *Guardian*, 17 August.

Stafford, L. (1992) London's financial markets: perspectives and prospects. In L. Budd and S. Whimster (eds) *Global Finance and Metropolitan Living*, London: Taylor & Francis, pp. 31–51.

Stevenson, J. (1984) *British Society 1914–45*, Harmondsworth: Penguin.

Stewart, J. (2014) *PwC/World Bank Report 'Paying Taxes 2014': An Assessment*, IIIS Discussion Paper No. 442, Dublin: Institute for International Integration Studies.

Taylor, P. (2005) Leading world cities: empirical evaluations of urban nodes in multiple networks, *Urban Studies* 42.9: 1593–1608.

Tellstrom, R., Gustafsson, I.-B. and Mossberg, L. (2005) Local food cultures in the Swedish rural economy, *Sociologia Ruralis* 45.4: 346–359.

Thrift, N. and Leyshon, A. (1992) *Making Money: The City of London and Social Power in Britain*, London: Routledge.

Trigilia, C. (2012) Why the Italian Mezzogiorno did not achieve a sustainable growth, *Cambio* 4: 137–149.

Waddington, D. and Parry, D. (2003) Managing industrial decline: the lessons of research on industrial contraction and regeneration in Britain and other EU coal producing countries, *Mining Technology* 112.1: 47–A55.

Weiss, L. (1988) *Creating Capitalism: The State and Small Business since 1945*, Oxford: Basil Blackwell.

Wickham, J. and Boucher, B. (2004) Training cubs for the Celtic Tiger: the volume production of technical graduates in the Irish educational system, *Journal of Education and Work* 17.4: 377–395.

Wickham, J, and Vecchi, A. (2008) Local firms and global reach: business air travel and the Irish software cluster, *European Planning Studies* 16.5: 693–710.

Wojcik, D. (2007) Geography and the future of stock exchanges: between real and virtual space, *Growth and Change* 38.2: 200–223.

Zuliani, J.-M. (2008) The Toulouse cluster of on-board systems: a process of collective innovation and learning, *European Planning Studies* 16.5: 711–726.

7 From labour immigration to European mobility

Viewed from America, immigration is often seen as the great failure of contemporary Europe. Such criticism takes two mutually contradictory forms. For some writers, political absent-mindedness has allowed Europe to be swamped by Muslim immigration. Thus Caldwell asks 'whether you can have the same Europe with different people' and answers in the negative (2009: 22). For others, Europeans are cutting themselves off from progress and innovation by creating barriers to mass immigration. From this perspective, Europe becomes 'the incredible shrinking continent' (Theil 2010). As so often, part of the issue is that Europe (like the rest of the world) cannot be understood by simply applying American arguments.

This chapter begins by showing how the European experience of migration is different from that of the USA. In particular, population movements both within Europe and into Europe have often been – and continue to be – the direct result of war and violence. The second section contrasts migration in the fordist and post-fordist periods: contemporary post-fordist migration is very different to that of the 'classical' post-World War II period through which the contemporary situation is often still understood. While fordist migration was regulated at national level, post-fordist migration, so the third section shows, is the result of both national and European level regulation. As the fourth section shows, in the new century there have also been new mass migrations within Europe from the new member states. These in turn are sometimes interwoven with other forms of mobility (such as 'circular' mobility), other occupational categories (skilled, professional, etc.) and other motivations (from lifestyle to retirement). *Migration* into nation states is partly *mobility* within Europe.

7.1 Historical context: Europe is not America

Theorists of globalisation often draw parallels between the years around the beginning of the twenty-first century and the start of the twentieth century. Yet the movements of the late nineteenth century were the consequence of European world dominance; the export of people from Europe was a sign of Europe's pre-eminence on the world stage. This is hardly the case today.

The nineteenth-century migrations were *settler* migrations. They consolidated modern Argentina and Chile, but they created the Anglo-World, the *English-speaking* countries of the (then) British Isles, the United States and the 'white dominions' of Australia, Canada, New Zealand and (partially) South Africa (Belich 2009; Darwin 2009). These migration flows were not just *from* Europe. Many emigrants returned, and in Britain – far more so than in any other European country – a middle class career often included extensive 'sojourning' abroad (Darwin 2009: 98). One legacy of these movements is British exceptionalism in a European context today.

The period of globalisation before World War I also saw mass movements *within* Europe. Most Jews fleeing the pogroms of Tsarist Russia (and the claustrophobia of the shettl) went to the USA, but others joined established communities in Britain, France and Germany. Italians emigrated to France; within the German empire there was large-scale movement from what later became Poland to Germany, especially to the coal mines of the Ruhr. While most Irish emigrants went to the USA, some stayed within the British empire and many moved across the water to Britain.

Conflicts after World War I created very different movements. The Greco-Turkish war of 1918–1922 led to the expulsion of some 1.3 million Greeks from Asia Minor (Glenny 2000: 392). Some three million White Russians left their homeland, some ending up in Shanghai but most in Germany and France (Figes 2002: 528). After World War II there were even larger refugee movements. As the Red Army advanced into east Prussia in late 1944 it exercised a terrible vengeance for the seventeen million Russian civilians the Nazis had slaughtered (Overy 1997: 288); its soldiers were given licence to rape and pillage at will (Overy 1997: 260ff; Beevor 2002: 28). Entire populations fled westwards. This expulsion was repeated in Poland and the Sudetenland in 1945–1946. In total between twelve and fourteen million ethnic Germans fled or were forcibly expelled, mostly moving into what became West Germany; the dead numbered somewhere between 500,000 and 1.5 million (Snyder 2010; Douglas 2013). At the same time the few survivors of the Holocaust left the 'Continent of Death' for Palestine, expelling many of its indigenous people and creating the state of Israel in 1948.

Nothing like this happened in the USA. In the continent of peace there were no wars and no forced population movements. Mass immigration into the USA had ended with the imposition of quotas through the Immigration Acts of 1921 and 1924. Consequently, by 1930 a higher proportion of the population of France was foreign-born than that of the USA (Noiriel 2001: 105). As the proportion of foreign-born declined dramatically the American melting pot could begin to bubble: ethnic neighbourhoods first consolidated and then became the launching point for the ethnic integration of the subsequent generations. The American fordist growth, interwoven with the popular mobilisation of World War II, turned ethnic Americans into Americans.

The USA also had no equivalent of the post-World War II European emigration. After the end of the war there was emigration from Continental Europe, such as from Croatia to Australia. British emigration to the Dominions continued. According to one estimate, between 1966 and 2005 there was a net loss of UK nationals of 2.5 million, so by the turn of the century only China and India had a larger diaspora (Sriskandarajah and Drew 2006). Finally, the colonial migrations reversed. The other forgotten story of European migration is those who returned home, sometimes to a home they themselves had never seen. By the end of 1962 about one million *pieds-noirs* (French Algerians) had returned from Algeria to France in one of the 'biggest population transfers of the twentieth century' (Evans 2012: 320); in the early 1970s well over half a million Portuguese *retornados* (returning settlers) came back from Africa (Carrington and de Lima 1996), joined almost clandestinely from the 1980s by many of the British (and Irish) white population of southern Africa.

7.2 Fordist immigration and beyond

The population movements of the immediate post-war period created a labour reserve for the rebuilding of West European industry. Nonetheless, by the early 1950s labour shortages were becoming endemic, and Europe began what can be seen as a period of fordist immigration. It can be contrasted with a longer post-fordist period lasting from the 1970s until the present day, within which the early 1990s form another dividing point. Up until then most immigration into Europe was essentially through the family members of those who had arrived before labour migration ended in 1973, whereas later new immigration streams developed, both from other less developed countries (above all sub-Saharan Africa) and from Eastern Europe (Castles and Miller 2009: 96).

In the fordist period immigrants entered quite specific areas of the labour market. The expansion of the economy created spaces at the bottom of the occupational hierarchy for semi-skilled work in public services (hospitals, street cleaning) and above all in manufacturing industry. Immigrants, whether Turks or Italians in Germany or West Indians or Irish in Britain, tended to work in large establishments in the private or the public sector and were frequently unionised (since these workplaces were traditional centres of trade unionism). They were usually legally resident in the host country and sometimes had access to full citizenship. Finally, these migration flows were relatively structured: immigrants came from particular origins to particular destinations, West Indians to Britain, Algerians to France, Turks to Germany, etc. Table 7.1 highlights the contrast with the contemporary situation.

Early scholars assumed that immigrants' economic role explained this fordist immigration (e.g. Castles and Kosack 1973). However, historical research highlights the specificity of the British experience. 'Coloured' immigration occurred largely because of the legal heritage of the British empire (Hansen 2000). British immigration is also often classed with France as *imperial* immigration, with the implication that in both countries immigrants came from colonies whose inhabitants retained rights of entry and even of citizenship in their destination. Yet this is simplistic. First, in both countries immigrants also came from the less

Table 7.1 Fordist and post-fordist population movements

	Fordist	*Post-fordist*
Skill level of employment	Mostly semi-skilled	Mainly low skill, but increasingly professional and managerial
Sector	Manufacturing and services	Services, some light manufacturing, agriculture
Ownership	Private and public	Private
Establishment size	Large	Small
Unionised	Sometimes	Rarely
Legal status	(Usually) legal residence, citizenship possible in some countries	Multiple: illegal entry, legal residence, full citizenship
Migration flows	Discrete (from specific origin to specific destination)	Diverse (from multiple origins to multiple destinations)
Cause	Demand driven	For low skilled, supply driven; for others, both demand and supply

developed areas in Europe. In Britain there was massive immigration from Ireland, while in France the ONI (Office National d'Immigration) was set up in 1945 to recruit workers from southern Europe, not from the colonies (Castles and Miller 2009: 99). Second, only in Britain was this immigration directly linked to legal entry and easy access to citizenship.

The *non-imperial* countries, by contrast, had no historic colonial possessions as natural recruiting grounds. In countries such as Germany or Switzerland immigration was usually sponsored. Acting on their own or through a government agency, employers directly recruited labour in the labour exporting country. This in turn enabled immigrants to be admitted on temporary permits, on the assumption that they would eventually return home – and of course, could be sent home when they were no longer needed. In all the German-speaking countries of Europe, immigrants were known as *Gastarbeiter* (guest workers).

In Britain, Germany and France, immigrants were employed on the assembly lines of the car factories such as in London–Dagenham (Ford), Cologne–Deutz (Ford) and Paris–Billancourt (Renault). In Sweden also, Finnish immigrants were crucial to the car factories; in Turin the Fiat factories employed immigrants from the south of Italy. Like European immigrants to the United States half a century before, differences of language and culture did not prevent them from carrying out work for which the key requirement was being prepared to tolerate monotony and close supervision. Of course, most immigrants did not work in car factories as such, but such employment can be taken as emblematic of the immigrant labour market experience: *relatively* secure employment with large employers.

This immigration established the contemporary ethnic minorities of Western Europe which by 1975 amounted to between 5 and 10 per cent of the population in France, Germany (FRG), Sweden and the UK (Castles and Miller 2009: 101). Because the immigrants came to earn money and perhaps to return home, they mostly were male (the crucial exception being Irish immigrants to Britain, where women just outnumbered men) and almost all young and single. Simply because of this demographic structure, they were more likely to be in employment than the 'host' population; they also moved to areas where they were likely to find employment. Just when the indigenous population was settling down after the war (or leaving Europe altogether), the new immigrants provided labour market flexibility.

The *Gastarbeiter* generation of the 1960s solved Europe's labour shortage. To some extent this meant that industries remained viable which otherwise would have disappeared. Textiles in northern England or coal mining in Belgium and northern France probably only survived into the 1970s because they were able to utilise the low paid work of immigrants. If that labour had not been available, the industries would have had to invest in labour-saving machinery and/or close. An alternative would of course have been to use other people. Thus, confronted with a growing labour shortage from the 1960s, Sweden relied not so much on immigration but on the mobilisation of women. Conversely West Germany, the *Gastarbeiter* country par excellence, remained also the land of *Kinder, Küche, Kirche* (children, kitchen, church): women stayed at home, the immigrants arrived instead (Naumann 2005) – and this was even more the case in Switzerland.

With the oil shocks of the 1970s the era of permanent expansion and full employment juddered to an end. Of fourteen million one-time immigrants to Germany between 1955 and 1973, fully eleven million eventually returned home (Friedrichs 1998, citing Bade 1995: 54). However, a minority of the 'guests' not only intended to stay, they now wanted to be joined by their families. The 1970s began the period of 'family reconstitution': joining a family member (usually husband or father) became the only ground for admission. The demographic structure of the immigrant population changed. Still younger than the host population, it now included more women and children.

The end of fordist employment meant the run-down of large-scale manufacturing industry. New jobs were far from the heartlands that had drawn people in the 1950s and 1960s. At least in France, the shift towards service sector employment meant that established immigrants were likely to become unemployed or only access the most low skilled of the new jobs (Marie 1994). Whereas their parents went where there were jobs, now immigrant children were likely to be stuck in areas of high unemployment. For the first time, unemployment and welfare dependency among the immigrant population began to exceed that of the host population. And for the immigrants and their children, Europe became – almost – home.[1]

7.3   European immigration policy: from immigration subi to immigration choisie?

A democratic nation state is partly defined by the right to control who enters the national territory. To the extent that European governments have abandoned this right they have risked losing legitimacy with their own citizens. The member states of the EU have committed to the free movement of EU citizens across their national borders. To varying degrees they – and the EU itself – have increasingly tried to attract skilled immigrants from outside the EU. Finally, they have to varying degrees and at different times tolerated extensive entry from outside, mostly by unskilled immigrants arriving as family members, asylum seekers or simply illegals. Even compared to the contemporary USA, let alone Australia or Canada, the European states have not chosen their immigrants. To a large extent President Sarkozy's description of French immigration applies to European immigration as a whole: *immigration subi*, not *immigration choisie* (imposed immigration, not chosen immigration).

Free movement for European citizens

Since the Treaty of Rome freedom of movement of labour has been integral to the European project. Freedom of movement of labour was one of the four freedoms – of goods, of capital, of services *and of labour* – which defined Europe as a common *market*. It is also a freedom that is taken for granted and internalised by ordinary European citizens (TNS Qual+ 2010). The origin of EU freedom of movement is not a common political citizenship, but participation in a common labour market. Today EU citizens now also have the right to live elsewhere in the Union in order to seek work, the right to study and even (subject to some restrictions) the right to retire. Nonetheless, EU citizens have no general right of residence in another EU country, not least because they cannot take up residence in another country if they are going to be a burden on its social services.

Freedom to move means freedom to take employment, but access to jobs usually depends on qualifications – and these are produced by *national* educational and training systems. Increasing mobility depends on mutual recognition of qualifications. After decades of attempts to agree equivalences between national qualifications, a 1991 directive imposed on member states a general obligation for mutual recognition of all state-regulated professional qualifications. Yet such formal recognition has its limits. Sections of public employment, in particular the military and the national civil service, are usually reserved for citizens not of the EU but of the national member state. In many countries, teachers or even (in the past) post office workers have been legally civil servants, and such traditions still survive. Many jobs, especially in the public sector, require not just linguistic knowledge but contextual knowledge – an Irish-trained social worker might have fluent Italian, but without formal *and informal* knowledge of the Italian social services, he or she would be an incompetent social worker in Italy (Harris and Lavan 1992).

The right to move is a right held by European citizens, but European citizenship is a derived consequence of national citizenship of a member state of the Union. Since each member state has its own nationality laws, European citizenship itself reinforces the importance of each national member state. Inhabitants of a European country who do not have this citizenship thus become 'third country nationals'. Third country nationals have tended to acquire rights if they have long-term legal residence: the right to residence itself, the right to economic activity, the right to economic participation at the workplace, and above all, access to social rights. Since such rights are also defined at the national state level, the intersection of national and European law prevents any simple hierarchy of rights across the EU as a whole. German Turkish workers in Germany have more employment rights than British workers in Britain, but will have fewer political rights than British citizens if they move to the UK.

The EU is composed of distinct *national* welfare states. Certainly, the EU does ensure limited rights to universal healthcare through the EHIC (European Health Insurance Card) but the EHIC is the exception. Each national welfare state involves different entitlements and different contributions. What matters is not just the benefits but how they are funded. As the current British attempt to restrict recent Polish migrants' access to benefits shows, where the welfare state (whether social democratic or liberal) pays benefits funded from general taxation, payments to new arrivals will appear illegitimate. New arrivals are by definition not (yet) members of the national community which has over generations created 'our' welfare state. Conversely, insurance-based systems should be more exportable: to the extent that benefits depend on prior contributions, benefits can be paid out anywhere to anyone who has paid into the system. Once again, what matters is the national welfare state.

Skilled immigration

During the twentieth century the traditional immigrant countries such as the USA and Canada developed immigration policies that explicitly favoured the more skilled. Australia and Canada operate points-based (PBS) immigration systems: potential immigrants are awarded points for attributes such as qualifications and English-language competence. Above a certain level of points the applicants gain entry. A points-based system runs the risk that once in the country immigrants will find that their qualifications are actually underused or not even recognised. The alternative is an employer-based system where the employer applies for the visa and the immigrant is essentially tied to the job for which they entered the country. Thus under the US H1B programme applicants are required to have the equivalent of a bachelor's degree, but they enter the USA sponsored by a specific employer. During their stay such immigrants are entitled to apply for permanent residency (the 'Green Card') and thus, like entrants to Canada through the PBS system, can ultimately apply for citizenship.

Within Europe there are major differences which can partly be explained by the different 'varieties of capitalism' (Chapter 3). The UK has always been relatively open to skilled labour and its service class is the most cosmopolitan in Europe (see Section 5.4). Working within a liberal market economy, British employers will buy rather than make skilled labour – and demand access to the international labour market to get it (Devitt 2011). Since 2008 the UK has operated a points-based system for potential immigrants from outside the EU and the UK is often held up as a model for other European countries (Menz 2009). By contrast, in co-ordinated market economies such as Sweden or Germany trade unions have more power and these countries have been slower to import skilled labour (Cerna 2009). In 2000 Germany tried to attract Indian software workers with special work permits, but the initiative was a complete failure.[2] Subsequently the immigration law of 2005 granted skilled immigrants immediate permanent residence, but the results have been limited.

Given the plethora of national schemes within the Schengen Zone, in 2007 the European Commission proposed a common EU 'Blue Card' to standardise entry procedures and allow skilled immigrants access to the entire European labour market. The Blue Card was more restrictive than the American Green Card after which it was named (it would not have given the right to permanent residency). Furthermore, member states were unwilling to give up their national control over migration and the Blue Card is hardly used (Cerna 2014). Skilled immigration remains overwhelmingly shaped within national states (McGovern 2007).

Plugging the holes in fortress Europe

In 1985 the Benelux countries, France and Germany signed the Schengen Agreement which committed them to remove all mutual border controls. Apart from Ireland and the UK, all EU states are now committed to implementing Schengen; the non-EU states of Norway, Iceland and Switzerland have also joined. Since this means that there is freedom of movement right across Continental Europe, it has created pressure for a stronger common external frontier. From the Dublin Asylum Convention of 1991 onwards member states have been moving towards common procedures towards asylum seekers and for mutual support in policing external borders, especially in southern Europe. Schengen also pushes European states to adopting a common visa policy, so that new controls are erected not just • on the border but in the country of origin.

It is frequently claimed that states cannot control migration flows. In a classic argument (Hollifield 2004) claimed that liberal democratic states are constrained by their own liberal principles and by international law. A more sociological argument is that migration flows become self-perpetuating: elite attitudes are generally pro-immigration, ethnic networks ensure a continual flow of new recruits, a growing and well-organised 'migration industry' (including employers, traffickers, lawyers and NGOs) depends on continued migration (Czaika and de Haas 2013). However, migration flows depend partly on the situation in origin countries: refugees are produced by wars, especially civil wars. The collapse of the Soviet empire and the consequent Balkan wars produced the mass movements of the 1990s; between 1990 and 2000 over three-quarters of a million inhabitants of the former Yugoslavia entered the European Union (Castles and Miller 2009: 194); the conflicts in Iraq, Afghanistan, Libya and Syria are producing refugees today.

Nonetheless, tighter admission procedures can reduce the flow of asylum seekers, and European co-operation does now ensure that applicants can no longer make multiple applications to different countries. National policies have become more differentiated: restraining unskilled immigration, attracting qualified immigrants (de Haas *et al.* 2014). The UK experience shows how migration flows are influenced by policy. As late as 1994 emigration from the UK exceeded immigration (ONS 2015). Then immigration increased dramatically as a result of decisions by New Labour: (1) relaxing restrictions on family reunification, (2) facilitating foreign students who worked part-time, and somewhat later (3) opening the labour market immediately to immigration from the new member states of the EU.

One reason for the continued inflow of unskilled immigrants is family reunification of *some* ethnic groups. Whereas the term 'family reunification' suggests a once-off movement whereby an immigrant is reunited with his or her family, now 'reunification' is used to continually replenish the immigrant community through marriage to spouses from outside. This is especially the case for the poorer Muslim families of Germany and Britain. This, however, is not immutable: in the UK the 1990s changes have been reversed and 'New Commonwealth' immigration has been falling (ONS 2015).

Perhaps Fortress Europe is therefore under construction, despite the fact that at the moment so many new arrivals can tunnel under its walls or even just walk through the gate. While the term 'fortress' is used in a derogatory way, a fortress is after a place of safety and of refuge. So long as immigrants have easy access to welfare state resources, access to such benefits has to be controlled, in the first instance by more effective policing of the borders. The very importance of social cohesion in Europe (Brochmann 1999: 15) – as compared to the USA – places a stark choice between easier entrance and social cohesion. International evidence suggests that increased immigration is only acceptable if immigrants' social rights are restricted (Ruhs and Martin 2008). Given that this is so difficult to do, it is difficult to see how continued mass immigration can be publicly acceptable.

7.4 Post-fordist migration

The combination of tighter controls and economic downturn reduced immigration into Europe in the 1980s. At the end of the decade, however, new forms of immigration began. Migration became again partly the result of war, economic crisis and political collapse. In these terms migration today is more reminiscent of the post-World War I period than of the high peak of the previous wave of globalisation before World War I with which it is often compared.

The new migration flows

The EU's southern border is a dramatic income precipice. Whereas there is a large gap between living standards in Mexico and the USA, the gap between Africa (especially sub-Saharan Africa) and Europe is a multiple of this. Even in the age of globalisation, geography still matters: emigrants from Africa try to cross the Mediterranean, few try to cross the Atlantic. The physical frontiers are also the most porous in southern Europe. Greece, Italy and Spain, traditionally countries of emigration, have now become the destination for large numbers of illegal immigrants.

Especially in Africa, many states are not just poor, they have collapsed into civil war and banditry. Wars in the Horn of Africa and in the Middle East have also generated literally millions of refugees, including at the time of writing (2015) 3.5 million Syrians. Most remain close to their original homes, and the numbers reaching Europe are absolutely trivial in comparison. This does not alter the fact that the pressure at the gates is mounting. In 2014 over 3,000 illegal immigrants died trying cross the Mediterranean; in 2015, in scenes prefigured forty years ago by Jean Raspail's apocalyptic novel *Le Camp des Saints* (Raspail 1977), thousands of migrants crowded onto unseaworthy boats hoping that they would be duly rescued by European authorities and NGOs.

The new immigrants are therefore different from the 'fordist' immigrants: more diverse in terms of origin, motivation and destination. With the crucial exception of immigrants from the new member states of Eastern Europe, unskilled migrants now enter as family members of those already legally resident ('family reunification'), as various forms of refugees and asylum seekers, and as illegals. According to one estimate, in the year 2000 fully half a million foreigners entered the (then) EU illegally, a fivefold increase on 1994 (King 2002). However, the most systematic attempt to count the uncountable suggested that the number of illegal immigrants living in the EU15 actually fell between 2002 and 2008 to somewhere between 1.9 million and 3.8 million. This was partly because of changes in the *geographic* inflow (fewer people entering) but crucially because of *status-related* flows (significant numbers being legalised, in particular in amnesties in Italy, Greece and Spain). 'Illegal' is not necessarily a permanent status: migrants can become legal, but they can also become illegal again, especially if status is linked to employment (Clandestino 2009; Reynieri 2004).

In recent decades a crucial international trend has been the rise of skilled migration. Indeed, by 2005 across all OECD countries 28.2 per cent of immigrants had a tertiary education compared to 20.9 per cent of the indigenous population (OECD 2008). This difference is especially clear in countries such as Canada and Australia with selective immigration policies. In most EU member states, recently arrived immigrants are better educated than those who arrived more than ten years ago, but France and the southern member states continue to receive immigrants from outside the EU27 with only minimal education (Eurostat 2011).

In the fordist period immigrants were overwhelmingly employed men: compared to the host population immigrants had higher activity rates. Those times are long gone. Everywhere, male immigrants from poor countries are more likely to be unemployed than native men. Immigrants who have recently arrived in Europe are more likely to be unemployed than those who have been here some time: in the Swedish case, recently arrived immigrants have an unemployed rate of fully 27 per cent, but this falls to 13 per cent of those who have been in the country for eight or more years. Now many immigrants are women and they are less likely to be looking for work than women from the host population. As Figure 7.1 shows, this is especially the case for women from less developed countries. The extreme case is Germany, where in 2008 84 per cent of all women aged between 25 and 54 were active on the labour market, but among immigrant women from poorer countries outside the EU the activity rate was only 55 per cent. Although there has been a feminisation of labour immigration, with women from countries such as the Philippines or Morocco entering to work, many other women are entering for family reunification and their families do not expect (or allow) them to work.

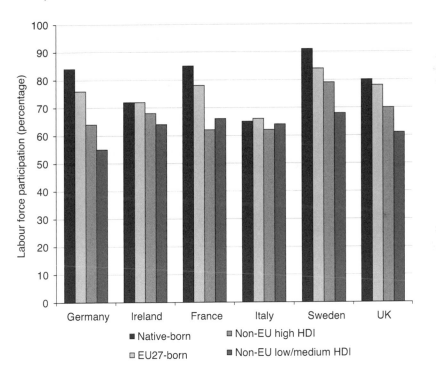

Figure 7.1 Women, immigration and labour force participation (derived from Eurostat (2011: Table 1.4)).

Note
'High HDI' and 'low/medium HDI' are proxies for 'high income' and 'low to medium income' countries respectively.

New migration and income distribution

New immigrants are very different to established ethnic minorities. Initially at least, immigrants compare their wages and their working conditions with what they could have received 'at home' rather than with wages and conditions of native workers in their new country. Furthermore, to the extent that they see their stay in the new country as temporary, so issues like job security, promotion, etc., are of less importance. This 'dual frame of reference' (Waldinger and Lichter 2003) means that immigrants are prepared to accept wages and conditions that might be unacceptable to natives (Ruhs and Anderson 2010). Employers therefore often see new immigrants as 'good workers' and contrast their 'work ethic' favourably to that of the natives (Gomberg-Muñoz 2010).

In the current context the mass immigration of unskilled workers (or more precisely, of immigrants taking unskilled jobs) undermines wages at the bottom of the income distribution. In the short term this form of mass immigration will, ceteris paribus, therefore make the society more unequal. It *may* be the case over time that there is both an overall increase in GDP and that enough of this increase is at the bottom of the income distribution to cancel out the natives' loss of earnings, but even this does not necessarily cancel out the impact on inequality. In other words, it is possible that everyone may end up better off, but the gap between poor and rich has nonetheless increased.

Any empirical study of the impact of immigration that focuses only on the impact on average wages will be misleading. Thus an initial review concluded that:

> The available evidence suggests that immigration has had a small negative impact on the lowest-paid workers in the UK, and a small positive impact on the earnings of higher-paid workers. Resident workers whose wages have been adversely affected by immigration are likely to include a significant proportion of previous immigrants and workers from ethnic minority groups.
>
> (House of Lords 2008: 28)

More recent empirical work in economics has disaggregated the impact of immigration and clearly suggests that immigration has different impacts on different groups of wage and salary earners. For the UK Dustmann *et al.* (2013) show that in the period 1997–2005 immigration led to an overall increase in average wages in the UK, but had a negative impact on wages of the lower paid. As they say, immigration has a 'sizeable negative impact of immigration on the lower wage quantiles' (160) and again, 'Overall, these results suggest that immigration tends to stretch the wage distribution, particularly below the median' (161). Equally, a recent report by the UK Migration Advisory Committee concludes that 'Wages for the low-paid may be lowered as a result of [low skill] migration, although … this effect is moderate at the national level but possibly larger in London' (MAC 2014: 31f.).

New migration and occupational structure

More, however, is involved than overall wage levels. The new availability of large numbers of people ready to work long hours in unpleasant and even unregulated environments changes the jobs that are available. The transformation of the US social structure is indicative here. Crucial sectors of agriculture have become dependent on low wage immigrant labour; the wages are low partly because the labour is illegal. Meatpacking used to be heavily unionised with a wage premium because of the dangers involved. Now firms have moved to rural areas and some of the largest firms in the industry employ large numbers of illegal immigrants (Martin 2009: 94). Employers – sometimes joined by immigration advocates – argue that American food production can only occur if there is (cheap) immigrant labour. As the leading researcher comments with reference to American nineteenth-century debates: 'History is littered with predictions that there are no alternatives to slaves or guest workers to produce food and fiber' (Martin 2009: 139).

In the UK the use of newly arrived immigrant labour merely continues the long-established 'low road' strategy of British industry, with firms in mature sectors competing on cost rather than on quality and innovation. One case study describes a bottle recycling factory in north-east England with a workforce of nearly 300 workers, 90 per cent of whom are now migrants. When indigenous workers were no longer prepared to tolerate the wages and conditions, management began to recruit local women, then young workers, then migrants, first refugees from the Balkans, then from Eastern Europe. The expansion of the EU in 2004 allowed the firm to recruit workers from Poland and Latvia, this time without infringing any immigration laws (MacKenzie and Forde 2009). In food processing and food packing about 40 per cent of the workforce is now foreign, with over 90 per cent of employers citing such workers' 'work ethic' as their main attraction (Ruhs and Anderson 2010: 204). The supermarket chains that now dominate British food retailing exert continuous price pressure on their suppliers, and this in turn puts pressure on wage costs. This is a relatively labour-intensive industry, and the few ethnographic studies we have report relatively simple levels of mechanisation, little capital investment and harsh supervision – conditions which reminded at least one Polish worker of a 'labour camp' (Wilczek 2012: 144).

In the UK the new availability of migrant labour has contributed to firms' continuation of the low technology option. Rather than changing their production technology, firms innovate in their recruitment strategy to ensure a ready supply of what they consider to be the appropriate workers. The fact that one new source of labour is the accession states of the EU is ambiguous. On the one hand such workers are clearly prepared to take more arduous work at lower levels of pay than are native workers (including members of established ethnic minorities), but on the other hand as EU citizens they have been granted full access to the labour market. This means that they cannot be tied to individual employers in the way that is normal for holders of work permits, let alone for illegal immigrants. Union organisation is difficult but not impossible and minimum wage legislation is operative (Fitzgerald and Hardy 2010). While the so-called gangmaster system allowed a new class of non-EU labour to develop, it too has been restricted by recent legislation (Cohen 2008).

Everywhere in Europe the new immigrants contribute to the workforce of the private service sector, in catering and hotels, domestic cleaning and domestic caring work, In southern Europe immigration allows the continuation of social relations that would otherwise disappear: low skill and low productivity firms in manufacturing and 'traditional' small-holding farmers. Especially in southern Italy, a ready supply of illegal labour allows elderly people to be looked after at home without any modernisation of state-funded social care services (Finotelli and Sciortinno 2009; Reynieri 1998). For men a main destination has been the construction industry, especially in Spain. Here too immigration has been interwoven with a transformation of employment relations. The employment of illegal immigrants has been both cause and effect of the shift to more extensive sub-contracting and, in some countries, 'false' self-employment, all of which makes regulation of building sites much more difficult (Fellini *et al.* 2007).

Some workplaces are emerging which appear to be outside even minimal restraints and thus closer to actual slavery. In France and Italy Chinese entrepreneurs have entered the clothing and textile industry and imported their own labour. The Sedain-Poppincourt area of Paris has become filled with Chinese-owned workshops finishing clothes for the Parisian *prêt-à-porter* trade. In Italy much of high fashion production is now partially controlled by Chinese and Italian criminal gangs (Saviono 2007). This is a world of micro-firms who often utilise the labour of family members: leisure and family life are sacrificed to extraordinarily long working hours (Ceccagno 2007). In some Italian industrial districts, of which the most famous is Prato, Chinese firms have essentially supplanted indigenous firms in the entire production chain of *pronto moda* (ready-to-wear fashion) (Ceccagno 2003; Mallet and Dimone 2011).

Even more difficult to document, but clearly now employing many thousands of women, particularly from Eastern Europe, is the growing sex industry (e.g. Lazaridis 2001; Glenny 2007). Here the new criminal enterprises are only doing more brutally what many employers do: using the illegal status of their employees to ensure compliance. Indeed, illegality is one central aspect of post-fordist European immigration. In countries such as Germany, the *Gastarbeiter* were *recruited* either by government agencies or by large companies. Although they had restricted rights, they were nonetheless legal and worked in regulated labour markets. By contrast, most low wage immigration today in Europe is supply-driven and in lightly regulated labour markets where illegality is more likely. Finally, in the fordist period there was full employment and those not at work were overwhelmingly women outside the labour market. By contrast, today virtually all of Western Europe has high unemployment, especially among the descendants of the earlier generation of immigrants (Section 8.2). When the welfare system provides a minimal standard of living, immigration and unemployment can co-exist, often in the same geographical areas.

7.5 East–West migration and the European Union

Interwoven with the new movement *into* Europe has been new movement *within* Europe. In what used to be Eastern Europe and the Soviet Union the implosion of authoritarian state socialism led not to a market economy but to a form of bandit-capitalism. Apart from in what had been East Germany, there was no expansion eastwards of the European social model. Lacking the self-confidence and the moral responsibility to put forward its own solution for the reconstruction of Eastern Europe, the European Union ended up as merely the destination for new migrant flows as living standards in the East collapsed. Astonishingly, it took nearly twenty years – the same length of time as between the world wars of the first half of the last century – before there was any real end in sight to this haemorrhage.

Immediately after the revolutions of 1989, emigration from the East was possible and, despite entry restrictions in the West, movement from East to West increased dramatically. Much movement was temporary, sometimes in a traditional way, as in short-term seasonal work in agriculture. Other movements, such as 'tourists' who filled suitcases with Western goods to sell back at home, had a pre-history in the last years of some communist regimes (Cyrus 2006: 27). The extent of this new short-term migration suggested that East–West movement did not fit within the traditional paradigms that had dominated the understanding of immigration in Western Europe since the 1950s (see especially, Favell 2008). This became clear once EU membership meant that NMS citizens had the right to move within the EU. As a Polish resident in Ireland remarked: 'It's not that anybody gives you anything, they don't do you a favour, the fact that you are here, [not that] you need a visa or you need to bow low to everybody around. It's my right to be here.'[3]

Such mobility takes different forms. One extreme is movement to Italy, where East Europeans work almost entirely in low skill jobs, especially domestic service and care work. Here the migrant is usually sending remittances home and his or her migration may well have been a collective decision on the part of the family remaining in Poland. Migration to the UK is predominantly in low skilled jobs but in all sectors of the economy; it also includes a higher proportion of students and those with some educational qualifications; it includes more family members. Finally, in the mass movement of East Europeans to Ireland between 2004 and 2008 Poles in particular were spread throughout the occupational hierarchy with a significant number entering directly into 'white-collar' administrative and even professional jobs (Krings *et al.* 2013: 46).

This right to movement is made real by changes in transport technology. Deregulation of air transport allowed the growth of low cost carriers across Europe such as Ryanair, German Wings, etc., and this growth has been fastest in the new member states. Most obviously, flights became cheaper. However, thanks above all to online booking, air travel became much simpler, so that booking a flight across Europe became easier than buying a long-distance train ticket. In the past, airline routes had been focused on a few major hubs, but low cost carriers initiated point-to-point flights from one regional airport direct to another (Williams and Balaz 2009) and this creates a certain flattening or suburbanisation of European travel. Just as in the city mass car ownership means that most journeys are now suburb to suburb (and not suburb to city centre), so air travel is increasingly local (regional) airport to local airport.

This decentralisation is exacerbated by the dramatic increase of electronic communication, from mobile phones to web-based social networking. Whereas not everyone can have an airport at the end of the road, everyone can have a mobile phone. An earlier generation of immigrants pointed their satellite TV dishes eastwards and southwards; now Polish migrants logged on to Nasza Klasa (*Our Class* – Polish social networking site) wherever they were. Stories of parents reading their children bedtime stories on Skype are doubtless somewhat exaggerated, but new electronic media do allow routine and casual communication with home in a way that was not possible before (Krings *et al.* 2013: 117).

In this context notions of emigration as a one-way permanent move become problematic. Migration can be a series of repeated visits, as in seasonal work in agriculture, but it can be a series of continued return visits. As we have seen above, return migration itself is not new: it was one untold story of the *Gastarbeiter period*; it was important part of European settlerism. However, the combination of new technologies and a common European legal framework allows a new level of fluidity.

East–West migration has further features which differentiate it from traditional migration. Polish migrants are not restricted to the lower end of the labour market: in Dublin migrants have worked on building sites, but also in architects' offices; many of them form part of 'middling migration'. When Favell (2008) defines the new NMS migrants as 'a new servant class' he is therefore focusing on only one part of this migration. However, while social networks are important, they are now thinner and more transient since migrants can access the market directly both because they are legal and because of electronic media. And crucially, many of these migrants have not simply moved from one country to another to remain there permanently. Many young migrants are 'free movers', ready to move on somewhere. Migration is not only the search for a new home to replace the old.

This migration is not, however, free of constraints and does not involve the creation of a simple European space within which people move. East–West migration was greatest to the UK and Ireland because these countries had relatively flexible labour markets which were relatively easy for migrants to enter (unlike the more regulated labour markets, where migrants are more likely to be locked at the bottom). Furthermore, these countries were also preferred by some as a gateway to the Anglosphere beyond the seas – to the USA, but also to Canada or Australia. State boundaries remain important and indeed structure these movements. And finally, language still matters. Lacking Continental European language proficiency, young Irish fleeing their crisis-ridden economy are largely restricted to the Anglosphere: they travel to Australia, not to Germany (Wickham *et al.* 2013).

7.6 From European migration to European mobility?

Despite such increased movement, mobility within the EU itself remains far lower than movement within the USA (Section 1.3). For a long time this has been defined as a problem: one policy objective has been to increase the physical mobility of labour within the EU. Yet it is immigrants from outside the EU15 and from outside the EU altogether who have largely ensured this form of flexibility. Within the old EU the least important migrations are those most desired by traditional policy: movement from areas of high unemployment to areas of labour shortage.

Within the EU15 adequate social welfare ensures that few low skilled Europeans are prepared to move. The rewards are greater – and the obstacles probably less – in more privileged areas of the private sector. Already by the early 1990s the growth of French investment in south-east England led to an influx of French managers and professionals (Boyle *et al.* 1994), while on a Friday evening at the Gare du Nord young French professionals in the City of London were returning home to spend their British salaries in civilisation (e.g. Vinen 2002: 584). By the 1990s managerial labour markets were Europeanising to some limited extent, enabling people to move between countries but within similar business milieux. And the European project itself has generated some novel forms of transnational service class mobility, from the polyglot population of Brussels to movement between Bristol and Toulouse within Airbus Industrie. Today, 'movers' within the old EU are now more likely among the well educated and the well paid. And yet again, there is British exceptionalism. Movers both from and even to Britain are more 'Euro-sceptical' than other EU movers (Rother and Nebe 2009). Yet this same British service class is more international than that of other EU15 European countries (see Section 5.4).

Even less undocumented in the formal literature is the growing phenomenon of *lifestyle mobility*. Official student exchange programmes, above all Socrates. have enabled over one million students to spend part of their studies in another European country (Teichler 2004). And while most of this mobility is very short-term, it generates and cross-cuts with longer-term migration. The lifestyle attractions of some cities such as Dublin or Barcelona, let alone London or Paris, now attract a transient youthful population, sometimes working in the designer end of the service sector, sometimes in the more down-market areas where they often merge with illegals. And such lifestyle migration can generate its own curious forms of investment: in the mid-1990s US call centres were setting up in Dublin to take advantage of the language skills, not of the indigenous Irish population, but of such migrants (Richardson and Marshall 1999).

At the other end of the life cycle, the expansion of property ownership in the service class and beyond (Section 4.3) often involves the purchase of a second home in a second country. This has led to hundreds of thousands of people buying a second home which becomes either their main home on retirement and/ or the starting point of a second career. For some time the population of Spain has included hundreds of thousands of German and UK expatriates (O'Reilly

2000). Rural areas of south-west France are home to British, Dutch and Irish expatriates (e.g. Benson 2010). More generally, an increasing number of Europeans move country for personal reasons, sometimes simply because they find another country more interesting or more pleasant, but usually in order to join a partner or relative (Santacereu *et al.* 2009). Such moves are not restricted to the service class, but they are more likely among those with educational qualifications (Recchi 2008).

From this perspective, migration to take up permanent residence in another country is a limiting case within contemporary Europe. The mass movement from the NMS at the start of the century highlighted new features of migration: electronic communication, frequent movement from country of origin to destination, the likelihood of moving on to another destination. Equally, a focus on skilled migration highlights not only different groups but different forms of movement, ranging from students spending a semester abroad to visiting scholars working for a few years in a foreign university or research laboratory (Salt 1997; Mahroum 2000). For example, a study of the Irish software industry discovered air travellers ranged from project team members working for a few weeks on a client's site to managers commuting between offices (and apartments) in Dublin and Munich and entrepreneurs commuting to work in Ireland from homes in the UK or France (Wickham and Vecchi 2009). Migration is no longer – if it ever was – coterminous with the poor and exploited moving from one country to another, there to settle in a new ethnic ghetto.

Notes

1 However, not everyone stayed. There has long been considerable return migration, both of the original immigrants on retirement (Ireland, Jamaica) and of their descendants (e.g. Sriskandarajah and Drew 2006).
2 It was criticised by German politician Jürgen Rüttgers with the slogan '*Kinder statt Inder*' (children instead of Indians). As the slogan spread around the internet, many potential applicants drew the obvious conclusion that they would not be welcome in Germany.
3 Excerpt from interview (participant 13, interview wave 6) in Migrant Careers and Aspirations Project on Polish migrants in Dublin (Krings *et al.* 2013).

Bibliography

Bade, K. (1995) *Ausländer, Aussiedler, Asyl. Eine Bestandsaufnahme*, Munich: C.H. Beck.
Beevor, A. (2002) *Berlin: The Downfall 1945*, London: Viking.
Belich, J. (2009) *Replenishing the Earth: The Settler Revolution and the Rise of the Anglo World 1783–1939*, Oxford: Oxford UP.
Benson, M. (2010) The context and trajectory of lifestyle migration: the case of British residents of Southwest France, *European Societies* 12.1: 45–64.
Boyle, M., Findlay, A.M., Lelievre, E. and Paddison, R. (1994) French investment and skill transfer in the United Kingdom. In W. Gould and A. Findlay (eds) *Population Migration and the Changing World Order*, Chichester: Wiley, pp. 47–65.

Brochmann, G. (1999) Controlling immigration in Europe. In G. Brochmann and T. Hammar (eds) *Mechanisms of Immigration Control*, London: Bloomsbury Academic, pp. 297–334.

Caldwell, C. (2009) *Reflections on the Revolution in Europe*, London: Allen Lane.

Carrington, W. and de Lima, P. (1996) The impact of 1970s repatriates from Africa on the Portuguese labor market, *Industrial & Labor Relations Review* 49.2: 330–347.

Castles, S. and Kosack, G. (1973) *Immigrant Workers and Class Structure in Western Europe*, Oxford: Oxford UP.

Castles, S. and Miller, M. (2009) *The Age of Migration: International Population Movements in the Modern World*, London: Palgrave Macmillan (first edition 1993).

Ceccagno, A. (2003) New Chinese migrants in Italy, *International Migration* 41.3: 187–214.

Ceccagno, A. (2007) Compressing personal time: ethnicity and gender within a Chinese niche in Italy, *Journal of Ethnic and Migration Studies* 33.4: 635–654.

Cerna, L. (2009) The varieties of high-skilled immigration policies: coalitions and policy outputs in advanced industrial countries, *Journal of European Public Policy* 16.1: 144–161.

Cerna, L. (2014) The EU Blue Card: preferences, policies and negotiations between member states, *Migration Studies* 2.1: 73–96.

Clandestino (2009) *Clandestino Project: Final Report*, Athens: European Commission.

Cohen, S. (2008) Modern migrants and new slaves. In Council of Europe, *Trends in Social Cohesion no. 19*, Strasbourg: Council of Europe, pp. 63–90.

Cyrus, N. (2006) Polish emigration: permanent and temporary patterns. In A. Triandafyllidou (ed.) *Contemporary Polish Migration in Europe*, New York: Edwin Mellen Press, pp. 25–46.

Czaika, M. and de Haas, H. (2013) The effectiveness of immigration policies, *Population and Development Review* 39.3: 487–508.

Darwin, J. (2009) *The Empire Project: The Rise and Fall of the British World System 1830–1970*, Cambridge: Cambridge UP.

de Haas, H., Natter, K. and Vezzoli, S. (2014) *Growing Restrictiveness or Changing Selection? The Nature and Evolution of Migration Policies*, International Migration Institute Oxford, Working Papers, Paper 96, Oxford: IMI.

Devitt, C. (2011) Varieties of capitalism, variation in labour immigration, *Journal of Ethnic and Migration Studies* 37.3: 579–596.

Douglas, R. (2013) *Orderly and Humane: The Expulsion of the Germans after the Second World War*. New Haven: Yale UP.

Dustmann, C., Frattini, T. and Preston, I. (2013) The effect of immigration along the distribution of wages, *Review of Economic Studies* 80.1: 145–173.

Eurostat (2011) *Migrants in Europe: A Statistical Portrait of the First and Second Generation*, Luxembourg: Publications Office of the European Union.

Evans, M. (2012) *Algeria: France's Undeclared War*, Oxford: Oxford UP.

Favell, A. (2008) The new face of East–West migration in Europe, *Journal of Ethnic and Migration Studies* 34.5: 701–716.

Fellini, I., Ferro, A. and Fullin, G. (2007). Recruitment processes and labour mobility: the construction industry in Europe, *Work Employment and Society* 21.2: 277–398.

Figes, O. (2002) *Natasha's Dance: A Cultural History of Russia*, London: Allen Lane/ Penguin.

Finotelli, C. and Sciortinno, G. (2009) The importance of being southern: the making of policies of immigration control in Italy, *European Journal of Migration and Law* 11.2: 119–138.

Fitzgerald, I. and Hardy, J. (2010) 'Thinking outside the box'? Trade union organizing strategies and Polish migrant workers in the United Kingdom, *British Journal of Industrial Relations* 48.1: 131–150.

Friedrichs, J. (1998) Ethnic segregation in Cologne, Germany, 1984–1994, *Urban Studies* 35.10: 1745–1763.

Glenny, M. (2007) *McMafia: A Journey through the Criminal Underworld*, London: Bodley Head.

Gomberg-Munoz, R. (2010) Willing to work: agency and vulnerability in an undocumented immigrant network, *American Anthropologist* 112.2: 295–307.

Hansen, R. (2000) *Citizenship and Immigration in Post-war Britain: The Institutional Origins of a Multi-Cultural Nation*, Oxford: Oxford UP.

Harris, R. and Lavan, A. (1992) Professional mobility in the new Europe: the case of social work, *Journal of European Social Policy* 2,1: 1–15.

Hollifield, J. (2004) The emerging migration state, *International Migration Review* 38.3: 885–912.

House of Lords (2008) *The Economic Impact of Immigration, Vol. 1*, House of Lords Select Committee on Economic Affairs, London: The Stationery Office.

King, R. (2002) Towards a new map of European migration, *International Journal of Population Geography* 8.2: 89–106.

Krings, T., Moriarty, E., Wickham, J., Bobek, A. and Salamońska, J. (2013) *New Mobilities in Europe: Polish Migration to Ireland post-2004*, Manchester: Manchester UP.

Lazaridis, G. (2001) Trafficking and prostitution: the growing exploitation of migrant women in Greece, *European Journal of Women's Studies* 8.1: 67–102.

MAC (Migration Advisory Committee) (2014) *The Growth of EU and Non-EU Labour in Low-skilled Jobs and its Impact on the UK*, London: Migration Advisory Committee.

McGovern, P. (2007) Immigration, labour markets and employment relations: problems and prospects, *British Journal of Industrial Relations* 45.2: 217–235.

MacKenzie, R. and Forde, C. (2009) The rhetoric of the good worker versus the realities of employers' use and the experience of migrant workers, *Work Employment and Society* 23.1: 142–159.

Mahroum, S. (2000) High skilled globetrotters: mapping the international migration of human capital, *R&D Management* 30.1: 23–30.

Mallet, V. and Dimone, G. (2011) Europe: hidden economy, *Financial Times*, 8 June.

Marie, C.-V. (1994) L'immigration en France dans les années quatre-vingt dix: nouvelle donne pour l'emploi et nouveux enjeux de société, *Sociologie du Travail* 36.2: 143–163.

Martin, P. (2009) *Importing Poverty? Immigration and the Changing Face of Rural America*, New Haven: Yale UP.

Menz, G. (2009) *The Political Economy of Managed Migration: Non-state Actors, Europeanisation and the Politics of Designing Migration Policies*, Oxford: Oxford UP.

Naumann, K. (2005) Child care and feminism in West Germany and Sweden in the 1960s and 1970s, *Journal of European Social Policy* 15.1: 46–63.

Noiriel, G. (2001) *État, nation et immigration*, Paris: Gallimard.

OECD (2008) *A Profile of Immigrant Populations in the 21st Century: Data from OECD Countries*, Paris: OECD.

ONS (Office of National Statistics) (2015) *Long-term Migration into and out of the United Kingdom, 1964–2013*, www.neighbourhood.statistics.gov.uk/HTMLDocs/dvc123/index.html. Accessed 27 July 2015.

O'Reilly, K. (2000) *The British on the Costa Del Sol*, London: Routledge.

Overy, R. (1997) *Russia's War*, London: Penguin Books.

Raspail, J. (1977) *The Camp of the Saints*, London: Sphere.

Recchi, E. (2008) Cross-state mobility in the EU: trends, puzzles and consequences, *European Societies* 10.2: 197–224.

Reyneri, E. (1998) The role of the underground economy in irregular immigration to Italy. Cause or effect? *Journal of Ethnic and Migration Studies* 24.2: 313–331.

Reyneri, E. (2004) Immigrants in a segmented and often undeclared labour market, *Journal of Modern Italian Studies* 9.1: 71–93.

Richardson, R. and Marshall, J. (1999) Teleservices, call centres and urban and regional development, *Service Industries Journal* 19.1: 96–116.

Rother, N. and Nebe, T. (2009) More mobile, more European? Free movement and European identity. In E. Recchi and A. Favell (eds) *Pioneers of European Integration* Cheltenham: Edward Elgar, pp. 120–155.

Ruhs, M. and Martin, P. (2008) Numbers vs rights: trade-offs and guest workers programs, *International Migration Review* 42.1: 249–265.

Salt, J. (1997) *International Movements of the Highly Skilled*, International Migration Unit Occasional Paper no. 3, Paris: OECD.

Santacreu, O., Baldoni, E. and Albert, M. (2009) Deciding to move: migration projects in an integrating Europe. In E. Recchi and A. Favell (eds) *Pioneers of European Integration*, Cheltenham: Edward Elgar, pp. 52–71.

Saviono, R. (2007) *Gomorrah: Italy's Other Mafia*, London: Macmillan.

Snyder, T. (2010) *Bloodlands: Europe Between Hitler and Stalin*, London: Bodley Head.

Sriskandarajah, D. and Drew, C. (2006) *Brits Abroad*, London: IPPR.

Teichler, U. (2004) Temporary study abroad: the life of ERASMUS students, *European Journal of Education* 39.4 395–408.

Theil, S. (2010) The incredible shrinking continent, *Newsweek*, 18 February.

TNS Qual+ (2010) *European Citizenship – Cross-Border Mobility: Aggregate Report*, Brussels: European Commission.

Vinen, R. (2002) *A History in Fragments: Europe in the Twentieth Century*, London: Abacus.

Waldinger, R. and Lichter, M. (2003) *How the Other Half Works: Immigration and the Social Organisation of Labor*, Berkeley: California UP.

Wickham, J. and Vecchi, V. (2009) The importance of business travel for industrial clusters – making sense of nomadic workers, *Geografiska Annaler: Series B Human Geography* 91.3: 245–255.

Wickham, J., Bobek, A., Daly, S., Krings, T., Moriarty, E. and Salamońska, J. (2013) Learning from Poland? What recent mass immigration to Ireland tells us about contemporary Irish migration. In L. Brennan (ed.) *Enacting Globalization: Multidisciplinary Perspectives on International Integration*, London: Palgrave, pp. 146–155.

Wilczek, B. (2012) 'Neither here nor there: choice and constraint in migrant worker acculturation', PhD thesis, Bournemouth University.

Williams, A. and Balaz, V. (2009) Low-cost carriers, economies of flows and regional externalities, *Regional Studies* 43.5: 677–691.

8 Ethnic diversity and the national welfare state

When in the 1990s Bundeskanzler Kohl remarked that Germany 'is not a country of immigration' (Kohl 1991) he was widely pilloried for ignoring that at the time over 8 per cent of the country's population did not have German citizenship (European Commission 1998: 67). Yet Kohl's statement was factually correct in at least one sense – and applied to all Europe. The USA is based on an immigrant population, just as it is also based on the genocide of the indigenous population. In the USA everyone, with exception of the descendants of Native Americans, can legitimately claim to have *come from somewhere else*. By contrast, in Europe, just as even more so in China or Japan, national identity is linked to a claim to a common historical past in a shared geographical place. In the words of traditional French school textbooks, '*nos ancêtres les Galles*' (our ancestors the Gauls).

The chapter begins by differentiating between structural assimilation and cultural integration. On this basis the next section of the chapter shows that, while some immigrants and their descendants often share a disadvantaged situation in the social structure, there are major differences both between groups and between countries; there has been much more successful structural assimilation than is normally assumed. The third section suggests that national models of integration are now converging on what could be called 'civic republicanism' which loosens the connection between ethnicity and national identity. Integration in Europe is in fact integration not into Europe but into specific national states. These European national states are also national welfare states and this may make integration more difficult than in the more individualistic USA.

8.1 Conceptualisating integration

Europe's 'immigrant problem' is often understood as the failure of integration. Yet what that term means is often unclear. Does it mean that immigrants (or their descendants) are disadvantaged in terms of jobs or education, or does it mean that immigrants (or their descendants) have different values and different identities to indigenous Europeans? In what ways if at all are these issues related to political participation, to the exercise of the rights and duties of citizenship and, most fundamentally of all, to loyalty to the specific nation state in which Europeans all live?

Most accounts of integration begin with some differentiation between structure and culture. Thus an early study of Irish immigrants to Britain defined 'structural assimilation' as involving 'occupational distributions, fertility rates and settlement patterns ... and also marriage', and contrasted all of these to the 'normative belief system' of the Irish and British groups (Hornsby Smith and Dale 1988). Other writers (e.g. Dubet 1989, cited in van Zanten 1997) differentiated between socio-economic integration, cultural assimilation and political participation.

Table 8.1 shows one widely conceptualised interaction of the first two dimensions with four logical possibilities. An immigrant group is structurally assimilated (right-hand column) when it has the same 'objective' position as the host population, so that members of the group have similar occupations to the host population; conversely, if this does not happen (left-hand column) the group is concentrated in particular areas of the occupational structure (usually, of course, the least skilled and the least prestigious). Similarly the minority group can achieve a similar culture to the host population (lower row) or retain a distinct culture (upper row).

Putting these two dimensions together generates four cells. These are related to conventional understandings of the dominant immigrant experience in different European countries. Thus in the case of 'ethnic exclusion' (upper left cell) immigrants are excluded from occupational equality and maintain a separate culture (while a separate culture can act as a defence against discrimination and hostility, it will nonetheless be used by the host society to justify exclusion). The polar opposite is 'merger' (lower right cell) where both immigrant and host groups share a common culture and have the same structural positions. On the other diagonal are situations where only one dimension is positive. Thus the immigrant population may accept the values of the host population but nonetheless be objectively excluded from high occupations (lower left cell). In this situation ethnic politicians and cultural nationalists will describe their own group in terms of 'false consciousness' since they believe that members are denying the reality of their own situation. Finally, immigrants may achieve occupational parity with the host population but nonetheless maintain their own identity (upper right cell). A positive evaluation would describe this situation as a successful multi-cultural society or a nation of communities. European commentators label the same configuration more negatively as one of parallel societies. In

Table 8.1 Conceptualising integration

		Structural assimilation	
		NO	YES
Cultural integration	NO	Ethnic exclusion	Multi-cultural nation Parallel societies (Europe) (Segmented assimilation (USA))
	YES	Illusionary equality	Merger

the USA many new immigrants fill the same structural position as the native underclass: this combination of cultural separation with occupational equality has been termed 'segmented assimilation' (Portes and Zhou 1993).

Reality, of course, is far more complex than this simple framework. Even in the same country and at the same time, there are many different groups of 'immigrants'. As the next section shows, even the apparently objective issue of structural assimilation is not only multi-dimensional but often entangled with issues of culture and identity. And finally, the notion of assimilation can be seen as normative. The determined imposition of a new American identity on nineteenth-century immigrants grates with contemporary sensibilities: being boiled in a melting pot is hardly pleasant (Rumbaut 2005). Today members of many ethnic groups in Europe find the equation of integration with assimilation a denigration of their traditions, memories and identity (e.g. Moran 2012).

8.2 Structural assimilation: the European melting pot?

Structural assimilation involves positions in the social structure occupied by individuals: positions in the education system, the occupational structure, the housing market. Here it appears straightforward to compare immigrants and natives: do the two groups live in similar housing areas, reach the same levels of education, achieve similar jobs? On at least the last two of these three dimensions, there would be general agreement that *assimilation* is desirable. Indeed, failure to achieve assimilation (defined as the lack of difference between immigrants and non-immigrants) could be taken as showing discrimination or exploitation. By contrast, assimilation in terms of values, national identity or religion may be desired by some host societies but rejected by immigrants themselves.

Under-achievement does not *prove* discrimination, even though this is the assumption of ethnic monitoring. Some ethnic groups face hostility and discrimination but over-achieve relative to the host population. For example, in the early twentieth century Jews were over-represented in the economic elites of Europe by a factor of thirty-three in Germany, and nine in Russia (Ferguson 2002: 378),[1] but still faced overt social hostility. By the 1980s second generation Irish immigrants in Britain were more successful occupationally than the overall British population (Hornsby-Smith and Dale 1988) and by 2001 'White Irish' women were significantly better placed in the occupational structure than 'White British' women (Walter 2004). None of this proves that Britain had magically been cleansed of anti-Irish prejudice. In the USA some recent immigrant groups also over-achieve relative to the indigenous population (Portes and Zhou 1993). 'An appeal to racism by itself may have little explanatory value without considering how a target group reacts to exclusion' (Modood 2004: 94, cited in Heath *et al.* 2008). If over-achievement does not prove that racism has disappeared, it follows that under-achievement is not necessarily the result of racism or discrimination.

Some forms of structural 'segregation' may at least in part be actively chosen by the immigrant population. For example, immigrants may well prefer to live next to people like themselves. Equally, although we assume educational success is desired by all, historically many European working class children have been discouraged by their parents from attempting to go to university (Jackson and Marsden 1962) just as today some immigrant parents may regard education for their daughters as less important than finding a suitable husband.

The term 'immigrant' is also problematic. An assessment of structural assimilation should compare the *second* generation of an immigrant population with the host population. New arrivals may have some advantages in the labour market compared to 'natives' (e.g. greater mobility) but they are also likely to face disadvantages, ranging from language to lack of local knowledge, which can hardly be blamed on discrimination. Furthermore, the vast majority of the fordist immigrants entered Europe as unskilled workers (Section 7.1), so their initial position was lower than that of the host population as a whole. What matters is therefore the position of their children, who were not immigrants but now members of an ethnic minority. And to complicate the situation still further, strictly speaking this second generation should be compared not to the host population as a whole but to *the children of comparable individuals within the host population.*

Notions of integration and of assimilation assume that the host population provides the measure of achievement; they assume that the host society is itself unchanged by immigration. Yet in Europe immigration has altered the society itself. Such changes range from the obvious, such as definitions of national identity and culture, through to less obvious but fundamental changes in the occupational structure (see Section 7.1), the housing market and even the welfare system. If immigrants had not arrived in Europe, Europe itself would be different.

And the historical context changes. For the *Gastarbeiter* generation the growth of middle mass jobs generated the possibility of social mobility. For some time now in the USA – and perhaps more recently in Europe – the structure has begun to change as the middle contracts and the society moves from diamond to hour-glass. For the immigrants' children, social mobility now means clawing their way into a contracting middle mass.

Finally, comparisons necessarily require definitions of who is being counted. Studies of the 'second generation' often make a pragmatic decision to focus on the children of foreign-born residents. This now underestimates the number of people who might be described by some others as 'immigrants' and might be classified by themselves as members of ethnic minorities – even though they were born in Europe and are citizens of a European nation state. The British term 'BME' (Black and Minority Ethnic) or the German expression *Menschen mit Migrationshintergrund* (people from migration background) are closer to the reality of European ethnic minorities than the term 'immigrant' which is best reserved for those who have actually immigrated in their own lifetimes.

Housing

Immigrant 'ghettoes' are widely seen as one of the most negative possible consequences of immigration. Yet ghettoes as such are created by the host society. In Germany early *Gastarbeiter* were housed in factory barracks; in France and in Britain the new arrivals were pushed into the most marginal accommodation. In Britain this meant the cheapest private rented accommodation; in France it meant literally shanty towns – *bidonvilles*. Everywhere immigrants subsequently gained access to state housing such as the French HLM – *habitations à loyers modérés* (low rent housing) which had initially been created for the 'local' working class (and, at least in Paris, for the lower middle class).

In the new century there was a fear that Europe was becoming segregated. In the major cities more and more housing areas appeared to be dominated entirely by immigrants and/or the more established ethnic minorities: Rosengraben in the Swedish city of Malmo, La Courneuve in Paris, Kreuzberg in Berlin. After the race riots in Bradford in 2001 British media reported that whole areas of the city had a Muslim population living a separate life to the rest of society. Articulating such concerns, after the 7 July terrorist murders in London by three British Muslims in 2005 the then chair of the British Commission for Racial Equality, Trevor Philips, claimed that Britain was 'sleepwalking towards segregation'. Many European cities have concentrations of ethnic minorities, but do such concentrations amount to 'ghettoes' and is it the case that the population is increasingly segregated on ethnic and/or religious lines? Is Europe becoming like the USA?

Historically blacks in American cities have been concentrated in *ghettoes*. Ghettoes are doubly exclusive: they are inhabited entirely by one group, and all members of the group live in the ghetto. Furthermore, ghettoes are constrained: the ghetto population is compelled to live in the ghetto by law, discrimination or whatever. After all, the term 'ghetto' derives from the small area of European mediaeval cities where *all* Jews were *compelled* to live. An ethnic enclave by contrast is very different: not only does just a minority of the minority live in the enclave, but even within the enclave this group does not predominate. Given that in 2000 two-thirds of Chicago's black population lived in census tracts that were 90 to 100 per cent black, 'the assertion that Bradford and Leicester are more segregated than Chicago and Miami simply cannot be sustained.' (Peach 2009: 1391).

For writers like Peach, the term 'ghetto' is appropriate for the black quarter of an American city, but not for the ethnic areas of British cities. First, most members of the minority population do not live in areas which are dominated by one minority: most are minorities within 'white' areas. Second, the concentration can be a matter of choice. Members of ethnic minorities are often *less* segregated (in the sense of living close to members of their own ethnic group) than they would like to be. People may want to live near family, friends and familiar facilities such as ethnic shops and established mosques; in the enclave they are safe from hostility or worse from the majority. There is also no longer a simple division between a white majority and one homogenous ethnic minority, since there is a multiplicity of ethnic *minorities* and different minorities have clear tenure preferences greater than can be explained just by their occupation. Constraint cannot explain everything. In Britain the minority population is growing and some groups (especially Pakistani and Bangladeshi) are far more concentrated than others, but in *all* groups there is a trend towards dispersal (e.g. Finney and Simpson 2009). If the countryside remains almost entirely white, the suburbs are decreasingly so. In these terms there is a trend towards structural assimilation in the UK.

The situation elsewhere in Europe seems more ambiguous. Rhein (1998) reported increasing concentration of 'foreign' population within Paris, while contrasting results have been found for German cities (Friedrichs 1998; Kemper 1998). In France the Loi Borloo (2003) aimed to renovate over a quarter of a million units in the housing areas from the 1960s and the explicit objective was not to improve housing conditions but to combat segmentation (*communautarisme*). Paradoxically, the policy may have actually increased segmentation since it makes good social housing more expensive (Gilbert 2009; Blanc 2010). As in France, public policy in Germany and Sweden now explicitly tries to limit residential segregation (Phillips 2009). Yet inhabitants of some Swedish model housing projects from the 1960s are now almost entirely first or second generation immigrants (in Rosgraben in Malmo, for example, 90 per cent of the 22,000 inhabitants) (Stothard 2012). Nonetheless, a focus on 'immigrants' ignores the extent of diversity within the minority population. There are extreme cases, for instance northern English cities such as Bradford, where most of the minority population is from one ethnic group, but this itself is quite unusual.

In the USA cities are far more ethnically segregated than in Europe. This is not just because of the historic legacy of race, but also the peculiar combination of an extensive housing market, localised control over land use zoning and extreme income inequality. If almost all housing is provided through the market, this ensures that the most affluent can purchase in the most desirable areas, so that areas are stratified by income; local control of zoning ensures that communities can restrict housing types; the affluent can segregate themselves while the poor have very few resources to spend on housing. European cities are very different. In the second half of the twentieth century much housing was provided by the state or by non-profit organisations, although this has been reduced in most countries (Section 4.3); state employment provides more regular low to medium paid jobs; urban planning constrains unrestricted suburbanisation and more extensive public transport maintains the city core. The extremes of poverty remain restricted by the welfare state (Häussermann 2005; Kazepov 2005). At least to date, Europe is not America (Musterd 2005; Van Kempen and Murie 2009).

Education

One reason for the creation of mass education at the end of the nineteenth century was the creation of the next generation of national citizens. In the USA this was crucial for immigrants, or rather for their children: American schools turned the children of European immigrants into Americans. Contemporary understandings of education are more narrowly utilitarian: education is seen as valuable for its assumed linkage to employment. Nonetheless, as studies of the curriculum show, national ideologies of education remain different across Europe (e.g. Faas 2007). Another intra-European difference is the institutional structure of the educational system: where and how educational selection occurs, the extent of stratification within higher education, etc. Thus a system where children who are to continue education are selected early will disadvantage those with least resources (e.g. Hochschild and Cropper 2010). Within Europe Germany selects children for academic progress very early, while countries such as Sweden and France have more comprehensive systems; the UK and France have elite third-level institutions (Oxbridge and the Russell Group versus the rest, grandes écoles versus universities).

Much also depends on the resources and aspirations with which children enter the system – something which largely but not exclusively reflects their own background and varies massively by ethnic group. Some young people and indeed their parents may actively reject education, in a manner reminiscent of young manual working class males in the mid-twentieth century (e.g. Willis 1977) and develop an anti-school culture. Some immigrant groups, such as Indians in the UK, themselves have high educational qualifications and it is hardly surprising that their children do relatively well. Other parents may see education as a mobility project – as the key route for their children to achieve social promotion – but they may lack the resources and knowledge to translate these aspirations into reality.

Such differences between national European educational systems and differences within the immigrant population combine to ensure very diverse experiences even for the established ethnic minorities. Overall, the second generation immigrants have higher education than their parents but their educational achievements remain below those of the host population (Eurostat 2011). However, this is by no means universal. Within Britain, children of both Irish and Indian parents now match or out-perform the native population, as does the smaller Chinese minority (Heath *et al.* 2008; Berthoud 2000). Nearly everywhere there is a crucial gender difference, with girls doing better than boys. With many British commentators now suggesting that the key educational issue is the failure of young working class white *boys*, increasingly it is the interaction of ethnicity, gender and *class* that is decisive. Turkish girls in Germany achieve more than Turkish boys, and Afro-Caribbean girls in Britain are outpacing girls from the majority population (Modood *et al.* 1997: 74). Indeed, Bangladeshi girls in East London are now performing better than white children in local schools, even though they come from a community with one of the lowest educational levels of all British immigrant groups (Dench *et al.* 2006).

Far from fleeing a system that discriminates against them, ethnic minority children tend to use the educational system as much as possible. In Britain even Caribbean young men stay slightly longer in the educational system overall than young white men, although achieving slightly lower qualifications (Berthoud 2000). In Germany Turkish boys with the Abitur are more likely to go to university than boys from the majority population; the same applies to those of Maghrebi origin in France (Heath *et al.* 2008). Such young people see education as a route to employment: they are more likely than their majority peers to choose applied and apparently vocationally relevant subjects.

With mass higher education, ethnic minorities are now entering third-level education. However, especially where higher education is itself highly stratified, the elite institutions remain largely the preserve of the children of the native elite (and of rich foreigners). As the director of policy of the UK Commission for Racial Equality remarked in 2007: 'London Metropolitan University has more Afro-Caribbean students than the whole Russell Group combined' (Tahir 2007). While students of Maghrebi origin are common in French universities, they are almost completely absent from the elite grandes écoles (Sabbagh and van Zanten 2010).

It is in Britain that ethnic minorities and immigrants have progressed furthest within education. However, this is in part because Britain's widely varying ethnic groups include some immigrants who have entered the country with high educational qualifications. Germany stands at the other extreme, with the children of immigrants being even less likely to succeed in education than in other established countries of immigration. For example, children from an immigrant background are less likely to enter third-level education in Germany than in any other European country for which there is data (Eurostat 2011: 129). Partly this is because of specific institutional features of German education: the relatively small proportion of all children who go to university coupled with the highly selective schooling system. Partly, however, it is because German immigration lacks the higher qualified groups that are so significant in Britain.

Educational achievement can also be measured not by participation rates or even qualifications but by direct measures of learning such as reading ability. The PISA studies allow comparisons of the achievements of native, immigrant and second generation immigrant children in reading, maths and science. Using this data, Hochschild and Cropper (2010) suggest, once account is taken of immigrants' starting point, that France is the real European success story. Even more so than the British case, the French case shows that in Europe ethnic minorities are achieving structural assimilation in education.

Employment and work

The extent to which immigrants and ethnic minorities have the same jobs as the host population is the central test of structural assimilation. An ethnically defined underclass in Europe would mean that immigrants, whatever their qualifications, were less likely to be looking for work, were less likely to get jobs and, compared to the host population, had little chance of good jobs, let alone of entering the service class.

The first issue therefore is labour market participation. Among established minorities there is considerable diversity, especially in the UK. By the 1990s

Afro-Caribbean mothers were more likely to be in employment than white women in a similar household situation while, at the other extreme, Bangladeshi mothers were unlikely to be in any form of formal employment at all (Holdsworth and Dale 1997). More generally, there is a clear trend among *most* groups for women's labour market participation to increase over time (also Laurence and Vaisse 2006: 45)

Everywhere in Europe, ethnic groups are more exposed to unemployment than the host population and young people from ethnic minorities are significantly less likely than 'native' young people to be able use their educational qualifications to gain access to employment. According to one study of French young people in 2000, while 'autochthonous' and Maghrebi had almost identical educational qualifications, unemployment among the former was 20 per cent, but fully 40 per cent among the latter (EFFNATIS 2001).

Employment leads finally to the key question of occupational achievement: what sort of jobs do ethnic minorities hold? Full structural assimilation would have occurred if the occupational distribution of ethnic minorities and natives was identical. Yet again, given that immigrants mostly (and the exceptions are important) entered at the bottom of the occupational structure, structural assimilation would require that their children were *more* occupationally mobile than those of natives.

Clearly full structural assimilation has not been achieved, but in Europe as a whole second and third generation immigrants have a much wider range of occupations than their parents and grandparents. For example, a first generation Turkish immigrant in Germany would have started his career in a large factory. The height of occupational mobility would be to become a works councillor, trade union official or social worker (Joppke 1999: 211). Today there is a small but growing Turkish–German middle class. This clear progress can co-exist with continued relative disadvantage. Reviewing the recent research literature, Heath *et al.* (2008) suggest that an ethnic penalty is *almost* universal across Europe. However, there are very significant exceptions. Defined as entry to the service class (the 'salariat'), there are now few penalties in Britain and even some cases of ethnic premium (in Britain, Afro-Caribbean and Irish women have a disproportionately *high* chance of accessing such jobs). Elsewhere, however, with the apparent exception also of Sweden, ethnic minorities remain disproportionately *unlikely* to enter the service class.

Historically, where ethnic groups face discrimination, such as blacks in the USA or Catholics in Northern Ireland, they have usually generated an *enclave middle class*: doctors, lawyers, shop-owners, etc., who serve their own community. Similarly, ethnic groups often develop ethnic businesses – most obviously in restaurants. Such ethnic businesses utilise their community as a resource, but ethnic entrepreneurship is often a response to discrimination (Ram 1992). What seems to be significant about contemporary Europe is that the dominant mobility route is that of the native population: educational qualifications and access to white-collar jobs, particularly in the state sector. Nonetheless, apart from a very small number of individuals in Britain, members of ethnic minorities are completely absent from the senior management of large private sector companies.

Repeating America?

Reviewing the difference between Europe and America, one author comments: 'It is a demographic certainty that an ethnically and religiously distinct lower class in Europe will grow in decades to come' (Baldwin 2009: 226). Such a lower class would presumably be doubly separated: members of the ethnic/religious minority would be at the bottom of the hierarchies of housing, education and employment, and at the same time these lower positions would be filled exclusively by this minority.

At least so far, that has not happened in Europe. There is residential segregation, but Europe does not have ethnically homogenous ghettoes on the scale of the USA. This is partly, but only partly, explained by the ethnic and religious diversity within the minority population itself. Educational achievement is the success story, especially perhaps in France: nearly everywhere (Germany is the key exception) ethnic minorities are at least level-pacing with the native population of similar class background. Unemployment is disproportionately high among young people in some ethnic minorities and access to well-qualified jobs is not very impressive, and here ethnic minorities' relative disadvantage continues. Yet relative disadvantage (sometimes involving overt discrimination) is not large enough to rule out significant occupational advance. What distinguishes Britain is not progress in education but progress in employment. This in turn suggests that the cause of British success is not the country's much-debated multi-cultural policies, but rather its more effective anti-discrimination legislation (see below Section 8.3) and perhaps even its flexible labour market.

The historic success of the USA in the integration of its immigrants used to be a model for Europe. Today, however, in the USA immigrants increasingly appear to either experience 'segmented assimilation', joining the existing underclass, or use ethnic cohesion for occupational mobility, joining the service class but remaining culturally segregated. Neither fate appears so decisive for immigrants to Europe, who, so Thomson and Crul (2007) suggest, may be returning to 'the classical, linear model of assimilation' exemplified by the historic success of the USA in the integration of its immigrants. That assimilation occurred in the historically specific context of growing middle mass occupations and an effective halt to further immigration. This benign scenario certainly does not operate in Europe today: the number of low skilled jobs is growing and the inflow of unskilled immigrants continues. This combination could provide the basis for an ethnically and religiously distinct underclass – but it has not yet done so.

8.3 National models of integration

Since the 1980s a series of writers have argued that different European countries have different conceptions of national citizenship and national belonging. This has been central to comparisons of the immigrant experience across Europe. Brubaker (1992) compared the construction of national citizenship in France and Germany; Rex (1998) claimed that there were three main models of citizenship in contemporary Europe. Each involved different definitions of the nation and consequently different ways in which immigrants can become citizens. Rex's argument is part of the tradition that stresses the continued importance of the national state. Until recently, the main alternative position was the globalist argument which claimed the growing irrelevance of the nation state and hence the emergence of 'trans-' or 'post-'national citizenship (Soysal 1994). Once again, although discussion is often phrased in terms of 'immigration', the crucial issue here is the integration (or lack of it) of their descendants – Europe's ethnic minorities.

According to Rex, in the *assimilationist* model citizenship is based on the principle of *jus solis* (law of the territory), in which a person's birthplace determines their nationality. While citizenship for the children of immigrants is therefore automatic, immigrants themselves are expected to become as similar as possible to the host population ('assimilate'). The state does not recognise any differences between citizens in terms of their culture, ethnicity or national background. In these terms all citizens are equal members of the nation as a civic community. For Rex, France was a clear example of this model and he cited the (in)famous issue of the *foulard* (headscarf) as evidence: 'It is no way surprising that Muslim girls in a French school with a black French headmaster should have been sent home merely for wearing the scarf which was a normal part of Algerian Muslim dress' (Rex 1998: 113).

To the Anglo-American tradition, this refusal to accept the validity of a different culture is heinous and even 'racist'. Such apparent neutrality, so it is claimed, masks an ethnic or racial hierarchy in which immigrants are trapped at the bottom of society. Not only is there a gap between law and reality, the law makes it difficult to challenge discrimination. Such assimilationism locates France unequivocally in the bottom left cell of Table 8.1. French citizenship law hardly bans cultural difference, but it does insist that where citizens deal with the state they are dealt with on the principle of equality. Anglo-American criticisms ignore that, in historically Catholic countries such as France and to a lesser extent Italy and Spain, the very creation of the modern state and of national sovereignty was won against the extra-territorial claims of the nineteenth-century ultra-montanist Vatican. The freedom of the individual citizen is based on *laicité* which ensures that the individual is not controlled by an undemocratic organisation based outside the state.

The *ethno-nationalist* model corresponds to the upper left cell in Table 8.1, for here citizenship depends on prior membership of an ethnic group. Within this model, citizenship is inherited according to the principle of *jus sanguinis* (law of blood). This model was exemplified by (West) Germany, in which the large immigrant population were classified as 'foreigners' and non-citizens, even if they had been born in the country. Not surprisingly, West Germany had the lowest naturalisation rate in Europe, while about 10 per cent of the adult population were denied full citizenship, including the right to vote. Ethnonationalism is therefore seen as creating permanent second-class citizens – and not just in political terms.

In the *multi-cultural* model citizenship is also based primarily on birthplace, but there is a much stronger separation than in the previous model between identity and national citizenship. The state recognises differences between ethnic groups and so facilitates the retention of different ethnic traditions (upper right cell in Table 8.1). The objective here is not assimilation but integration. For Rex, Britain and the Netherlands were exemplars of this approach, epitomised by their educational policies which explicitly recognised and valued the different traditions of children's parents.

Rex's account is a typology of citizenship models, but the stress on political citizenship arguably underestimates the importance of social citizenship, particularly in the German case. Until recently, it was very difficult for second or third generation Turkish immigrants to achieve German *political* citizenship, but first generation immigrants achieved all the social rights of the welfare state. All across Europe, access to social rights largely depends on residence, not political citizenship. And furthermore, such long-term residence, even for non-EU citizens, has become increasingly difficult to revoke. In Germany, for example, since the 1970s German immigration law had increasingly given non-citizens resident in Germany protection against expulsion, and these decisions were codified in the 1990 Foreigner Law.

National differences remain today, but arguably all three countries are converging on what could be called 'civic republicanism' (Joppke 1999) where relatively easy access to citizenship is counter-balanced by explicit commitment to the nation state. Thus in Germany access to citizenship is now defined by residence in Germany and not by ethnic heritage. In this sense, anyone can *choose* to be German. On the other hand, citizenship is seen as requiring a commitment to Germany, epitomised by the requirement that the applicant must demonstrate facility in the German language and a knowledge of German history and society. As Table 8.2 also shows, Germany is one of those countries that now – like the classic immigrant societies such as the USA – positively celebrate citizenship through a public ceremony.

Table 8.2 Access to citizenship in selected countries, 2015

Country	Length of residence (years)	Language test	Knowledge test	Oath and ceremony
France	5	Yes	Interview	Yes
Germany	8	Yes	Yes	Yes
Ireland	4	No	No	Yes
Italy	10	No	No	No
Sweden	5	No	No	No
UK	5	Yes	Yes	Yes

The French model of assimilation is not simply an imposition. Certainly the French state does insist that schools and other public institutions remain a public space where no religious identity is recognised. For some commentators, especially outside of France, this is seen as simply anti-Muslim or anti-immigrant prejudice. While there may be an element of truth here, it is also the case that the ban on the *foulard* is supported by many self-professed Muslims, including an actual majority of those aged between twenty-five and forty-nine (Laurence and Vissier 2006: 169). While there is undoubtedly some re-Islamisation among younger people of Maghrebi origin, there is also widespread support for the fundamentals of French *laïcité*. Access to citizenship has been relatively easy, requiring only five years' residency and a language test and interview; new citizens are invited to a welcoming ceremony in the local prefecture.

Yet there are clear limits to such assimilationism. For some time ethnic organisations have been an important part of French public life. Thus the origins of Beur FM, a radio station appealing primarily to young people of Maghrebi origin, go back to 1983. For several decades the French state has recognised and negotiated with Muslim organisations over questions of religious policy. By 2003 the French government had helped to create the Conseil Français du Culte Musalman (CFCM) (French Council of the Muslim Religion). These semi-official representational structures often explicitly parallel those of longer-established religions in France, such as those of the Jewish religion. Affirmative action as such remains taboo, but in some policy areas affirmative action is disguised within universalistic arguments. Since 1981 areas of socio-economic deprivation have been designated Zones d'Éducation Prioritaire (ZEPs) and receive additional state funding for schools. Even the elite Science Po has initiated a programme to ensure a small number of applicants from the ZEPs. It is common knowledge that such areas will usually have high immigrant populations, but this is not the explicit reason why they gain extra resources. There is also some willingness to move beyond such formal universalism. President Sarkozy himself at times praised American *discrimination positive* (affirmative action) in employment, while some large companies, including the many US-owned multinationals, have explored US-style diversity management.

At times British policy has come closer to notions of group rights and hence to multi-cultural *policy*. For example, it has been argued that Britain is especially prone to restrict criticism of Islam as a religion in the name of good 'race relations' (Caldwell 2009; Scheffer 2011). Indeed, the very term 'race relations' posits the existence of distinct 'racial' groups whose relationship has to be managed! British schools, for example, continue to attempt a multi-cultural education (Faas 2007); some local authorities continue to use ethnic minority languages in public communication. Totally unlike Germany, Britain has long been 'relaxed' about dual nationality (e.g. Hansen 2000). More recently, however, the UK introduced policies which demand greater commitment of potential citizens: there is a compulsory language test and civic knowledge test, along with a rather low-key naturalisation ceremony.

Especially since the July 2005 terrorist mass murders – committed by second generation immigrants with full British citizenship – multiculturalism has been increasingly questioned. Yet this intellectual challenge has had little effect on actual policy. Curiously the focus on British multi-culturalism has distracted attention from the other distinguishing feature of the British experience, namely the deeply embedded use of the law to prevent discrimination. Long before any other European country, Britain introduced 'race relations' legislation (Race Relations Acts 1965, 1968 and 1976) (Hansen 2000). Not only did British law ban discrimination in public places (1965) and employment (1968), it created bodies to ensure compliance. Over the long term, this has created a climate where overt discrimination is much less acceptable than in most other European countries. Whereas most Britons believe ethnic discrimination is widespread, most also find it unacceptable (e.g. British Council 2007: 187).

Yet if Britain is multi-cultural, this is in the sense of 'everyday multiculturalism' and not the multi-culturalism of group rights as put forward by theorists such as Kymlicka or sometimes demanded by ethnic and religious organisations. Anti-discrimination law defines certain forms of difference between individuals (e.g. those of race or religion) as irrelevant and inappropriate in certain contexts, and thus effectively creates individual citizens in a way which would be consistent with a republican policy. It is one of the paradoxes of European integration that this British tradition logically appears as part of the French tradition!

Other countries have also retreated from official 'multi-culturalism'. This is especially clear in the Netherlands, which now demands that even applicants for long-term residence pass a tough integration test. Yet the extent of this change can be exaggerated. Sweden still has no integration test, no language test and no citizenship ceremony (Table 8.2). Arguably, in southern Europe, in Spain and especially in Italy multi-culturalism never became public policy at all. It is in southern Europe, just as in most of the new member states, that the linkage between ethnicity and citizenship remains, and any notion of European republicanism meets its limit.

8.4   European multi-culturalism or a Europe des patries?

In the nineteenth century the British built red-brick gothic churches in India; by the end of the twentieth century at least one Victorian church in Ireland had been turned into a mosque. In Britain, France and Germany weekly attendance at a mosque is nearly as frequent as attendance at church. The arrival of Islam in Western Europe is the most dramatic example of the extent to which the activities of many inhabitants of Western Europe depart from assumptions of 'normal' national culture. Such cultural diversity is indisputable, but its political implications – if any – are a matter of debate.

Trust, diversity and the welfare state

After World War II European nation states became welfare states. Whereas in the past (male) citizens were defined by their obligation to fight for the state

('*Aux armes, citoyens*' in the Marseillaise, 'The Soldier's Song' for Ireland) now men and especially women became defined by their involvement in the systems of mutual support (education, health, social welfare …). The welfare state is, however, a *national* state with clear territorial boundaries: taxes are raised from within its borders to fund benefits distributed to citizens (or more precisely, to residents) within the same borders. This suggests that in unexpected ways welfare states are demanding states.

Any society needs some common values, and in any nation state this has to include some vague and usually changing national story that links people and place. The national story says who 'we' are, how 'we' came to be 'here'. In addition, a democratic nation state requires some particular common values – democratic tolerance, individual citizenship and freedom of speech. Like the national story, these democratic values change over time, but in the current period they include gender equality and a public space free from religion. Such values are actually quite limited and make few demands on citizens. A democratic national welfare state is actually more demanding: the state asks its citizens to *pay* for each other, to look after each other and to contribute towards the next generation. Although the welfare state involves some 'vertical' redistribution (from the rich to the poor), it also involves massive 'horizontal' redistribution, such as from those at work to those either too young or too old to work. The welfare state therefore makes enormous demands on all its members. Liberal nationalist theorists (e.g. Miller 2006) accordingly argue that a strong national identity which ensures both trust and sympathy for co-nationals is an essential prerequisite for a welfare state. Certainly there is evidence that, *in countries with strong welfare states*, a strong national identity bolsters individuals' support for the welfare state (Johnston *et al.* 2010).

Following the same logic, in the new century social scientists have begun to suspect that increased ethnic diversity itself has undermined support for the welfare state. A landmark study of American distinctiveness argues that in the USA, where ethnic or 'racial' divisions are strong and politicised, welfare is seen as transferring resources to 'them' and has little political support; conversely, the most advanced welfare states in Europe, those of Scandinavia, were built when these societies were remarkably homogenous in terms of religion and ethnicity (Alessina and Glaser 2004). This general argument was reinforced in a much cited paper by Robert Putnam (2007). Putnam argued that diversity (measured in terms of ethnic origin) leads to what he termed 'hunkering down': in diverse areas social trust is lower, not just between the different groups but also *within* them. Putnam was careful to stress that new identities can be created from diversity, so that diversity can diminish and trust can rise – but this of course assumes that diversity per se is a problem.

Such a decline is often assumed to be a particular problem for welfare states, because a welfare state requires stronger shared values than a society where the values of the market predominate. If it is assumed that these 'shared values' are the opposite of cultural diversity, then progressives face a stark choice:

This is America versus Sweden. You can have a Swedish welfare state if you are a homogenous society with intensely shared values.... In the US you have a very diverse, individualistic society where people feel fewer obligations to fellow citizens. Progressives want diversity but they thereby undermine part of the moral consensus on which a large welfare state rests.

(David Willetts in 1998, quoted in Goodhart 2013: xxi)

Nonetheless, such views seem to be overly based on the experience of the USA. Unlike Europe, the USA has a historically entrenched racial divide. Perhaps even more importantly and nearly always ignored, the US has never had any social democratic presence in national government and so remains fundamentally undemocratic in terms of social rights (Taylor-Gooby 2005). Once the USA is excluded, analysis of international survey data suggests there is little or no relationship between racial or ethnic 'fractionalisation' (an index of ethnic diversity), low social trust and lack of support for the welfare state (e.g. Gesthuizen *et al.* 2009; Hooghe *et al.* 2009)

Multi-culturalist politics and the welfare state

A rather different argument focuses on the issue of multi-culturalist politics and the welfare state. Here multi-culturalism does not mean everyday tolerance but a specific form of politics: on the one hand groups mobilise on the basis of ethnicity and/or religion to demand recognition and resources, on the other hand the state negotiates with such groups and distributes resources to them.

At its most pronounced, multi-cultural politics prioritises the ethnic or religious community over the nation. Ethnic identity becomes crucial for members of minority groups, since it is through that identity that they achieve recognition as members of the broader society. The community is 'represented' by leaders who are effectively self-appointed and in turn reinforce the control of the family over its members. Once resources are distributed on the basis of ethnicity, then ethnic headcounting becomes central and competition between groups becomes inevitable. Since the community is prioritised, acquisition of the national language gets little priority and this in turn exacerbates male unemployment and women's low labour market participation.

It is clear that some areas of the UK come close to this ideal type. Nearly twenty years ago Kepel pointed out that the ability of local authorities to fund local 'cultural' initiatives had created what he termed an 'interrelationship between religious communalism and electoral clientelism' (1997: 115). There seem to be no clear parallels to this in France, despite widespread citizenship and political participation among the minority population. In this rather unexpected way, the UK has moved closer to the USA than to Continental Europe: like the Democratic Party of the USA, the British Labour Party's popular appeal has less and less to do with the universalistic traditions of social democracy, and more to do with the distribution of favours to organised ethnic groups.

Furthermore, the recognition (or at least acknowledgement) of some ethnic claims has led to *some* 'Yugoslav' ethnic fragmentation. Again, this seems to be most advanced in Britain, where Muslims have increasingly organised in terms of religion to distinguish themselves from both the white majority and other minorities. In France, the state's increasing readiness to negotiate directly with Muslim organisations has quite clearly led to Jewish organisations beginning to define themselves in ethnic rather than purely religious or cultural terms. This has been interwoven with increased tensions between French Jews and French Muslims, concentrated around the Palestine–Israel conflict. In a similar disengagement, in Britain Irish groups successfully demanded minority status with monitoring by the Race Relations Commission.

It is here that the antipathy between multi-cultural politics and the welfare state becomes clear. Ethnic minorities tend to have higher unemployment and thus to be more dependent on welfare benefits, but in countries such as Sweden or the Netherlands multi-culturalism exacerbates this because it puts no pressure on minorities to learn the national language (Koopmans 2010). When claims are made and resources distributed on a 'community' rather than universal basis, the welfare state becomes understood as handouts for ethnic groups rather than the nation's mutual support system. The welfare state belongs to 'them', not to 'us' (see Section 5.2).

Escaping to the European nation?

Democratic societies allow spaces, born of the separation of private and public worlds, which allow individuals some chance to define themselves. Multi-culturalism is often compared to the world of the Ottoman empire, where the *millet* system allowed each subordinate religion to regulate its own affairs providing it paid taxes (in money and in soldiers) to the sultan. Such toleration ensured a 'multi-racial' empire where relations between the groups were relatively peaceful, but there was no equal citizenship and within each group the power of religious authorities was consolidated. By contrast, in democratic market-based societies ultimately only the state can legally exercise coercive power over individuals. Such states ensure that all have access to the market for property, goods and services. To these basic 'civil' rights of all inhabitants, European societies tend to add social and economic rights and, increasingly, common political citizenship (Section 10.2). Hostility to ethnic minorities can exclude them from these markets and from these rights, but equally, communitarian bonds, from informal cohesion to overt violence, can keep individuals locked away from the freedoms and choices which the national state provides. To what extent are ethnic minorities part of the nation: in terms of shared practices, associations and even shared identities?

Cultural integration is partly a question of national identity: do people *consider themselves* French, German, or whatever? This identity is related to, but not reducible to, two further dimensions: broadly speaking *cultural practices* which may mark people as different and *social relations* through which people are restricted within group boundaries. Modood *et al.* (1997) term the first 'behavioural identity' and the second 'associational identity'. In the same vein, an EU comparative project (EFFNATIS 2001) referred to *cultural preferences* (media, food, language, moral attitudes, fertility behaviour, religious beliefs) and *cultural integration* (friendship patterns, partnership and marriage choices). This study showed that in the first sphere widespread integration has occurred. The most obvious shift is in terms of language. Indeed, other studies also show that by the second generation nearly all immigrants are completely competent in the host language (e.g. Thomson and Crul 2007); young people use it among themselves, though this is less so among Turks in Germany. By contrast, in terms of media use, food and clothes some British minorities are more likely to be distinctive from the host population. Particularly here differences between minorities are important: the poorest and most recently arrived group, the Bangladeshi, are more likely to use 'ethnic' clothes from tradition, while among others there is sometimes a deliberate choice to *return* to 'ethnic' clothes, especially on special occasions. Facility with the host country practices does not necessarily mean that other practices are abandoned.

While *some* members of *some* British groups insist on their own identity in this way, this is less likely in Germany and even less so in France. While there is some use of 'ethnic' food and clothes, the similarities across the nation are more striking. Furthermore, in France those of immigrant origins include a proportion who define themselves as having 'no religion', while nearly all celebrate holidays such as Christmas to some extent. Again, it is the British immigrants who are more likely to celebrate distinctive religious festivals and to diverge from the host nation in terms of moral attitudes (e.g. divorce, homosexual partners, etc.). And finally in terms of demographics the aspirations of the young in terms of fertility are very similar to those of native young people, although again some British groups do diverge more.

While such choices depend in the first instance solely on the immigrant group, social relations by definition involve members of the host society. Here the integration of some groups is dramatic. British Afro-Caribbeans are the extreme case, with over half of the men and one-third of the women having a white partner and nearly half of all 'Caribbean' children have one white parent (these are rates of inter-marriage far higher than those between Afro-Americans and whites in the USA). In this case to talk of 'ethnic minority' in any clearly defined sense is becoming increasingly strained. Also in Britain, among African Asians and Indians around one-fifth have a white partner (Modood *et al.* 1997: 355). In France about one-third of all second generation immigrants (i.e. the sons or daughters of parents both of whom immigrated to France from the same country) choose an indigenous partner. However, in France, as in the UK, endogamy among the Muslim groups is far higher and indeed there is some evidence that mixed marriages are now less likely than before (Santelli and Collet 2012).

Despite fears of native racism, it does seem now to be the case that often resistance to such social relations comes from the minority population rather than the host population, although yet again differences between groups are often more important than differences between minority and host population. Thus in Britain, whereas fully 90 per cent of whites aged 16–34 'would not mind' if a close relative married a non-white person, for all except Afro-Caribbeans the figure is far lower among minorities themselves (Modood *et al.* 1997: 315). Although ethnographic studies in France suggest that marriage to a 'French' partner is frowned upon or worse by most Muslim parents of Maghrebi origin (Santelli and Collet 2012), survey data suggests tolerant attitudes are more prevalent (Laurence and Vaisse 2006).

'There are no British Muslims, only Muslims', claims a radical Islamic student movement in the UK. Critics of multi-culturalism claim that it encourages political fragmentation of the nation state, destroying those political loyalties on which ultimately the nation depends. Such fears appear realised when British Muslim citizens willingly join jihadi groups. Yet given that jihadis are recruited from everywhere in Europe, from multi-cultural Britain to assimilationist France, this is an issue that cannot be traced back to national models of integration. In any case, such national disloyalties by some members of some ethnic minorities are not new. Insurgency in Palestine immediately after World War II or in Northern Ireland until the Good Friday Agreement also forced ethnic minorities in the UK to make choices of allegiance (as opposed to identity). Whatever their sympathies, most Jews and most Irish, like most Muslims today, remained in this specific sense loyal.

If extremist politics cannot be explained by different national models of integration, the nation state remains an important influence on more mundane issues. The cultural and associational definition of 'minority' is partly shaped by the nation state itself. This is clearly shown by national self-identities as documented in the EFFNATIS project. Not only do British minority members overwhelmingly have British passports, they are also more likely than minorities in other countries to identify with the host country. In this sense, British multi-culturalism is clearly successful. By contrast, French assimilationism is marginally less successful in creating a new French national identity for immigrants. The German case here is particularly dramatic. Social and economic rights may be widely available, but it is presumably the absence of political citizenship that explains the fact that less than 10 per cent of German Turkish young people in the study considered themselves 'German' (EFFNATIS 2001). The nation state still matters, not least in terms of defining who belongs to it.

As ethnic minorities enter the broad middle mass (Section 5.2), their political allegiances move away from the left-wing parties which in the past could count on their automatic support. The process seems most advanced in the UK, but is not unique to it. While there are several MPs from minority backgrounds in the British Labour Party, the British Conservative Party is beginning to attract support from ethnic professionals and business people. As some Conservatives have pointed out, in the nineteenth century the party produced Britain's first Jewish prime minister and in the twentieth century the country's first woman prime minister; it is probable that in the twenty-first century it will produce the country's first non-white prime minister. In France, it was the conservative government of Nicholas Sarkozy that appointed most ministers from ethnic minorities. In Germany there are now estimated to be just less than half a million German citizens of Turkish origin (1 per cent of the electorate) and the CDU, despite its opposition to dual citizenship, has begun an active campaign for their support. Perhaps the ultimate indication of achieved assimilation would be if ethnic minorities (as opposed perhaps to their self-appointed representatives) no longer were identified with the political left.

These changes suggest that Europe is not becoming like the Ottoman empire, an assemblage of self-contained ethnic groups. Instead, political freedoms, a market economy and social and economic rights allow people to increasingly develop multiple identities, retaining ethnic heritage, even national identity while also joining new ones. This is far from the world of group rights, but it is also far from cultural assimilation: it is practical or everyday multi-culturalism. Despite the multi-cultural lobbyists and the self-appointed guardians of communitarian identity, European democratic states still provide freedom for ordinary individuals. At the end of Monica Ali's novel *Brick Lane*, Nazneen, born in (then) East Pakistan, having spent her early adulthood in East London, is taken by her (English-born) daughters and her friend to realise a dream born from her first encounter with English television:

'Here are your boots, Amma.'
   Nazneen turned round. To get on the ice physically – it hardly seemed to matter. In her mind she was already there.
   She said, 'But you can't skate in a sari.'
   Razia was already lacing her boots. 'This is England,' she said. 'You can do whatever you like.'

(Ali 2003: 413)

Note

1 The figures are cited by Ferguson from an unpublished paper by David Rubinstein.

Bibliography

Alesina, A. and Glaeser, E. (2004) *Fighting Poverty in the US and Europe: A World of Difference*, Oxford: Oxford UP.

Ali, M. (2003) *Brick Lane*, London: Doubleday.

Baldwin, P. (2009) *The Narcissism of Minor Differences: How America and Europe are Alike*, Oxford: Oxford UP.

Berthoud, R. (2000) Ethnic employment penalties in Britain, *Journal of Ethnic and Migration Studies* 26.3: 389–416.

Blanc, M. (2010) The impact of social mix policies in France, *Housing Studies* 25.2: 257–272.

British Council (2007) *Migration Integration Policy Index*, London: British Council.

Brubaker, R. (1992) *Citizenship and Nationhood in France and Germany*, Cambridge, MA: Harvard UP.

Caldwell, C. (2009) *Reflections on the Revolution in Europe*, London: Allen Lane.

Dench, G., Gavron, K. and Young, M. (2006) *The New East End: Kinship, Race and Conflict*, London: Profile.

Dubet, F. (1989) *Immigrations: que savons nous?* Paris: La Documentation française.

EFFNATIS (2001) *Final Project Report*, Bamberg: University of Bamberg for European Commission.

European Commission (1998) *Employment in Europe 1997*, Luxembourg: Office for the Official Publications of the European Communities.

Eurostat (2011) *Migrants in Europe: A Statistical Portrait of the First and Second Generation*, Luxembourg: Publications Office of the European Union.

Faas, D. (2007) Turkish youth in the European knowledge economy, *European Societies* 9.4: 573–599.

Ferguson, N. (2002) *The Cash Nexus: Money and Power in the Modern World, 1700–2000*, London: Penguin.

Finney, N. and Simpson, L. (2009) *'Sleepwalking to Segregation?' Challenging Myths about Race and Migration*, Bristol: Policy.

Friedrichs, J. (1998) Ethnic segregation in Cologne, Germany, 1984–1994, *Urban Studies* 35.10: 1745–1763.

Gesthuizen, M., Van der Meer, T. and Scheepers, P. (2009) Ethnic diversity and social capital in Europe: tests of Putnam's thesis in European countries, *Scandinavian Political Studies* 32.2: 121–142.

Gilbert, P. (2009) Social stakes of urban renewal: recent French housing policy, *Building Research and Information* 37.5–6: 638–648.

Goodhart, D. (2013) *The British Dream: Successes and Failures of Post-War Immigration*, London: Atlantic Books.

Hansen, R. (2000) British citizenship after the empire: a defence, *Political Quarterly* 71.1: 45–49.

Häussermann, H. (2005) The end of the European City? *European Review* 13.2: 237–249.

Heath, A., Rothon, C. and Kilpi, E. (2008) The second generation in Western Europe: education, unemployment and occupational attainment, *Annual Review of Sociology* 34: 211–235.

Hochschild, J. and Cropper, P. (2010) Immigration regimes and schooling regimes: which countries promote successful immigrant incorporation? *Theory and Research in Education* 8.1: 21–61.

Holdsworth, C. and Dale, A. (1997) Ethnic differences in women's employment, *Work Employment and Society* 11.3: 435–457.

Hollifield, J. (2004) The emerging migration state, *International Migration Review* 38.3: 885–912.

Hooghe, M., Reeskens, T., Stolle, D. and Trappers, A. (2009) Ethnic diversity and generalised trust in Europe: a cross-national multi-level study, *Comparative Political Studies* 42.2: 198–223.

Hornsby-Smith, M. and Dale, A. (1988) The assimilation of Irish immigrants in England, *British Journal of Sociology* 39.4: 519–544.

Jackson, B. and Marsden, D. (1962) *Education and the Working Class*, London: Routledge.

Johnston, R., Banting, K., Kymlicka, W. and Soroka, S. (2010) National identity and support for the Welfare State, *Canadian Journal of Political Science* 43.2: 349–377.

Joppke, C. (1999) *Immigration and the Nation State: The United States, Germany and Great Britain*, Oxford: Oxford UP.

Kazepov, Y. (2005) Cities of Europe: changing contexts, local arrangements, and the challenges to social cohesion. In Y. Kazepov (ed.) *Cities of Europe*, London: John Wiley, pp. 3–42.

Kemper, F.-J. (1998) Restructuring of housing and ethnic segregation: recent developments in Berlin, *Urban Studies* 35.10: 1765–1789.

Kepel, G. (1997) *Allah in the West*, Cambridge: Polity Press.

Knapper, B. (2003) Beur FM, agent of integration or ghettoisation? University of Westminster, MS. http://wjfms.ncl.ac.uk/KnapperWJ.htm. Accessed 24 August 2010.

Kohl, H. (1991) Regierunserklärung 30.01.1991, http://helmut-kohl.kas.de/index. php?menu_sel=17&menu_sel2=&menu_sel3=&menu_sel4=&msg=609. Accessed 05 January 12.

Koopmans, R. (2010) Trade-offs between equality and difference: immigrant integration, multiculturalism and the welfare state in cross-national perspective, *Journal of Ethnic and Migration Studies* 36.1: 1–26.

Laurence, J. and Vaisse, J. (2006) *Integrating Islam: Political and Religious Challenges in Contemporary France*, Washington: Brookings Institute.

Miller, D. (2006) Multiculturalism and the welfare state: theoretical reflections. In K. Banting and W. Kymlicka (eds) *Multiculturalism and the Welfare State*, Oxford: Oxford UP, pp. 323–338.

Modood, T. (2004) Capitals, ethnic identity and educational qualifications, *Cultural Trends* 13: 87–105.

Modood, T., Berthoud, R. and Nazroo, J. (1997) *Ethnic Minorities in Britain: Diversity and Disadvantage*, London: Policy Studies Institute.

Moran, M. (2012) *The Republic and the Riots*, Frankfurt: Peter Lang.

Musterd, S. (2005) Social and ethnic segregation in Europe: levels, causes and effects, *Journal of Urban Affairs* 27.3: 331–348.

Peach, C. (2009) Slippery segregation: discovering or manufacturing ghettos? *Journal of Ethnic and Migration Studies* 35.9: 1381–1395.

Phillips, D. (2009) Minority ethnic segregation, integration and citizenship: a European perspective, *Journal of Ethnic and Migration Studies* 36.2: 209–225.

Portes, A. and Zhou, M. (1993) The new second generation: segmented assimilation and its variants among post-1965 immigrant youth, *Annals of the American Academy of Political and Social Science* 530.1: 74–98.

Putnam, R. (2007) E pluribus unum: diversity and community in the twenty-first century, *Scandinavian Political Studies* 30.2: 137–174.

Ram, M. (1992) Coping with racism: Asian employers in the inner city, *Work Employment and Society* 6.4: 601–618.

Rex, J. (1998) Race and ethnicity in Europe. In J. Bailey (ed.) *Social Europe*, London: Longman, pp. 106–120.

Rhein, C. (1998) Globalisation, social change and minorities in metropolitan Paris: the emergence of new class patterns, *Urban Studies* 35.3: 429–447.

Rumbaut, R. (2005) The melting and the pot: assimilation and variety in American life. In P. Kivisto (ed.) *Incorporating Diversity: Rethinking Assimilation in a Multicultural Age*, Boulder, CO: Paradigm, pp. 154–173.

Sabbagh, D. and van Zanten, A. (2010) Diversité et formation des élites: France–USA, *Sociétés Contemporaines* 3/2010 (no. 79): 5–17.

Santelli, E. and Collet, B. (2012) The choice of mixed marriage among the second generation in France: a life-course approach, *Papers: revista de sociologia* 97.1: 93–112.

Scheffer, P. (2011) *Immigrant Nations*, London: Polity Press.

Soysal, Y. (1994) *Limits of Citizenship: Migrants and Post-National Membership in Europe*, Chicago: Chicago UP.

Stothard, M. (2012) Spate of killings in Malmo highlights fears for Sweden's social welfare model, *Financial Times*, 21 April.

Tahir, T. (2007) For some, campus is still another country, *Times Higher*, 31 August.

Taylor-Gooby, P. (2005) Is the future American? Or can left politics preserve European welfare states from erosion through growing racial diversity? *Journal of Social Policy* 34.4: 661–672.

Thomson, M. and Crul, M. (2007) The second generation in Europe and the United States: how is the transatlantic debate relevant for further research on the European second generation? *Journal of Ethnic and Migration Studies* 33.7: 1025–1041.

Van Kempen, R. and Murie, A. (2009) The new divided city: changing patterns in European cities, *Tijdschrift voor Economische en Sociale Geografie* 100.4: 377–398.

van Zanten, A. (1997) Schooling immigrants in France in the 1990s: success or failure of the Republican model of integration? *Anthropology and Education Quarterly* 28.3: 351–374.

Walter, B. (2004) Irish women in the diaspora: exclusions and inclusions, *Women's Studies International Forum* 27.4: 369–384.

Willis, P. (1977) *Learning to Labour. How Working Class Kids get Working Class Jobs*, Farnborough: Saxon House.

9 Gender equality and social inequality

Although some of the key early feminist texts came from Continental Europe, above all Simone de Beauvoir's *The Second Sex*, from the 1980s onwards feminist social science became increasingly Anglophone and indeed American. Here as elsewhere, there is a real risk of imposing Anglophone concepts and even purely American concerns on Europe. This is paradoxical, since the situation of women in the world of work and family is one of key ways in which differences within Europe remain important – and at the same time in which Europe is not America.

Intra-European differences are most obvious in terms of women's employment, the subject of the first section of the chapter. Women's participation in paid work raises the question of non-paid work, especially the domestic labour of caring for children and (increasingly) older family members. The second section therefore examines work within the home, how it is divided between women and men and, crucially, the extent to which this work is outsourced to other institutions. As in the USA, and unlike in East Asia, in Europe equality (whatever that may mean) between women and men is official policy. The third section looks at the specific role of the European Union in attempting to make this a reality. However, gender equality faces a paradox. If gender equality were achieved, a logical corollary would be greater inequality between women unless counter-balanced by state caring policies. This makes state support for childcare a distinctive feature of the European social model.

9.1 Women's changing employment

For nineteenth-century feminists equality meant economic independence, and a long tradition in social thought took for granted that women's increased labour force participation was desirable. Given that progressive thought has also assumed that paid work was 'exploitation', this is only comprehensible if it was also assumed that exploitation in the workplace was preferable to exploitation in the home. It is, however, not clear whether working class women shared this view, and it certainly was not shared by working class men. In the Kaiserreich German social democrats were preaching women's equality, but for German social democratic male voters the fact that they earned enough for their wife not to have to work was a source of pride. Of course, this could be seen as typical male chauvinism, if it wasn't for the fact that these same men were moving towards companionate marriage and were making Bebel's *Woman and Socialism* one of the most popular texts of German social democracy.

One obvious lesson from this historical tale is that it cannot be assumed that women naturally want to work but are prevented from this by various obstacles. Equally, however, 'what women want' has itself to be socially and historically contextualised and explained. And finally, such aspirations have to be related to what actually does happen.

During the 1920s in most European countries more women were at work than in 1914, so there is some evidence of a very long-term increase in women's labour force participation through the twentieth century. Nonetheless, the variations between countries are considerable and the best explanation is in terms of national institutional systems. The role of women (and men) depends on the 'gender regime' in each particular country. National institutions and policies, such as the tax and social welfare system, the education system, the childcare system, the industrial relations and pay system, all tend to produce particular models of what women (and men) should be. We can find different breadwinner models of the household (Lewis 1992): the male breadwinner model, in which the male is the head of household and the woman makes little direct contribution to the household income; the modified male breadwinner model, in which the man's full-time employment is supplemented by the woman working part-time; and finally the universal breadwinner model in which both partners participate equally in the workforce.

This approach links to the tradition of comparative welfare state analysis. In terms of Esping-Andersen's 'three worlds of welfare' (see Section 1.3) the Anglo-Saxon liberal regime with its proclivity for market solutions allows women to enter the labour market, but at the same time the state makes no provision for childcare. A deregulated labour market and extensive unskilled immigration enables childcare to be provided through the market at prices that many can afford, thus ensuring that *some* women can participate in the labour market on terms that begin to approximate those of men, while at the same time ensuring that most women are under pressure to seek employment even though this may have to be compatible with extensive family obligations. The social democratic system provides extensive childcare and support services, enabling all women to participate in the labour market, but this requires high levels of taxation. Finally, the conservative or corporatist model limits women's participation at work. It focuses benefits and rewards on the male head of household, penalises second earners in the tax system and does not de-familise childcare (see also Esping-Andersen 2009).

Across Europe there are therefore differences in the extent to which women participate in the labour force. Thus the Swedish social democratic gender regime ensures over three-quarters of all women are active in the labour market, whereas this is the case for only about a half of all Italian women (see Figure 3.6). These differences have, however, been diminishing. Figure 9.1 shows that

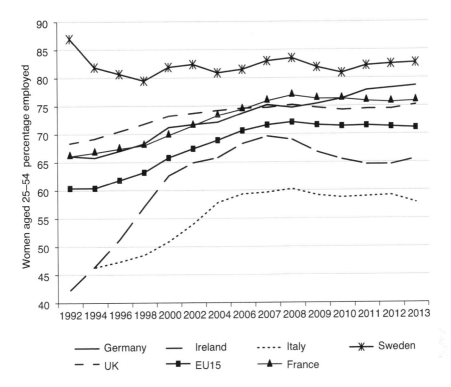

Figure 9.1 Women's 'core age' employment, 1992–2013 (derived from European Commission (2004, 2014)).

in Germany, Sweden and the UK a majority of so-called core-aged women have been at work for some time. In 1992 employment rates of these four countries ranged from 87 per cent in Sweden to 66 per cent in Germany; then, too, Italy was different, with 46 per cent (1994) at work. Subsequently women's employment fell somewhat in Sweden, but rose everywhere else. There is a clear long-term trend for women to be at work, whether or not they have children (Rubery *et al.* 1999: 111).

Europe's current austerity crisis has not pushed women back into the home. Indeed, with falling household incomes women's earnings have become more important. In most European countries most women stopped being housewives several decades ago. As of 2009, male breadwinner households (i.e. where the male was the only income earner) comprised only about a fifth of all partner households. Within the EU such male breadwinner households are most common in Greece (37.0 per cent of all partner households) and Italy (35.9 per cent). At the other extreme male breadwinner households comprise only 10.7 per cent of all Swedish partner households and 11.3 per cent of all such Danish households. With male breadwinner households at 22.4 per cent in Germany and 20.8 per cent in the UK, most other EU15 countries are closer to the Nordic than the Mediterranean models (see Bettio and Verashchagina 2014: 70).

Everywhere a significant minority of employed women work part-time. Gender regimes also help explain the differences in the level and form of women's part-time work. Thus Table 9.1 shows how women's part-time work has increased in those countries where women's employment was historically low. In Italy in 1998 only 14.3 per cent of all employed women were working part-time (column 1) but as of 2013 this had risen to 31.9 per cent (column 4). Table 9.1 also shows how in countries such as the UK and Germany, the presence of children had meant that women reduce their hours and work part-time (column 2). In these countries part-time work often means marginal part-time work (defined as nineteen hours or less per week) (column 4). Marginal part-time work is widespread here because on the one hand the lack of affordable childcare means that women have to juggle employed work in the labour market and caring work in the home, and because on the other hand labour market regulations allow or even encourage firms to offer short part-time jobs. By contrast, in Sweden the presence of children in the household makes little difference to women's working hours: motherhood does not affect how women participate in the labour force. In both Sweden and France women with children can work full-time – partly because there is extensive childcare, partly because short (thirty to thirty-five hours per week) full-time work is widely available.

A final convergence is the extent to which women's participation varies over the life cycle. In the 1980s the UK was unusual in Europe for its 'M-shaped'

Table 9.1 Extent and form of part-time work: women in selected EU countries, 1998 and 2013

	Part-time employment % of all employment (1998)	Hours worked: difference between households with/without children (1998)	Marginal part-time % of all dependent employees (1998)	Part-time employment % of all employment (2013)
	(1)	(2)	(3)	(4)
France	31.6	−1	9.0	30.6
Germany	36.4	−6.5	18.0	46.1
Ireland	30.0	−5.5	10.0	35.6
Italy	14.3	0.0	8.0	31.9
Sweden	33.1	+0.1	6.0	38.8
UK	44.4	−6.0	21.0	42.6
EU15	33.5	−3.4*	14.0*	38.5

Sources: Column (1): European Commission (2004); Columns (2) and (3) derived from Bielenski *et al.* (2002); Column (4) European Commission (2014).

Note
* EU15 + Norway.

age-related activity curve: women before childbearing were mostly at work; of those with children fewer were at work; older women were again more likely to be at work. This was never the pattern in most other European countries, where women either left the workforce once they had children and did not return (most of Continental Europe) or worked for the entirety of their lives (the Scandinavian pattern). During the 1990s a 'plateau-shaped' activity curve became almost universal with indeed Scandinavia, France and Germany all showing an activity peak during the forties (Rubery *et al.* 1999: 82).

One cause of the increased participation has undoubtedly been changes in education. The higher the woman's education level, the more likely she is to work and indeed the more likely she is to work full-time. Today in most countries young women have the same or even higher educational qualifications as men. Within higher education there have also been important changes in horizontal segregation (the extent to which women and men are in separate areas). Science and in particular technology remain male-dominated, just as arts and the softer social sciences are dominated by women. The significant change has been that young women have entered academic areas that lead to well paid employment – in law and medicine in particular, but also areas of business and management studies. The concentration in professional degrees is particularly significant: here anti-discrimination legislation (see Section 9.3) and the linkage between career entry and formal qualifications have enabled women to use education to prise open areas of employment that were previously reserved for men. Given these trends, a new division is opening up: on the one hand educated women, likely to work full-time, and on the other hand less educated women working part-time or indeed not at all (e.g. Konietzka and Kreyenfeld 2010).

Given these changes, it is not surprising that economic inequality between the genders has changed its form. In the early years of the life cycle there is in now little economic difference between women and men. Overall, young women and young men have increasingly similar work experiences and financial rewards. On the one hand women have used the 'qualifications lever' (Crompton and Sanderson 1990: 65) to gain access to well paid employment; on the other hand the decline of skilled manual jobs has removed a traditional source of well paid jobs for men without educational qualifications. At the same time, for women entering their middle years, inequality continues to exist, not least because it is then that the effects of children and household begin to take effect.

Since the 1970s, Sweden and other Scandinavian countries have stood out from the rest of Europe as countries where it has been normal for nearly all women to work. The Scandinavian welfare states have concentrated on providing services to the population that in other countries are provided either by the family or by the market: pre-school childcare, high levels of after-school care, extensive elderly care. On the one hand this means the 'de-familialisation' of much caring work. There is less pressure on women to stay at home in order to look after children or elderly relatives, so it is easier for women to go out to work. On the other hand, the provision of such services within the state sector has meant the creation of new areas of 'women's work'. The Scandinavian system ensures that such work is relatively 'good work', especially in terms of working conditions. As state employees, women have had job security and regular pay. Movement from full-time to part-time work and vice versa has been relatively easy (Wickham 1997). Working hours have usually suited women; in particular, 'flexibility' has been to accommodate employees' needs rather than those of the employer and overall working time has been 'short full-time'. In this situation, women can take their generous parental leave entitlements, knowing that they will not be penalised when they return to work. The state sector has become, more so than in other countries, the preferred area of employment for women (Hansen 1997). Women's greater equality with men has increased horizontal segregation, with women concentrated in the public sector and men in the private sector. Partly for this reason, women are now the majority in the trade unions and have increasingly high representation in politics – perhaps when decisions are made increasingly in the private sector.

There are of course differences between the Scandinavian countries. For example, Norway has a much more 'conservative' stress on the importance of motherhood (see Duncan and Strell 2004) despite extensive welfare state facilities. Nonetheless, the Scandinavian states share a high level of taxation and extensive welfare state services. These services are seen as entitlements of all citizens, rather than a safety net for the poor as in 'liberal' regimes. Because they are also of high quality, this binds the middle class into the welfare state. Unlike their compatriots elsewhere, they have no direct interest in reducing state expenditure. The same mechanism also works for women: most women benefit from the welfare state. This generates a gender division in politics, with women significantly more likely to support parties (usually the social democrats) that maintain the welfare state.

All of this may have involved trade-offs between class and gender equalities. Thus there is evidence that the glass ceiling is actually tougher in Scandinavia than in countries such as the USA. Compared to American women, Scandinavian women are less likely to achieve extremely well paid positions – which are overwhelmingly at the top of the private sector. The concentration of Scandinavian women in the public sector has come at the cost of opportunities for well-education women (e.g. Mandel and Shalev 2009). Although this is disputed (Korpi *et al.* 2013), on balance it would seem to be the case that in Scandinavia equal opportunities benefit large numbers of ordinary women, while in the USA they especially benefit a few privileged women.

9.2 Gendered aspirations at home

With the end of 'housewifery', what has happened to work within the home? Before discussing the domestic division of labour (the division of work between women and men) it is important to discover what work actually has to be done in the home. One major issue here is of course the number of children and hence Europe's alleged fertility crisis. A related issue is the extent to which this work can be outsourced – to the market, to the state, to extended kin or even voluntary organisations. Important here is the role of the state in providing childcare. Just as with women's participation in the formal labour force, understanding the domestic division of labour involves acknowledging the effect of institutional systems, without assuming that women are sisters of that well-known sociological fallacy, the over-socialised model of man.

Fertility

It is frequently argued that Europe needs immigration because the European populations are ageing and without immigration the population will actually decline.[1] In fact this is only half-true: *some* European countries do face population decline, but not all. Furthermore, the most serious declines are not in Western Europe but in some countries of the former Soviet bloc, where the 'transition' to a market economy had disastrous consequences for the living standards of ordinary people. The decline of fertility has several different dimensions. A growing number of women choose to have no children at all (Tanturri *et al.* 2015). Of those women who do have children, on average they are having them older and they are having fewer of them. However, differences between countries are crucial here (Figure 9.2).

In the 1990s, when there began to be talk of Europe's demographic crisis, it also became noticeable that the crisis was much less severe in Scandinavia. Irritatingly for American ideologues who think that Europe is dying from too much equality, egalitarian countries also now have high birth rates. A Total Fertility Rate (TFR) of around 2.1 is normally assumed to be necessary to ensure population stability in the absence of migration. Figure 9.2 shows that between 1960 and 1980 the TFR fell in France and above all in Italy. Since then fertility has

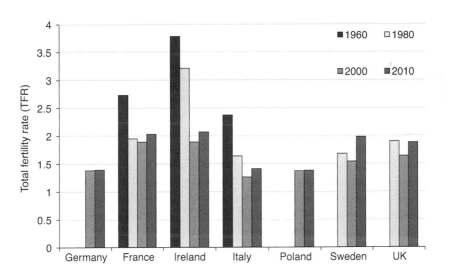

Figure 9.2 Total fertility rate, 1960–2010 (derived from European Commission (2013b)).

remained well below ZPG (Zero Population Growth) in Italy and in Germany, but France, the UK and Sweden all have fertility levels which are almost or completely high enough to ensure population stability. There is also no reason to believe that fertility levels are unchangeable. Most women in Europe already have fewer children than they would like to have – the so-called 'child gap' (Bernardi 2005) and it is clear that unemployment and employment insecurity make people less likely to want to become parents (Pailhé and Solaz 2012; Vignoli *et al.* 2012).

Across the OECD the relationship between women's fertility and women's employment has reversed in recent decades. In the 1960s fertility was high where women's employment was low, whereas now the opposite is true (Castles 2003; European Commission 2013a). Today women are prepared to have children where this can be *combined* with labour market participation. This participation in turn depends on two factors. First, it must be possible to outsource some of the burden of childcare from the household to either the state (as in Scandinavia) or to the market (as in the UK and the USA). Second, there must be forms of employment available which can be combined with raising children. The most obvious issue here is part-time work, but also relevant are family-friendly working arrangements, parental leave, etc. Through such measures the Nordic welfare states have ensured that fertility rates are at approximately replacement level (Ellingsaeter 2012). Equally, one explanation for the relatively high birth rates of all Anglophone countries seems to be women's easy access to the labour market (McDonald and Moyle 2010). Conversely, it is the lack of parent-friendly employment and the lack of childcare that explains the low fertility levels of Germany and Italy.

Outsourcing

Care work involves not just young children but also increasingly the care of elderly dependents. Reproducing a household also involves relatively straightforward domestic labour (cleaning, cooking, household maintenance), activities of caring and mutual concern which are perhaps problematically labelled 'work' but which nonetheless do involve responsibilities that cannot be abandoned at a whim; there are even the mechanics of dealing with state bureaucracies and service suppliers. As Figure 9.3 shows, all this work can be either done within the household (and divided in different ways between the household members) *or* outsourced to the state, the market, to kin or to the third (voluntary) sector. What women – and men – do in the home depends on the much-discussed domestic division of labour, but also on the totality of work that stays within the household. This in turn depends massively on the relations between the household and the broader society.

The comparative welfare state literature provides quite extensive data on *state*-provided childcare, but less on that provided through the market, even less on that provided informally outside the household by kin, and almost nothing on the specific role of the voluntary sector. Figure 9.4 shows the extent of *formal*

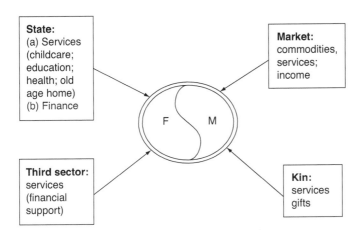

Figure 9.3 Supporting the household.

Note
Each of the four 'boxes' can provide specific services and finance to the household; the extent and form to which it does this depends on different forms of regulation (law, charity, finance, familial norms), and in turn this affects domestic division of labour.

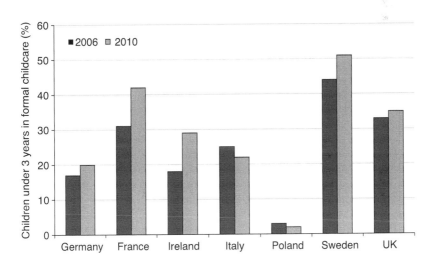

Figure 9.4 Formal childcare, 2006 and 2010 (derived from European Commission (2013: Table 2.2.2).

Note
Figures for Poland 'are based on small samples and therefore not considered statistically reliable'.

childcare in different European countries. Here 'formal' means largely state-provided care in Sweden and France, but the market can also remove childcare work from the household. In the UK in particular, the private sector is very important and growing: nurseries were the fastest growing small business sector of the late 1990s (Quarmby 2003: 51). In countries such as Ireland, the expansion of childcare has involved state funding of childcare places provided by private companies.

Similar outsourcing opportunities apply to care for elderly dependents. The combination of low state provision and an unregulated labour market ensures that care workers in the UK are some of the worst trained in Europe. while conversely high quality work is most present in Scandinavia (Cameron and Moss 2007). In Italy, the private sector is important for elderly care, with frequent reliance on new immigrant labour (Reyneri 2004). Other aspects of domestic labour can be outsourced in rather more restricted ways. All forms of housework, from cleaning to cooking, can be outsourced to the market, but not usually (except perhaps in the case of people with disabilities) to the state, kinship networks or the voluntary sector. Another option is for the activity to be financially rewarded within the home. Thus, Norway was one of the first countries to give the choice of either placing their young child in a day care centre or receiving a cash allowance which was the same value as the cost to the state of providing that care. Especially in Scandinavia, such policies have been opposed by social democratic parties and supported by their opponents (Leira 2015).

The voluntary or third sector can provide services to the household. This is particularly important where the state essentially sub-contracts social services to religious or charitable organisations, as in Italy or Germany. In the UK government policy also supports this, and this should be seen in the context of the UK's very specific ethnic politics (Section 8.2). Where multi-culturalism is institutionalised, reliance on the third sector runs the risk of further ethnicising and fragmenting citizenship, making access to services dependent on religion, ethnicity or even gender and undermining any universal social citizenship (Peña-Ruiz 2004).

Focusing on the different forms of outsourcing shows that different countries reduce the burden of caring work to differing extents and in different ways. While UK households do not have access to state services on the same scale as in Sweden, they may more than compensate by using other sources – the market, kinship and the third sector. However, reliance on the market means that facilities are used by those who can afford them, while others have to juggle paid work and domestic obligations. Thus in the UK formal childcare is used by only 20 per cent of households in the lowest income quintile, but by fully 53 per cent of households in the richest quintile (European Commission 2013a). By contrast, the more universalist Swedish approach facilitates all women, especially those on more average incomes.

Whereas childcare is a service provided to the household, parental leave can be based on the very different assumption that caring is not simply a burden, there is a *right to time to care* (Boje and Almquist 2000; Ellingsaeter 2007). Certainly, European countries have increasingly moved from the narrow conception of maternity leave, acknowledging only the physical impact of childbirth on the mother, to the much more general concept of parental leave, acknowledging mother and father as individuals with caring responsibilities and aspirations. The initial EU Parental Leave Directive set down baseline rights, but there has been a wide variation between countries. For example, in 2000 maternity leave ranged from over a year in Sweden with financial compensation at over 70 per cent to only forty weeks with lower compensation in the UK. Whereas Swedish fathers had ten days' paternity leave, British fathers had none (Boje and Almqvist 2000: 60f.). The revised Parental Leave Directive (2010) specifies minimum periods of leave for both parents, but the right to paid paternity leave still depends on member states. At a time of alleged retrenchment of the welfare state, it is noticeable that parental leave has also become the norm in Anglophone countries from the UK to Australia, with the USA the significant exception (Baird and O'Brien 2015).

Parental leave and childcare are often justified as facilitating women's employment. Parental leave enables parents (but especially women) to take time off from employment but to maintain their job and so their connection to the labour market. Childcare can be justified in terms of educational benefit to the children, but the prime justification now appears to be that it enables the mother to take paid employment. This focus on facilitating employment is considered a hallmark of the *social investment state.* According to its advocates, the social investment state does not simply support the poor, redistribute resources and protect individuals from the market, it *enables* citizens to participate in the market (Jenson and Saint-Martin 2003). While until the crisis social expenditure was broadly maintained in most countries (see Figure 1.6), expenditure has been redirected towards such active policies and services. As Figure 9.4 shows, formal childcare has continued to expand even in the crisis.

State-funded childcare is also seen as helping more women into employment and thus lifting households and children out of poverty. The extent to which this actually happens is variable. A comparison of state-funded childcare provision in Sweden and Flanders shows that usage of the Flemish system rises with parental income; in Flanders, unlike in Sweden, state support works through tax credits to users, which further benefits those with higher earnings (Van Lancker and Ghysels 2012). The social investment state is not necessarily a redistributive state (Van Kersbergen and Hemerijck 2012). Parental leave raises related issues, since again it tends to be used by those parents who are well educated and already in full-time employment (Ghysels and Van Lancker 2011).

Distributing domestic labour

Taking the total quantity of domestic work, all evidence points in the direction of an overall decline in unpaid work by women and a rise in that by men. Combining data sets from different countries from the 1960s through to the mid-1980s, Gershuny found that in all countries the gap between women and men in terms of time spent on unpaid work by women and men was narrowing, while at the same time class differences within the genders also narrowed. Time budgets also show that the major source of change is households where women work full-time. While part-time work makes very little difference to women's domestic labour, women working full-time work significantly fewer hours at home. Equally, in partnership households where women work full-time, men are particularly likely to increase their labour input. These changes do not necessarily occur overnight, but there is a clear lag effect: the reduction of the household workload (through outsourcing and/or mechanisation) combined with the growing employment of women, has led to a general softening of the domestic division of labour (Gershuny 2000).

National contexts, however, continue to matter. Thus Scandinavian households do have a more egalitarian division of labour than British households. This can be seen as part of the Gershuny's contrast between the 'Nice North' and the 'Wild West' (Mingione 2005). If men work shorter hours, then they have time to contribute at home. Conversely, if women are facilitated in working full-time (or 'long' part-time), then the pressure on men to contribute is increased. Certainly the change in Swedish households has been dramatic: 'By the late 1990s, 85 per cent of fathers were participating in changing nappies, dressing children and other child-related tasks, compared to only about 1 per cent in the 1960s' (Bergqvist and Jungar 2000: 170).

And this pressure is often welcomed. Studies of parental leave in Scandinavia show that men welcome the opportunity to spend time with their young children, and a legal right to do so protects them against employers' demands that they do not take time off work (Brandth and Kvande 2001). The so-called Daddy Leave thus contributes towards the development of the Scandinavian earner–carer (Korpi *et al.* 2013) in which both parents are employed and both parents are carers. This not only means a more egalitarian division of labour within the home, it also means that some carework is retained within the home. The work that occurs within the home and how it is distributed is partly shaped by national social policies as well as by the extent of the market for goods and services.

Aspirations in context

Focusing on national social structure and national state policy and comparing states leads to looking for differences *between* states, and downplaying differences *within* them. The gender regime approach is 'top down', seeing women (and men) as simply shaped by structures and institutions. It says little about how these systems are actually used, interpreted or simply ignored by real women, thus ensuring social change. For example, in both Germany and the Netherlands mothers' labour force participation began to rise *before* changes in policy (Pfau-Effinger 2005). Equally, the earlier massive decline in the Italian birth rate occurred despite strong policies and ideologies that defined women as mothers (Hantrais 1999).

In a series of works, Catherine Hakim has fruitfully challenged the orthodoxies of comparative gender regimes. She argued that a series of fundamental changes have created new opportunities for women to make choices about their lifestyle. The contraceptive revolution enabled women to control their own fertility (including the choice not to have children at all and expanding the possibilities of recreational sex). In all Western countries women have legal protection against overt discrimination in employment; the growth of white-collar jobs makes paid work less linked to physical strength, while the growth of secondary employment enables women who spend time at home still to have some economic independence. Using Eurobarometer data, Hakim argued that in this historically novel situation, women's aspirations essentially divide into three types: a home-centred group, for whom home and children have priority, a work-centred group, for whom participation in the labour market is their priority, and an adaptive group, wishing to juggle the two (Hakim 1999, 2000).

That many women actively value motherhood is also suggested by the high take-up of 'payment for parenting' forms of benefit. In France the Allocation Parentale d'Education was introduced in 1985 and provided paid leave for a parent who chose to stay at home to look after young children (Laufer 1998); this is now part of the PAJE – *Prestation d'accueil du jeune enfant* – a comprehensive package of benefits for parents of young children (Martin 2010). Even where childcare facilities are high quality and extensive, as in Sweden, Denmark or France, many women want to work shorter hours in order to spend more time with the children. Nonetheless, these aspirations are not as free-floating as Hakim's 'preference theory' would seem to suggest, since there remain clear national variations in preferences as well as in actual outcomes.

9.3 Gender equality and social engineering

Although the European Union has very limited powers in social policy compared to the member states, in the past it played an important role in gender equality, especially in relation to equal opportunities in the workplace. However, as organisations have changed away from traditional bureaucratic structures and internalised the market, so this has rendered equal opportunities less effective for ordinary women.

The EU and gender equality

The Treaty of Rome was signed in 1956 by twelve men – and not a single woman. At the time this was hardly unusual, but there have been times when the EU has actively undermined existing gender inequalities. Article 119 of the Treaty of Rome committed the original six member states to the principle of equal pay at the insistence of the French negotiators as compensation for the removal of tariff protection from French industry. They believed that, without such a clause, German industry would enjoy a competitive advantage. In fact, the article does not seem to have made any contribution to equalising pay rates within Europe for over ten years. Nonetheless, the mere existence of Article 119, as well as institutions such as the European Social Fund (originally set up to support and retrain workers made redundant by industrial structuring) did provide a legal basis for more active social policy in the future.

In the UK the strike of women workers in Ford Dagenham in 1968 led directly to the Equal Pay Act. In the late 1960s strike movements in Belgium included a strike by women engineering workers for equal pay which explicitly appealed to Article 119. This was the context for the celebrated Defrenne case: Gabrielle Defrenne, a Sabena air hostess, challenged the right of her employers to impose retirement at forty for women but at fifty-five for men. Feminist lawyer Elaine Vogel-Polsky brought the case to the European Court of Justice, arguing Article 119 had 'direct effect': in other words, that it did not require national legislation to come into force. The ECJ finally ruled on the case in 1976, awarding Mme Defrenne all of 12,716 Belgian francs (about St£240). The award may have been trivial, but the judgement showed the legal importance of the Treaty, consolidating the principle that European law supersedes national law, even in the area of social policy.

By the time the Defrenne case came to final judgement, the then EEC had developed its first Social Action Programme in which women's issues were given a key role. Equal opportunities were ideally suited for European action. On the one hand, this was a new area of policy, so that it was not yet defined by national interests and national institutions. On the other hand, once 'women's issues' were defined as equal opportunities in the workplace and in the labour market, they were indisputably part of the Community's responsibility for ensuring economic integration. From this context came the three key directives ensuring for women equal pay, equal treatment at work and equal treatment in social security systems. The Equal Pay Directive was relatively uncontroversial, for by this time the abstract principle of equal pay was becoming as accepted as women's right to vote, and Britain and France already had equal pay legislation. However, the Commission was determined to do more than simply harmonise existing legislation, since it insisted that equal pay should also mean work of equal value, thus in principle making it more difficult for women to be segregated into low paid jobs. The Equal Treatment Directive outlawed discrimination in recruitment and promotion. In particular, it used the concept of indirect discrimination, thus providing a legal basis for challenging some socially embedded definitions of women's work and men's work. The Social Security Directive enforced equal treatment in social security. This was far more complex and controversial. It threatened to have massive cost implications, especially in the area of pensions, while the proposal that social security benefits should be individualised hit directly at the gender contract of some states. It was finally passed only once individualisation was abandoned and occupational pension schemes excluded.

By the end of the 1970s the EU had a framework of equal opportunities legislation that made explicit discrimination against women illegal. The very fact that this is now taken for granted itself indicates the importance of the achievement (Walby 1999). Equal opportunities have been built into what is now the Union's *aquis communitaire.* Long before the Maastricht Treaty first used the term 'EU citizen', the European Economic Community was creating legally enforceable social rights. These rights were acquired by women not because of their political citizenship (nationality) or even residence, but because of their participation in the labour market. Where overt discrimination against women was entrenched, as in Italy or in Ireland, 'Europe' could become identified with women's issues.

During the 1980s the 'women's issue' was one of the clearest cases of multi-level politics and governance (Marks *et al.* 1996). Pressure groups working within national boundaries now targeted 'Brussels' as well as their national governments and this common objective created new horizontal European links. At the same time the Commission itself deliberately stimulated new European-wide organisations. As early as 1976 an Equal Opportunities Unit was created within the then DGV (Employment) (Rees 1998: 59); in 1981 the Commission set up an Advisory Committee on Equal Opportunities for Women and Men; the European Network of Women followed in 1983 and soon established contacts with the Commission and with MEPs. In 1984 the European Parliament created its Women's Rights Committee, which consistently raised issues going beyond the Commission's narrow focus on employment; finally the Women's Committee of the ETUC also argued for more activist policy. This network meant that the Commission – or at least DGV – was linked to the women's movement across Europe, but also meant that the Commission, and to some extent the Parliament, themselves contributed to developing and to Europeanising the women's movement.

Initially this activity did not lead to substantial further gains. For example, a Parental Leave Directive was proposed in 1983 and failed because of the 'unremitting hostility' of the British government (Hoskyns 1996: 147) and was abandoned in 1986. During the 1990s women's issues and employment became linked through a new focus shifted on 'reconciling work and family life'. Compared to the initiatives of the 1970s, this involved the use of 'soft law' (Section 1.2). There were agreed objectives, but member states were merely encouraged to achieve them in their own way. However, new directives on part-time work and parental leave did finally emerge. The expansion of childcare is now EU policy: in 2002 the so-called Barcelona objectives committed member states to ensuring that by 2010 one-third of all children under the age of three were in formal childcare. This, with other targets, was not achieved by most member states. They have been reasserted in the Commission's Europe 2020 strategy, but national variations remain dramatic (Figure 9.4) and most states have still not reached these targets (European Commission 2013a).

If the 1990s saw women's issues linked to – and arguably subordinated to – employment policy, by the end of the decade gender had been 'mainstreamed'. In theory this means that all policies are assessed for their implications for gender, but in practice it seems that gender has simply become one aspect of 'diversity'. For decades the EU had been officially blind to ethnic and religious discrimination, even though this was covered by some member states' laws (e.g. the Race Relations Act and its subsequent amendments in the UK). Now that the EU has some social policy competence, the new Equality Directive creates separate grounds (gender, ethnic origin ...) on which discrimination is illegal. As such, EU equality legislation approximates US-style managing for diversity as developing in the private sector. It is all a far cry from those women strikers of the 1960s.

Organisational changes

For most of the twentieth century, work increasingly occurred within large bureaucratic organisations which generated an increasing number of clerical, administrative and professional jobs (Section 5.4). Many of these jobs were filled by women, but until at least the 1970s the gender division within these organisations was synchronised with a male breadwinner gender model: women were concentrated in routine jobs which they often left when they married or had children, while men were often on a career track moving up through the organisation.

From the 1970s this situation began to change. Especially in the public sector – and this was a period of expanding public sector employment – women entering employment were less likely to want to leave when they married or had children. Many women also began to demand careers rather than just jobs and started to compete with men on the career path up into managerial grades. Given their clear hierarchy of posts, these organisations were ideally suited to the 'classic' equality directives: direct and even indirect discrimination could be relatively easily identified, and women's progress could be monitored statistically. Because posts were clearly separate from people, women could even take extended maternity leave and be assured that their job would still be there when they returned. And finally, as *state* employers these organisations often had to be seen to be doing something about women's issues, and so were quite easily pressurised into actively promoting women: appointing equality officers, developing special training programmes and attempting to recruit women into non-traditional posts (Wickham *et al.* 2008).

The shift to increased graduate entry also helped women. Not only was third-level education expanding, but so too was women's educational participation, so there were now plentiful potential women recruits. Of course, this external recruitment meant increased competition for those working their way up the hierarchy from below, but this was softened by the overall expansion of this type of employment which created more promotional posts.

These changes started earliest and went furthest in the Scandinavian countries. Here the expansion of state employment, particularly in state services, occurred precisely when gender equality became a political issue. In the UK, Halford and Leonard (2001: 196) describe how in the late 1970s local authorities introduced equal opportunities programmes, usually initiated by 'femocrats' – the term 'femocrat' itself intriguingly indicates the compatibility of 'feminism' and 'bureaucracy'. Reforms came later in Italy, France and Germany. For example, in Germany, although men continued to dominate the upper ranks of the state bureaucracies, there was a consistent rise in the percentage of senior posts held by women from 1986 until 1999 (di Luzio 2001).

These transformations of bureaucracies have allowed many European women to access relatively well-remunerated and secure employment; many of them have been able to combine this employment with having children. For those with career ambitions, extended parental leave and secure job tenure has allowed them to temporarily step back from their work without being shunted onto what the Americans term the 'Mommy track' (Hill *et al.* 2004). Such extensive rights, however, can be integrated into large-scale bureaucracies carrying out relatively stable tasks.

Just when large bureaucracies were being – in some countries – made more woman-friendly, private sector organisations began to change into marketocracies (Section 5.4). Unlike in reformed bureaucratic organisations, here women cannot temporarily downshift to have children. The simplest solution is therefore for them to remain childless. If they want to have children and a career they must either have an extremely supportive husband or partner and/or purchase plentiful domestic labour, whether through outsourcing or by employing servants. Flatter hierarchies, individualised and performance-related pay and even more interesting work, all make work more and more demanding. As always, there are national variations here, with the UK (as usual) an outlier with longer working hours than other EU countries, in particular for professional and managerial workers. Thus women, especially in the UK, are placed in the situation that career progression and a sustainable domestic life become increasingly difficult. One comparative study of women in retail and financial services in eight European countries reported that women were frequently turning down promotion because 'promotion entailed longer working hours, which they could not manage in conjunction with their private lives' (SERVEMPLOI 2002: 132). Accordingly, such organisations are increasingly employment for those without dependents – of whatever gender

In many ways, and against normal assumptions, it has proved easier to reform bureaucratic organisations than expected (see also du Gay 2000). By contrast, contemporary forms of private sector organisation increasingly offer managerial careers to women, but only at a high personal cost which relatively few are pre-pared to take. For US MNCs in particular, equal opportunities are often now subsumed into 'managing for diversity', the private sector analogue of main-streaming. In theory, managing for diversity encourages firms to be more flex-ible and imaginative on working time issues, and hence can genuinely lead to working time becoming more compatible with other obligations for women – and perhaps even for men. In general, however, such changes cannot be left to the goodwill of enterprises, but require changes in legislation and social security. For example, international comparisons show that the gender gap within house-holds in terms of hours worked is lower where working time regulation is stronger (Landivar 2015).

9.4 Gender equality and social inequality

This section begins showing how, especially in the UK, women have been able to enter previously male domains such as even private sector management, while in politics women have been more successful in Scandinavia. The obverse of women's success is men's growing failure: their early exit from the labour force, their entry into low paid jobs previously reserved for women, the increasing educational under-achievement of working class boys. Where these trends of success and failure occur most together, there social inequality is strongest, with at the top more households with two good incomes and at the bottom households with no income at all apart from state support.

Women in management

Next to the military, the world of senior management is the paradigmatic men's world. Nearly all senior managers are men, and as one goes up the hierarchy there are fewer and fewer women. Equal opportunities legislation has made overt discrimination against women increasingly rare, precisely because at this level women are able *and willing* to use their formal qualifications and equal opportunities legislation. Nonetheless, it is a standard finding (e.g. Wajcman 1998) that whereas male managers believe that in their organisation women have the same chances as men, women themselves are much less likely to believe this.

National comparisons here are extremely difficult, not least because the definition of 'manager' varies between countries. Some data from around 1990 show that by then a few women had already reached senior management. Thus Olivares reported that in Italy women comprised 3 per cent of senior management, but this ranged from 10 per cent in public administration to 2 per cent in industry (1993: 164). In 1989 in France women comprised 33 per cent of all 'directors', but only 6 per cent of heads of companies employing ten or more staff (Laufer 1993: 112). In Sweden, according to 1990 figures, women comprised 19 per cent of all managers, but only 9 per cent of private sector managers as opposed to fully 29 per cent of all public sector managers (Ministry of Health and Social Affairs 1995: 28). For the UK Wajcman (1998) cites the Institute of Management's 1995 National Management Salary Survey: in 1995 women comprised 9.8 per cent of all managers. Finally, senior German management remained effectively closed to women:

> The preponderance of men in German boardrooms comes as a surprise to many foreign executives and one British corporate lawyer based in Berlin recently complained that, in two years representing one of the city's biggest firms, she had never negotiated with another woman.
>
> (Staunton 1995)

Twenty years later the rather disparate evidence suggests that the USA differs from *all* European countries in the extent to which women have entered junior management jobs, although the UK is not far behind. By contrast, and despite the large numbers of women in the workforce as a whole, management in the private sector in Scandinavia remains a man's world and women remain what early researchers (Dahlerup 1988) termed a 'skewed' group. These differences broadly continue into senior management. Once again it appears that women's entry into very senior management occurs more in the USA than elsewhere, though even here a female senior executive remains unusual. Within Europe, women in senior management seem to be more commonplace in the UK than elsewhere, while in Germany management remains almost over-male.

Women appear to enter senior management most easily in two very different contexts. First, the liberal market economy of the UK is close to that of the USA. Here, individualism ensures that liberal equal opportunities laws are enforced enough to allow ambitious individual women to force their way into the male managerial preserves. Although many opt to remain childless, an extensive low wage service sector allows them to outsource domestic labour including child-care. Individual women are facilitated by companies, particularly US-owned MNCs, pursuing 'managing for diversity'-type policies. Second, in the social democratic Scandinavian situation the preponderance of women in the public sector feeds through into promotion within the public sector.

In the specific case of membership of company boards Norway took the lead with 2006 legislation setting a mandatory gender quota, and there are now similar mandatory quotas in Spain. In this area the European Commission has been active, calling in 2011 for mandatory quotas if there is not sufficient pro-gress. In France there are also mandatory gender quotas for the boards of large companies, and this is part of a general 'stepping up' of legislative measures with the civil service now required to set gender quotas for top posts (Bender *et al.* 2014). The threat of mandatory quotas seems to be one reason why every-where, including in voluntaristic countries such as the UK, women's representa-tion on company boards has increased (Fagan *et al.* 2012).

In all European countries, young women now acquire educational qualifica-tions at least to the same level as men. Furthermore, these qualifications give them entry to private sector management careers; the day is long past where women only gained third-level qualifications in humanities, equipping them for the marriage market or for the caring professions. By the start of the century in most EU countries women were nearly as likely as men to graduate in business and law, and indeed in Spain and Portugal were more likely to do so (Wirth 2001: 75). Equally, in France for example, women already comprised about 50 per cent of graduates of the grandes écoles business schools (Laufer 2000: 28). As a consequence, young women's share of management and professional jobs is similar to that of young men. It is no longer management work that is gen-dered, but *senior* management work.

It would be tempting to claim, as many male executives do, that it is therefore only a matter of time before women's share of senior management also dramat-ically increases. However, this ignores that there are not only 'glass ceilings' but 'glass walls' – women are under-represented in those financial and line manage-ment jobs which are seen as the essential area *within* middle management for promotion to the senior levels and over-represented in support areas such as human resources (e.g. McDowell 1997: 79). Above all, however, many women experience having to *choose* between their career and their family. As women managers increase their earnings they are therefore likely to outsource as much as possible, but for many this is not early enough to fund their career. Disproportionately, such women are not likely to marry and are particularly likely not to have children. A UK study of women managers reported over two-thirds had no children, whereas two-thirds of comparable male managers had children living with them (Wajcman 1998: 83) Once again, comparative studies suggest that conflicts between family and career are particularly acute for British women managers, just as they are particularly likely to 'solve' them by remaining childless (e.g. Windebank 2001).

Nonetheless, three major changes were in process by the new century. First, the constraints of caring work are no longer inevitable. Educated and ambitious women are not only putting off having children, they are increasingly not having children at all. Focusing on the problem of caring work ignores that women can opt out of it. To the extent that care is an actual constraint, it is decreasingly gendered. It is dependency, not gender, that counts:

> Pressures towards economic competitiveness have generated organisational restructuring ... these pressures have been passed on to individuals who, if they wish to improve their chances of a successful career, are constrained to behave in ways that can make family life difficult.... Thus a model of employment is perpetrated in which the 'best' jobs also happen to be those least compatible with employment and caring.
>
> (Crompton and Birkelund 2000: 349)

Second, there is evidence that qualified young women are becoming much more ambitious. A review of French research showed that whereas in the 1980s studies suggested that women entering management were uninterested in power or male-style management, now

> While a taste for 'power' was not supposed to exist on the part of women managers in the past, younger women managers emphasise that power in its various forms is needed if they are to make something of their working lives.
>
> (Laufer 2000: 30)

Third, as a quick perusal of any of the glossier women's magazines reminds one, the workplace is exciting and where people meet their sexual partners. Rather grudgingly, academic research is beginning to notice this egalitarian sexualisation of the workplace, even though old-fashioned sexism is far from dead. Wajcman quoted one of her sources: 'Chip UK is quite incestuous, there was a lot of affairs going on ... they were all screwing with each other' (1998: 115). And work is more exciting at the top. Power has its own pleasures, as well as its sexual frisson. Power and sexuality are no longer the private property of men.

Women in politics

Mrs Thatcher made it acceptable for a woman to be an international stateswoman. In fact, until then women in developing countries were more likely to be leading politicians than women from the developed worlds, just as in many developing countries women have for long been less segregated within professional occupations (Hakim 1979). Yet Mrs Thatcher was notoriously surrounded by 'traditional' men, and today women's representation in UK politics remains low by European standards. Today Angela Merkel, often described as the most powerful woman in the world, leads a very different cabinet to Margaret Thatcher.

For the last forty years women have formed a higher percentage of national parliamentarians in Scandinavia than elsewhere in Europe. Thus even in the early 1960s, when woman parliamentarians were lone individuals in Britain or the USA, they already comprised around 15 per cent of the Finnish or Swedish parliaments (Dahlerup 1988). This proportion then climbed rapidly in all Scandinavian countries, while showing no major change elsewhere. More recently women have made substantial gains in France and above all Germany, where 37 per cent of all *Mitglieder des Bundestages* (members of parliament) are women (Inter-Parliamentary Union 2015). And while women are usually less likely to be ministers, and even less likely to be ministers of finance, foreign affairs or defence, this is no longer always true. Anna Lindt was Swedish foreign minister when she was murdered in 2003; in 2004 Michèle Alliot-Marie was the French minister of defence; in 2015 Ursula von der Leyen is the minister for defence in Germany.

In some countries, women's representation has been increased by political parties imposing quotas. In Germany the Greens were the first to do this, and also to 'zip' their candidate lists by putting males and females in alternative positions, thus ensuring that women were not always at the bottom of the list. The SPD first introduced a quota in 1988 and the CDU finally followed suit in 2001, even though the party's chairwoman, Angela Merkel (just like Margaret Thatcher earlier) is herself not interested in 'women's issues' (McKay 2004). At a European level women have also made progress. In the 1999–2004 session of the Parliament, 30 per cent of all MEPs were women, more than the average of the national parliaments (Wirth 2001: 50); the proportion has continued to rise, reaching 37 per cent in the 2014 session (European Parliament 2015). Nonetheless, women MEPs are still disproportionately involved in conventional women's issues, being significantly under-represented in committees such as the Security and Defence Committee. Jacques Delors presided over an all-male Commission but in 2015, of the twenty-eight members of the Commission, nine were women (European Commission 2015). Such women European politicians have not yet had such a clear impact as their sisters have had in Scandinavia, but many contribute to the strengthening of European-wide women's networks and hence have ensured that the women's movement has a strong European dimension. Even if only indirectly, European political institutions have contributed to gender equality.

Decline of men

In different ways in different countries, European women have been entering well paid and/or powerful occupations. At the same time, the situation of some men (again with national variations) has deteriorated. Unskilled men in particular now frequently leave the workforce before official retirement age since welfare systems often allow them to define themselves as unfit for work. Even though they will still be dependent on state income support, such illness has the politically useful function of reducing the unemployment figures (Webster 2000). The personal implications depend on the welfare system. In Germany until the Hartz IV reforms, income support allowed such men to maintain their previous standard of living, whereas in the UK it simply means the poverty of unemployment at a marginally better standard of living and with less stigmatisation. Paradoxically, even if income support appears adequate, as in Scandinavia, older men are more at risk than women from social exclusion if this means exclusion from social networks, in particular given that such men are likely to no longer have a functioning family (Andersen and Larsen 1998). Scandinavian women, have better coping strategies to deal with low income than Scandinavian men, not least because of the feminisation of the welfare state.

Less noticed than the entry of women into higher occupations has been the undoubted degendering of *some* traditionally low paid female jobs. This is interwoven with the casualisation of *some* areas of traditionally relatively secure women's jobs. The rollback of the welfare state in the UK from the 1980s onwards pushed women into bad work, destabilising routine but good women's work and contributing to the 'feminisation of poverty'. By 1999 fully one-third of all British children were growing up below the poverty line (Franks 1999: 227), and these were disproportionately concentrated in single-parent families. The well-documented collapse of traditional male working class jobs (Section 5.1) has been followed, in countries such as the UK and the Netherlands, by the emergence of many jobs more accessible to groups such as students (Doogan 2009: 161; Hofman and Steijn 2003). The erosion of traditional male jobs and the new displacement of young working males contributes to their educational under-achievement, in particular compared to young working class women and young women from ethnic minorities.

In this situation, desegregation means that the inequalities among women begin to mirror those among men. In the age of housewifery, women were hardly equal, but their inequalities depended on their being dependent on different men. To an increasing extent, women now generate these inequalities in their own right and this in turn contributes to greater inequalities between households. At the lower end of the occupational structure, worklessness and part-time and temporary work are increasingly concentrated in the same households. A new division emerges between workless and work-intense households. Somewhat bizarrely, the subsidised childcare and parental leave initiatives of the social investment state can even exacerbate this division, since such supports are utilised by the better educated and more fully employed women (Cantillon 2011).

At the top end of the occupational structure, service class households increasingly contain two full-time working adults both with professional incomes or salaries. As early as 1980 in the UK a growing proportion of households comprised two full-time earners with both wife and husband in professional class jobs. If gender equality was defined as the increasing access of women to professional jobs hitherto reserved for men, this also meant that income disparities between households were increasing (Bonney 1988). Today such dual-earning couples are making their own dual contribution to greater inequality between households.

9.5 Conclusion: a European approach?

Since the 1970s and 1980s women's experiences in Europe and the USA have diverged. At its simplest, American (and to some extent British) women have achieved greater economic independence but at the cost of exposing themselves to a deregulated market. This market imposes costs on those who wish to have children and have a career, while it also makes it very difficult for mothers to stay at home. Even if flexibility is more beneficial to the employer, these countries' flexible labour market means that most women can find employment. This seems to be the main reason why the Anglophone countries today continue to have relatively high fertility. Yet precisely because this independence depends upon the market, it is intertwined with greater social inequality between people – and between women.

Yet Scandinavia offers an alternative model, with echoes in France and even, rather surreptitiously, in Germany. Here the state supports women to have children, but at same time facilitates entry into work. This does run the risk of creating new female ghettoes in the public sector, but they are nonetheless ones in which women do have real independence. Through accessible childcare services, through taxation and benefits and through labour market regulation (e.g. parental leave) it is possible for the state to support parenting – including by men. Given that even the UK now has paid paternity leave it is possible to see this area as one where there really is a distinctively European approach. And furthermore, while as always these social policies are implemented (and largely funded) by the national states, they have been promoted by the European Union. Unlike in the USA, at least in some areas of Europe equality between the genders does not have to come at the cost of greater social inequality.

Note

1 There are obvious reasons to reject the conventional wisdom that the population of European countries needs to grow (Coleman and Rowthorn 2011). Growing populations impose high environmental costs, especially if the population is also affluent: there are strong ecological arguments in favour of some *reduction* of population size over time. There is evidence that growing population is already experienced by some Europeans as damaging their quality of life: population pressure on the environment ('overcrowding') is now one reason Europeans give for emigrating (Van Dalen and Henekens 2013).

Bibliography

Andersen, J. and Larsen, J. (1998) Gender, poverty and empowerment, *Critical Social Policy* 18.55: 241–258.

Baird, M. and O'Brien, M. (2015) Dynamics of parental leave in Anglophone countries: the paradox of state expansion in liberal welfare regimes, *Community, Work and Family* 18.2: 198–217.

Bender, A.F., Klarsfeld, A. and Laufer, J. (2014) Equality and diversity in years of crisis in France. In A. Klarsfeld (ed.) *Country Perspectives on Diversity and Equal Treatment*, London: Edward Elgar, pp. 87–100.

Bergqvist, C. and Jungar, A.-C. (2000) Adaption or diffusion of Swedish gender model? In L. Hantrais (ed.) *Gender Policies in Europe: Reconciling Employment and Family Life*, London: Macmillan, pp. 160–179.

Bernardi, F. (2005) Public policies and low fertility: rationales for public intervention and a diagnosis for the Spanish case, *Journal of European Social Policy* 15.2: 123–138.

Bettio, R. and Verashchagina, A. (2014) Women and men in the 'Great European Recession'. In M. Karamessini and J. Rubery (eds) *Women and Austerity: The Economic Crisis and the Future for Gender Equality*, London: Routledge, pp. 57–81.

Bielinski, H., Bosch, G. and Wagner, A. (2002) *Working Time Preferences in Sixteen European Countries. Report for the European Foundation for the Improvement of Living and Working Conditions*, Luxembourg: Office for the Official Publications of the European Communities.

Boje, T. and Almquist, A.L. (2000) Citizenship, family policy and women's patterns of employment. In T. Boje and A. Leira (eds) *Gender, Welfare State and the Market: Towards a New Division of Labour*, London: Routledge, pp. 421–70.

Bonney, N. (1988) Dual earning couples: trends of change in Great Britain, *Work Employment and Society* 2.1: 89–102.

Brandth, B. and Kvande, E. (2001) Flexible work and flexible fathers, *Work Employment and Society* 15.2: 251–267.

Cameron, C. and Moss, P. (2007) *Care Work in Europe: Current Understandings and Future Directions*, London: Routledge.

Cantillon, B. (2011) The paradox of the social investment state: growth, employment and poverty in the Lisbon era, *Journal of European Social Policy* 21.5: 432–449.

Castles, F. (2003) The world turned upside down: below replacement fertility, changing preferences and family-friendly policy in 21 OECD countries, *Journal of European Social Policy* 13.3: 209–227.

Coleman, D. and Rowthorn, R. (2011) Who's afraid of population decline? A critical examination of its consequences, *Population and Development Review* 37 (Supplement): 217–248.

Crompton, R. and Birkelund, G. (2000) Employment and caring in British and Norwegian banking: an exploration through individual careers, *Work Employment and Society* 14.2: 331–352.

Crompton, R. and Sanderson, K. (1990) *Gendered Jobs and Social Change*, London: Unwin Hyman.

Dahlerup, D. (1988) From a small to a large minority: women in Scandinavian politics, *Scandinavian Political Studies* 11.4: 275–297.

di Luzio, G. (2001) Reorganising gender relations in the German civil service: administrative reform and the decline of the male breadwinner model, *German Politics* 10.3: 159–190.

Doogan, K. (2009) *New Capitalism? The Transformation of Work*, Cambridge: Polity Press.

du Gay, P. (2000) *In Praise of Bureaucracy*, London: Sage.

Duncan, S. and Pfau-Effinger, B. (2000) *Gender, Economy and Culture in the European Union*, London: Routledge.

Duncan, S. and Strell, M. (2004) Combining lone motherhood and paid work: the rationality mistake and Norwegian social policy, *Journal of European Social Policy* 14.1: 41–54.

Ellingsaeter, A. (2007) 'Old' and 'new' politics of time to care: three Norwegian reforms, *Journal of European Social Policy* 17.1: 49–60.

Ellingsaeter, A. (2012) Childcare politics and the Norwegian fertility machine. In D. Mayes and M. Thomson (eds) *The Costs of Children: Parenting and Democracy in Contemporary Europe*, Cambridge: Polity Press, pp. 70–91.

Esping-Andersen, G. (2009) *The Incomplete Revolution: Adapting Welfare States to Women's New Roles*, Cambridge: Polity Press.

European Commission (2004) *Employment in Europe 2004: Recent Trends and Prospects*, Luxembourg: Office for the Official Publications of the European Communities.

European Commission (2013a) *Barcelona Objectives*, Luxembourg: Publications Office of the European Union.

European Commission (2013b) *EU Employment and Social Situation: Quarterly Review March 2013 Special Supplement on Demographic Trends*, Luxembourg: Publications Office of the European Union.

European Commission (2014) *Employment and Social Developments in Europe 2014*, Luxembourg: Publications Office of the European Union.

European Commission (2015) The Commissioners, http://ec.europa.eu/commission/2014-2019_en. Accessed 31 July 2015.

European Parliament (2015) European Parliament Elections, www.europarl.europa.eu/elections2014-results/en/gender-balance.html. Accessed 13 July 2015.

Fagan, C., González Menèndez, M. and Gómez, S. (eds) (2012) *Women on Corporate Boards and in Top Management: European Trends and Policy*, London: Palgrave Macmillan.

Franks, S. (1999) *Having None of It: Women, Men and the Future of Work*, London: Granta.

Gershuny, J. (2000) *Changing Times*, London: Sage.

Ghysels, J., and Van Lancker, W. (2011) The unequal benefits of activation: an analysis of the social distribution of family policy among families with young children, *Journal of European Social Policy* 21.5: 472–485.

Hakim, C. (1979) *Occupational Segregation*, Research Paper no. 9, London: Department of Employment.

Hakim, C. (1999) Models of the family, women's role and social policy, *European Societies* 1.1: 33–58.

Hakim, C. (2000) *Work–Lifestyle Choices in the 21st Century*, Oxford: Oxford UP.

Halford, S. and Leonard, P. (2001) *Gender, Power and Organisations*, London: Palgrave.

Hansen, M. (1997) The Scandinavian welfare state model: the impact of the public sector on segregation and gender equality, *Work Employment and Society* 11.1: 83–99.

Hantrais, L. (1999) Socio-demographic change, policy impacts and outcomes in social Europe, *Journal of European Social Policy* 9.4: 291–309.

Hill, E., Märtinson, V., Ferris, M. and Baker, R. (2004) Beyond the Mommy track: the influence of new-concept part-time work for professional women on work and family, *Journal of Family and Economic Issues* 25.1: 121–136.

Hofman, W., and Steijn, A. (2003) Students or lower-skilled workers? 'Displacement' at the bottom of the labour market, *Higher Education* 45.2: 127–146.

Hoskyns, C. (1996) *Integrating Gender*, London: Verso.

Inter-Parliamentary Union (2015) Women in national parliaments, www.ipu.org/wmn-e/classif.htm. Accessed 13 July 2015.

Jenson, J. and Saint-Martin, D. (2003) New routes to social cohesion? Citizenship and the social investment state, *Canadian Journal of Sociology/Cahiers canadiens de sociologie* 28.1: 77–99.

Konietzka, D. and Kreyenfeld, M. (2010) The growing educational divide in mothers' employment: an investigation based on the German micro-censuses 1976–2004, *Work Employment and Society* 24.2: 260–278.

Korpi, W., Ferrarini, T. and Englund, S. (2013) Women's opportunities under different family policy constellations: gender, class, and inequality tradeoffs in Western countries re-examined, *Social Politics: International Studies in Gender, State and Society* 20.1: 1–40.

Landivar, L. (2015) The gender gap in employment hours: do work-hours regulations matter? *Work Employment and Society* 29.4: 550–570.

Laufer, J. (1993) France. In M. Davidson and C. Cooper (eds) *European Women in Business and Management*, London: Chapman, pp. 107–132.

Laufer, J. (1998) Equal opportunity between men and women: the case of France, *Feminist Economics* 4.1: 53–69.

Laufer, J. (2000) French women managers. In M. Davidson and R. Burke (eds) *Women in Management*, London: Sage, pp. 26–39.

Leira, A. (2015) From poverty relief to universal provision: the changing grounds for childcare policy reforms in Norway. In H. Willekens, K. Scheiwe and K. Nawrotzki (eds)*The Development of Early Childhood Education in Europe and North America*, London: Palgrave Macmillan, pp. 112–131.

Lewis, J. (1992) Gender and the development of welfare regimes, *Journal of European Social Policy* 2.3: 159–173.

McDonald, P. and Moyle, H. (2010) Why do English-speaking countries have relatively high fertility? *Journal of Population Research* 27.4: 247–273.

McDowell, L. (1997) *Capital Culture: Gender at Work in the City*, Oxford: Blackwell.

McKay, J. (2004) Women in German politics: still jobs for the boys? *German Politics* 13.1: 56–80.

Mandel, H. and Shalev, M. (2009) How welfare states shape the gender pay gap: a theoretical and comparative analysis, *Social Forces* 87: 1873–1912.

Marks, G., Hooghe, L. and Blank, K. (1996) European integration from the 1980s: state-centric v. multi-level governance, *Journal of Common Market Studies* 34.3: 341–378.

Martin, C. (2010) The reframing of family policies in France: processes and actors, *Journal of European Social Policy* 20.5: 410–421.

Mingione, E. (2005) Urban social change: a socio-historical framework of analysis. In E. Kazepov (ed.) *Cities of Europe*, Oxford: Blackwell, pp. 67–89.

Ministry of Health and Social Affairs (Sweden) (1995) *Shared Power and Responsibility: National Report by the Government of Sweden for the Fourth World Conference on Women in Beijing 1995*, Stockholm: Government of Sweden.

Olivares, F. (1993) Italy. In M. Davidson and C. Cooper (eds) *European Women in Business and Management*, London: Chapman, pp. 161–173.

Pailhé, A. and Solaz, A. (2012) The influence of employment uncertainty on childbearing in France. A tempo or a quantum effect? *Demographic Research* 26: 1–40.

Peña-Ruiz, H. (2004) Laïcité et égalité, leviers de l'émancipation, *Le Monde diplomatique*, February.

Pfau-Effinger, B. (2005) Culture and welfare state policies: reflections on a complex interrelation, *Journal of Social Policy* 34.1: 3–20.

Quarmby, K. (2003) The politics of childcare, *Prospect*, November.

Rees, T. (1998) *Mainstreaming Equality in the European Union*, London: Routledge.

Reyneri, E. (2004) Immigrants in a segmented and often undeclared labour market, *Journal of Modern Italian Studies* 9.1: 71–93.

Rubery, J., Smith, M. and Fagan, C. (1999) *Women's Employment in Europe: Trends and Prospects*, London: Routledge.

SERVEMPLOI (2002) Innovations in Information Society Service Sectors: Implications for women's work, expertise and opportunities in European workplaces. Final Report, http://cordis.europa.eu/documents/documentlibrary/70777261EN6.pdf. Accessed 7 August 2015.

Staunton, D. (1995) Abrupt halt of march to top by women, *Irish Times*, 8 March.

Tanturri, M., Mills, M., Rotkirch, A., Sobotka, T., Takács, J., Miettenen, A., Faludi, C., Kantsa, V. and Nasiri, D. (2015) *State-of-the-art Report: Childlessness in Europe*, FamiliesAndSocieties Working Paper Series 32, Brussels: FamiliesAndSocieties for EU Seventh Framework Programme.

Van Dalen, H. and Henekens, K. (2013) Explaining emigration intentions and behaviour in the Netherlands 2005–10, *Population Studies* 67.2: 225–241.

Van Kersbergen, K. and Hemerijck, A. (2012) Two decades of change in Europe: the emergence of the social investment state, *Journal of Social Policy* 41.3: 475–492.

Van Lancker, W. and Ghysels, J. (2012) Who benefits? The social distribution of subsidized childcare in Sweden and Flanders, *Acta Sociologica* 55.2: 125–142.

Vignoli, D., Drefahl, S. and De Santis, G. (2012) Whose job instability affects the likelihood of becoming a parent in Italy? A tale of two partners, *Demographic Research* 26: 41–62.

Wajcman, J. (1998) *Managing Like a Man: Women and Men in Corporate Management*, Cambridge: Polity Press.

Walby, S. (1999) The European Union and equal opportunities policies, *European Societies* 1.1: 59–80.

Webster, D. (2000) The geographical concentration of labour-market disadvantage, *Oxford Review of Economic Policy* 16.1: 114–128.

Wickham, J. (1997) Who wants what where? Part-time work in Ireland and Europe, *Work Employment and Society* 11.1: 133–155.

Wickham, J., Collins, G., Greco, L. and Browne, J. (2008) Individualization and equality: women's careers and organizational form, *Organization* 15.2: 211–231.

Windebank, J. (2001) Dual earner couples in Britain and France: gender divisions of labour, *Work Employment and Society* 15.2: 269–290.

Wirth, L. (2001) *Breaking Through the Glass Ceiling: Women in Management*, Geneva: International Labour Organisation.

10 Conclusion

The end of the European social model before it began?

Europeans are unequal, but in European ways. This final chapter begins by summarising the distinctive forms of European inequality, and highlights the distinctiveness of the UK within Europe. Indeed, the European project might actually be strengthened if Britain were to leave the European Union. The converse of social division is social integration. If inequality in Europe is distinctive, does the same apply to integration in Europe? Within a market-based society the divisions of inequality have to be bandaged by citizenship to ensure some social integration. Here the EU is largely ineffective: European social citizenship is minimal and increasingly marginalised by financial integration. There are few cultural resources and social links from which a European identity could be constructed; European social processes are largely the prerogative of the service class. Indeed, the failure of the EU to secure any meaningful economic and social rights for ordinary Europeans increasingly undermines any legitimacy for the European project. We face the paradox that European elites are now destroying the only real basis for a distinctive popular European identity.

10.1 European social inequalities

Defining what Europe is – or even where Europe is – turns out to be open to many different answers. This book started with the suggestion that *one* definition of Europe is its *social model*. This is especially the case when Europe is identified with the European Union.

All human societies are unequal, and the twentieth century demonstrated that attempts to completely extirpate economic inequality involve extreme violence and generate new and more extreme political inequalities. Radical egalitarianism is certainly incompatible with any form of representative democracy. This is true but unimportant given that over time societies which combine a market economy and parliamentary democracy have varied enormously in the extent and form of inequality: compare, for example, the income inequality in Britain in the 1950s with that of today (Section 4.2). In the same way, as shown schematically in Figure 1.8, Europe today comprises national societies which are more inclusive – and also more cohesive – than the USA. European societies differ from the USA not just in terms of income inequality, but also in terms of social rights and economic rights. In Europe, more so than in the USA, there is an acceptance of a strong backbone state which can maintain a public sphere distinct from the dictates of the market.

This story is, however, complicated by the variety within Europe. Some scholars argue that this means it is simply impossible to contrast Europe and the USA, yet if the focus is on the old EU15 this is certainly invalid. Furthermore, such an argument ignores that Europe is not *simply* a collection of independent nation states, for Europe is also that political project known as the European Union. While the EU is clearly not a super-national state, it is nonetheless also a political entity in its own right with its own institutional structure and its own common policies.

The distinctiveness of Europe thus involves both features of the national member states *and* those features that derive from the European Union. The core sociological chapters of the book examined inequalities within Europe, largely in the old EU15: inequalities of income, occupational class, region, migration, ethnicity and gender. The nature of Europe as a unit becomes clear if it is contrasted with the USA. This comparison also highlights one major difference within Europe, namely the very distinctive role of the UK.

During the 1980s (West) European societies changed from societies based on manufacturing to societies dominated by service industries. As Chapter 2 showed, this transition was most rapid in the UK and took a specific form. Services can mean many things, and in the UK more so than elsewhere have meant financial services plus privatised personal services. As a consequence the UK led the way in Europe to a low wage service sector as had been developing in the USA. Whereas literature within the welfare state modelling tradition highlighted variety within Europe, the 'varieties of capitalism' approach within political economy operated with a dichotomy between liberal market economies, epitomised by the UK and the USA, and co-ordinated market economies, identified with Germany. Indeed, analyses of financialisation often treat the UK and USA as isomorphic (e.g. Langley 2009). Within Europe the UK initiated the move away from the mixed economy of class compromise of the mid-twentieth century. British firms now follow US firms in their notorious focus on shareholder value and are furthest away from any form of stakeholder involvement. For ordinary people the change has been most directly experienced through the labour market: the growth of low wages, the lack of employment protection (exacerbated by UK opt-outs from several EU directives) and the collapse of trade union bargaining coverage.

Given these changes it is hardly surprising that since the 1980s the UK has become one of the most unequal societies in Europe in terms of its income distribution and, despite considerable amelioration under the New Labour governments (1996–2010), has some of the most extreme poverty. In these terms within the EU15 the UK is closest to the USA. The UK is also closest to the US in terms of the importance of light wealth (Section 4.3). While other European countries, especially the southern ones, also have extensive private property, the UK is unique in the extent to which this property has been made fungible by the financial services industry. This is liquid lite wealth, to be bought and sold, to be amortised and borrowed against, connecting the household directly into a global system of finance. It is very different to the illiquid family property of so many Italian or Greek households. Equally, while the UK is hardly the only European country with extremely rich individuals (the heavy wealth of Section 4.4) it is distinctive in that so many of them derive their wealth from the financial services industry.

Very recently Robert Putnam has documented the growth of what he terms the 'split screen nightmare' of the USA, where the most affluent third and the poorest third of the population live totally different lives in mutual ignorance (Putnam 2015: 1). While the self-image of USA is that it is classless compared to Europe, in fact no country in old Europe reaches this level of division – not even Britain. Yet in many ways the British social structure is now less European than before. The degradation (and denigration) of its traditional working class has gone furthest, its management is the most Americanised. In the past Italy, with its north/south divide, was the European country with the greatest regional differences. Now the growing gap between London and the south on the one hand and the northern cities on the other hand means that Britain begins to resemble a US slash-and-burn pattern of economic growth (Section 6.2).

Within Europe London is the success story global city. Despite or perhaps because of its extremes of inequality, it pulls in migrant labour from across Europe and the world; illegal migrants from sub-Saharan Africa clean the offices where highly paid financial specialists from France (or even from India) work. In the early 1990s Sassen identified London and New York as both having an extremely polarised occupational structure. The comparison was wrong at the time, but subsequently the decline of the British welfare state has made it accurate, just as transport and digital links have made the two cities more inter-twined than ever before (Section 6.4). Indeed, the success of women in the upper echelons of these two cities shows how in the UK gender equality has become an option for the affluent, while elsewhere in Europe gender equality has especially benefited ordinary women (Chapter 9).

While most of these issues cast the UK (and the USA) in a negative light, the UK's distinctiveness in terms of immigration and especially ethnicity seems more positive. Its immigration policy has oscillated wildly, but of all European societies it has probably come closer to becoming a multi-ethnic society where ethnic diversity is simply an accepted fact of life and even part of national identity (Chapter 8). The very individualism of British society and the very weakness of the welfare state may well make the UK especially open to ethnic minorities. Even more so than in other European countries, discussion of 'immigration' often takes little account of whether or not migrants are EU citizens. Revealingly, there is no British equivalent of the Italian term *extracommunitari* (people from outside the [European] community). Indeed, the planned referendum on EU membership will use the normal franchise for UK parliamentary elections: British, Irish and Commonwealth citizens resident in the UK will be allowed to vote, EU citizens resident in the UK will not (a Pakistani citizen resident in the

UK can vote on British EU membership, a French citizen resident in the UK cannot). This apparent anomaly highlights how the post-Thatcher distinctiveness of Britain in Europe builds upon much older historical differences.

10.2 European integration and the European social model

European inequalities lead to the question of European bonding. Societies are unequal, but they are also integrated or bonded. If the European social model involves distinctive forms of inequality, it is plausible that it also involves distinctive forms of integration. Such integration should not be confused with social cohesion as discussed in Chapter 1 for, especially where traditional authority is respected, a society can be both cohesive and very unequal. In the contemporary world the nation state bonds or integrates the national society: the nation state generates much of the social glue that holds the society together. This involves citizenship and, in Europe, social policies as broadly conceived.

Within modern Europe nation states have been coterminous not only with national societies but also with national economies. The creation of a national economy involved the creation of a single national market with its own currency and a common external tariff. As the market deepened internally, the national state put in place national institutions which made people not just economic actors but also national citizens. During the twentieth century these national institutions were increasingly the institutions of the welfare state, and the strength of these differentiated Western Europe from the USA (Chapter 1). Thus whereas the EU and the European nation state are usually seen as opposed, this suggests that they are potentially reinforcing. If so, the strength of the European social model depends on both European and national institutions. First, are there now European – as opposed to national – institutions of integration? Are there Euro-bonds as well as national bonds? Second, what is happening to member states' integrative abilities? Is the European Union undermining or enhancing its constituent national states?

Marshall's classic account of citizenship differentiated between civil, political and social citizenship (Marshall 1950). The initial form of the Union, the European Economic Community, already contributed to European citizenship. To the extent that the original Common Market necessarily involved some common legal rights and a mechanism (the European Court of Justice) to enforce these, the *burghers* of the EEC did share a common citizenship. However, this was a citizenship that was only a legal basis for economic activity, not for political participation. It was the civil right to be a member of a market economy, but not the political right to be a member of a liberal democratic society.

The Maastricht Treaty created European 'citizens' for the first time with explicit rights (Article 8) that could be taken as political rights. The rights are limited, the most important being that all European citizens have the right of movement and residence within the Union, and the right to vote and stand in municipal and European elections in the place where they reside. However, these rights do not apply to elections for the national parliament, and national parliaments remain crucial.

Many key European institutions are either simply intergovernmental (e.g. the Council of Ministers) or chosen by national governments (e.g. the Commission). Although the European Parliament is undoubtedly more assertive and has shown itself to be a serious restraint on the appointment of commissioners, for most Europeans it remains far less important than their national parliament. Furthermore, a European citizen is simply a citizen of a member state, but each member state retains the sole prerogative to decide its rules of citizenship: once again a decision taken by a national parliament.

During the 1970s, the equality directives began to create social rights (Section 9.3): women acquired the right to equal pay and equal treatment in employment. These social rights were therefore created at the 'European' level before any political rights (whereas in Marshall's typology social rights come after civil and political rights). Furthermore, because these rights only applied to the world of formal work, those people to whom they applied were not coterminous with national citizens. On the one hand, they were more restrictive: those outside the formal economy were not affected. On the other hand they were more extensive: they applied to all employees, whether or not they were national citizens (see Meehan 1993).

Today the Union's Charter of Fundamental Rights, promulgated in 2000 and finally made legally binding in the Lisbon Treaty of 2009, includes various social rights such as the 'right to social and housing assistance' (Article 34). In practice these rights seem to be fairly meaningless. Certainly specific European Union policies and programmes have marginally enhanced economic citizenship (Section 1.3): the Works Council Directive gives some minimal rights of representation to some employees, the Working Time Directive has had some impact on working hours. Yet revealingly, the various recent bail out programmes for countries such as Greece took no account of their social impact. Since these programmes ensured that many citizens were denied any social assistance, the EU's programmes were in breach of the Union's own Charter – and nobody ever bothered.

The anti-poverty programmes have made little overall impact on the distribution of income within the member states (Chapter 4). However, they made noticeable innovations in encouraging local participation and in involving non-governmental organisations and local authorities in the design and execution of programmes. The poverty programmes have both directly and by example made some contribution to social inclusion, considered not just as lack of income but as lack of democratic participation. The anti-poverty programmes of the European Commission have certainly facilitated the measurement of poverty and supported more sophisticated social research. In this policy area the Open Method of Co-ordination has probably facilitated some limited policy learning and policy transfer – there is for example evidence of movement towards active labour market policies instead of passive support for the unemployed. Nonetheless, in the last decade there has been a growing gap between aspiration and reality, epitomised by the bluster of the so-called Youth Guarantee which was meant to bring unemployed youths (the NEETs) into employment but in practice has had virtually no impact. The Europe 2020 poverty targets equally seem now to be effectively ignored.

In most other areas of inequality the European Union has also ceased to build institutions of integration. The heyday of regional policy is now long past. Compared to the structural funds received by the states that joined in the 1980s, funding to the new member states has been trivial. Here the expansion of the market itself is seen as the most direct route to greater regional equality. In terms of gender equality the glory days of the 1980s are also a distant memory. Certainly, with the exception of the UK and Ireland, the Union is hesitantly developing a common frontier policy and the maintenance of citizens' freedom of movement remains a major achievement for ordinary Europeans as workers and as consumers. Whatever the consequences may have been for the host countries, the right of their citizens to move and work anywhere within Europe has been an important contribution to the economic development of the new member states. While ethnic and racial discrimination appear to be outlawed by the Charter (Article 21) this seems to have provided little protection to ethnic minorities and the Roma within the new member states and it is doubtful whether this European citizenship right has any relevance to Western Europe's established ethnic minorities. For Europe's ethnic minorities what matters, positively or negatively, is the nation state, not 'Europe'.

Just as within nation states, the deepening of the European market initially involved compensating social policies and institutions. Today within the Eurozone market integration has been supplemented by financial integration, by the attempt to build common financial regulatory institutions and by the growing role of the European Central Bank. Yet such financial integration is one-sided. It is market-making, not social bonding. By only strengthening the market, it will end up further undermining social integration. Indeed, the bail-out programmes were remarkable for their total lack of interest in the maintenance of social integration, and in the social sphere the prime concern appeared to be further labour market changes (so-called reforms) to remove the rights of a few slightly privileged groups of employees. It is therefore perhaps appropriate that it was the President of the European Central Bank who announced the death of the European social model (see Section 1.5).

10.3 European identities

One response to the crisis has been calls for greater European integration, but popular support for the European project is stagnant or even declining. Any stronger political union would require a common European *demos*, a 'public' which debates what 'we' should do (Siedentop 2000). Since the nineteenth century European national states have been the framework for political debate. Despite the party alliances within the European Parliament, there is precious little sign of such debate at European level. Indeed, political debate was arguably more Europeanised in the inter-war years of the twentieth century than it is today. Researchers have looked hard for anything resembling a European public sphere (Koopmans and Erbe 2004). Public discussion of 'European' politics is in terms of national interests: 'the' Greeks, 'the' Germans or whatever. This has clearly been exacerbated by the current crisis, with policy made by national government/bargaining with each other. As Europe faces its political crisis, national governments have sidelined European institutions. This section now asks first whether there are any social and cultural resources on which a European identity could be built, and second which social groups or social classes within Europe are in any meaningful sense pro-European.

European culture and European social links

If we look to the past, Europe can be defined in terms of its history, in particular its cultural history. While this is the core of academic courses in 'European Studies', it has little popular resonance today. For better or worse, the European high culture of painting, architecture and classical music has become simply another form of consumption and has long lost its moral value. In 1880 the frieze of the new opera house of Frankfurt dedicated the building to *Dem Wahren, Schönen, Guten* (To Truth, Beauty, Goodness). Unfortunately perhaps, such a slogan could not be made without irony today.

We could look to the future, seeing 'Europe' as something to be made.[1] Whereas in the nineteenth and twentieth centuries national states were legitimated by constructing unitary national myths of a historical past ('the Irish people', *'nos ancêtres les Galles'* or whatever), Europe could be understood in terms of its future: the 'ever closer union of peoples' hailed in the Treaties, even 'the European project' itself. From this perspective Europe's boundaries are not fixed but fluid and expanding: European integration is ongoing because there is no defined end apart from the process itself. In all sorts of ways, legitimacy through perpetual motion defines 'Europe'; it highlights the curious fact that despite one crisis after another 'Europe' keeps getting bigger (Voruba 2005). Yet this ever closer, ever bigger Union was never actively supported by those same peoples in whose name it is being constructed and it has few enthusiasts today. In terms of expansion the Turkish question highlights that increasingly the only important advocates of Turkish entry are precisely those who argue for a 'thin' Europe where union means little more than a customs union.[2]

Part of the problem with building a European identity is the lack of available cultural resources. National identities may have built from the top down by determined intellectuals, but these seized on folk dances as popular symbols with which to do it. Today European civilisation is symbolised by high culture (e.g. opera, even wine) but this hardly has the popular purchase of the Americanised global mass consumption of Levi's jeans and Coca-Cola. And while the creation of the European nations certainly involved imposing a national language on many people who would never have spoken it, it's impossible to imagine any one single European language playing the same role in the creation of Europe as individual national languages did in the creation of the nation states.

And 'Europe' is above all a politicians' and an administrators' Europe. In the consolidation of the nation states of Europe the negative integration of the trade unions and social democracy was crucial, for these movements linked together members from different areas of the nation in common opposition to the status quo. This nationalising role of the opposition is clear in the Germany of the Kaiserreich but was also clear in imperial Britain, where British trade unions and above the British Labour Party integrated the Scottish and Welsh working class into a national polity and made their national identities a component of a wider one. The creation of a European political space for economic rights has stimulated the development of European lobbying, but this remains far removed from the world of mass action and mass identities.

Within Europe up until World War II there was a working class movement which was a social force. For political and trade union activists it could even transcend national loyalties and certainly generated an intellectual milieu for oppositional intellectuals. When the Nazis seized power in Germany in 1933 the first concentration camp inmates were political opponents, communists, trade unionists and social democrats (gays, gypsies and then of course Jews followed after quite a long gap). The Nazis were determined that they would extirpate Marxism from Europe. When the social democrats and communists emerged from the ruins of the Third Reich to rebuild the labour movement the Nazis had tried to destroy, the cultural conditions were very different. As mass consumption spread in the 1950s the age of the working class autodidact was over, and the cultural space in which the working class movement had developed its institutions of working class sport and theatre was increasingly occupied by the new forms of mass entertainment. A popular Europeanism was no longer possible.

For the Nazis, Marxism was Jewish. There was, of course, the disproportionate contribution of Jewish intellectuals to the movement, particularly in Germany and Russia (Marx himself, Rosa Luxemburg, Leo Jogiches, Eduard Bernstein, etc.). There was, however, a more fundamental reason. In the twentieth century Marxism was the most powerful anti-national ideology, far eclipsing the older religions in both its popular purchase and its ability to escape the nation state. For all the attempts at assimilation, for all those German Jews clutching their iron crosses, for all those British knighthoods, to be Jewish was to share an identity with someone beyond the boundary of the nation state. This identity was not narrowly European, being massively Eastern European and trans-Atlantic, but European Jewry was one of the social bonds of pre-Nazi Europe (others included the old European aristocracy). The Nazis did not succeed completely, but enough of European Jewry was destroyed to ensure that it could not become a component of European identity.

Who are the Europeans today?

For Europeans to debate European politics as Europeans would also require some form of common European identity. Here the signs are rather more mixed: a European identity does now co-exist with national identities. While only a small minority of Europeans (never more than about 10 per cent in any member state) identify themselves in exclusively European terms, about 40 per cent

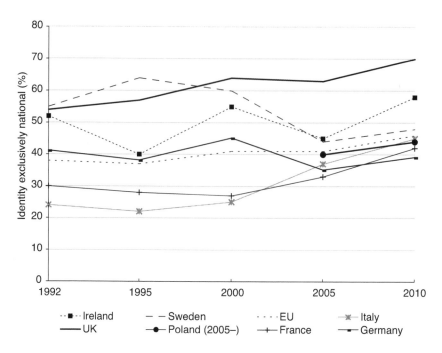

Figure 10.1 Identity as exclusively national, 1992–2010 (derived from Eurobarometer database).

consider themselves as having at least partly a European identity (Fligstein 2008: 144). However, nearly half of Europeans define themselves in purely national terms, and as Figure 10.1 shows, this proportion has been growing decisively since the onset of the crisis. Conversely, as exclusively national identity has been growing, so the proportion of people who think Europe to be good for their country is declining in most countries (Figure 10.2).

Who are these Europeans and who are the non-Europeans? Self-ascribed European identity is linked to support for the European Union and somewhat linked to relatively left-wing views. One of the most pro-European groups is those EU citizens who have migrated from one EU state to another. Such internal migrants are especially likely to think of themselves as Europeans: they are likely to be well informed politically and to support greater European integration. Intriguingly, they tend to be more left-wing than would be expected on the basis of their occupational backgrounds and display 'a certain reticence towards economic liberalism' (Muxel 2009: 163).

Such migration within the borders of the EU has been taken as an example of a process of social Europeanisation – the creation of social relations across national borders and so a Europeanisation from below. Migration within the EU is now very different to traditional forms of immigration. Whereas migration

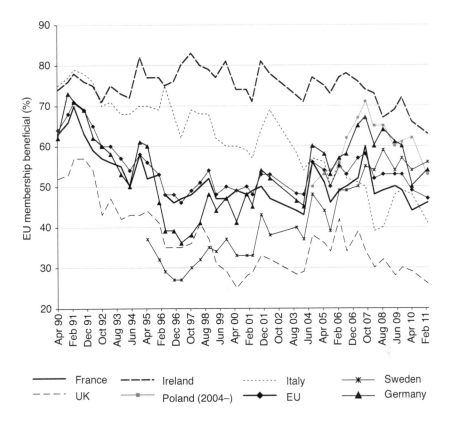

Figure 10.2 Support for EU membership, 1990–2011 (derived from Eurobarometer database).

Note
Proportion considering membership of the European Union is a good thing for their country.

used to mean the unskilled moving from poor countries to rich countries, now *within Europe* it is above all the educated and skilled who move, and such mobility is not just for employment (Section 7.6). Equally, the Erasmus programme of student exchange between European universities has made a stay abroad part of the normal experience for young Europeans (Section 2.3). However, it is all too easy to assume that the new service class mobility or the new student exchanges are specifically 'European' when in many ways they are merely 'international'. Arguably what is happening in both domains is a process of *internationalisation* in relation to the UK, but a process of partial *Europeanisation* for other member states.

Many Europeans are now involved in organisations and institutions that function on a European, not a national, scale. Euro-2012 might have meant the latest stage of the European financial crisis, but it also meant hundreds of thousands of football supporters travelling to matches, national fans in other European countries and a European TV audience of millions. Football clubs like Barcelona or even Manchester United have a European, not a regional, fan base and play on a European stage (Martin 2005). And everyone talks about Eurovision, even if nobody knows who is taking it seriously ... (Raykoff 2007). For many members of the 'service class' (managers and professionals), their everyday working life involves not just contact with colleagues in other countries but participation in European professional organisations, everything from the European Association of Archaeologists to the European Association of Zoo and Wildlife Veterinarians.

Just as for Eurovision and for UEFA, for professional organisations 'Europe' is often bigger than just the European Union. In other respects, however, the European football and television organisations are unusual in that they involve the participation of ordinary Europeans. If Europe is being integrated through migration, through education and through civic society organisations, even through shopping and foreign property purchase, then this is a very uneven process. Football may be increasingly European, but most popular culture is either national or global/American. Most processes of Europeanisation, by contrast, disproportionately involve the service class.

European integration is described by researchers as an elite process in the sense that it has been always been driven from the top (Haller 2008) with the passive tolerance of the population. This has made European unification very different to the great nineteenth-century national movements of Germany or Italy. Italian unification was certainly created by political elites, but they did at least aspire to popular mobilisation. The heroic images of the Risorgimento may in retrospect appear as romantic posturings, but they had some plausibility at the time. Such images are totally foreign to European unification.

Nonetheless, in terms of social groups or even social classes it is misleading to focus on the European 'elite' as the most pro-European. If elite means those with heavy wealth and those on incomes of (say) several hundred thousand euros a year, such people have little interest in 'Europe' for they are increasingly disconnected from any national society (see Section 4.4). For them, the national state is something with which they have only the most utilitarian relationship, an institution which irritatingly still tries to tax them and from which they escape as much as possible. Such elite cosmopolitans are certainly not interested in developing a larger European state.

In terms of identity and politics it is therefore not so much the elite as the broader service class that is European. It is thus reasonable for Fligstein to ignore any 'upper class' or 'socio-economic elite' in his account of the linkage between European identity and social structure, reporting that: 'The upper-middle-class are the most European, the middle classes are more national but still partly European, and the working and lower classes are the least European' (Fligstein 2008: 18).

Pro-Europeans often explain hostility to Europe in terms of prejudice, but this is arrogance instead of analysis. Given the differential involvement in European processes, it is hardly surprising that the less skilled and the more welfare-dependent are becoming more hostile to 'Europe'. Like it or not, such people have a realistic perception of their economic interests (e.g. Gabel 1998; also de Vries and van Kersbergen 2007). Increasingly it is the service class that is gaining from Europeanisation, it is the working or lower class that is losing. For many of the latter, Europe has meant the destruction of secure employment and the undermining of their national welfare state. Above all, Europe means for them the erosion of the limited but real protection which the national welfare state provided against the uncertainty of the market. It is not surprising that in France or in Germany such people are drifting to the nationalist right-wing parties. Although political commentators often ignore this, nationalist parties such as the Front National in France promise to protect national *welfare* states – against 'Europe'.

10.4 Conclusion

The founding fathers of Europe (Jean Monnet, Robert Schuman, etc.) were mostly Christian democratic politicians who were committed to European unity as the solution to intra-European rivalry. Their explicit objective was to end wars between European states. Perhaps their covert ambition to use a united Europe to reassert the European influence on the global stage that was now beyond the reach of any single European state. As they clearly stated, economic integration was a tool with which to achieve the political objective of European unity. Today, traces of this orientation still linger on, especially perhaps within the German CDU/CSU. For many of those who promote European integration, however, the relationship between economics and politics has long since been reversed. Now political structures are used to achieve economic objectives, and those objectives are not so much the creation of a *European* market as the universal *generalisation* of the market.

Any history of the European Union reiterates how the 'lesson' of the war was the need for European unity. Slipping out of sight now is what was then another obvious apparent lesson of history. Political extremism of the inter-war period was seen as the result of mass unemployment (and to a lesser extent) of untrammelled social inequality. This opened the door for the class compromise of the post-war decades: Keynesian economics and the welfare state, which together ensured not just rising real incomes but, crucially, less inequality. Christian democrats (and, in Britain, One Nation Conservatives) now modernised their unitary conception of the national society to acknowledge popular interest representation. This compromise was ruptured in Britain by the Thatcher revolution. Thatcher famously declared that 'there is no such thing as society'. Yet in the 1980s and 1990s this belief remained an Anglo-Saxon eccentricity: outside of Britain national welfare states were consolidated while the first attempts were also made to create the institutions and policies of a European society. Today however, for European business and political elites, what seems to really matter is the global *market*, certainly not European *society*.

The neo-liberal elites that now dominate Europe have abandoned any commitment to 'Social Europe' and have turned European institutions into market-making mechanisms. In so doing they are trashing everything that made Europe distinctive and they are chipping away at popular tolerance of European unity. The neo-liberals appropriated the European project for their own purposes and in so doing now risk destroying it completely. Today only a social Europe can rescue Europe.

Notes

1 The great republican revolutions of the eighteenth century, the American and the French, also have this future orientation in their appeal to the realisation of universal human rights.
2 Turkish entry is also supported by various 'multi-culti' lobby groups and (some) immigrant lobby groups, as well as those well-known European enthusiasts, the British and American governments.

Bibliography

de Vries, C. and van Kersbergen, K. (2007) Interests, identity and political allegiance in the European Union, *Acta Politica* 42.2–3: 307–328.
Fligstein, N. (2008) *Euroclash: The EU, European Identity and the Future of Europe*, Oxford: Oxford UP.
Gabel, M. (1998) Economic integration and mass politics: market liberalization and public attitudes in the European Union, *American Journal of Political Science* 42.3: 936–953.
Haller, M. (2008) *European Integration as an Elite Process: The Failure of a Dream?* London: Routledge.
Koopmans, R. and Erbe, J. (2004) Towards a European public sphere? Vertical and horizontal dimensions of a Europeanised political communication, *Innovation* 17: 97–118.
Langley, P. (2009) *The Everyday Life of Global Finance: Saving and Borrowing in Anglo-America*, Oxford: Oxford UP.
Marshall, T. (1950) *Citizenship and Social Class and Other Essays*, Cambridge: Cambridge UP.
Martin, P. (2005) The 'Europeanization' of elite football: scope, meanings and significance, *European Societies* 7.2: 349–368.
Meehan, E. (1993) *Citizenship and the European Community*, London: Sage.
Muxel, A. (2009) EU movers and politics: towards a fully fledged European citizenship? In E. Recchi and A. Favell (eds) *Pioneers of European Integration*, Cheltenham: Edward Elgar, pp. 156–178.
Putnam, R. (2015) *Our Kids: The American Dream in Crisis*, New York: Simon & Schuster.
Raykoff, I. (2007) Camping on the borders of Europe. In I. Raykoff and R. Tobin (eds) *A Song for Europe: Popular Music and Politics in the Eurovision Song Contest*, London: Ashgate, pp. 1–12.
Siedentop, L. (2000) *Democracy in Europe*, London: Penguin.
Voruba, G. (2005) *Die Dynamik Europas*, Wiesbaden: Verlag für Sozialwissenschaften.

Appendix
Statistical sources

Table 2.1 Industrial employment

Coal – UK

UK 1940–2000: National Coal Mining Museum for England, online table. Accessed 5 November 2013.

2012 Source: Department of Energy and Climate Change, *Digest of United Kingdom Energy Statistics 2013*, page 43, www.gov.uk/government/uploads/system/uploads/attachment_data/file/225067/DUKES_2013_published_version.pdf. Accessed 5 November 2013.

(For 2012) Employment includes contractors and is as declared by licensees to the Coal Authority at 31 December each year.

Coal – Germany

Coal figures received from email correspondence with Federal Statistical Office Germany, reference number: 326259/436610 karl-dietrich.fischer@destatis.de Germany.

Figures for 1950s–1980s are for Früheres Bundesgebiet (West Germany); 1990s for Federal Republic including former East Germany.

Railways – UK

UK (1950–2001) employment in the railway industry figures are for England and Wales only. Source: www.neighbourhood.statistics.gov.uk/HTMLDocs/dvc12/railway.html. Accessed 23 October 2013.

Railways – Germany

Germany and Italy 1975 and 1985 figures from Eurostat – number of people employed in principal railway enterprises – includes general administration, operating traffic, rolling stock, maintenance of ways and work, etc. [rail_ec_emplo_a].

Germany railway figures 1996–2004, source: European Foundation for the Improvement of Living and Working Conditions, *Profile of the Rail Transport Sector in Germany* (2005), page 24 (based on data from the Federal Statistical Office, Germany), www.eurofound.europa.eu/emcc/publications/2006/ef0540enC5.pdf. Accessed 5 November 2013.

Railways – Italy

Italy 1998–2004 railway figures, source: European Foundation for the Improvement of Living and Working Conditions, *Profile of the Rail Transport Sector in Italy* (2006), www.euro-found.europa.eu/emcc/publications/2006/ef0540enC2.pdf. Accessed 5 November 2013.

The Italian 2000s figure is for year 2004: 102,000 employees are broken down into 56,000 employed in Trenitalia, the passenger and freight transport division of the Fer-rovie dello Stato group, and 46,000 employed in other FS companies.

Railways – UK, Germany and Italy

Railway employment 2009–2011, source: UNECE United Nations Economic Commis-sion for Europe, http://w3.unece.org/pxweb/. Accessed 25 October 2013 – employment in principal railway enterprises.

Autos – UK

UK 1950s figure is for 1956 and includes British vehicle manufacturers and suppliers concentrating on work for them. Source: Maxcy, G. and Silberton, A. (1959) *The Motor Industry*, London: George Allen and Unwin, page 33.

UK 1960s figure is for 1968 and includes only those employed in British Leyland. In 1968 British Leyland had 188,000 employees, peaking at 208,000 employees in 1974, and in 1983 British Leyland had 103,000 employees. Source: William, P. (1986) Labour relations strategy at BL Cars. In S. Toliday and J. Zeitlin (eds) *The Automobile Industry*, Cambridge: Polity Press, page 307.

UK 1970s figure is for 1975 and includes UK employees of the big four assemblers. Source: Wilks, S. (1984) *Industrial Policy and the Motor Industry*, Manchester: Man-chester University Press, page 76.

Autos – Germany

Germany auto figures received from email correspondence with Federal Statistical Office, Germany, query reference number: 326259/436610 karl-dietrich.fischer@destatis.de Germany. Figures prior to 1995 include territory of Früheres Bundesgebiet, 1995 onwards figures for territory of Federal Republic.

Autos – Italy

Italy 1975 and 1985 figures for number of people employed in Italian automobile and autoparts industry. Source: Silva, F., Ferri, P. and Enrietti, A. (1987) Robots, employ-ment and industrial relations in the Italian automobile industry. In S. Watanabe (ed.) *Microelectronics, Automation and Employment in Automobile Industry*, Chichester: John Wiley and Sons, page 132.

Autos – UK and Germany 1980s

Figure is for 1985: the number of people employed in manufacture of motor vehicles, trailers and semi-trailers. Source: Eurostat detailed economic activity (NACE Rev. 1.1, DM34).

Autos – UK, Germany and Italy

Figures for 1990s onwards are for 1995, 2005 and 2012: manufacture of motor vehicles, trailers and semi-trailers. Source: Eurostat detailed economic activity (1992–2008, NACE Rev. 1.1, two digit level [lfsa_egana2d]) (from 2008 onwards, NACE Rev. 2 two digit level [lfsa_egan22d]), http://epp.eurostat.ec.europa.eu/portal/page/portal/ employment_unemployment_lfs/data/database. Accessed 5 November 2013.

Sources for Figure 3.1 Annual car production

France 1957–1997

From Freyssenet M., *The World Automobile Production by Continent and by Some Countries, 1898–2012.* Inquiry document: four tables and seven graphics, comments. Digital publication, freyssenet.com (2007 and updatings), http://freyssenet.com/?q=en/ node/654. Accessed 22 November 2013.

Germany 1957–1997

From VDA, Domestic production of passenger cars by German manufacturers (1957–2011), www.vda.de/en/zahlen/jahreszahlen/automobilproduktion/. Accessed 21 November 2013.

Italy 1957–1997

From Associazione Nazionale Filiera, Automobile in Cifre, http://webmail.anfia.it/autoin-cifre/ProduzioneItalia.htm. Accessed 22 November 2013.

UK 1957–1994

Figures for 1957–1994 figures relate to Britain, figures from Wood, J. (1996) *The Motor Industry of Britain Centenary Book*, London: The Society of Motor Manufacturers and Traders, pages 155, 169 and 185.

Sweden 1995–1997

Car production 1995–1997 from email correspondence with Mats Mattsson, BIL Sweden.

Other periods

All figures for 1980 and 1990 relate to passenger car production for France, Italy, Sweden and UK, from page 56 of www.ccfa.fr/IMG/pdf/ccfa_ra_2011_gb.pdf. Accessed 21 November 2013.

Figures for 1961, 1971, 1981, 1991 for France, Italy, Sweden and UK are from RITA Table 1–23: World Motor Vehicle Production, www.rita.dot.gov/bts/sites/rita.dot.gov. bts/files/publications/national_transportation_statistics/html/table_01_23.html. Accessed 21 November 2013.

All 1998 figures from OICA www.oica.net/wp-content/uploads/2007/06/europepc.pdf. Accessed 21 November 2013.

All 1999–2012 figures from OICA www.oica.net/category/production-statistics/1999-statistics/. Accessed 21 November 2013.

Index

Page numbers in *italics* denote tables, those in **bold** denote figures.

Taylor & Francis eBooks

Helping you to choose the right eBooks for your Library

Add Routledge titles to your library's digital collection today. Taylor and Francis ebooks contains over 50,000 titles in the Humanities, Social Sciences, Behavioural Sciences, Built Environment and Law.

Choose from a range of subject packages or create your own!

Benefits for you

- » Free MARC records
- » COUNTER-compliant usage statistics
- » Flexible purchase and pricing options
- » All titles DRM-free.

REQUEST YOUR **FREE** INSTITUTIONAL TRIAL TODAY

Free Trials Available
We offer free trials to qualifying academic, corporate and government customers.

Benefits for your user

- » Off-site, anytime access via Athens or referring URL
- » Print or copy pages or chapters
- » Full content search
- » Bookmark, highlight and annotate text
- » Access to thousands of pages of quality research at the click of a button.

eCollections – Choose from over 30 subject eCollections, including:

Archaeology	Language Learning
Architecture	Law
Asian Studies	Literature
Business & Management	Media & Communication
Classical Studies	Middle East Studies
Construction	Music
Creative & Media Arts	Philosophy
Criminology & Criminal Justice	Planning
Economics	Politics
Education	Psychology & Mental Health
Energy	Religion
Engineering	Security
English Language & Linguistics	Social Work
Environment & Sustainability	Sociology
Geography	Sport
Health Studies	Theatre & Performance
History	Tourism, Hospitality & Events

For more information, pricing enquiries or to order a free trial, please contact your local sales team: www.tandfebooks.com/page/sales

 Routledge
Taylor & Francis Group

The home of
Routledge books

www.tandfebooks.com